AJIKISTAN'S

DIFFICULT DEVELOPMENT PATH

MARTHA BRILL OLCOTT

TAJIKISTAN'S

DIFFICULT DEVELOPMENT PATH

CARNEGIE ENDOWMENT

FOR INTERNATIONAL PEACE

WASHINGTON DC ▪ MOSCOW ▪ BEIJING ▪ BEIRUT ▪ BRUSSELS

Carnegie Endowment for International Peace
1779 Massachusetts Avenue, N.W.
Washington, D.C. 20036
202-483-7600, Fax 202-483-1840
www.ceip.org

The Carnegie Endowment does not take institutional positions on public policy issues; the views represented here are the author's own and do not necessarily reflect the views of the Endowment, its staff, or its trustees.

To order, contact:
Hopkins Fulfillment Service
P.O. Box 50370, Baltimore, MD 21211-4370
1-800-537-5487 or 1-410-516-6956
Fax 1-410-516-6998

Cover design by Jocelyn Soly
Composition by Cutting Edge Design
Printed by United Book Press

Library of Congress Cataloging-in-Publication Data

Olcott, Martha Brill, 1949-
  Tajikistan's difficult development path / Martha Brill Olcott.
      pages ; cm
  Includes bibliographical references and index.
  ISBN 978-0-87003-273-8 (paperback)—ISBN 978-0-87003-274-5 (cloth)
  1. Economic development—Tajikistan. 2. Tajikistan—Economic policy—1991-
3. Tajikistan—Economic conditions—1991- 4. Tajikistan—Politics and
government—1991- I. Title.

  HC421.3.Z9E445 2012
  338.9586--dc23

                                         2012024785

MIX
Paper from
responsible sources
FSC® C010236

CONTENTS

FOREWORD

Tajikistan's post-Soviet transition has not been easy. Shortly after independence, this landlocked and mountainous country plunged into a civil war that magnified the economic and political difficulties of building a viable state from the fragments of a unitary Soviet economy. Ever since, Tajikistan has teetered on the brink of failure.

The country's struggles are brought into sharper relief as international forces prepare to withdraw from neighboring Afghanistan in 2014. Soon, the states of Central Asia will be faced with the burden of ensuring regional stability. Yet, Tajikistan has not yet proved it can overcome its challenges on the domestic front.

There is no one better equipped to illuminate the complex problems confronting Tajikistan than Martha Brill Olcott. *Tajikistan's Difficult Development Path* is fully up to date, but it is the product of over two decades of research in the region. It provides a comprehensive overview of the country's transition from communism to independence and of the challenges barring the road ahead.

Today, Tajikistan's economy is dominated by inefficient state-owned enterprises. Its hierarchical political system is controlled by President Emomali Rahmon and his supporters, who also seek to manage media and religious activities in this traditionally Islamic society. A broad swath of the country's population is struggling with unemployment, with up to a million of its 7 million inhabitants forced to travel abroad to find work. Many face frequent electricity shortages and deteriorating environmental conditions, and the quality of health care and education is often low.

Tajikistan's proximity to Afghanistan creates another set of problems, such as drug trafficking, that are compounded by unsecured borders and corruption.

Although the Tajik leadership has introduced some reforms, it has shown little commitment to economic liberalization or to fostering a participatory political system. Instead, it chooses to get by on promises of dramatic relief in the future from infrastructure projects like the construction of the Roghun hydroelectric station.

Tajikistan has accepted substantial foreign assistance from international organizations and bilateral donors since the end of its civil war in 1997, including the International Monetary Fund, World Bank, Asian Development Bank, European Bank for Reconstruction and Development, and United Nations Development Program as well as the United States, the European Union, Switzerland, Japan, China, and Russia. However, donor-led efforts at reform have been hampered by inefficient dispersal of assistance and lack of political will.

In this timely and well-researched volume, Martha Brill Olcott traces the path of Tajikistan's political, economic, and social development since independence. As *Tajikistan's Difficult Development Path* makes clear, the country's leadership faces an urgent choice between fully embracing reform or continuing on its current failed track with all the attendant negative consequences for Tajikistan's citizens.

The choice the country makes will have very real implications for this troubled region. The country's economic and political weaknesses threaten to be a serious liability not just for itself, but for all of its neighbors if the security situation in Afghanistan deteriorates following the U.S. withdrawal.

−JESSICA T. MATHEWS
President
Carnegie Endowment for International Peace

CHAPTER 1

INTRODUCTION: A COUNTRY AT RISK

Tajikistan, probably the most remote of all the former Soviet republics, has been a country at risk since achieving its independence twenty years ago. It is the poorest country in Central Asia, with an average per capita income of $780 in 2010, when it was ranked 183 of 213 countries by the World Bank.[1]

This mountainous and landlocked country has a population of approximately 7.7 million.[2] Tajikistan has over 700 miles of border with Afghanistan, much of which is fully porous along the Pyanj River; a border of similar size with even fewer natural geographic obstacles with Uzbekistan; and one that is similarly porous and slightly smaller with Kyrgyzstan. Until December 1991, these last two were Soviet administrative boundaries. Tajikistan also shares a border with China, which was not fully demarcated until 2011, when Tajikistan surrendered slightly over 1.1 square kilometers to China.[3]

Tajikistan's first years of independence were marked by a four-sided civil war between two competing, regionally based elite groups from the Soviet-era Tajik Communist Party, a prodemocratic group, and Islamist elements.[4] The unrest began in early September 1991, triggered by Tajik party leader and president Kakhar Makhkamov's public support for the failed Communist Party coup in Moscow just weeks earlier.

Makhkamov's predecessor, Rahmon Nabiyev (who had been removed by Mikhail Gorbachev in 1985 shortly after the latter took over as general secretary of the Communist Party of the Soviet Union), aligned and mobilized his supporters with two other rising groups. One of these was an active prodemocracy movement that had been gaining support in Dushanbe, the nation's capital, and the other was a group of charismatic Islamic leaders and their devout village followers (this group later became the Islamic Renaissance Party, the first religious party in Central Asia). Together, the three groups formed a powerful alliance and staged demonstrations to oust Makhkamov. The protests succeeded, and Makhkamov resigned and was replaced by Nabiyev in 1991. Yet Nabiyev, who came from the Khujand region in northern Tajikistan—the home of most of the republic's Soviet era leaders—quickly clashed with the leaders of the other two movements. In March 1992 demonstrations began against Nabiyev, mostly by citizens from Tajikistan's southern regions, largely those from Kulyab, who were unhappy with seeing another northern ruler in power. In May 1992, fighting broke out in Dushanbe as Nabiyev attempted to break up these protests.

To ameliorate this situation, Nabiyev formed a new coalition government, but it quickly fell apart and in June 1992 fighting escalated. That September, Nabiyev resigned, and in November of that year the coalition that succeeded Nabiyev was ousted by supporters of Emomali Rahmon, who serves as Tajikistan's current president.[5]

Two main groups emerged from the various coalitions jousting for power: the Popular Front and the United Tajik Opposition (UTO). The Popular Front supported Rahmon, a former state farm chairman born in Dangara, a town in the Kulyab region, and whose support was drawn from that region's Communist Party elite. The UTO was made up of religious forces and some secular prodemocracy groups and was led by Said Abdullo Nuri.

Fighting remained intense through February and March 1993, during which period an estimated 50,000 to 100,000 people died.[6] The number of refugees was somewhat easier to count, as most were registered by some international agency. The United Nations Development Program (UNDP) reports that during this period 60,000 people fled to Afghanistan, 195,000 went to countries within the Commonwealth of Independent States (CIS),[7] and 697,653 were internally displaced within Tajikistan.[8]

In 1994, presidential elections were held, and Rahmon, in what was considered a widely contested election, emerged victorious. With pressure from the international community and surrounding states mounting, the UTO and Tajik government began a series of peace talks. In 1997, they signed the General Agreement on the Establishment of Peace and National Accord in Tajikistan, which finally officially concluded the war.

Rahmon was able to consolidate his power through the process of National Reconciliation. The 1997 agreement has since atrophied, however, and thus the opposition is now denied the 30 percent quota of government positions that was established in that agreement.

The resolution of the Tajik civil war created a greater public role for Islam in Tajikistan than in any other country in Central Asia, and during Rahmon's first term in office it seemed that Tajikistan might evolve into a democracy under his leadership. Tajikistan has eight registered political parties, including the Islamic Renaissance Party, the only legal religious party in the Central Asian region. In addition, in the late 1990s non-governmental political organizations, including some that represented independent media, played a key role in the country's political life. But over time Tajikistan has moved much closer to one-man rule; it is now somewhere between Uzbekistan and Kazakhstan in its degree of "democratization." Rahmon's commitment to democratic change has decreased as his political power has grown, and Tajikistan's deteriorating rankings in Freedom House's governance ratings are testimony to this; the country's democracy score deteriorated from 5.63 to 6.14 between 2002 and 2011 (the higher the score, the less democratic the political system), and Tajikistan is now considered to be "not free" (see Appendix).[9]

With time, Tajikistan's presidency has grown stronger, and its Parliament has become both weaker and less representative of the full spectrum of its political forces. Its elections have grown increasingly flawed and its media more constrained, and restrictions on the practice of religion have increased. Judicial reform has proceeded slowly, and there is no civilian oversight of the country's various security institutions. Prison conditions remain dire, and political opponents of the regime are at risk of arbitrary arrest.

For virtually all of the 1990s, the security situation in Tajikistan kept the international community and especially international financial institutions from much engagement in the country. But since the late 1990s, legions of technical experts have been coming to the country to advise its central government in Dushanbe on programs to address its economic and political challenges. The pace of engagement further increased after the beginning of the NATO operation in Afghanistan, because enhancing Tajikistan's own security was seen as necessary for fostering success in Afghanistan itself.

Despite the fact that events in Tajikistan are presumed to have an impact on the stability of all its Central Asian neighbors, relatively little that has been written has focused on the development challenges this country has faced since the end of its civil war in 1997, although the history of the war itself has attracted a lot of attention.[10] By contrast, this book focuses on the engagement of the international community to help stave off the economic and political collapse of Tajikistan, and it evaluates the successes and failures that have been achieved, along with the risks that remain.

In the past fifteen years, the country has accepted substantial international intervention in its economy, including a macroeconomic stabilization program sponsored by the International Monetary Fund and substantial engagement by the World Bank, as well as the Asian Development Bank, the European Bank for Reconstruction and Development, the United Nations Development Program, and a large number of bilateral donors, such as the United States, the European Union, Switzerland, Japan, China, and Russia.

Although the first years of economic reform (through the mid-2000s) brought a period of rapid economic growth, Tajikistan remains a country with severe economic problems. The period of rapid growth made noticeable changes to lifestyles in Dushanbe, and new buildings and businesses sprouted up in most of the other larger urban centers as well, as the country's service sector grew in response to new consumer demands. Tajikistan's economy was also benefiting from Russia's economic growth, and to a lesser extent from that of Kazakhstan, as remittances provided an important source of income for many Tajik households.

But international assistance has still left Tajikistan's economy only partially reformed. The incomplete reform of the agricultural sector is one of the major causes of poverty in the country. The old Soviet-era collective farms have been broken up, and farmers thus now have the right to work their lands; but they still cannot transfer ownership, leaving the agrarian sector hostage to a largely unreformed and increasingly less productive but debt-ridden cotton sector.

Little progress had been made toward realizing the goal of energy self-sufficiency, not to speak of creating a large income stream through exporting hydroelectric power. The country's largest industrial enterprise, Tajik Aluminum, is controlled by the state or state-assigned actors and has only limited prospects for future development. Both Tajik Aluminum and the national electric company, Barki Tojik, have done little to introduce international management principles. To make matters worse, in late 2007 the International Monetary Fund discovered that Tajikistan had a substantial (close to $500 million) undisclosed public external debt, which was almost entirely linked to pledges made by the state-owned National Bank for the financing of the cotton sector by private institutions (and presumably thus to private individuals). The country's debt burden had been steadily growing, and even international debt relief has not been able to keep its national savings from declining.

The most serious test came in the winter of 2007–2008, when a drought, combined with unusually cold weather, led to crisis conditions in much of the country, wreaking havoc on agriculture and leading to shortages of food and energy. Snowfalls were up to 245 percent over the average in November, and temperatures from December through most of February were far below normal. For example, daytime temperatures in January averaged –15 degrees Celsius, instead of the range of –1 to +3 degrees that had been common in previous years. Temperatures in Dushanbe dipped to –15 degrees at night, and in some rural areas (including relatively low-lying ones) the temperature dropped to –25 degrees.

Between this severe weather and a loss of production due to electricity blackouts, Tajikistan incurred some $250 million of winter-related damage, a loss of 7 percent of its gross domestic product (GDP).[11] Electricity production in Tajikistan dropped by 8 percent in 2008, which may explain why industrial production in the country dropped by 4 percent in 2008.[12]

The situation was worst in rural areas, where (except in the Gorno-Badakhshan region, which is served by a local electric company) electricity was available for a maximum of six hours per day. For the first time in a decade, moreover, electricity was limited in the same way in Dushanbe as it was in all the country's other cities, where enforced blackouts had been common but never as extreme. The shortage occurred despite the fact that Sangtuda 1, a long-promised major hydroelectric power station, had just begun to be commissioned; eventually, this station would provide the country with an additional 670 megawatts of annual capacity, but it still lacks a stable market for all that it produces.[13]

Tajikistan's energy shortages helped highlight the incompetent (and some would add corrupt) practices of the country's electricity monopoly, Barki Tojik, and the generally unreformed practices of the country's economic monopolies. It also made starkly apparent the continued interdependencies of northern Tajikistan with Uzbekistan, which was a source of natural gas (for electricity and heating in winter) either directly or through transit from Turkmenistan, and the negative impact that this had on Barki Tojik's ability to offer an unbroken supply of energy to its clients.

In the harsh winter of 2007–2008, the electricity shortage did more than dampen economic activity. It led to the illness and death of hundreds and possibly even thousands of elderly citizens, newborns, and young children, who struggled to survive the winter in unheated homes, hospitals, and schools. Moreover, the state-run institutions found it a challenge to keep operating. School attendance dropped by almost half, many hospitals sent home all but the most critically ill patients, clinics worked shortened hours, and the facilities of the small sector of orphanages, homes for the elderly, and other related institutions struggled to keep their residents alive.

Cold weather was not the only reason for the increased mortality. Rising food prices, which grew by 26 percent in Tajikistan during 2008, were at least as important a cause. The harsh winter led to the loss of both winter and spring crops, which are so crucial for Tajikistan's food security after the dry summer, causing the country to put out an appeal for international food assistance to be distributed among the population. In many places food was obtainable, but people could not afford to buy it. Kyrgyzstan also fell victim to the same combination of climate extremes, and it also appealed for help, but the situation in Tajikistan was dire; according to the World Food Program, an estimated 1.5 million people in Tajikistan were food insecure in 2008, and 650,000 of them were severely food insecure.[14]

The international community did come forward with more than $28 million in humanitarian assistance, over and above its planned poverty alleviation and technical assistance support.[15] But the crisis did not lead the Tajik government to reconsider its political and economic strategies; nor did it get the international community to rethink the kinds of bilateral and multilateral assistance that it was providing to the Tajik government. Rather, as this book details, the Tajik government continues to muddle through, hoping that piecemeal improvements and the promise of dramatic relief in the future—in the form of the construction of the Roghun hydroelectric station to serve as a source of cheap electricity at home and of export earnings as well—will allow Rahmon and his family and friends to remain in power.

Tajikistan's economy was further damaged when Russia and Kazakhstan both began suffering the effects of the global economic crisis, which left hundreds of thousands of migrant workers from Tajikistan without employment, causing a substantial decline in the country's economic growth rate and leading to inflation and pressure on the Tajik currency, the somoni.

The country's less and less democratic political system was also facing a legitimacy crisis, as charges of economic malfeasance were being lodged against key members of the president's economic team, and President Rahmon left himself increasingly open to charges of nepotism as more and more of his family members were offered official posts. Tajikistan was rated 152 of 182 countries on the 2011 Transparency International Corruption Index.[16]

The country's international situation had also changed, and in some ways become more precarious, as fighters from the Islamic Movement of Uzbekistan and other Islamic extremist organizations started making forays into the country again in 2009.

Generally speaking, NATO's International Security Assistance Force (ISAF) operation in Afghanistan has had a positive impact, creating new opportunities for Tajikistan through its support of international coalition activities, through benefits accruing from international recovery efforts in Afghanistan, through the creation of new trade networks, and even more important, through the enhanced security situation in Afghanistan itself. But even after ten years of active engagement by ISAF, the security situation in Afghanistan has not been fully stabilized, and Taliban-led insurgent activities have begun in areas that are relatively close to the Tajik border, making Tajikistan once again (as it was until 2002) a transit point for insurgent groups that oppose the Uzbek government of President Islam Karimov and increasing the already-strained relationship between these two states.

On the plus side, Tajikistan has grown closer to both China and a number of the Gulf states. This has led to more development money coming into the country but it has left the future of Tajikistan's political and economic reform even more in question.

It is hard to know how much time President Rahmon has before he could begin to feel strong popular pressure for change. A 2010 survey done by the International Foundation for Electoral Systems (IFES) shows that overall satisfaction with the situation in Tajikistan is much higher than it was in 1996, when it did its first survey, but has decreased slightly since 2006, although it remains very positive.[17] Moreover, the overwhelming majority of those surveyed said that they thought that Tajikistan was a democracy, although, ironically, a smaller percentage of the sample said that they thought that "democracy is preferable to any other form of government."[18]

Until now, one of the things working to Rahmon's advantage has been the memory of the losses incurred during the country's civil war. But more and more people in Tajikistan are too young to remember this period, and if the Arab Spring of 2011 is any indicator, the members of this new generation could decide to hold their country's leadership to very different standards of behavior. The study done by IFES makes clear that Tajikistan's citizens will judge their government's performance by how well it responds to the country's economic problems. More than 50 percent of those surveyed answered that elected officials' priorities should be to create jobs, fight poverty, and improve the economy in general.[19] And the respondents in the study made clear what a precarious economic situation most Tajiks face, with only 30 percent reporting that they had enough money for food and shelter.[20]

This book looks at how Tajikistan ended up in such a dire situation in 2008 and what has been done since then to alleviate its problems, exploring its unresolved economic and social challenges. The volume concludes with a discussion of the challenges facing Tajikistan as the ISAF operation plans to draw down its troop levels, including how Tajikistan's neighbors might react to its still incomplete reform agenda.

One's perspective on Tajikistan very much depends upon when one made his or her first trip there. For those who visited for the first time right after the end of the civil war, it is easier to be a bit optimistic about Tajikistan's chances for success, for no matter how many problems still confront the country's decisionmakers, there has been a marked degree of recovery.

However, longtime Tajik hands have a more sober view, for they remember the country's rich intellectual life, which was so visible even to foreigners during the political thaw of the 1980s. For those who knew this earlier Tajikistan, it is hard not to focus on the "brain drain" that has occurred and to be concerned about what are likely to be the long-term effects of these lost opportunities of the first two decades of independence.

For the past twenty years, Tajikistan has always seemed to be on the precipice of becoming a failed state, but then either good luck or public lethargy has given the government enough time to right its course, or to at least maintain enough public confidence to allow its leadership to remain in power. Although it is difficult to predict whether Tajikistan has some version of the Arab Spring in its future, one can only hope that the country will right its course without its population being plunged into a civil war like the one it suffered through in the early 1990s.

The book builds on more than a quarter century of travel to Tajikistan, including numerous trips from 2005 through 2010, when the bulk of the research for this book was completed. The book has benefited from the counsel of many people, including Johannes Linn and Saodat Olimova, who read a draft and provided detailed and thoughtful comments and suggestions for its improvement. Several junior researchers at the Carnegie Endowment also made strong contributions, in particular taking responsibility for all the figures and tables. Daria Anichkova, Diana Galperin, and Alyssa Meyer deserve special thanks.

CHAPTER 2

POLITICS AND RELIGION

POLITICAL LIFE: THE GROWTH OF DYNASTIC POLITICS

Tajikistan's political life is dominated by a strong presidential system. Although the civil war slowed the process of political consolidation, today the presidency in Tajikistan is a stronger office than that in Kazakhstan, and may even be stronger than the institution of the presidency in Uzbekistan. Moreover, unlike in Uzbekistan, where Islam Karimov is slowly vesting the Parliament and prime minister with some of the presidency's powers, in Tajikistan the prime minister is a weak figure and parliamentary powers are being steadily curtailed.

Emomali Rahmon—who dropped the Russified ending to his last name in 2007 as something of a snub to Moscow, and has begun to be referred to as "his highness" (*ego vysochestvo* in Russian; *padahshah* in Tajik)—is behaving in ways reminiscent of Turkmenbashi (President Saparmurad Niyazov of Turkmenistan). He has not changed the days of the week or the months of the year to terminology of his own invention, as his Turkmen counterpart did; nor is he the creator of his own religious doctrine. But the Tajik leader's face is displayed on many of the country's roadways and streets, and he has put himself forward as a leading religious thinker.

Rahmon was first elected president in 1994, and then reelected in 1999, in a presidential campaign marked by irregularities. This was his second and, according to Tajikistan's constitution, his final term of office, but the document was amended in 2003. It now provides for the election of a president to serve a maximum of two seven-year terms. In other words, under Tajikistan's current constitution Rahmon can now remain in office through reelection until 2020.

He was elected to a seven-year term in November 2006, with 79 percent of the vote, in an election judged less flawed than the one in 1999, but also one in which he lacked a serious opponent. As elsewhere in the region, it is hard to gauge a president's popularity from election results. In Tajikistan, as in neighboring states, the political landscape has been constructed to ensure that only one person, the president, is viewed as a credible political figure, and anyone who emerges as any kind of potential rival is pressured off or removed from the political stage. So while local election commissions may "round up" numbers to the benefit of the president to impress him with the victory scored in their districts, as an incumbent Rahmon is unlikely to ever face serious competition at the ballot box. Moreover, given the deeply ingrained patrimonial culture in Tajikistan, most of the population will likely continue to vote for their "*padahshah.*"

A Swiss government report from 2006, prepared by the Swiss Agency for Development and Cooperation and the State Secretariat for Economic Affairs to set forth the country's "Cooperation Strategy for the Central Asia Region for 2007–2011," described the challenge posed by Rahmon's government to those interested in engaging in development work in Tajikistan:

> Since the end of the civil war in 1997, President Emomali Rahmon has grown from a compromise candidate at the end of the conflict to the little-contested leader of the country. This is also due to weak and divided opposition parties, as well as to keeping them as part of the power system. Staying supreme since 1994, President Rahmon has also secured his power for the future. Peace and stability has [*sic*] been a crucial condition for increased international support and has [*sic*] allowed remarkable economic development in the recent past, with annual growth rates of 8–10 percent in recent years.

The downside of this development is an increasingly self-centered government with considerable and accelerating elements of arbitrariness, an endemic corruption with little progress for improvement, the exploitation of profitable economic assets by a minority of the society, and a general neglect of the people's basic development needs in the overall policy making.[1]

Rahmon appears keen to remain in power. He is expected to run for a second seven-year term in 2013. His critics speculate that he will either change Tajikistan's constitution to make himself president for life, or perhaps even transform the country's presidency into a hereditary office. The latter option seems implausible, however, unless someone else in Central Asia were to opt to do this first.

The Constitutional Law on Election of the President of the Republic of Tajikistan, which was adopted in 1994 and modified in 1999 and 2005,[2] states that presidential candidates can only be nominated by political parties,[3] by the Federation of Trade Unions, by the Union of Youth of Tajikistan, by the councils of Tajikistan's oblasts and Dushanbe's City Council, and by representatives of councils of towns and districts. The law does not permit self-nomination, which places Tajikistan in violation of the Organization for Security and Cooperation in Europe's (OSCE's) Copenhagen Convention of 1990, which allows all individuals to seek public office without restriction. In addition, the law requires all candidates to get signatures of 5 percent of the country's eligible voters on their nomination petitions, or some 150,000 to 160,000 voters—a very high number to have to collect, especially given the roughly three-week window allotted for signature collection. A further problem with the presidential election system is that it is based on a model of negative voting; on the ballot, the voter must strike out the names of all candidates that he or she does not want elected rather than simply indicating his or her choice.

As noted above, President Rahmon was reelected on November 6, 2006, with 79 percent of the vote. The election was the first to feature ballots in Uzbek, Russian, and Kyrgyz, as well as in Tajik. The procedure for monitoring the casting and counting of votes was as flawed for the presidential election as it was for the preceding and subsequent parliamentary elections. That said, there is no reason to assume that the percentage that President Rahmon received was substantially altered, although it is very possible that turnout figures were inflated.[4]

From start to finish the conduct of the election was undoubtedly skewed in Rahmon's favor, despite the fact that no serious political figure was running against him. Instead, the Tajiks conducted a presidential election designed to meet the letter rather than the spirit of the law, and whose outcome was known from the beginning.

Six candidates were nominated during the presidential election of 2006; neither the Socialist Party of Tajikistan (SPT) nor the Islamic Renaissance Party of Tajikistan (IRPT) was willing to nominate a candidate.[5] All six candidates met the threshold of required signatures (they began collection 50 days before the election and had to complete the process 30 days before). In all, 47 percent of registered voters signed one of these election petitions, a figure that the election report from the OSCE and its Office for Democratic Institutions and Human Rights (ODIHR) considers implausible, and thus a product of election fraud.[6] Equally implausible, in their opinion, were the claims of Tajikistan's Central Commission for Elections and Referendums (CCER) that only 444 of these signatures were missing data and that only 1,494 of them were duplicates.

One other serious problem with the election was the restrictions on campaign spending; each candidate received 3,600 somoni (about $1,000) from state funds and could spend another 100,000 somoni (under $30,000) from party funds on his campaign. Even though Tajikistan is a poor country, $31,000 for an electorate of over 3 million voters means that candidates could spend on average about one cent per voter, a rather comically small sum.

The election law requires that all candidates get up to 30 minutes of free air time on state television or radio and that up to fifteen proxies per candidate can get up to 10 minutes of additional free air time. In addition, the candidates and their proxies can publish up to ten double-spaced pages in the country's newspapers, giving President Rahmon an inordinate publicity advantage, as his presidential activities could be covered without restriction; in the three weeks before the election, the state-owned TV stations devoted 69 percent of their total news coverage to Rahmon's activities (and one station, TV Safina, gave him 83 percent of its news time), whereas the other candidates got between 6 and 10 percent each. And on the eve of the election, the interview broadcast with President Rahmon ran roughly four times longer than that conducted with any of the other candidates. Even so, the Tajik authorities blocked five websites for ten days beginning on October 9,[7] and prevented the Tajik newspaper *Adolat* (Justice) from publishing (starting October 12) and detained its editor, Rajiab Miro, for fifteen days (starting November 4) after he began picketing the Ministry of Justice in protest.[8]

In the years since the election, Rahmon's family has gone from playing large roles behind the scenes in the country's economy to holding prominent public office. His daughter, Ozoda Rahmonova, was named deputy foreign minister in 2009,[9] and his brother-in-law, Hasan Sadulloev (Hasan Azadullozoda), runs Orienbank, one of the country's largest banking institutions.[10]

With nine children, the Tajik president is well placed to create a political dynasty. In February 2010, the ruling People's Democratic Party of Tajikistan (PDPT) announced that Rahmon's eldest son, Rustam, would run for Dushanbe's City Council from the Somoni District, for a seat in which the incumbent was from the IRP. Rustam subsequently won the seat. A graduate of Tajik State University, he has served as an adviser on the State Committee on Investments and State Property, and he is a member of the Central Committee of the PDPT. In March 2011, he gave up his seat in the Dushanbe City Council to take a senior position in the State Customs Committee, where he now heads the department in charge of countering smuggling.[11] This gives him valuable experience in managing some of Tajikistan's security forces, which is obviously important if he is to eventually move to assume his father's powers.

Rustam has been a rather colorful figure in Tajikistan's political landscape, having allegedly shot his uncle, Hasan Sadulloev (his mother's brother), in May 2008. The latter was initially (and incorrectly) reported to have died. Rustam is said to have acted in a thwarted effort to help his sister, Takhmina (who owns a major construction company), gain control of Orienbank.[12] Rumors abound about the shooting, including that it had led to a rift between Rahmon and his wife, as the latter is said to have put her brother's economic interests above those of her children.[13] The division of power (and economic opportunities) within such a large ruling family is ripe with the potential for ongoing splits.

TAJIKISTAN'S PARLIAMENT

The Parliament is designed to maximize strong presidential power, and the use of the strong presidency to secure informal as well as formal advantage for progovernment candidates. Not surprisingly, then, parliamentary elections have also failed to meet the OSCE's standards in a number of critical areas.

The Supreme Assembly of the Republic of Tajikistan (Majlisi Oli) has two chambers. The Assembly of Representatives (Majlisi Namoyandagon), the lower house, has 63 members who are elected for five-year terms, of whom 22 are elected from party lists based on a proportional representation system with a 5 percent threshold, and 41 from single-mandate systems in which a 50 percent majority is needed (in a second round if necessary). These 41 single-mandate parliamentary districts (*okrugs*) vary considerably in size; for example, the Isfara District in Sughd (an area home to many who are seen as disloyal to the president) has 188,000 residents, or some 100,000-plus voters, while Vanj in Gorno-Badakhshan Autonomous Oblast (GBAO) has roughly 31,000 residents and has been combined with Shugansky, Rushansk, and Darvazsk regions to create a parliamentary election district of fewer than 50,000 voters. These kinds of districts are in violation of the country's election law, which allows for deviations of only 15 percent (20 percent in remote rural regions) in the size of election districts.

The upper house, or National Council, has 33 members, 25 appointed by local councils and 8 members chosen by the president. Since 2000, the National Council has been headed by Mahmadsaid Ubaydulloyev, who also serves as mayor of Dushanbe. He is generally viewed as the second most powerful politician in the country. Like Rahmon, he is from Kulyab and has extensive business interests, some of which are generally assumed to have been funded by money paid to him by drug traders shipping merchandise through the country. This, of course, has never been substantiated. Ubaydulloyev and Rahmon have a very uneasy relationship, largely because of the Dushanbe mayor's untouchable power base. But Ubaydulloyev clearly has his share of enemies, as he lost a leg in a bombing attack in February 2000.[14]

The Parliament still does not function as a very professional body. Legislators do not employ professional staff to help them perform their legislative duties, so the legislation that is drafted is often of a declarative nature rather than in a form that is designed for implementation. In addition, it is not easy to access copies of legislation, in either their draft or completed form, because unlike in Kyrgyzstan and in Kazakhstan, the idea of e-government is virtually nonexistent in Tajikistan, and there is currently little stimulus to do so as the Internet is very poorly developed in the country.

Parliamentary elections are regulated by provisions of the 1994 Constitution and the 1999 Constitutional Law on Elections to the Majlisi Oli, as well as relevant provisions from the Law on Citizens' Complaints (1996), the Law on Political Parties (1998), the Law on Public Meetings (1998), the Criminal Code (1998), the Civil Procedures Code (2008), and all the laws relating to media, religion, and public association. The multiplicity of legal acts governing elections has given opposition groups a large number of avenues through which to try to assert their grievances, but it has also given the judiciary numerous reasons to void their claims.

The election law was amended in 2004, after considerable public debate in which opposition figures took a vocal part, and incorporated enhanced provisions for political parties to observe the voting process, as well as opening up electoral commission meetings to the public and to the mass media. However, the amendments did not address criticisms regarding the lack of inclusiveness in the membership of electoral commissions, left the inadequate system for handling complaints untouched, and made no new provisions for collecting and managing voter lists.

Tajikistan's elections are administered by a three-tiered system of election commissions: the CCER, 41 district election commissions, and 2,953 polling station commissions.[15] The CCER is a permanent body with a chairman, deputy chairman, and thirteen other members who are chosen by the lower house of the Parliament after nomination by the president. This ensures that the body solely reflects the will of the president, while district commissions are dominated by the senior officials from local governments.

Problems with the electoral system begin with the compilation of voter lists and carry on through the counting of ballots. There is no computerized voter registry in Tajikistan, and these lists are generally handwritten and are supposed to be publicly displayed. The polling station commissions are charged with updating voter registration lists before every election, by going door to door, and while some polling station commissions are reported to do this very diligently, this is not always the case.[16] Although the election law makes provision for out-of-country voting, in reality only about 5 percent of the Tajik population living abroad appears to vote, and roughly a third of all Tajik males of working age are employed out of the country.

Although the contradictory nature of legislative and constitutional provisions has been pointed out to the Tajik authorities, they have had little interest in doing anything about this. For example, some of the provisions of the election law and the criminal code as they relate to elections are in conflict with constitutional guarantees on freedom of expression. In fact, the political organization around the president has worked to keep any reform of the electoral process from occurring. For example, a series of working groups composed of members of Tajikistan's registered parties, the CCER, Parliament, the Office of the President, and the Center of Strategic Studies (under the president) all met to work up reforms to the electoral law, but the PDPT refused to support the proposed measures, which, when reported out by the Communist Party of Tajikistan (CPT) in 2009, were defeated in committee.[17]

During the 2005 elections, 231 candidates were registered, including 170 for the 41 single-mandate seats and 61 put forward by the six parties that were registered to compete in the contest. The PDPT supported 62 candidates; the IRPT, 37; and the Communist Party, 20. In addition, 80 were self-nominated candidates (and these included people who were pro-PDPT). However, there were only 195 candidates left in the race on election day. A large number of the withdrawals occurred within 48 hours of the election, suggesting that their candidacies had been fielded by progovernment forces to dilute public attention from those who were running in opposition to government policies. The IRPT won 2 seats,[18] the CPT won 4 seats, and independent candidates got 5 seats, leaving Rahmon's PDPT with 52 seats. The OSCE found numerous problems with the election process, which, in its opinion, did not meet international norms for transparency or fairness. Observers from OSCE/ODIHR complained that they were not given access to even the most basic documents of the CCER.[19]

The operation of the CCER itself was seriously flawed, as it held no public meetings during the month before the election, so that it failed at its mandate calling for transparency. Moreover, in the preparations for and aftermath of the election, the CCER settled almost no complaints in favor of the complainant; they did so in just 3 of 23 complaints relating to registration. And of those complaints that were referred by the CCER to the Prosecutor's Office, none resulted in charges being filed.[20]

During the 2005 election, progovernment forces resorted to exerting pressure to ensure that prominent opposition figures were not elected to Parliament, and that their parties fared poorly on the list system. Two prominent opposition candidates—Sulton Kuvatov, the head of the unregistered Taraqqiyot (Development) Party; and Mahmadruzi Iskandarov, the leader of the Democratic Party of Tajikistan (DPT)—were both excluded from contesting the election because they fell afoul of the country's legal system just before the election campaign, and then were banned from running because they had been charged with criminal offenses.[21]

The arrest of Iskandarov in particular threw a serious wrench into his party's election campaign and appears to have been designed to split the DPT and render it ineffective nationally. The DPT had benefited from Iskandarov's wealth, making it better able to fund a national campaign. His arrest and imprisonment were very controversial, as he was picked up on a Moscow street in April 2005 and was extradited back to Tajikistan, where, on April 22, 2005, he was convicted of misusing state funds, organizing illegal groups, and illegally using weapons and was sentenced to twenty-three years in prison. His family protested his treatment under incarceration, which they allege included torture, and the U.S. ambassador to the OSCE also filed an objection to the way Iskandarov was treated by the Tajik judicial system.[22]

There is no question that the DPT's electoral chances were seriously diminished by Iskandarov's imprisonment. For example, Tajikistan's television stations refused to broadcast paid advertisements by the DPT because they included footage of Iskandarov. Tajikistan's Ministry of Justice also refused to recognize the party's choice of new chairmen on at least two occasions in 2006.

Several other minor figures were also jailed in the year or so preceding the parliamentary elections. They included Rustam Fayziev, deputy head of the Taraqqiyot Party, who was arrested in August 2004 and charged with slandering the president, and was still awaiting trial at the time of the 2005 parliamentary election; and Shamsiddin Shamsiddinov, a deputy head of the IRPT, who was arrested in 2003 and charged with multiple crimes, including forming illegal groups, murder, and treason, in addition to illegal border crossings and polygamy, for which he was convicted and sentenced to sixteen years in prison.[23]

In addition, opposition candidates, especially in the last phase of the election campaign, claimed that they had been subject to various forms of harassment and that in general their ability to campaign freely was thwarted by the local authorities. It is certainly the case that Tajikistan has no culture of political campaigning, and that most candidate meetings, organized by the district election commissions, were rather formal affairs, with candidates receiving their allotted time, but no give-and-take with the potential voters. Some candidates apparently preferred to go directly to the voters on an informal basis, going door-to-door or meeting in *chaikhanas* (teahouses) or in settings in the *mahallas* (traditional neighborhood subdivisions), but this also made them more vulnerable to harassment. ODIHR also received complaints that candidates were pressed to withdraw, and if not they or their proxies would be attacked. Again, it is hard to know if this was because of pressure from the very top or the desire of lower-down supporters of the president to deliver proregime landslides, in the hope that they could turn this into further advancement for themselves or for family members after the election.

Unequal access to the media was also a serious handicap, with equity issues being compromised both by the imprecision with which the electoral code deals with media access issues and by how requirements are set for free time that must be provided but no instructions are given for how it is to be allocated. Candidates also often did not seem to know how to take good advantage of the media opportunities afforded to them. Only 25 percent of the candidates took advantage of the opportunity to publish material without cost in state newspapers. And in at least one case, the government seems to have directly interfered with the ability of one candidate in particular to publicize his own candidacy. One week before the elections, the State Committee for Radio and Television decided to suspend the license of Sughd's TV Guli Bodom, which is owned by Yusuf Ahmedov, an independent candidate for Parliament. After Ahmedov registered his candidacy, a new state TV station, Anis, began broadcasting in the region, covered the campaigns of all the candidates save Ahmedov, and then suddenly ceased broadcasting right after the election.[24]

Most privately owned media outlets provided only minimal election coverage, and the opposition charged that state-run television stations in particular provided very limited or even skewed coverage of the campaign, shortening and editing their presentations without permission.[25] All this led to low public interest in and knowledge about the 2005 campaign.

On March 1, 2005, just two days after the first round of balloting, three opposition parties—the IRPT, the DPT, and the Social Democratic Party of Tajikistan (SDPT)—all held separate news conferences, claiming that they did not accept the results of the elections, and a similar announcement was made by the CPT two days later. These parties also made similar objections to the local legislative elections. Both the CPT and IRPT originally announced that they would not take up the seats that they were offered, although both did reverse this and their elected representatives were seated.

If anything, the 2010 parliamentary elections were conducted even less democratically. The passage of new laws on civil society institutions, new laws on religious organizations, and increased pressure on the media all contributed to an atmosphere of greater public apathy. In a survey done by the International Foundation for Electoral Systems (IFES), only 26 percent of those questioned in a national survey responded that they expected the election to be completely fair.[26] At the same time, however, popular identification with the PDPT seems to have increased, as 68 percent of the respondents in the 2010 survey said that they intended to vote for Rahmon's party, as opposed to 41 percent in the 2004 survey.[27]

In addition, none of the flaws described by the OSCE with regard to the 2005 elections had been rectified. These included restrictions on the admissible size of election funds. These are set at less than the actual costs of elections, creating conditions in which candidates are basically forced to submit fraudulent reports or risk disqualification. Similarly, candidates are not permitted to begin accumulating campaign funds until just three months before an election, when the formal campaign period begins; to do otherwise is to commit fraud.[28]

Candidates are either nominated by political parties (both for inclusion on party lists or for single-mandate districts) or by themselves. In the latter instance, they must obtain a minimum of 500 signatures. In addition, all candidates must pay an electoral deposit (in the 2010 election, this amounted to 7,000 somoni, almost $1,700),[29] which is forfeited if the candidate does not receive a minimum of 5 percent of the vote and is a substantial barrier to some candidates.[30]

As provided by the law, candidates had to register in the period beginning 45 days before the election, and ending 20 days before the first round of voting. In 2010, there were 129 candidates registered in the 41 single-mandate districts. The PDPT competed in all but 2 of the single-mandate districts, and they ran unopposed in 9 districts. The IRPT competed in 20 districts (and won in 2), the CPT in 7, the Party of Economic Reform of Tajikistan (PERT) in 6, the Agrarian Reform Party of Tajikistan (APT), in 4, and the SDPT in 2, while the DPT and Socialist Party only ran party lists.

The CCER was supposed to provide opportunities for public debate, but candidates complained that they were not notified of such meetings or permitted to hold any other public meetings. Candidates complained that their posters and electoral materials were not displayed prominently (especially in comparison with the posters that were displayed for the public collection of funds for the construction of the Roghun hydroelectric station). Government employees in both the Sughd region and in Dushanbe complained to the OSCE that they were being pressed to vote for PDPT candidates; additionally, two election proxies reported that they had been threatened with job loss if they continued to serve as electoral representatives for opposition candidates.[31] Although the observer mission was unable to confirm the claims, it expressed concern over "the number of such allegations."[32]

Tajikistan's media paid little attention to the election. There is very little media in Tajikistan; there are only four state-run television stations and one independent station known as Independent Tajik Television (ITT), which is unable to broadcast full time in Dushanbe because it shares its frequency with the Russian military.[33] There are no daily newspapers, and only a handful of newspapers or radio stations pay any attention to political issues.[34] By law, each station has to award 30 minutes of free airtime to registered parties and 15 minutes of free airtime to single-mandate district candidates. State-funded newspapers must set aside up to eight pages of newsprint for candidates. But the OSCE found that there was virtually no election coverage other than this, although the media continued to bombard the airways with articles about the accomplishments of President Rahmon and the ruling party.[35]

The official turnout for the 2010 election was 85.2 percent, and the OSCE assessed that the election was properly conducted in 74.8 percent of the polling stations visited. This was partly because, once again, the CCER had inadequately prepared the district election committees for their duties.[36]

In a survey done just weeks before the election, there was also substantial dissatisfaction with the way the actual voting process was conducted. The OSCE observers positively assessed voting in only 74.3 percent of the precincts that they visited, and in 21 percent of the polling stations there were serious violations. There were various kinds of violations found, including numerous cases where a single person cast numerous ballots, one for each member of his or her family (demonstrated by the fact that a single hand clearly wrote numerous signatures for people sharing a last name on the voters' lists). This was facilitated by the fact that voters were not always asked for proper identification (in 36.6 percent of the polling stations visited). In addition, unsigned protocols were delivered by the precinct election commissions, as well as those completed in pencil. Ballot boxes were not always properly sealed, and in just over 10 percent of the cases observed secrecy in voting was also not observed. In fact, the OSCE observers found that in a full third of the precincts they visited, members of the precinct election commissions did not know how to properly fill out ballots. Spoiled and unused ballots were not always discarded, and in 25 instances OSCE observers found that properly cast ballots were not reported. In addition, observers were only able to partially view the ballot-counting process.[37] Nonetheless, the performance of Tajikistan's electoral officials appears to have been slightly better in 2010 than in 2005.

TAJIKISTAN'S LOCAL GOVERNMENTS

Tajikistan has only had very limited reform of its national-level executive institutions. The country's civil service remains only partially modified. As Tajikistan's own authorities admitted in their March 2007 National Development Strategy:

> The decisionmaking mechanism employed by government authorities remains complicated and is not transparent as far as the public is concerned. Effective mechanisms for civil monitoring of government agencies have not been developed and the low wages earned by employees in the public sector encourage corruption.[38]

The government has long promised that it would offer a new law on self-government, which, when passed, should facilitate the operation of local water users' associations. A great deal of international assistance has been devoted to their development, both to facilitate better agricultural practices and simultaneously develop more support for the norms of civil society, building democratic institutions at the grass roots.

Tajikistan's Constitution left most of the Soviet administrative divisions unchanged, with the country divided into four oblasts (or provinces), and each oblast divided into districts (*rayoni* or *nohiyaho* in Tajik), with 22 cities, 47 towns, 354 villages, and 3,570 settlements. The heads of local governments remain appointed. Elections to local and regional legislatures are generally held at the same time as those for the national Parliament.

There are three major levels of local government in Tajikistan—oblasts, cities and regions, and villages and towns—although there is considerable variation as to how power is divided across the country. At the local-most level, several villages or towns can be grouped together as a single *jamoat* (municipality), and larger cities are divided into several districts. At the next level up, there are cities and *rayons*, and then above them are two oblasts (Sughd and Khatlon), the Gorno-Badakhshan Autonomous Oblast, and the Region of Republican Subordination (RRS), which consists of the city of Dushanbe and a large swath of cities and rural districts surrounding it. This highest tier of local government represents a substantial recentralization of power as compared with the Soviet period, when Tajikistan had four oblasts, as well as GBAO and Dushanbe city (with the status of an oblast). The boundaries and makeup of the current subnational divisions of the country were designed to reward President Rahmon's civil war supporters and punish those who supported the United Tajik Opposition.

There is considerable duplication between the responsibilities of these levels of government, and the differentiation between them is not always clearly elaborated. One of the challenges for the institutions at the most local level (towns and villages) is that they have a host of fiscal responsibilities, including augmenting central government financing for local school support, pensions, and municipal services such as clean water, but they are sharply restricted in the ways that they are able to raise money through the levying of taxes and fees.[39]

The rights and responsibilities of the various levels of local self-government were set forth in the 1994 Law on the Bodies of Local Self-Government in Settlements and Villages, were modified somewhat in 2008, and were intended to be replaced by a new law that was drafted and circulated in communities in 2008 and 2009. Legislation on agricultural reform introduced in 2008 also modified the powers of self-governing bodies in towns and villages; these bodies lost the right to allocate land plots (largely taken from vacant lands that are found between communities and are owned by the state). This responsibility was granted to city and rural districts, representing a serious loss of authority. This was designed to help facilitate agricultural reform, as most local authorities were viewed as being most vulnerable to pressure from large landowners.[40]

The changes proposed in the new law include the requirement that local communities elect a council based on representation by distinct districts (of at least one representative per village), through secret ballot. A report from the U.S. Agency for International Development (USAID) on Tajik local government reforms criticized the draft law for not clarifying the qualifications for office and system of voting, or guaranteeing that the officials represent roughly similarly sized districts.[41]

Tajik voters, however, expect their elected local councils to improve the economic and social conditions in their communities. The 2010 IFES survey asked respondents who were aware of upcoming local elections what they expected of their new deputies. Free to name multiple goals, 72 percent of those responding said improved electricity supply, and 49 percent said better roads and safer drinking water.[42]

It is quite another thing to expect Tajik local deputies, or the appointed local government officials who serve in these communities, to have the intellectual, let alone the financial, wherewithal to address these problems. There are a number of Tajik, as well as international, projects designed to boost local government capacity and to broaden the dialogue on these questions to include representatives of civil society.

The goal of local government reform is also encompassed in the Public Administration Reform Strategy approved by the Office of the President in 2006, which runs through 2015. Most particularly, it contains a Project on Local Governance and Citizen Participation, which is designed to facilitate a dialogue on decentralization and lead to greater local participation in local development planning and budgeting. In addition, U.S. officials continue to work with local Tajik government officials through a local governance project that was launched in April 2010; termed the "local development initiative," the program makes small grants for infrastructure projects available to local officials who go through good governance training.[43]

The UNDP has also done extensive work trying to build government capacity at the local community level while simultaneously engaging civil society, through what it terms its Communities Program. This program has supported the development of district development councils, initially in 19 areas, to be extended to 67 districts by 2015. These councils focus on engaging civil society actors, the private sector, and local government to develop resource mobilization and developmental strategies that focus on poverty alleviation. They also support the initial establishment of some 100 *jamoat* resource centers, to be expanded to 400 *jamoats* by 2015,[44] which are to foster community-driven development.[45] These centers and councils, which are subsumed in the UNDP's Joint Country Partnership Strategy and are funded by a host of UNDP donors, are found in Sughd, Khatlon, the districts of the RRS, and in GBAO.[46]

In many ways the most important institution of local authority remains the traditional institution of "local" power, the *avlod* (an extended family that is formally constituted). The respondents in the IFES survey on civic participation, done in January 2010, were twice as likely to say that they had contacted a local *avlod* or *mahalla* official to address or solve a problem than a public official.[47]

The *avlod* is an informal patrimonial institution that reaches into most ethnic and especially rural Tajik communities. A 2007 study commissioned by the Aga Khan Development Network estimated that 60 to 65 percent of the country's population was part of the more than 12,000 *avlods* in the country.[48] These institutions function much like the Uzbek *mahalla*; but unlike the *mahallas*, Tajikistan's *avlods* lack any legal recognition of their authority by the state. The power exercised by the head of the *avlod*, who is a family elder in every sense of the word, is nearly absolute, and the reach of the *avlod* has expanded as more and more families are divided—initially by the conditions of the civil war in the 1990s, and now more frequently as a result of labor migration to jobs in Russia or elsewhere in Central Asia. Although lacking legal authority to do so, *avlod* leaders successfully compel members to allocate their income to the benefit of more impoverished members of the community. They can prevent marriages they disapprove of and force community members to leave the country to work as migrant labor.

Muzaffar Olimov and Saodat Olimova argue that part of the reason that the Tajik people have accepted the strengthening of President Rahmon's authority is that most Tajiks, especially those in rural areas, have been socialized to accept patrimonial authority from childhood. Those who are able to see the presidency as the extension of the *avlod* to the national level are not only able to accept Rahmon's authority, but they can also identify with the public manifestations of his power, such as the ubiquitous posters with his face, his increased presence on television, and the large volume of his writings. His public presence, then, is seen as a natural manifestation of his power.[49]

LAW AND ORDER IN TAJIKISTAN

The reform of Tajikistan's legal system has been very incomplete. In many places, Soviet-era laws remain on the books. More important, however, a Soviet-era mentality still dominates many of those who work in the legal system. What this means is that Tajik lawmakers have been willing to accept the recommendations of Western specialists when drafting legal reforms, but those in key positions of power have not been willing to back up these reforms with formal or informal directives that press for their enforcement. The will to reform is further compromised by the fact that anyone trained under the old legal system is used to the continental style of jurisprudence, rather than the Anglo-American one, which is key in so many of the reforms. The continental system places much of the burden on the defendant to prove that he or she is not guilty as charged, rather than on the state to demonstrate his or her guilt. Continental law also places primacy on the use of legal precedents in making decisions, rather than on the sanctity of the law itself.

Tajikistan has a large number of institutions with shared authority in the area of law enforcement, with unclear differentiation of their various responsibilities. These include the Ministry of the Interior, which has primary responsibility for public order and has supervisory responsibility for the police; the State Committee on National Security, which is the main intelligence-gathering agency and controls the Border Service; the Drug Control Agency, the Agency of State Financial Control and the Fight Against Corruption, the State Tax Committee, and the Customs Service, which all have mandates to investigate specific kinds of crimes and report directly to the president; and the Prosecutor's Office, which is able to supervise the investigations that all of these offices perform.

Tajikistan still operates under an amended version of the Soviet criminal procedure code of 1961. The country's criminal courts are organized into district, city or regional, and national courts, and most criminal cases are heard in civilian criminal court, although the state has the discretionary power to send cases to military courts. One modification that has been introduced is that Tajikistan has accepted the European Union's standards insofar as introducing a moratorium on capital punishment.[50]

Trials are public, with the exception of those involving national security, and the state is largely free to invoke the claim to national security at will. Those charged with a crime are technically innocent until proven guilty and have the right to a free public defender; but in practice, anyone who wants to have a competently prepared defense must hire a private attorney. Defendants and their attorneys have the right to examine all aspects of the government's case and to confront witnesses. Nonetheless, the bias of the court, as during the Soviet period, will lie with the prosecution. Nongovernmental organizations (NGOs) have been able to send representatives to observe many trials, although sometimes judges demand that formal requests be made and approved by the Council of Justice.

Tajikistan's legal system provides the prosecutor and police with discretionary power to make arrests and to hold suspects for extended periods before trial. Prosecutors can issue warrants on their own authority, and despite the fact that the accused are supposed to go before judges within 28 days, prosecutors can authorize pretrial detentions of up to two months, and with special permission from higher authorities they can extend this for a total of fifteen months, with judges rarely willing to review petitions from defendants claiming that they have been subject to excessive pretrial detention.[51] During this period, family members are not allowed any contact with the accused. Prosecutors also have a variety of "supervisory" powers, which allow them to protest judicial decisions outside of the normal appeals process, and they are able to force decisions that go against them to be reviewed by a higher court, even after the period for appeal has expired. This effectively means that anyone who has ever been arrested on a criminal charge is at risk of being returned to court for an indefinite period of time, even if the case against him or her has been dismissed. Tajikistan's search-and-seizure provisions require prior approval from prosecutors in most cases, but this requirement is said to be frequently ignored.

There have been periodic allegations of corruption made against the various levels of law enforcement, including the traffic police, whose practice of extorting bribes from Tajikistan's drivers is an everyday occurrence and has been witnessed by this author on many occasions.

However, little has been done to address this practice—such as introducing a competitive pay structure for the traffic police and other law enforcement officials—and the Tajik authorities content themselves with the occasional arrest of relatively low-ranking police officials.

In addition to this absence of political will to seek out and punish violators, efforts to address corruption are further complicated by an atmosphere of intimidation that makes people unwilling to file criminal complaints against individuals in positions of authority and their family members. There have been accounts, for instance, of pressure from regional prosecutors on citizens to drop complaints against prosecutors' relatives. Tajiks are hesitant even to seek help from the Office of the Ombudsman for Human Rights, a position that was created in 2009 but that remains underfunded and understaffed; the legislation that established this office did not guarantee its independence from interference by the government.

There also appears to be little confidence in Tajikistan's Agency of State Financial Control and the Fight Against Corruption, which was named among the top five most corrupt structures in the country in a nationwide public opinion survey carried out by the Center for Strategic Studies in 2010.[52] In the first nine months of 2008, the anticorruption agency investigated 677 corruption-related crimes, including 122 cases involving various law enforcement officials, including four judges and three judicial system employees.[53]

In July 2011, the Tajik government took as yet unproven steps to improve this situation through the creation of an "Accounts Chamber" (modeled after the similar one in the Russian Federation), which is intended to conduct independent financial inquires and report its results to the president and to the lower house of the Parliament. The Accounts Chamber is able to examine any level of government, or any organization in which the government participates, as well as the National Bank. Those who serve in it are immune from prosecution, a provision that is designed to keep those under investigation from threatening members of the Chamber to get them to back off their inquiries.

As a result of the government's soft stance on corruption, at least according to the U.S. Department of State's 2009 human rights report for Tajikistan, Tajikistan's criminal authorities are not effective in their efforts to control the activities of organized crime groups, and "serious abuses—particularly those committed by high-ranking officials—[have gone] unpunished."[54] The report makes specific reference to the refusal of Tajikistan's government to investigate allegations of misconduct made against Murodali Alimardon for his behavior as head of the National Bank of Tajikistan, in the matter of the bank's misuse of funds from the International Monetary Fund.

Tajikistan's judicial system remains very weak. The president has nearly complete control over the national-level judiciary through the Ministry of Justice, if he decides to exercise it. He appoints judges and prosecutors with the consent of Parliament, but Tajikistan's legislative body is not inclined to exercise this power. Since 1999 oblast- and district-level courts have fallen under a nominally independent "Council of Justice."

Judicial reforms were introduced in 2004, extending the term of judges from five years to ten years and giving part of the Supreme Court's authority to oblast courts, which themselves were pressured to introduce circuit riding practices. Some 240 Tajik judges had gone through some form of judicial retraining by 2005 through a USAID program on legal reform introduced in both Kyrgyzstan and Tajikistan; the program, however, had more resonance in the former country.[55]

Not all Tajikistan's justices made it through the retraining courses or the examinations that Soviet-era judges had to undergo in order to be retained. But the dismissal rate of less than 15 percent was judged too high by the Council of Justices, which then discontinued the examination process.[56]

Thus, in 2004 the Association of Tajik Judges adopted a Code of Judicial Ethics, which introduced three levels of sanctions—warning, censure, and dismissal—to be administered by the Council of Justice; in its first year of operation, the council issued warnings to eight judges and censured three others in the eleven cases that they were asked to deliberate on.[57] In 2010, three judges were arrested for corruption.[58] The Code of Judicial Ethics, however, remains unevenly applied.

Overall, the judiciary remains poorly trained. There have been international assistance projects designed to create and expand access to legal reference materials, and USAID has funded the development of seven regional libraries with legal materials. It has also offered computer training to judges and helped fund the development of electronic court records that were based on standardized forms. Nonetheless, the country still lacks a comprehensive electronic database for legal records, and most judges make their decisions without much access to judicial precedent. The intent of the Tajik government is to introduce lifetime tenure. The salaries of judges remain low, as do those of prosecutors, making them prone to taking bribes.

Although Tajikistan maintains that it has no political prisoners, there are several individuals in jail whom it is hard to consider anything else. And some political figures have been killed under unclear circumstances, raising suspicions that their deaths may have been politically motivated. In June 2009, former minister of the interior Mahmadnazar Solehov died, having allegedly committed suicide, after government security forces entered his house. Less than a month later, in July 2009, Mirzo Ziyoev, a former commander in chief of the UTO and the minister of emergency situations, was fatally shot near Tavildara, allegedly by rebel forces, while traveling with government forces. Both deaths were considered suspicious enough that they were included in the U.S. Department of State's human rights report for 2009.[59]

Moreover, some prisoners have fared rather poorly while in incarceration, raising suspicions over the treatment of prisoners. For example, Rustam Fayziev, deputy chairman of the unregistered Party of Progress, died in prison in February 2008, after four years of incarceration for a letter that allegedly defamed and insulted President Rahmon. The letter itself was never published.

Several other political prisoners also remain in prison. They include the well-publicized case of Mahmadruzi Iskandarov, the head of the DPT, who formerly headed Tojikgaz and was convicted on charges of corruption in 2005 after being extradited from Russia.[60] Former minister of the interior Yakub Salimov remains in prison, having been sentenced to fifteen years of incarceration for crimes against the state and high treason during a closed trial in 2005. In December 2008, several family members of the late UTO commander Mirzo Ziyoev received prison terms on unknown charges.[61]

There remain periodic reports of torture of both political and ordinary prisoners. There is no legal definition of torture provided, and there are no systematic mechanisms for Tajik authorities to investigate allegations of torture. In fact, those who bring forward such complaints are at risk of further punishment from the judicial system. The situation is so bad that Human Rights Watch reports that "experts agreed that in most cases there is impunity for rampant torture in Tajikistan."[62] Beatings and threats to the safety of the family of the accused seem to be regularly used to extract confessions. Despite the fact that the law formally recognizes a defendant as innocent until proven guilty, a confession is a virtual guarantee that the accused will be sentenced to prison; hence the importance for Tajik prosecutors and investigators to secure confessions. This was apparently what occurred in the case of Muhammadi Salimzoda, who received a twenty-nine-year sentence when convicted of espionage after being accused of spying for Kyrgyzstan in 2009, after he is said by his relatives to have confessed because he was subjected to physical and psychological torture.[63]

The UN Human Rights Committee has found against Tajikistan (in the April 2008 case *Rakhmatov et al. v. Tajikistan*), with regard to the violation of the human rights of three adults and two minors, and international observers have been denied access to detention centers since the judgment, making it hard to know if any improvements have occurred.[64] In general, it has been very difficult for international observers to gain access to prisons and detention facilities, and Tajikistan failed to sign an agreement with the International Red Cross to cover prison visits, although international missions and NGOs have been able to review medical facilities in prisons and to discharge their consular responsibilities. They have observed that there are high rates of HIV/AIDS and tuberculosis in the prisons, with medical treatment generally being poor.

Prison conditions are harsh, and the country has eight prisons (including one for women) and four pretrial detention centers. The new prison at Sughd, however, is considered to be a considerable improvement over those that date from Soviet times. Prisons are said to be generally overcrowded, and generally have unsanitary conditions. The government periodically offers amnesties to large numbers of prisoners, largely to deal with some of this overcrowding. This was largely the reason why President Rahmon pardoned some 10,000 prisoners in November 2009, generally those who had completed at least three-quarters of their sentence, or were minors when they committed the crime, and men and women over fifty-five years of age. In June 2011, in honor of the upcoming twentieth anniversary of independence, President Rahmon sent Parliament a new law on amnesty that led to the release of 15,000 additional prisoners, including those who were convicted of "extremist" activities receiving sentences of five years or less, some members of Hizb ut-Tahrir, and some lesser-known political prisoners.

Sentences are often arbitrary, or at least seem so. For example, Judge Nur Nurov sentenced 31 residents of Isfara District to between ten and twenty-five years for a variety of crimes including theft, embezzlement, and membership in a criminal organization. Most of these individuals were relatives of an Isfara official who had fallen out of favor with local officials. Isfara is a part of the country where Islamic groups are seen as active, and where the government in Dushanbe views the locals with considerable suspicion. These sentences were apparently rendered even though the state prosecutor did not ask for lengthy incarcerations; the U.S. Department of State's 2009 human rights report stated that the defense attorney produced a tape in which Judge Nurov claimed that the chief of the Supreme Court had demanded that he sentence these defendants to the maximum penalty provided by law.[65]

The lack of clarity in Tajikistan's laws is another reason for the inadequate legal protection accorded to the country's citizens. Particularly problematic is the legal protection of property, because it is very difficult to establish clear titles to either agricultural lands or urban property. The situation with regard to agricultural lands is discussed at length below, but it is important to underscore that urban landowners are as vulnerable to the risk of expropriation by the government as their agricultural colleagues.

The best-publicized case involved the destruction of Dushanbe's only working synagogue in 2008 to make way for the new Presidential Palace (which is still unoccupied due to structural flaws) in a main downtown area. The case attracted international attention.[66] The city administration offered the Jewish community a plot of land elsewhere in Dushanbe. Eventually, Hasan Sadulloev, chairman of Orienbank, donated a building in downtown Dushanbe to the Jewish community to be used as a new synagogue, and it opened in May 2009.[67] Some of the other businesses and landowners who were affected by the building of the palace and a new downtown park were not as well compensated. In December 2010, the deputy chairman of the Committee for Religious Affairs claimed that the synagogue had failed to fulfill registration requirements and was therefore operating illegally.[68]

FREEDOM OF THE PRESS

Reporters Without Borders ranked Tajikistan 113 out of 175 countries in terms of press freedom, based on violations of press freedom from September 1, 2008, through August 1, 2009.[69] As of 2010, there were 244 registered newspapers and magazines published in Tajikistan, of which 128 were privately owned. The most frequently any of these publish is weekly; the only exception is a small English-language daily. All newspapers and magazines with circulations that exceed 99 are required to register with the Ministry of Culture before beginning publication. Tajikistan also has eight information agencies, seven of which are privately owned. In addition, the government controls most of the country's printing presses and access to newsprint.[70]

In theory, media organizations are guaranteed free access to information about government activities by the Law on Access to Information, which was passed in June 2008. But in reality, it has been very difficult for journalists to be able to actually secure better access. Most government ministries and agencies still require written requests for information before they will agree to answer questions from journalists. Moreover, the government continues to seem to feel that journalists should report what casts authorities in a positive light, rather than serving as an independent source of information.

According the U.S. Department of State's 2009 human rights report for Tajikistan, independent journalists complain that they frequently encounter pressure from the government, and that they receive threats from the prosecutors' offices (sometimes made by telephone, and other times when they drop in to editorial offices), and that their publications are subjected to more than the ordinary number of tax inspections.[71] Pressure on independent journalists has traditionally been especially strong in the weeks before elections.

In addition, journalists are at risk of having criminal proceedings lodged against them, often arbitrarily. In recent years, a number of cases against journalists and publishers have been launched by the Tajik authorities. For instance, in 2007 the government of Tajikistan charged Tursunal Aliyev with slander, for criticizing the authorities in Sughd in his local newspaper, *Tong* (Morning). After local prosecutors dismissed these charges, the case was pursued anew by regional officials.

The most celebrated case in recent years has been the criminal proceedings brought against Dodojon Atovulloyev, the editor in chief of *Charogi Ruz* (Daylight)—an opposition, Tajik-language newspaper that is published in Russia. He was charged with public defamation of the president and seeking to overthrow the constitutional order of Tajikistan in September 2008, and the Tajik authorities made an unsuccessful demand for his extradition from Russia. Atovulloyev currently lives abroad and heads the opposition Vatandor (Patriot) movement.[72]

The country lacks a national daily newspaper. Pressure on independent weeklies has been acute, with their owners and publishers subject to costly penalties if they are found guilty of libel, which is a charge that is frequently levied against them by prominent individuals in or close to the government when they are implicated in articles about corruption. For example, in January 2010 *Paykon* (Arrowhead) was subject to substantial damages (300,000 somoni or $63,000) in a judgment lodged by Tajikstandart after its appeal failed. The newspaper had printed an open letter from a group of Tajik businessmen addressed to President Rahmon, in which they accused Tajikstandart, which monitors the quality of imported goods, of corruption and of crippling the development of foreign trade. Shortly afterward, two Supreme Court judges and a judge from Dushanbe City Court brought libel suits against three separate weeklies (*Asia-Plus*, *Ozodagan*, and *Farazh*), with a total of $1.2 million in damages being sought, and the Ministry of Agriculture brought suit against the newspaper *Millat* (Nation) for roughly $250,000 in damages.[73]

Television remains the most important source of information for Tajik citizens.[74] Four state-run television stations operate nationally, four state-run television stations operate regionally, and there are one state-run national and several state-run regional radio stations. In recent years, the government has been seeking to squeeze out both independent and foreign-owned radio and television stations, and the U.S. Department of State's human rights report for 2009 noted that, according to the National Association of Independent Media in Tajikistan (NANSMIT), in the previous five years 20 independent broadcasting groups had been denied operating licenses by the State Committee on Radio and Television. Both NANSMIT and the Union of Tajik Journalists have called for the disbanding of the state broadcasting committee, which has the authority to grant all radio and television licenses.[75] Opposition politicians regularly complain that their activities get no coverage on state-run radio and television.

In addition, the independent TV station Somoniyon was shut down in 2004, and despite the fact that it successfully took the State Committee on Radio and Television to court, it received neither compensation nor a new license to operate, and then in October 2009 it once again lost a court case. Another independent television station, Guli Bodom, in the Sughd region, was denied an extension of its license, seemingly because some of its broadcasts had a critical political tone.

The independent Radio Imruz lost its ability to transmit in August 2009, when it was charged with broadcasting information on sensitive topics. It was able to return to broadcasting some three weeks later, but only after its editor in chief resigned.[76]

Foreign-owned media outlets have also fallen afoul of Tajik officials. The BBC has had the most trouble in this regard. After being denied a renewal of its FM license, it began offering its Persian-language broadcasts through satellite transmission. Although Russian television and radio programs are frequently rebroadcast on Tajikistan's state-run channels, RTR's Planeta network lost its license in March 2009, allegedly for unpaid fees.

The state also licenses all Internet cafes, and on occasion it has blocked access to particular websites that are seen as "undermining state policies," such as the site that had been run by the *Charogi Ruz* newspaper referred to above. In addition, in 2007 Tajikistan's criminal code was amended to criminalize libel and defamation of character on the Internet, making it punishable by up to two years in prison. However, as of late 2009 there had been no prosecutions based on that law.

In May 2011, the government further tightened controls over the communications network, requiring that all electronic and cellular telephone service providers go through Tajiktelekom, the state monopoly, for access to foreign countries. All licenses that allowed for direct international hookups were annulled.

In addition, in the wake of the "color revolutions" in Central and Eastern Europe, in May 2007 Tajikistan's government introduced a new Law on Civil Society Organizations, which forced all NGOs to reregister; this allowed the government to push from public life some of the political organizations that had been registered in the immediate aftermath of the National Reconciliation process. At the time of the adoption of the law, there were some 2,000 NGOs operating in the country, of which roughly 1,000 applied for and received reregistration. Of them, approximately 50 are offices of international groups.

In 2011, Parliament passed two laws that increased the risks associated with holding unsanctioned public meetings, which makes political protests by unregistered groups in particular more problematic. The first, "On Peaceful Meetings, Gatherings and Demonstrations," allows the government to charge participants in unsanctioned peaceful protests or meetings with an administrative crime, with a fine of $100 to $150, roughly equivalent to a month's salary. It also makes participation in hunger strikes (something that political protesters often do) a crime. A piece of legislation, "On the Militia," permits security officers to use rubber batons to break up demonstrations.[77]

RELIGION IN POLITICS AND SOCIETY

The conduct of the Tajik civil war led to a different role for Islam in Tajikistan than elsewhere in Central Asia. It is the only country in the region with a registered religious party, the IRPT. Tajikistan's 1994 Constitution established the country as a secular state, and although the 1998 Law on Political Parties precluded the formation of parties along religious lines the IRPT was able to gain registration when President Rahmon vetoed this version of the law.

Within a few years of the signing of the National Reconciliation Agreement, the Tajik government sought to limit the role of the Islamic opposition and to influence the practice of Islam in the country to make it better conform to the national ideals that Rahmon was seeking to perpetuate.

Amendments to the Constitution made in 1999 further elaborated the relationship between church and state, providing for a separation of the two. At the same time, however, the amendments guaranteed "political and ideological pluralism," which most took as consistent with a role for "political Islam" or participation of Islamic actors in political life. Religious thinkers tried to respond to this; highly influential in this regard were a series of articles published in 1998–1999 by IRPT leader M. Himmatzode, titled "On the Compatibility of a Secular Government with a Religious Party," which elaborated how the values associated with an Islamic government could also be associated with a secular government. And in September 1999, the leaders of the IRPT, in conjunction with the other leaders of the UTO, agreed to support the changes proposed in the constitutional amendments, and endorsed the idea of a secular Tajik state as in accordance with their own political principles. The leaders of the IRPT considered their support for a secular state to signify a rejection of the "transnational project" traditionally associated with political Islam, in that they were effectively disavowing the ideal of a single global *umma* (Muslim community) to replace existing national states.[78] The participation of the IRPT in Tajik political life cemented its transition from a political-military organization to a parliamentary political party with a religiously inspired program in a participatory (at least on paper) political system.

Since the 2006 presidential election, the pressure on nonconformist Islamic institutions and leaders has increased. In 2007 the new Law on Observing National Traditions and Rituals took effect, requiring clerics to pass a formal exam designed to test their knowledge of Hanafi teachings.[79] Although some defended the new policy as an attempt to eliminate clerics with limited religious training or knowledge, others complained that it was a way to discriminate against those who sought to instruct their congregations in the Salafist tradition.[80] In the chaos of the war and its aftermath many mosques "spontaneously" emerged in community centers or other informal settings, and more or less anyone was able to anoint himself a mullah and to seek a following. But the introduction of an examination (administered by mullahs under state authority) gives the state new powers to curtail the activities of troublesome clerics.

In August 2007, tests were administered to imams in Dushanbe. However, even earlier, the state was able to label the preaching of those who criticized the government as "posing a threat to the stability" of Tajikistan. This was the charge leveled against Nuriddin Qahhorov, who led a congregation in the Dushanbe suburb of Vahdat, in May 2007, when recordings of Qahhorov's sermons were confiscated from stores.[81]

A new law on religion, which was sent to Parliament in November 2008 and took effect in April 2009, replaces the 1994 legislation that had been amended in 1997, 1999, and 2001. This new law met with strong criticism from the OSCE, because it introduced further restrictions on freedom of conscience and made few positive changes. The law increases the role of the state in religious affairs in general, and in particular was designed to create more favorable conditions for the Hanafi school of law to play the dominant role in religious affairs, as opposed to Salafi teachings or the Ismaili sect, which is not recognized as consistent with Islam by most Sunnis.[82] The law notes "the special role for the Hanafi school of Islam in the development of the national culture and moral life" of the Tajik people.[83]

Under the new law, the registration process for religious organizations was made much tougher, and required ten citizen founders to obtain a certificate from local authorities that they had lived in the area for at least ten years; and these citizens could also be required to give accounts of their attitudes toward education, family, and marriage. These requirements were seen as particularly onerous by members of Protestant Evangelical groups. All religious organizations were required to reregister (having until January 1, 2010, to do so) and were now required to report on all their activities annually; special restrictions were applied to mosques, whose locations now required special approval by state religious authorities.

There were limits set on the number of mosques that could be opened in any community, with one Juma mosque (that is, Cathedral or Friday mosque) for every 10,000 to 20,000 people, and in Dushanbe one for every 30,000 to 50,000 people. Similarly, there could be one ordinary mosque for daily services for every 100 to 1,000 people, and for every 1,000 to 5,000 people in Dushanbe. The state also took over the organization of Tajik participation in hajj, for the hajjis (pilgrims) who are traveling as part of Tajikistan's official quota. The state also assumed responsibility for clearing foreign religious groups interested in visiting Tajikistan, and for granting permission for Tajik clerics to participate in international religious activities outside the country. Many religious institutions were unable to meet the deadline and now operate in a gray zone, liable for fines and at risk of closure, while others had their documents returned to have "errors" corrected, and still others were denied registration.[84]

The law also seeks to regulate the number of guests at religious life-cycle gatherings, like weddings and funerals, setting a maximum number of 250 people who can be invited. This is designed to reduce expenditures for such occasions—which frequently required extensive borrowing from family members and others and could cost up to several years' income for an entire family. Ironically, the idea of such restrictions is more popular among Salafi or neo-Salafi clerics than among traditional Hanafi clerics, because Salafist thinkers are more focused on the purity of ideals rather than the public presentation of observance.

The law also introduces new restrictions on religious literature, requiring state approval for its importation, export, sale, and distribution. Individuals are left largely free to own what they like. However, only registered religious associations are authorized to produce, import, and distribute religious literature, still of course only with state permission, and only the most national religious organizations would be able to set up publishing houses or access printing presses. It is clear that these regulations were primarily focused on Islamic groups, which are responsible for the overwhelming majority of religious materials published in the country, and particularly targeted Salafi groups and Islamic schismatics, such as Hizb ut-Tahrir. But it will also affect the importing of Evangelical Christian texts.

Although the law allows believers to spread their faith, it sharply restricts the conditions under which they may do so. It bars proselytizing in schools and other public places. Restrictions on religious leaders holding office were also introduced. This latter provision creates a point of possible tension for the IRPT's continued participation in public life, giving the courts grounds for the exclusion of parliamentarians and officeholders openly identified with this party if they decide to pursue such a course of action.

President Rahmon has sought to make the Hanafi tradition of Islam an important component of Tajik national identity, in part because many people are contesting Islamic space in Tajikistan—the Hanafi clerics attached to DUM (Muslim Spiritual Administration) Tajikistan, the remaining members of the civil-war era IRPT, Salafi clerics, members of Hizb ut-Tahrir, the fragments of the Islamic Movement of Uzbekistan (IMU), the Aga Khan (at least for the Ismaili population), and increasing numbers of Shi'a clerics from Iran (who though they do not proselytize much are identified by a growing number of Tajiks as being an integral part of the Iranian/Persian culture to which the Tajiks view themselves as heirs). Moreover, there is a question as to whether ordinary Tajiks view President Rahmon as a worthy representative of the faith, given his position during the Soviet period.

It is one thing for Rahmon to be seen as a personification of Tajik nationhood, but it is quite another for him to appear as the personification of the faith. For a time, Rahmon seems to have toyed with the idea of becoming an imam, and certainly at the time of the jubilee for Imam Azam, the Tajik president made himself the centerpiece and the leading author and commentator.

At the same time, the members of Tajikistan's legally recognized religious establishment are working hard to create a place for themselves in society. And they have had to press the state hard to be able to do this. For example, Tajik educational officials announced in August 2009 that starting with the coming school year, all eighth graders would be required to take 34 hours of instruction on the history of Islam in order to keep young people from being attracted to "extremist" forms of the faith—on the express order of the president. The weekly class on "Understanding Islam" went into the school curriculum during the 2009–2010 academic year.

As Sayid Umar Husayni of the IRPT noted in an interview with Radio Free Europe/Radio Liberty, none of Tajikistan's noted religious scholars were invited to take part in the working group that prepared the required teaching materials for this course.[85] Moreover, the Ministry of Education rather than religious authorities implemented special training in Dushanbe to prepare 400 history and literature teachers to teach the course. Abdujalol Alizoda, the rector of Tajikistan's Islamic University, could do was to express his hope that graduates of his university might be hired to teach such a course in the future.[86] This discussion became moot, as the course was removed from the curriculum the following year, and more time was instead spent on "the history of the Tajik people."[87]

The 2008 Law on Freedom of Conscience and Religious Organizations placed the Islamic University directly under the administration of the Ministry of Education, where it was downgraded to an institute, the equivalent of a junior college. The now–Islamic Institute's teachers had to requalify to retain their positions. There are also 20 madrassas (high schools) that prepare students for study at the Islamic Institute, and a secular madrassa as well.

Tajikistan's religious establishments' efforts have also included trying to offer spiritual support for their coreligionists living in Russia. Interesting in this regard was the November 2009 visit of Abdulkasim Abdulloev, head of the religious organization Nur (Light) in Komsomolsk-na-Amur, who came to Tajikistan as the representative of the Muslim Spiritual Administration of the Asian part of Russia (DUMACHR) to talk with leaders in Tajikistan about importing from Tajikistan more religious literature in the Tajik and Uzbek languages for Tajik citizens working in Russia, and to explore whether Russian students could come to study in the religious academies in Tajikistan.[88]

This is an interesting development, especially if it augurs increased cooperation by leading Tajik and Russian Islamic officials (at least those associated with the formally sanctioned "spiritual administrations") in order to dampen growing popular fervor for radical ideas. Clerics from Tajikistan are settling in Russia among those Tajiks who are living in ethnically consolidated communities. However, most seasonal laborers do not live in these established communities but reside in workers' dormitories. There they do not have the spiritual support structure of a *mahalla* or *jamoat* and have no communally based mosque on which to rely. This is said to make them more willing to experiment with radical forms of Islam that are not organized around a mosque, such as Hizb ut-Tahrir, whose recruiters often live among them.[89] Many of these young people had been practicing Muslims before their departure, and in some cases had even received counsel from community elders, including clerics, before deciding to migrate to Russia.

Russian and Tajik security officials are cooperating closely on trying to identify radical and terrorist elements, both from Hizb ut-Tahrir and from the IMU. Meanwhile, the IRPT, the former religious opposition, is making an effort to maintain a role for itself, one that is at least institutionally separate from the Council of Ulema, the country's highest religious body. The Council of Ulema, though technically independent, is under the supervision of the government's Department of Religious Affairs and functions as Tajikistan's DUM. It certifies the country's Islamic clerics and sets the direction of religious instruction, decides what religious literature is acceptable, and sets the themes for sermons. The IRPT's position was somewhat marginalized after the death of Said Abdullo Nuri, which left it without a charismatic figure with authentic religious credentials.[90] Some close to the IRPT maintain that the procedures for reregistering imams are designed to push out those who supported the former IRPT leader and mufti, Akbar Turajonzoda, and his brother, Eshon Nuriddinjon Turajonzoda.[91]

The government and official religious hierarchy tries to keep the IRPT isolated. For example, it was very noticeably not included in the celebrations for the 1,310th anniversary of the birth of Abu Hanafi. Since then, there has been increased government pressure on the party. Pressure has included a police raid on the party's headquarters in October 2010 and statements by officials accusing the party of fundamentalism.[92]

In January 2011, the head of the Center for Strategic Studies of the President of Tajikistan, Suhrob Sharipov, said that the IRPT was receiving too much media attention.[93] The one-third of government positions guaranteed to the opposition by the National Reconciliation Agreement has steadily eroded; since the 2010 parliamentary election, the IRPT holds 2 of 63 seats in the Assembly of Representatives, and controls no ministerial portfolios. The party was optimistic going into the 2010 parliamentary election, having remade its image by expanding its traditional support base of rural religious conservatives from the east of the country to include young, educated Tajiks and women. But once again, it won only two seats in an election marred by allegations of mass electoral fraud.[94] The IRPT is chaired by Muhiddin Kabiri, who has held the post since 2006.

Although the IRPT's leaders might be nervous about the vigor with which government officials go after Islamic "extremists," they, too, maintain a staunch public profile against these antistate elements, which have become an increasing target of Tajikistan's judicial system in recent years. In their ongoing campaign to keep a firm grasp on religion, the Tajik authorities have also been closing mosques. In Sughd Oblast alone, some 300 mosques lacked registration and were threatened with closure, and two mosques in Dushanbe were razed. In 2010, fifteen mosques in GBAO were shut down temporarily for failing to reregister in accordance with the Freedom of Conscience and Religious Associations Law.[95] Moreover, in 2011 the Council on Religious Affairs announced the publication of a list of acceptable sermon topics for imams, which was developed in conjunction with theologians and the Islamic Council.[96] Predictably, the announcement was met with criticism that the government is trying to pressure imams and control their message.[97]

Religious affairs in Tajikistan are also regulated in part by the country's 2003 Law on Extremism,[98] which lays out the organizational and legal basis for its counterextremism effort.[99] This legislation has allowed the Tajik government to go after members of Hizb ut-Tahrir, of which there are presumed to be several thousand in the country, along with the IMU, and to monitor the activities of the unregistered Islamic Jamaat ut-Tabligh.

Hizb ut-Tahrir was founded in the 1950s. Its objective is the overthrow of governments in Muslim countries and the creation of a caliphate. Hizb ut-Tahrir maintains that it does not condone violence and that its focus is primarily ideological, but opponents of the organization say that it radicalizes members and sets them on the path to violence.[100] The organization is recognized as extremist and banned by numerous countries, including all the Central Asian states, Russia, and states in the Middle East and North Africa. Germany has also banned it. Tajikistan banned Hizb ut-Tahrir in 2001.

The exact number of Hizb ut-Tahrir's members in Tajikistan and Central Asia is unknown, but it is generally assumed that they are in the thousands. Alleged members of Hizb ut-Tahrir are periodically arrested and sentenced to lengthy jail terms for extremist activities. In 2010, local prosecutors in Sughd brought charges against 90 alleged Hizb ut-Tahrir members, and criminal proceedings had been started against 29 members in the first quarter of 2011. In January 2011, the leader of Hizb ut-Tahrir in Tajikistan was sentenced to eighteen years in prison on charges of inciting ethnic and religious hatred and attempts to overthrow the government.[101] In March 2011, eleven members in Sughd were given terms ranging from four to twenty years.[102]

Jamaat ut-Tabligh has also been under attack, even though this group accepts the teachings of Sunni Islam's Hanafi school and works at the grassroots level to promote Sunni values. It is this grassroots work that has increasingly made them seem threatening first to the Uzbek and the Kyrgyz, and now to the Tajik, authorities.

There is no evidence of any direct links between Jamaat ut-Tabligh and Islamic extremists, but it has some indirect connections with radical groups by, for instance, providing an easy link for recruitment by militant organizations. Jamaat ut-Tabligh itself, however, is most likely "not an intentional propagator of terrorism."[103] Jamaat ut-Tabligh's situation is not unique to Tajikistan; the group has also run into opposition elsewhere in Central Asia. In 2009, for instance, the Attorney General's Office of Kyrgyzstan filed a petition with the Bishkek District Court that Jamaat ut-Tabligh be recognized as an extremist terrorist organization.[104]

Members of Jamaat ut-Tabligh have opened schools and have been proselytizing in various parts of the country. The movement is said to be particularly active in the city of Kurgan Tyube and in the Bokhtar and Balijuvon districts of Khatlon Oblast, areas where support for the IRPT was strong during the civil war.

In contrast to Hizb ut-Tahrir, Jamaat ut-Tabligh is a transnational "loosely controlled mass movement rather than a centralized group" and does not have an explicitly political agenda.[105] It is active in countries like Bangladesh, Pakistan, and Malaysia.[106] Despite the group's apolitical nature and the fact that it represents the country's majority religion, the Tajik authorities see Jamaat ut-Tabligh as a threat to national security, similar to Hizb ut-Tahrir.[107] In 2006, the authorities allegedly imposed a ban on the group as an "extremist and terrorist organization," but it is unclear if this ban was really enforced.[108] Tajikistan has prosecuted numerous members for alleged extremist activities.[109] In April 2009, for instance, 129 members of Jamaat ut-Tabligh were arrested; all but 4, who were charged with being members of the IMU, were subsequently released.

Since January 2009, the Salafi movement has also been classified as an extremist group in Tajikistan. Related to this, the Tajik authorities have also been cracking down on unregistered religious schools and madrassas, and they have even gone to Pakistan to work with the Pakistani authorities to identify, register, and repatriate Tajik students who are studying in Pakistani madrassas.[110] There are also students in Turkey and in several Arab countries. In mid-2010, pressure was extended to all Tajiks studying abroad in Islamic universities and madrassas. In August 2010, Rahmon called on parents whose children were studying abroad to recall their children home, citing concerns that Tajiks studying abroad would be exposed to terrorism and extremism. This recall applied not only to students studying abroad "illegally" without the necessary paperwork from Tajik authorities but also those who had left the country legally.

The numbers on Tajiks studying abroad in religious institutions are not well known. In November 2010, the government put the official count of students at 1,400, of whom 800 were at Al-Azhar University in Cairo.[111] The real number is probably much higher, however, with an estimated 4,000 Tajiks studying in Pakistan alone.[112] Following Rahmon's statement, Tajik consulates in Islamic countries engaged in a push to locate and send students back to Tajikistan. As of January 2011, over 1,430 had come back from studying in Egypt, Iran, and Pakistan.[113]

This strategy of recalling Tajik students, which is supposedly aimed at preventing the spread of extremism and subsequent destabilization, has great potential to backfire. With one Islamic Institute and 20 official madrassas, Tajikistan cannot meet the demand from everyone seeking an Islamic education. The alternatives are either going abroad or joining an unofficial madrassa, which is generally cheaper. With the option of going abroad now effectively curtailed, the authorities are also shutting down unregistered religious schools at home, with the idea that religious education should be state regulated.[114] There have been many reports of government raids on unregistered religious schools.[115] There are not enough spaces in the Islamic Institute and official madrassas for returning students, who are faced with an inability to continue their education, along with other issues such as their country's high unemployment. Returning hundreds of students home, where they will have trouble pursuing their studies legally or finding employment, is a recipe for inciting instability.

The government's recall strategy may in effect force students to study illegally, even potentially pushing disgruntled students who wanted an Islamic education toward extremism instead.

The Tajik authorities try to control the outward signs of religious expression, particularly in schools. The Ministry of Education maintains a dress code, introduced in 2007, in schools and universities, which include a ban on wearing Islamic head coverings (traditional Tajik scarves that cover only the hair are allowed, as they are considered elements of traditional, rather than religious, dress).[116]

There have been cases reported of girls in hijab being harassed and insulted at school, and banned from attending class, although some 40 students dismissed from Tajik State University in 2009 were reinstated once they changed their dress.[117] Girls in hijabs have been denied diplomas at the conclusion of their studies, having unsuccessfully fought this in courts in Dushanbe and in Sughd.[118]

In January 2008, in an address to the nation, Rahmon labeled the hijab as culturally foreign to Tajiks, adding that traditional female dress—a dress just below the knee with pants underneath—was modest enough for praying in mosques and during prayers. Although not specified, a simple kerchief donned by married women was presumably still acceptable. Male students at the Islamic Institute are required to wear suits and ties and to shave their beards, and are barred from wearing "Middle Eastern" hats. There is also a dress code for teachers; beards are allowed only for men over 50.[119] And this is not limited to the education sphere, as evidenced by reports of the authorities in Dushanbe harassing and detaining men with beards.[120]

The Parental Responsibility Law introduced in 2011 prohibits children from attending religious ceremonies and activities, with the exception of funerals.[121] The government has defended the law as a necessary measure to protect children from undue religious influence and ensure improved school attendance. The law has met with resistance in both Tajikistan and among the members of the international community, because it violates Tajikistan's constitutional and international commitments to religious freedom.[122] After passing both chambers of Parliament, the bill was signed into law by President Rahmon on August 2, 2011.

However, it remains unclear how the law will be implemented and how the ban will be enforced.[123]

Women have been banned from Tajik mosques since 2004, as a result of a fatwa issued by the Council of Ulema, although the IRPT operates a special Juma mosque where women can pray. The strictness of this provision seems to be in conflict with the kind of "user-friendly" traditional Hanafi Islam that the government is advocating. It will be interesting to see if the government successfully pressures the Council of Ulema to reverse itself. Clerics who publicly preach against restrictions on women wearing hijab, such as Imam-Hatib Eshon Nuriddin, who leads a large mosque in Dushanbe, find themselves the objects of substantial official pressure.

RELIGION AND SECURITY

The Isfara District in eastern Sughd has been a center of what is alleged to be Islamic resistance. This district was one of the centers of the religious revival in the Ferghana Valley in the late 1980s and throughout most of the 1990s. The head of the local police command (the OVD, the office of internal affairs), Sidumar Saidov, was murdered execution style in September 2009, in a killing that was said to be in response to the arrest of Anvar Kayumov in Kabul in January 2009. Kayumov was alleged to have been the leader of the IMU cell in Sughd since 1997, and it was presumed that remnants of the IMU in Sughd were responsible for Saidov's murder, which occurred shortly before Kayumov's sentencing.[124] Anvar Kayumov, an alleged leader of the IMU, and five associates were sentenced to long prison terms for killing nine border guards and police officers. Kayumov received life in prison and the other five terms of eleven years.[125]

Saidov's murder was the fourth in a string of attacks against local police officials since August 2008. In response, four unnamed men suspected of being members of the IMU were killed in October 2009 as part of a "special operation" against the IMU launched by local and national security officials. The district is home to a number of current and former IMU members, possibly as many as 80 if the local authorities' assertions are accurate. They also claim that fifteen local residents have been killed fighting against NATO and government forces in Afghanistan.[126] The same month, Kyrgyz border guards stepped up their search for IMU members crossing from Tajikistan near Batken.[127]

In December 2009, three residents of Isfara were arrested and charged with membership in Islamic Jihad Union, which is considered by the Tajik authorities to be a terrorist organization.[128] And in February 2010, Tajikistan's Supreme Court sentenced Mahmed Said Mirzoev to eight years in prison for allegedly being a member of al-Qaeda. Mirzoev is said to have received military training in Afghanistan in the 1990s, presumably with the IMU, and was the eleventh Tajik to be receive prison time over the past two years for alleged ties with al-Qaeda.[129]

The Rasht Valley, a mountainous area located in the Region of Republican Subordination, was a UTO stronghold during the civil war. After the war, some UTO commanders were incorporated into state security services under the power-sharing agreement that gave the UTO one-third of government and military positions, but some have since been squeezed out. Other UTO commanders refused to deal with the government and went into hiding or left the country.

Following the civil war, the central government reasserted nominal control over Rasht, which remained home to some former opposition members who were given various positions under the power sharing agreement. But recent militant activity in the valley has undermined the credibility of central control there and has fueled concerns about Tajikistan's security.

In May 2009, the government launched "Operation Poppy," nominally a narcotics sweep, but in fact an incursion set to target insurgents, fueled by news of the return of Mullo Abdullo (Abdullo Rakhimov). Mullo Abdullo had been a UTO commander from Rasht who fled to Afghanistan after refusing to acknowledge the peace settlement, and while there forged ties with the Taliban. He supposedly returned to Tajikistan in May 2009 with a group of fighters, prompting the Tajik authorities to launch the search operation in Rasht, in which some insurgents were reportedly captured or killed. Some of those who were imprisoned then escaped in a jailbreak. In August 2010, 25 prisoners, including former opposition fighters and Islamic militants imprisoned for attempting to overthrow the government, escaped from a high-security prison in Dushanbe. Seven were still at large in May 2011.

Under the pretext of searching for the escaped prisoners, the government mobilized up to several thousand troops in Rasht.[130] In fact, this was an operation targeting the insurgents in the region. On September 19, 2010, a military convoy was ambushed in Kamarob Gorge, with 28 to 35 government troops killed in the attack. The government blamed the incident on Mullo Abdullo and Ali Bedaki (another former UTO commander), and it made a bargain with Mirzikhuja Akhmadov, a third former UTO commander—head of the anti–organized crime directorate (UBOP) in Rasht, and a man with a significant amount of influence in the region—to hunt down the warlords.[131] In December 2011, 53 people were sentenced to prison for terrorism in connection with the September 2010 attacks.[132] Ali Bedaki and Mullo Abdullo were killed in 2011.

Although Tajik government sources depict the victories that they have enjoyed in the military actions launched against such "terrorist groups" in recent years, most of the available evidence suggests that the Tajik troops encountered serious difficulties while facing what in some cases were fairly ragtag irregulars. The Tajik troops seem to have shown the effects of years of rampant corruption in the army, with conscripts bribing their way out—officially in 2011, there were 7,500 paramilitary and 7,300 soldiers; but in reality, the numbers were likely smaller.[133] In addition, in October 2010, a helicopter crash wiped out almost half the State Security Committee's Alfa Unit, Tajikistan's sole experienced counterinsurgency unit; it now has 32 people left.[134] Though foreign assistance money is being received for training, it is nowhere equal to what the Tajiks must have to meet their security needs, particularly in the face of the prevailing corruption in the country.

CHAPTER 3

DO TAJIK OFFICIALS HAVE THE WILL TO REFORM?

Tajikistan certainly faces challenges in maximizing its economic potential, given that it is landlocked; that it shares a border with Afghanistan, which has been in turmoil for more than 30 years; is on bad terms with neighboring Uzbekistan; and has a mountainous and largely impenetrable border with China and a mountainous, though somewhat more penetrable, border with Kyrgyzstan.

Although Tajikistan's leaders proudly point to its hydroelectric potential and mineral wealth, it lacks the resource base of fossil-fuel-rich states like Kazakhstan, Turkmenistan, and even Uzbekistan, and the development of those resources that the country does have is made more complicated by its remote geographic location.

This makes the quality of leadership of far greater importance for Tajikistan than in some of the region's other countries, and the problems posed by corruption of far greater potential magnitude. For this reason, the diffidence with which the country's top officials have gone about reform has further compounded its developmental challenges.

Tajikistan is considered by the European Bank for Reconstruction and Development (EBRD) to have one of the least-developed legal environments of any country where it operates; thus Tajikistan's own people are starkly aware of the fact that something is wrong with their political system, and many see widespread corruption as one of the causes for this.[1] In a survey done by the IFES on the eve of the 2010 parliamentary election, 89 percent of those surveyed saw corruption as serious, up 14 percent from 2004, on the eve of the previous parliamentary election.[2]

Tajik leaders have made a show of trying to respond to both public and international concerns, but generally more with declarative rather than substantive reforms. Perhaps both groups have not been vocal enough.

The international financial institutions working with Tajikistan have regularly chastised Tajik officials, but they have always had to moderate their tone because of their desire to continue to pursue an economic reform program with the country's leaders. Things came close to the breaking point in early 2008, after the National Bank of Tajikistan (NBT) revealed that it had "misreported" some of its loans, and as a result was about to run out of money to pay Tajikistan's bills.

However, with a NATO-led military operation just next door in Afghanistan, no one in the Western-dominated international institutions wants to leave the Tajik authorities fully to their own devices or risk toppling another government in an already-problematic region. So they continue to try to take heart from positive growth figures, and to praise those Tajik officials, usually technocrats, for the reform successes that do occur, in the hopes that this will serve to stimulate further reforms.

Tajikistan's proximity to Afghanistan has also been a source of the country's corruption, because it provides the northern route for the transit of the opium and heroin produced in Afghanistan. As the amount of opium being grown increased, so, too, did the temptations offered for cooperating with drug dealers. And once Tajikistan's drug lords began making heroin, the income potential for each kilogram transferred across the country increased exponentially.

Later chapters will explore some of the country's economic policy successes and failures in greater detail. The task here is to look at the pervasive atmosphere of corruption that dominates Tajik official life, both at the level of the presidency and around at least some of the men whom he has put into high office in the economy. This chapter also examines the trickle-down effect that this corruption has had on the economy more generally, creating an atmosphere in which bribe taking and bribe giving have become a way of life, and one that is often justified as a cultural practice that is decades and even centuries old.

"A FISH ROTS FROM THE HEAD DOWN"

Although the members of the Rahmon government certainly cannot be blamed for inventing corruption, which was prevalent in the Soviet Union, especially in its last years, they have deepened existing practices while claiming to be combating them. Nowhere is this more apparent than in the lifestyle of the head of state.

In the last several years, Emomali Rahmon has turned himself into a larger-than-life political figure, building a giant palace in the center of Dushanbe, and smaller palaces (or grand homes) in each oblast and principal city to allow him to "meet his people" throughout the country and still reside in the proper style.[3] Increasingly, he has tried to define himself as synonymous with Tajik independence, a modern-day Ismoili Somoni, Amir Adil (the just commander), who in the ninth century established the Samanid Dynasty in Bukhara, which the Tajiks consider the foundation of their modern state.

A 2007 WikiLeaks cable makes this point quite explicitly, describing how the Tajik government downplayed the sixteenth anniversary of independence in order to focus on the fifteenth anniversary of Rahmon's taking power, which was held some two months later, in November 2007 at the Arbob Palace in Khujand. This was the site of the peace negotiations at the end of the civil war, and where in November 1992 Rahmon had been named as chairman of the Supreme Soviet (it having been deemed too dangerous to gather in Dushanbe). At the fifteenth anniversary celebration a short film (following a nationally televised 90-minute speech) about Tajik history was shown that included a depiction of Amir Somoni, footage on the civil war, and then clips of Rahmon decked out in medals embracing a group of bearded opposition leaders.[4]

The Rahmon family's increasing domination of the country's economy appears to be part and parcel of this. There are repeated rumors about corruption related to President Rahmon, his children, and his brother-in-law, Hasan Sadulloev. The most pernicious, and potentially damaging, of these rumors relate to the decision of the government to not privatize key assets, such as the Tajik Aluminum Factory, and to run them for the benefit of offshore companies tied to the president or his family, such as TALCO

Management Company, which is nominally owned by several Tajik state entities, or for the benefit of the Orienbank, which Sadulloev heads.

There are also frequent rumors of improprieties in various national campaigns, such as the "voluntary" public subscription to the building fund for the Roghun hydroelectric station, in a campaign that was depicted as "extortion" in a WikiLeaks U.S. Embassy Tajikistan cable.[5] Money was collected from all nationally owned enterprises, and the employees of foreign-owned companies and agencies were also targeted, with their offices being threatened with closure and in some cases even closed if they did not meet their collective "goals," which were sometimes as high as all their annual salaries combined.[6] These "contributions" totaled tens of millions of dollars, which were under the loosest of supervision until the government decided to appoint an "independent" group to monitor the donations. The formal campaign was dropped shortly thereafter, but despite this the government is still finding ways to amass funds to support work on the early stages of the project.

Similarly, there were many rumors circulating about why the Tajik government announced that 2009 would be the "Year of Imam Azam," celebrating the 1,310th anniversary of the birth of Abu Hanafi, the founder of the Hanafi school of Islamic law. The year chosen was obviously not a traditional "jubilee" year, which is generally a centennial. Although the festivities, including a grandiose international conference held in November 2009, fit in beautifully with government policies designed to put the president and the state at the center of the country's policies with respect to Islam, it also brought in leaders from throughout the Muslim world, but most especially the rich nations of the Arab Middle East, who were reported to have funded this event.[7] Tens of millions of dollars were said to have been raised for the event, but when it came to paying the costs of foreign guests, the list of invitees was drastically cut, and even some who had responded were left waiting for promised e-tickets that never arrived. The organizers maintained that a lack of funds was the cause.

Those close to the president have also been able to use official positions with impunity. For example, there have been scandals involving key figures such as Murodali Alimardon, who headed the NBT and seemingly used his post to make uncollateralized loans to his friends in the cotton industry, and possibly even to himself. When a liquidity crisis within the bank forced him to reveal at least some of these improprieties to the International Monetary Fund, Tajikistan was forced to authorize an independent audit of the NBT, and Alimardon was removed, but he was then appointed deputy prime minister in charge of agriculture, with responsibility for supervising the reform of the cotton sector to which he had such strong personal ties.

In general, it has taken extraordinary efforts by international institutions to get the Tajik authorities to agree to international audits of their key state-run enterprises, with audits being conducted of Barki Tojik, the electricity company, and of Tajik Aluminum, only after years of pressure. Moreover, even after the audits have been conducted, it can take years for them to be published, and there has been very little follow-through on the recommendations made. A lengthy discussion of the Ernst & Young audit, which was required to be published as one of the IMF's conditions for continuing to provide funds to be administered by the NBT, is given below because it is a good window into the business practices of key state-owned businesses and institutions.

What is most noteworthy about the cases mentioned above, which are introduced in this chapter and developed further in later chapters, is that the international financial institutions and reputable international companies have been working with the individuals leading these Tajik businesses and institutions for many years now. This makes the latter quite distinct—at least in position, but perhaps not in behavior—from the allegedly ubiquitous Tajik drug lords, who have frequently been reported to have ties to key figures in the country.

Most officials of the international financial institutions will privately admit that dealing with the leaders of the Tajik government is challenging at best, but they defend their contact with them, claiming that there is little alternative to engaging with them. Most feel that the withdrawal of international financial assistance from Tajikistan would be impossible, given its location just beyond Afghanistan's borders and its status as one of the few currently dependable entry points for supplying or trading with Afghanistan. International advisers place their hope on training a new generation of technocrats to follow systems of control and accountability, such as audits, which they hope will become more commonly used in the future.

But it remains to be seen whether it is possible to move toward reform with such men in charge. In evaluating this situation, few are as blunt as Swiss development officials. Since 1993, the Swiss authorities have led a constituency group in the Bretton Woods institutions, coordinating assistance for Tajikistan, Kyrgyzstan, and Uzbekistan. Because of this special position, the Swiss authorities have taken the lead in working with the governments of Tajikistan and Kyrgyzstan in developing their poverty reduction strategies for the IMF and World Bank and their efforts to meet the UN Millennium Development Goals. In the Cooperation Strategy for the Central Asian Region 2007–2011, the third multiyear planning document that the Swiss authorities have prepared, they offered their "most likely" scenario for Tajikistan (as well as the other two countries) in which

- joint development efforts lead to positive poverty alleviation,

- social services do not substantially improve,

- reform stagnation and corruption remain limiting factors for economic growth, and

- civil society development and freedom of expression are restricted.[8]

CORRUPTION AND THE OFFICIAL FIGHT AGAINST CORRUPTION

The challenge of getting Tajikistan's government to move toward meaningful and sustainable reform is akin to the challenge of getting someone to push a heavy rock uphill. True, the government has introduced a variety of legislation that calls for the introduction of more transparency in government and throughout the bureaucracy, but much of what has been introduced is declarative in nature rather than being designed to set up a road map for how to actually achieve these nominally desired goals. Similarly, there have been various campaigns to weed out corrupt officials, but most have seemed more like efforts to find scapegoats, who are generally those who lack strong enough protection to be bypassed by such efforts, or are used as opportunities to get rid of one's rivals.

The World Bank acknowledges that, although Tajikistan did meet its targets in a four-year program to improve public-sector management and public service delivery,

Tajikistan is still considered to be among the least transformed and most poorly performing transition economies, and still has a considerable way to go in order to unlock its promising economic potential. Tajikistan has not yet built up a system of strong independent and accountable political institutions or established a strong governance framework that might other- wise anchor needed reforms.[9]

This is not a situation that is likely to lead to sustainable reforms. For although the World Bank positively notes that the Executive Office of the President performed satisfactorily on those guidelines agreed to by both the Bank and the government of Tajikistan, the Bank admits that it excluded the sectors most necessary for reform because of the unwilling- ness of the government of Tajikistan to even engage in a serious conversa- tion about reform in these sectors:

> Areas in which reform would have potentially high impact, such as actions to resolve cotton sector debt, or to enhance financial transparency and reform TALCO, the largest state enterprise, were deliberately left out of the program, because of a lack of government commitment to bring about the necessary improvements. The achievements under the PDGP [public-sector reform] program are due largely to the creative- ness of the Bank team in identifying entry points for reform, and then in giving reforms the support they needed through dialogue, analytical work, and technical assistance.[10]

Tajikistan's officials will admit that corruption is ubiquitous in their country, and that its pervasiveness has undermined political and eco- nomic reforms there, but they maintain that it tends to be caused by anonymous people, and certainly by "the other guy." To quote a 2006 study on corruption in the Republic of Tajikistan prepared by the Strategic Research Center Under the President of Tajikistan:[11]

> In previous years, corruption in our country has become wide- spread, leading to negative economic effects and social conse- quences, including the degradation of the society. In particular the large amounts of money in the interaction of corrupt officials with entrepreneurs and citizens of the Republic not

only results in direct social damages, but also destroys the constitutional foundations of society by violating the principles of
equality.[12]

Although often cited as a major source of this corruption, President
Rahmon's government has also pledged to fight it. During a 2005 speech
"On the Supremacy of Law, State Interests, and Citizen's Rights," delivered on the occasion of the eightieth anniversary of the Procurator's Office
of the Republic of Tajikistan (meaning the creation of this office during
the 1920s, itself a rather inauspicious event to celebrate the advancement
of human rights), the president made the following comment:

> Such a negative phenomenon as corruption is one of the
> gravest obstacles in the development of our society. We must
> conduct a comprehensive study and analyze factors and causes
> of corruption and mobilize all sound forces of our society to
> put corruption under restraint and reduce its level.[13]

The 2006 study distinguishes between individual and systemic forms
of corruption, and notes the following causes of corruption:

- Lack of experience and lack of professionalism in the government
  supports individual corruption.

- Lack of an institutional anticorruption strategy to combat systemic
  corruption and a reliance on piecemeal legislation instead.[14]

- Unfavorable economic conditions in general and low civil servant
  salaries in particular.

- Lack of understanding of what corruption is by the public, which
  many see as consistent with cultural norms, but in violation of
  the values of Islam, whose teachings could be used to combat
  corruption.[15]

- Lack of public support for fighting against corruption.

- Insufficient media coverage of corruption.

- Lack of political will compounded by the hidden interests of
  selected political groups (who oftentimes are in competition with
  the current government).

- Fear of critical changes that would occur when the country shifts from corrupt patterns to market forces.[16]

As the authors of the study unhappily note, corruption has been made systematic, with a well-established and well-known cost structure:

> One must admit that corruption in the Republic of Tajikistan has turned into an unwritten public norm of behavior for both its citizens and its entrepreneurs. It has formed models of mutually agreed procedural "enforcement" and understanding under the informal logo—"something is not allowed; someone has a great wish; then it is allowed"—in accordance with the existing price list for the "shadow" service of officials.[17]

The authors of the study emphasize the inadequacy of Tajikistan's political institutions to fight corruption, starting with the weakness of the legislative basis upon which such a "battle" would be based. For this reason, the World Bank has put increasing priority on programs designed to reform public-sector management and public service delivery, the latter being an area that has traditionally been particularly corruption ridden. These programs were designed to support the Tajik government's Public Administration Reform Strategy, adopted in March 2006, which was intended to implement a new transparent and predictable civil service wage system, a goal linked to improving the quality of people recruited into the civil service and reducing bribe taking among those already working in various state institutions.

But as the World Bank noted in its report on the implementation of these grants, "the November 2006 elections led to a shift in the government's approach to public-sector reforms, delaying the adoption of a new government structure."[18] This led the World Bank to substitute a set of measures related to improving the functioning of existing institutions, which included accepting a step-by-step approach to introducing an independent external audit capacity.

There were definitely some improvements in financial accountability; an Internal Audit Department was introduced in the Ministry of Finance, and internal audit units were introduced in the Education, Health, Agriculture, and Labor and Social Protection ministries, as well as in the Tax Committee.[19] Also, a standard set of bidding documents was introduced for tenders that ministries undertake to procure goods and services.[20] These measures do not meet the goal of full accountability, but do meet specific targets of the World Bank's program. In addition, the State Privatization Committee began posting information on the sale of assets on its website and in the press, including the names of successful and unsuccessful bidders.[21]

This "realistic" approach by the World Bank is probably responsible for whatever positive changes have occurred in the quality of Tajikistan's public administration, but it has also licensed the country's government to decide the pace of civil service reform and control the policies designed to increase government accountability. This of course is Tajikistan's right as a sovereign state, but it means that there are no "sticks" to fear and few limits placed on the available "carrots" when the government opts for a slow pace of reform.

As a result of these changes, the World Bank reports that Tajikistan's score on the World Economic Forum's Global Competitiveness Index rose from 3.01 to 3.38 between 2005 and 2009, but the country is still ranked 122 out of 134 countries.[22]

By the end of the grant period, in 2010, the World Bank reported that the responsibilities of civil service positions had been more clearly defined, but the government had not yet put a competitive wage system into place, although targeted gradual increases in salaries were generally met.[23] The Bank considers the latter critical to mitigate corrupt practices among state officials.

Some of the state agencies in Tajikistan remain notorious for their high level of corruption, with the traffic police coming out on top of virtually everyone's list of institutions that require change. The traffic police (GAI) are ubiquitous, they are on most major thoroughfares, and they have posts on the boundaries of administrative districts and regions. Their corrupt practices go back decades in most of Central Asia, and also in other regions of the former Soviet Union. Traffic officials receive low salaries and collect money for fines on the spot (along with payments for not levying fines), while anyone seeking to fight the fine must surrender his or her driver's license and then appeal in court. It is a rare day when a driver is not pulled over at least once for some real or imagined infraction, and many are willing to help the traffic police augment their salaries rather than pay a higher fine.

In a study on corruption by the Institute of Strategic Studies, passport offices were also frequently cited as corrupt (by 38.1 percent of the respondents). Their function, too, is still heavily influenced by Soviet-era practices, with long delays to get new passports, which generally must be replaced when the pages run out, or when someone reaches majority at the age of 25; in addition, renewals can almost never be done by foreign embassies, instead requiring that seasonal laborers or students return to Tajikistan. Officials, too, are underpaid, and are prone to create their own criteria for unofficial "expedited" service.

Electricity and gas officials were also viewed as corrupt (by 30.9 and 27.7 percent of the respondents, respectively), but here one wonders if money is changing hands to prevent service cutoffs for unpaid bills, the latter being a growing problem in Tajikistan because tariffs for communal services are steadily rising.[24]

Although those surveyed described public institutions as more corrupt than public associations, the picture that emerges from the survey is of a country where corruption is pervasive in all spheres of public life. For example, 27 percent of those interviewed said that trade unions were corrupt, 20 percent said that political parties and movements were corrupt, 20 percent that nongovernmental environmental organizations were corrupt, and, most interestingly, 25 percent of the respondents made the same claim about mosques. This last opinion speaks to the "business" that many think religion has become, with costly weddings and other religious ceremonies becoming the norm, practices the Rahmon government has been trying to cut back.

DO THE TAJIKS UNDERSTAND WHAT CORRUPTION IS?

Tajikistan's legal system is at the core of its corruption. This point is underscored by the results of a study done by the Strategic Research Center, as those surveyed believed that the judicial system "is neither interested in nor capable of" addressing the corruption, a conclusion borne out by the limited number of cases in which state officials are prosecuted or punished. The survey covered 24 cities and districts and included 2,054 individual respondents (1,769 individual citizens, 285 entrepreneurs)[25] and included an expert survey of 40 respondents. The survey results show confusion about what constitutes corruption (quite possibly including by those who drew up the survey).

For example, when asked what might define corrupt practices, 4.8 percent of those surveyed said "preelection grants for political parties." Another ambiguous category, "to lobby for one's own interests," was cited by 9.3 percent (but if this was a euphemism for bribery, it was not made clear). The "concealment of information to advance one's own interests" was chosen by 7.0 percent of those surveyed, and 6.8 percent said "pressure on the electorate during elections" (without specifying whether this meant buying votes or just campaigning).

The most frequently cited incidence of corruption was "making payments to traffic police," which was given by 14.9 percent, followed by 13.0 percent who said "acceptance of a bribe aimed at concealing or reducing applicable taxes."[26] The traffic police were generally considered to be the most corrupt institution in the country, with 53.4 percent of those surveyed answering that they considered them to be dishonest, and they were viewed as more corrupt even than the tax authorities (41.4 percent).[27]

Not all forms of "gift giving" were viewed as corruption. For example, 10.6 percent said that they considered giving gifts to doctors (a longtime Soviet-era practice, and sometimes the only way to ensure that one was seen) a form of corruption, but 58 percent saw gifts of flowers, candy, or brandy to teachers, doctors, or other useful persons as a normal "expression of gratitude." Similarly, nearly 60 percent of those interviewed thought that having dinner or a drink with someone who could help to resolve a business problem to be perfectly acceptable conduct, and two-thirds thought that it was acceptable to use connections or acquaintances for professional advancement. Most of these "gift-giving" practices are considered commonplace in Europe and America as well.

At the same time, 91.5 percent of the respondents thought that it was improper to bribe an official to get a problem solved quickly, while only 8.5 percent thought that bribing was appropriate, but 25 percent agreed with the statement that "bribing an official to suppress or evade unpleasant [treatment] and bureaucratic procedures in the interest of a firm or an organization" was "admissible." So although most Tajiks may think that it is inappropriate to bribe officials, they also view it as "admissible"—that is, they do it.

Similarly, although the Tajiks see giving relatively inexpensive gifts to educational officials as acceptable, many complain that they are compelled to cross a line and bribe educational officials. More than half the respondents (57 percent) reported that they "face[d] corrupt practices at schools and secondary educational institutions," and 17.9 percent responded that they faced them quite often or very often. (Bear in mind, this was in a survey based on the general population and not just those with school-aged children or family members.) Similarly, 40.3 percent of those surveyed complained about the level of corruption among the members of the administrations and staffs of higher educational institutions and secondary schools.[28]

If anecdotal accounts are to be believed, then the level of corruption in the Tajik educational system today is worse than it was in the late Soviet period, when those with the means frequently made payments to admissions committees to secure places for their children. Tajikistan is one of the last countries to abandon most Soviet-era admissions practices, in which each educational institution admits its own students through a system that relies on admissions tests that are institution-specific and based on largely nonstandard elements. Pilot projects have prepared by the United Nations Development Program and World Bank to support the introduction of a standardized nationwide examination system.

There were similar findings with regard to the health care system. Although most people reported that they had no problem giving small tokens of gratitude to doctors, 41 percent of those surveyed complained that the health care system was generally corrupt. The survey authors note that this finding was consistent with a 2006 report from Transparency International, which claimed that the

> abuse of funds, bribery and blackmailing deprive millions of people of medical assistance. Counterfeit drugs annually result in thousand[s of] victims and accelerate the spread of diseases resistant to medical treatment. Corruption in [the] pharmaceutical industry and health care deprives vulnerable groups of basic medical aid and facilitates the spread of diseases resistant to treatment.[29]

The study's authors go on to argue that corruption in the medical system is so bad that despite the scale of foreign assistance received from the donor community, the effectiveness of this sector has decreased over time. The cause, they maintain, is that officials "plunder" the funds allocated for public health. Sometimes, funds intended for purchasing medical equipment go astray; other times, the contents of cargo containers filled with medical supplies simply disappear—and few are ever held accountable for such transgressions. The blame, they argue, must be shared; civil society does not hold the government accountable, the government does not want to take control, and the donor agencies do not force the government to make public disclosures of the aid received and how it was disbursed.[30]

CORRUPTION IN THE COTTON SECTOR

A Christian Aid study of corruption in five countries quotes a May 2008 interview with Donald Bowser, a specialist on corruption with the UNDP in Tajikistan who claims that what occurred in the cotton sector of Tajikistan "was not privatization but rather a 're-nationalization into permanent public–private partnership, except that there is no divide between the state and the private sector.' In effect it was a 'move from state managers into private hands, whose only aim was to strip the assets of the sector.'"[31]

The information that emerged from an audit ordered by the International Monetary Fund strongly bears out this conclusion. In December 2007, IMF officials discovered that the NBT's hard currency reserves were only about a third of what they had assumed to be the case, because the funds had been used for unsecured loans to favored customers in the cotton sector.[32] This discrepancy appears to have come to light because the NBT found itself short of the funds necessary to meet its normal obligations because of an unexpected drop-off in foreign remittances.[33] As a result, the NBT sought to exercise its special drawing rights with the IMF, and this in turn alerted the IMF to problems with the NBT, which led its chairman, Murodali Alimardon, to admit that it had not been truthful in some of its earlier submissions to the IMF in December

2007. In fact the NBT maintained two sets of books, the one which recorded the actual loans made, and the other for showing to the IMF.

The IMF required the NBT to return $79 million that had been improperly drawn from the Poverty Reduction and Growth Facility (PRGF), which had run from 2002 to 2006 under an expedited timetable.[34] They were also required to hire an acceptable international auditing firm to audit the NBT's finances and publish the results. Ernst & Young carried out the audit, which when published in 2009 revealed a systematic pattern of unethical behavior on the part of NBT officials, who were effectively financing their friends, who were in turn dominating the cotton sector by financing small farmers so they could purchase seed, but were mortgaging their crops in the process. The main beneficiary in these transactions was KreditInvest, because it in turn lent money to the cotton factors (those that distributed seed and then collected and sold the harvested cotton from small farmers) and earned interest on these loans.

KreditInvest was a private financial institution established in 2004 when the Agroinvestbank split into the Agroinvestbank, a commercial bank, and KreditInvest (KI), a private bank (with only about $200,000 in capital, which was created to provide credit in the cotton sector). KI also received the nonperforming loans to cotton farms from Agroinvestbank. The senior management of KI came from the international department of the NBT.[35]

The NBT's chairman revealed that it had offered $241.2 million in pledges from foreign banks to secure financing for loans to cotton factors from 2001 to 2007, that it had provided $77.4 million in guarantees to foreign banks and foreign commercial institutions for financing received by KI, and had loaned KI (or its predecessor) some $250 million to finance cotton factors from 2002 to 2007.[36] The loans came from the main branch of the NBT, as well as the Khujand and Kurgan Tyube branches. The loans were classified as normal bank deposits rather than pledged assets in the NBT records so they were not noticed by PricewaterhouseCoopers when it did the original NBT audits.

The Ernst & Young audit discovered that the situation in the NBT was more dire than had originally been reported by the Bank to the IMF.[37] The auditors stated that at the time of the December 31, 2007, declaration by NBT chairman Alimardon there was still $264 million in outstanding loans to KreditInvest, of which $234 million had not been previously disclosed to the IMF.[38] The Ernst & Young auditors also complained that there had been a lack of cooperation from NBT officials with the audit. As Ernst & Young reported:

> Some key records had been deliberately destroyed, documents created which purported to be contemporaneous and multiple (and sometimes conflicting) responses were given to questions. These included the purported destruction of the notebook that had hand recorded all the loans given, a notebook which had previously been stored in the vault at NBT, and the spreadsheet on pledges and loans that was presented seems to have been created immediately before presentation to the auditing team.[39]

The report details how the auditors encountered a more difficult situation at KI, whose previous chairman (who was replaced in January 2008) admitted that he had ordered a number of documents destroyed because "they were no longer needed." The former head of the bank admitted that it had always kept two sets of books, one that recorded the loans it had concealed from the IMF and the other that was shown to its auditors.[40] The audit revealed that KI's bad debts totaled $584 million, as opposed to $20 million shown in its formal accounts, and there was only $52 million in collateral held against all the loans.[41] Moreover, the audit team was given no information about loans by KI's subsidiaries.

When the auditing team visited the cotton factors, they generally encountered even more hostile situations. Three enterprises were particularly criticized—HIMA Corporation, Tamer (where a Persian-speaking member of the team was entreated to not disclose the existence of loans that had not been reported by the banks involved), and Yare Resa Be Paraston (YRBP). The section of the audit pertaining to this last firm is reproduced in full, because it really testifies to the kind of "field conditions" one can encounter in Tajikistan:

> At Yare Resa Be Paraston, in addition to significant gaps in information attributed to the long-term illness of the chief accountant, we noticed documents were being burned in the

car park. The documents appeared to be original, stamped, financial information and spreadsheets, but we were not able to assess their significance. YRBP staff informed us that these documents had been used as toilet paper prior to burning, and we did not examine them further.[42]

The auditors' key findings were highly critical of how the NBT was organized in general and of Alimardon's leadership in particular. They criticized the lack of an independent and viable management board. Not only did Chairman Alimardon nominate new members of the management board for Rahmon's approval, he also cast the tie-breaking vote that approved their bonuses.

Alimardon also approved applications for funding by KI and for the cotton factors. More damaging still, he was reported to be a silent partner in HIMA, something that he vehemently denied, even though the initials of the company matched those of the public partner Ismatullo Hyoev, and those of Murodali Alimardon. Alimardon claimed to be just a close friend of the family, and someone who provided the management with "advice and assistance."[43]

There were also guarantees to two cotton trading companies, Axial Limited (registered on the Isle of Man) and Cottonex Anstalt (registered in Liechtenstein), whose ownership structures were opaque, both of which refused to cooperate with the audit,[44] raising the possibility that they were owned at least in part by those associated with the cotton factors from Tajikistan that were trading with them.[45] The Tajik companies also had financing from the NBT, which had absolutely no control over the amount, grade, or timing of the cotton shipments.

Moreover, the NBT did not require its borrowers to demonstrate that they had the required licenses to export cotton, so it is quite possible that these large cotton factors were also evading export fees and profit taxes. The large borrowers also do not appear to have been required to disclose information about their financial worth.

In addition, the NBT took no responsibility for trying to recover the KI funds. When the latter ceased operations in 2008 it was owed $497.2 million, of which $153 million was owed by Tamer and $116.5 million by HIMA, the firm rumored to be owned at least in part by Alimardon, and whose publicly recognized owner is Alimardon's close friend. Olim Karimzod owed $79.9 million and Khujand Invest Cotton owed $65.5 million, with eight other companies owing the remaining amount.[46] Olim Karimzod, Khujand Invest Cotton, and Tamer were all reported to have been minority shareholders in KI, as was HIMA.[47] All of the money owed to KI had been originally advanced to the bank by the NBT from foreign credits that the latter had received.

All these cotton companies had a number of subsidiaries—HIMA had ginneries, factories, and buildings; Olim Karimzod had ten subsidiaries in the cotton sector as well as a hotel, a construction company, and a sock factory; and Khujand Invest Cotton's subsidiaries included spinning factories. It seems a reasonable assumption that KI's loans were used to set up or maintain some of these subsidiaries, none of which (according to Ernst & Young) appear to have paid dividends to the parent company.[48]

Over the years, the debts of these large companies continued to grow because when loans came due, KI just lent them more money to pay their earlier loans in order to keep them from being labeled "bad debtors," and by doing this, these companies were able to draw out profits at a pace of their own choosing. Part of the way KI stayed in business was to make the majority of its loans to small cotton merchants, which were required to repay their loans in a relatively timely fashion.[49] The four largest companies—HIMA, Tamer, Olim Karimzod, and Khujand Invest Cotton— had repayment ratios of 15 percent, 12 percent, 20 percent, and 22 percent, respectively, as compared with a general borrower's repayment ratio of 41 percent, for the period from January 2004 to August 2008.[50]

The first audit of the NBT subsequent to the Ernst & Young audit was conducted by KPMG Audit LLC of Almaty in December 2009, and covered the financial years ending April 30, 2008, and April 30, 2009. It, too, found that the NBT was not yet fully compliant with international auditing standards because it was unable to get third party confirmations of borrowing amounts from China State Development Banks, Cottonex Anstalt Ltd., and Axial Ltd.[51]

In recent years, the Tajik government has sought to restore international confidence in the operation of the NBT, appointing officials with banking training and experience to its management, including Abdujabor Shirinov as its chairman in 2012. Shirinov had worked in the bank previously, and was well known to the international community through his diplomatic service, which included a stint as Tajikistan's ambassador to the United States.

There is the question of why the international community was caught by surprise when the NBT scandal occurred. The NBT had been the subject of earlier audits, and the EBRD's experience with various early projects should have been a warning for other lenders.

BRIBES ARE A WAY OF LIFE FOR BUSINESSMEN

Corruption has an impact on the conduct of businesses from the highest to the lowest levels in Tajikistan. Most Tajik businessmen are well aware that bribe taking, or "gift giving," reaches up to the highest levels, with few consequences for those who have been involved. In something akin to the old adage "what is good for the goose is good for the gander," this situation seems to encourage ordinary Tajiks to feel no compunction about operating outside the law themselves, and in many cases they appear to have little choice but to do so. This is either because without making bribes they cannot get their business done, or because there is simply no margin of profit if they do not do so.

The IMF is not alone in having been embarrassed by some of the projects with which it has been involved. The EBRD has also had some notable failures in its loan portfolio in which corrupt behavior played a conspicuous part. For example, in 2006, it developed an investment project with M&P, then the largest supermarket chain in the country, only to have the CEO (and main shareholder) arrested in 2007 on allegations of bribery and tax evasion. In April 2008, he was sentenced to eight and a half years in prison (the prosecutor had only asked for a one- to four-year sentence), and most of his private assets were confiscated.[52]

A second EBRD project, support for Geha Foods, a greenfield project to support the opening of a tomato-processing plant that was also supported by the International Finance Corporation (IFC), among other donors, was a less dramatic failure. In this case, the funds were never fully disbursed because supply was never ensured. The EBRD's 2009 report maintains that these projects (along with some earlier failures in mineral water and juice factories[53]) served as learning experiences that more and better due diligence, including market assessment, needs to be done in future projects.

The Central Asian American Enterprise Fund, a $150 million entity created by the U.S. government to stimulate investment in small and medium-sized enterprises in Central Asia, had such difficulty maneuvering in Tajikistan's corruption-dominated business environment that it suspended operations there and throughout the region, but not before some of its U.S. managerial staff members were sentenced to prison terms for fraud and violating the Foreign Corrupt Practices Act,[54] for schemes that were brought to the authorities' attention by its local employees.[55]

The World Bank reports on doing business in Tajikistan offer a troubling picture. Data from the 2008 Enterprise Survey shows that Tajikistan ranks at the very bottom of the World Bank's graft index (based on six indicators) for the entire Eastern European and Central

FIGURE 3.1

GRAFT INDEX IN THE EASTERN EUROPEAN AND CENTRAL ASIAN REGION

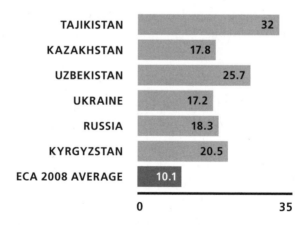

Source: 2009 Enterprise Survey, "Running a Business in Tajikistan," Country Note No. 4, Enterprise Surveys Country Note Series, World Bank Group, 2009, www.enterprisesurveys. org/Reports.

Asian region. These data, reproduced in figure 3.1, are from a survey of 360 firms that was done between May and August 2008. Thirty-two percent of all firms reported having to make informal payments to public officials in order to facilitate their business transactions, more than three times the average for the region as a whole, although the 2008 figure is lower than that for 2005 (table 3.1). Firms also, on average, each month experience 8.6 power outages lasting a total of 74 hours, during which these enterprises' activities essentially come to a halt. These data reflect a worsening situation from 2005.

TABLE 3.1
CONSTRAINTS ON THE AVERAGE FIRM, 2008

MEASURE	TAJIKISTAN	ECA	EU-10
Number of power outages in a typical month	8.6	5.8	2.5
Senior management time spent on government regulation requirements	11.7	10.6	9.5
Average number of visits or required meetings with tax officials	1.6	1.7	1.1
% of firms expected to pay informal payments to public officials	40.5	16.8	7.4
Incidence of Graft Index	32.0	9.9	4.7
Losses to theft, robbery, vandalism, and arson (% of sales)	0.3	0.5	0.4
% of firms paying for security	48.2	57.7	62.0

Note: ECA = Eastern Europe and Central Asia; EU-10 = Bulgaria, the Czech Republic, Estonia, Hungary, Latvia, Lithuania, Poland, Romania, Slovakia, and Slovenia—that is, the ten countries in the ECA region that belong to the European Union.

Source: 2009 Enterprise Survey, "Running a Business in Tajikistan," Country Note No. 4, Enterprise Surveys Country Note Series, World Bank Group, 2009, www.enterprisesurveys. org/Reports.

This picture is in line with the results obtained in an IFC survey of the business environment that was published in 2009, including data from 1,500 Tajik firms in the sector encompassing small and medium-sized enterprises (SMEs) reporting on business conditions in 2007, which was a follow-up to two surveys that the IFC did in 2003 and 2006. In these surveys, the IFC divided the SME sector into individual entrepreneurs (employing fewer than 5 people, of whom 114,676 were interviewed), *dekhan* (private) farmers (32,616), and owners of small and medium-sized companies (employing between 5 and 200 people, of whom 7,984 were interviewed). Over half the respondents in the IFC survey reported making at least one informal payment to tax officials, with individual entrepreneurs being the least reticent about admitting to making unofficial payments (that is, bribes), as figure 3.2 shows.

The survey done by the President's Strategic Research Center similarly describes a system in which payments are regularly made to facilitate decisions by the government for the delivery of services. The sums that change hands are substantial. Although only 5.3 percent of the total respondent pool surveyed remembered giving bribes or gifts of 1,000 to 3,000 somoni, 43 percent remembered giving gifts of between 50 and 100 somoni (compared with an average monthly salary of just over 100 somoni at the time).[56]

The businessmen surveyed described the pervasiveness of corruption, complaining that they were expected to make payments when starting a program, when resolving a bookkeeping problem, to get a faster turnaround from state agencies, to get orders from a state agency, to get a job in government for someone tied to one's business, to gain title to property, to gain legislative concessions, to receive leniency from inspection authorities, and to secure legal protection or to protect their property from rivals encroaching upon it.[57] Both businessmen and individual respondents complained that the amount of money spent on bribes, or "gifts," is increasing each year.

For many businessmen, the various payoffs offered to government officials constitute a significant portion of their business expenses. A total of 55.1 percent of those surveyed reported that they paid between 1 and 10 percent of their monthly turnover in spending to "stimulate the activity of government officials in [their] district"; an additional 23.9 percent said that they spent between 10 and 20 percent; and 10.9 percent said that they paid between 20 and 30 percent.

Most disturbing, 3.9 percent said that they were paying between 50 and 60 percent (2.1 percent spent between 40 and 50 percent, and 4.2 percent spent between 30 and 40 percent) of their business expenses for payoffs. Overall, the problem is so bad that 82.1 percent of the

FIGURE 3.2
INFORMAL PAYMENTS TO TAX OFFICIALS, 2007 (Percentage of Respondents)

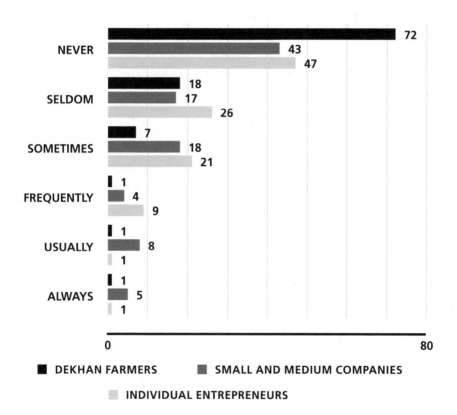

Source: International Finance Corporation, "Business Environment in Tajikistan as Seen by Small and Medium Enterprises," December 2009, www.ifc.org/ifcext/tajikistansme.nsf/Content/Survey.

entrepreneurs surveyed said that "the request for payments requested by authorities that were not stipulated by law" impeded their business development, and 93.2 percent listed "the supervision of private businesses by officials or their relatives" as another hindrance.[58]

A survey of Tajikistan's informal economy that was done during the same period (2006–2007) by independent scholars from the SHARQ research group offered similar conclusion.[59] Firms said that they paid 7.18 percent of their total annual sales in informal payments, of which 6.82 percent went to settle disputes (leaving the remaining 0.36 percent as payment to secure future favor). A total of 57.8 percent of those surveyed said that it was common practice (often, usually, or always) to make informal payments (monetary or in-kind) to state officials from the customs office, tax service, the registration and licensing committees, and to pay public utilities to "make sure that no unexpected problems occur," and 58.2 percent said that (often, usually, or always) the monetary value of the expected payment was known in advance, providing evidence of a well-developed payoff system.[60]

As the SHARQ study (done by Jafar Olimov) demonstrates, in a difficult business environment like that of Tajikistan, corruption can be the fatal blow that causes small and medium-sized businesses to go under. Of those interviewed, 71.4 percent cited corruption, 32.0 percent cited organized crime, and 31.0 percent cited street crime as a moderate or serious impediment, and 41.0 percent complained of an inefficient judicial system, as compared with 54.0 percent who noted the poor economic policy of the state as a reason for their failure to expand. The complaints regarding corruption as a serious problem were reported most frequently in general services (72.7 percent), construction (52 percent), and housing and health care services (50 percent each).[61]

DRUGS, ORGANIZED CRIME, AND CORRUPTION

The United Nations Office on Drugs and Crime (UNODC) estimates that upward of 100 tons of Afghan heroin are smuggled through Tajikistan every year, and that Tajik law enforcement agencies seize only about 2 percent of the heroin that transits the country, with heroin seizures declining in recent years.[62] Drug trafficking across Tajikistan has been a way of life for roughly two decades, ever since the collapse of the USSR and the advent of Tajikistan's civil war in 1992. During the civil war years, the proximity to Afghanistan and its burgeoning opiate industry provided a ready source of income to buy arms and feed soldiers for any regional commanders able to facilitate the transporting of narcotics across the country and get them to the drug traders further along the route to Europe, in Kyrgyzstan, Kazakhstan, and Russia. Many of these regional commanders then got jobs in the Tajik government, creating a link between government and the narcotics trade that has never been fully broken. Commanders from the People's Front of Tajikistan (PFT), the pro-Rahmon group, and the United Tajik Opposition both had ties to the narcotics trade, and some of these ties are still retained by fighters in the Islamic Movement of Uzbekistan living in Afghanistan and Pakistan.

Even for those in political favor, the ties that existed between officials and drug lords were not aired in public, but can be used when convenient to dismiss officials from power. In at least one case, that of Yakub Salimov, a reputed Soviet-era Dushanbe gangster who became a pro-Rahmon commander during the civil war and then was made minister of the interior, charged with eliminating criminal elements. He is reported to have used his time in office to organize one of the major trading routes across Tajikistan via the southern Vani District of Gorno-Badakhshan, which depended upon the cooperation of Russian military stationed in Tajikistan for the movement of drugs into Russia.[63] Salimov later served as ambassador to Turkey and head of the state customs agency.[64] As Rahmon's power grew, the Tajik president began moving against individuals with independent power bases, and in 2005 Salimov was arrested and sentenced to fifteen years in prison on charges of treason.[65]

General Gaffor Mirzoev, another former PFT leader who served as head of the presidential guard, and then head of the National Drug Control Agency (starting in 2003), was arrested in 2004 and was later sentenced to life in prison.[66] Mirzoev, from Kulyab, was also rumored to have had his own ring of drug traffickers.[67] Following his arrest, many of those who had worked with Mirzoev lost their jobs.

In May 2008, the Tajik authorities moved against two other powerful Kulyab families. At that time a vast police operation was launched against a major drug cartel operating in the Kulyab District headed by Suhrob Langariyev and Nurmahmad Safarov, the brother and son of Langari Langariyev and Sanjak Safarov, respectively, both deceased and former top commanders of the PFT. The operation followed closely on rumors that opposition to Rahmon was growing in the region.[68]

Former UTO leaders who went into the government also seem to have had ties to drug trafficking. Habib Sanginov, also from the UTO, who served as first deputy minister of the interior, also as part of the National Reconciliation accord, was reportedly killed in 2001 in a drug deal that went bad, and those charged with killing him were also accused of being drug dealers.[69]

Two more recent, and more celebrated, cases of former UTO officials are those of Mullo Abdullo and Mirzo Ziyoev. Mirzo Ziyoev, a leading commander in the UTO, is reputed to have been a major heroin smuggler, bringing his drugs in via the Pyanj District in the southern part of Tajikistan. After the signing of the National Reconciliation Agreement, he became minister of emergency situations, in 1998, and effectively was able to keep his own private army as part of his job. The ministry was disbanded in 2006, and Ziyoev died in July 2009, during a security operation in the mountainous and remote Tavildara region of central Tajikistan, having been alleged by Tajik authorities as reestablishing drug routes.[70] Mullo Abdullo, another former UTO leader, died in a security operation two months previously, after returning to Tajikistan from Afghanistan and Pakistan. The latter's death occurred during the May 2009 "Operation Poppy," when Tajik government forces set about eradicating poppies where they were not known to be grown but where opposition figures were presumed to be camping out.[71]

Although some of the former officials described above may actually have organized their own drug-trafficking networks, there are certainly networks operating in Tajikistan that are run by more traditional kinds of organized crime groups. The largest and most organized of them are generally assumed to have ties to senior people in both the regional and national governments, although attempting to prove this would be very risky to one's personal security.

Rumors abound as to who these people are—one name that is often mentioned is Mahmadsaid Ubaydulloyev, the longtime mayor of Dushanbe and simultaneously the speaker of the upper house of Parliament, who at one time was a close business associate of Mirzoev—but payoffs from drug dealers are presumed to make their way up to many who serve in the top ranks of government.[72] The Tajik military, its border guards, and before that Russia's border guards who served on the Tajik Afghan border until 2005 are also generally assumed to have had their cut.[73] Also, top officials of Tajikistan's Narcotics Control Service are seen by some as complicit, and some of the drugs seized by Tajik authorities are also reputed to find their way back to the street.

There is regular speculation that Ubaydulloyev, who is probably the greatest competitor for power with Rahmon, will be removed because of the competition that he poses, but he seems to have a sufficiently independent power base to explain his longevity in office.

Although Rahmon is able to use the drug authorities to move against his enemies, they seem to be unable to use their authority to move against any of Rahmon's relatives. This was made quite clear in 2007, when Rahmon was reported to have personally ordered the firing of Major General Faizullo Gadoyev, head of counternarcotics and counterterrorism in the Ministry of the Interior, a week after some of his officers pulled over a state security vehicle in which they discovered 60 kilograms of heroin (the third time that year that a search of a state security vehicle had yielded narcotics). The vehicle was driven by a distant relative of President Rahmon, all its occupants were arrested, and Gadoyev pressed for the prosecution of all the officers involved. The U.S. State Department reported that the minister of the interior met the president to plead that Gadoyev be retained, without success.

Gadoyev led the most effective counternarcotics organization in Tajikistan, UBNON (Upravleniye po bor'be s nezakonnym oborotom narkotikov, or the Bureau to Combat Drug Trafficking), and his police division seized several times as much heroin per year as the Drug Control Agency.[74] Gadoev joined the Ministry of the Interior (MVD) in 1982, had been working in drug control since 1995, and had headed UBNON since 2002.[75] He had been responsible for several well-publicized burnings of captured heroin stores.[76]

Although individuals and small, self-organized groups engaged in drug trafficking are relatively minor players in the drug trade, they are the ones most often apprehended by the Tajik authorities engaged in narcotics interdiction. One excellent study on the street-level drug trade in Tajikistan published in 2011, with data collected since 2005 by the Central Asian Drug Policy Center in Bishkek, suggests that the complicity of local police in the drug trade runs very deep.[77] The author of this study, Alexander Zelichenko, concludes that there is a "symbiotic relationship along the legal–illegal continuum."[78] As Zelichenko writes:

> Data regarding the disproportionate ratio of drug-related crime convictions to the number of registered drug-related crimes is strong evidence of the fact that in most cases the resulting investigation of the crime does not lead to the arrest and prosecution of criminal rings who are behind it. Instead the investigation and prosecution is limited to drug couriers or individual dealers, who are replaced on the streets almost immediately.[79]

He draws this conclusion from the interviews that he conducted. As one user he interviewed explained: "Law enforcement agencies do in fact supervise a 'drug policy' in the country—one where they provide the dealers with heroin." Another user quoted by Zelichenko explained:

> The cops need to meet quotas, which means that they need to arrest people, so the *baryga* (fixer-stoolie) provides a drug user; the cops need money, so the *baryga* provides a kickback; the cops need more money—so the *baryga* turns over someone else and he pays; they need drugs to plant on an addict—so the *baryga* provides some drugs; If the *baryga* has problems with some other cops, his cops will solve them. If they come looking for information about a drug addict—the *baryga* will provide it. In other words, the cops are "very" involved in this business.[80]

The profusion of Tajik agencies charged with combating drug trafficking means that no one is really in charge, and so it is easier for corrupt officers to go undetected, and for more honest ones to justify why they should not bother going after the "bad apples." Five separate Tajik agencies have responsibility in this sector: the Drug Control Agency, the MVD, the State National Security Committee (GKNB), border guards, and the customs service.[81]

Tajikistan receives funding for its drug-trafficking programs from the UNODC, the European Union, and the United States, among others. Capacity building in this sector has been a very slow process, no doubt in part slowed down by the lack of will in certain sectors of Tajikistan's security apparatus. For example, when the UNODC-sponsored working group "On the Financial Flows Linked to the Illicit Production and Trafficking of Afghan Opiates" met in Dubai in November 2011, the Tajiks had failed to even complete the questionnaire distributed at the meeting held in Tashkent two years previously, which was supposed to serve as a way to develop an action plan for work in this sector. The Russian Federation is Tajikistan's partner in this endeavor.[82]

In addition to motivations of personal gain, some of the Tajik authorities are also reluctant to see drug trafficking across the country end because of the money it puts into the Tajik economy. It is hard to know just how important a role the income from the drug trade has played in Tajikistan's economic recovery. Many engaged in the drug trade also have wide-ranging legitimate business interests, and even those that do not have nonetheless contributed to the economy through their purchasing power, including most visibly building large homes for themselves and family members.

A 2005 Oxford Analytic paper gives some notion of the value of the drug trade across Tajikistan, which it estimates at between $500 million and $1 billion (as against their figure of a gross domestic product of $2.1 billion at that time). This figure is derived from an estimate that 100 to 200 metric tons of heroin crosses Tajikistan each year, and the differences in the sale price on the Tajik–Afghan border, on the Russian black market, and the estimated amount of heroin sold within Tajikistan itself. The paper offers no conclusions as to how much of this money stays within Tajikistan, but enough does to provide substantial "bonuses" to Tajik officials ranging from lowly border control officers to senior government officials.

Enhanced drug control measures have reduced the number of the latter, as there must be interceptions made to prove that Tajik officials are cooperating with international efforts, but the available evidence—the low percentage of heroin intercepted—suggests that the systematic payments have not been substantially affected.

CONCLUSION: CORRUPTION OVERWHELMS THE WILL TO REFORM

The Strategic Research Center study showed substantial regional variation in how serious a problem those surveyed believed corruption to be. In Sughd, 30.4 percent of those surveyed listed corruption as the "biggest/ most important problem of the Republic of Tajikistan at the current development stage," a higher proportion than in any other region, and the population of Sughd saw it as second only to drug addiction (with 34.1 percent) in importance.[83] This finding is also consistent with the data collected by Jafar Olimov a year later.

Overall, the findings of the Strategic Research Center study are quite striking, especially when one takes into account that this report was issued by the president's own institute. They conclude that

> we witness the formation of [an] economic and political oligarchy which dictates its will to the society, paying no attention to the country's needs. This results in reduced political support of small business and social needs which in its turn leads to an acute decrease of socioeconomic funds [for] civil servants.

The authors add that this paralyzes government institutions, creates an informal tax on the population—especially vulnerable economic, political, and social groups—and causes environmental deterioration because groups use natural resources for personal and immediate profit, with an example of this being the cotton monopoly.[84]

The authors then go on to elaborate on the insufficiencies of the current Tajik legal system to deal with corruption, citing how the "Anti-Corruption Law of the Republic of Tajikistan" of December 1999 fails to make illegal some of the most prevalent corrupt practices in the country, such as officials engaging in commercial activity for personal benefit, or the use of official status to transfer state funds to commercial structures held by relatives or proxy owners. They describe the 1999 presidential decree "On Additional Measures Aimed at Crime Control and Fighting Corruption" as one of the "most ignored decrees in the whole history of state independence" because it provided no mechanisms for implementation, and created an opportunity to "fearlessly combine civil service with commercial activity," creating "not only a huge niche for corruption, but also a motivation to occupy public positions with the purpose of illegal enrichment." The number of bribery cases referred to the courts is small (only 86 cases in 2004–2005), and only a handful of cases resulted in prison sentences.[85]

Moreover, the kind of cases that do go to the courts clearly involve relatively minor government officials, who are charged with taking sums of money that, though large for ordinary Tajiks, are clearly small amounts in comparison with what senior officials are regularly rumored to have received. For example, during the first nine months of 2009, 115 officials were charged with misconduct, but one well-publicized case, involving the Prosecutor's Office in Jilikul region, Khatlon Oblast, involved a bribe of 26,400 somoni (about $6,000).[86]

It is difficult to know whether the scale of corruption is such that it serves as a damper on economic growth in the country. It definitely serves to circulate money in new ways, raising the salaries of some and deflating the profits of others, and at other times it is the only way to move things forward. One thing that is clear is that "corruption," broadly defined, has helped create a vast informal economy in Tajikistan.

The two reviewers who read earlier versions of this book both raised the question as to whether Tajikistan is so different from other Central Asian states with regard to corruption. I believe that in a critical way it really is.

In the last years of Communist Party rule, an informal economy flourished throughout the Soviet Union, and it was particularly vibrant in much of Central Asia. It served to fund the preservation of traditional (and costly) practices, like weddings and funerals, and allowed many Central Asians to live more comfortably than would have been the case if they had been dependent solely upon official sources of income. Local and even republic-level authorities were either indifferent to or even frequently complicit in the process as a kind of "in your face" to the authorities in

Moscow, whom the Central Asians generally believed looked down on them. Condoning and participating in corrupt practices allowed Central Asia's party leaders to build powerful patronage networks, which in turn they used to provide Moscow with the "deliverables" demanded of them, allowing officials in Moscow and in the republics to remain in power.

It has been hard for the governments throughout Central Asia to change the patterns of elite behavior, and the same human drives for enrichment and power have continued to fuel the perpetuation of corruption. Independence has brought new temptations, "incentive bonuses" from potential foreign investors, chances to profit from privatization schemes, and, with the deteriorating situation in Afghanistan, the opportunity to benefit from drug trafficking.

Although there have repeatedly been rumors of how senior officials in Turkmenistan and Uzbekistan have benefited from the drug trade, in Kyrgyzstan and Tajikistan the problem has been of a different scale. Drug traders and other criminal groups have been at the margins and sometimes at the very center of events that ousted two Kyrgyz presidents and of the violence in southern Kyrgyzstan in 2010. But nowhere in the region have corruption in general and drug trafficking in particular reached the levels of Tajikistan, where it is possible to talk in terms of the risk of "state capture," and where those serving the state engage in more illegal activities than legal ones.

Crudely put, the leaders and ruling elites of richer states, with more diverse economies and resources, have had more opportunities to balance the goals of personal enrichment with the broader concerns of national economic development. In Tajikistan, however, the choices presented to the ruling elite must seem starker; and given the choice, most seem to opt for what is good for them personally.

This same pattern is seen throughout Tajik society, and thus many in the middle and lower middle classes have learned how to work the current system, and this offers them some sense of security, while people at the bottom are simply focused on survival. This does not mean that no Tajiks are interested in political and economic reform. But many who have advocated it most strongly have decided to leave the country, to go to Russia or Israel or further afield, and to live in societies where other norms prevail. Those who remain have mostly resigned themselves to the idea that changing public and private behavior is going to be a very slow process.

CHAPTER 4

THE ECONOMIC ENVIRONMENT

This and the following two chapters look into Tajikistan's economic reforms in more depth. Once the poorest of the Soviet republics, Tajikistan is now the poorest of the Soviet successor states with a per capita gross domestic product of $780 in 2010, returning to pre–civil war levels at that time.[1] The country's pattern of economic growth was disrupted by the global financial and economic crisis of 2008–2009, whose effects were compounded by a harsh winter. Although the country has experienced economic recovery since then, with an annual growth rate of 6.5 percent in 2010 and 6.0 percent in 2011, up from 3.9 percent in 2009, this is substantially less than the 8.9 percent average increases in GDP that Tajikistan experienced from 2000 to 2006.[2]

Much of the improvement in Tajikistan's economy is the result of its recovery from the very deep recession of the 1990s that followed the breakup of the Soviet Union, favorable commodity price trends, and rapidly growing remittances from Tajiks working abroad, as well as continual prodding from the outside, in the form of lending and technical assistance provided by the various international financial institutions. In recent years, this has been augmented by a number of very large project-driven loans from the People's Republic of China, and smaller loans from other bilateral lenders. Tajikistan has also benefited from the growth in Russia's economy, and to a lesser extent in Kazakhstan's economy, which provide better-paid employment for Tajik workers than do jobs at home. There has also been a substantial reduction in poverty levels in

Tajikistan—more from remittances, the expansion of subsistence farming, and large infrastructure projects than from the creation of permanent new jobs or agricultural reform.

The government of Tajikistan launched its first serious effort at economic reform in 1998, signing an agreement with the International Monetary Fund on an Enhanced Structural Adjustment Facility, which was renamed the Poverty Reduction Growth Facility Arrangement in 1999. This reform agreement was complemented by a structural adjustment credit from the World Bank. The reform process was given a further impetus in 2001, when the country's monetary reform was completed and the Tajik somoni became, effectively, a convertible currency.

Tajikistan initially took something of a fast track to reform, undertaking price and trade liberalization, financial-sector reform, the privatization of small enterprises, and restructuring land to enhance the rights of family farmers. The government also tried to improve the conditions for starting and maintaining privately owned small and medium-sized businesses, a theme developed later in this chapter.

The country's annual growth rate reached a high of 10.2 percent in 2001 and then averaged 7 percent through 2005.[3] Yet despite this positive economic growth, its GDP did not surpass 1991 levels until 2006.[4]

The lingering effects of the civil war, the government's lackluster approach to reform, Tajikistan's limited amount of arable and overworked agricultural lands, and its relatively limited natural resource base have made the country heavily dependent upon remittances from foreign workers, which declined in 2008 due to the global economic crisis. Railroad stoppages by Uzbekistan—the product of deteriorating relations between the two countries rather than of global economic factors—also contributed to Tajikistan's problems in those years.[5]

Tajikistan's economic crisis in 2007–2008 led the international financial institutions active in the country to substantially reexamine their country strategies, as well as to try to better coordinate donor activity and international relief efforts. The terms of this reexamination were also strongly influenced by the financial irregularities involving the National Bank of Tajikistan (NBT) that were discovered by the International Monetary Fund in late 2007, when the NBT was using international credits and misreporting macroeconomic benchmarks as they related to the debt relief programs provided by the IMF from 2004 through 2006. This situation resulted in an international audit of the NBT, and the IMF putting Tajikistan under a staff-monitored program to supervise the repayment of the misused funds.

Once Tajikistan's government met the conditions imposed by the IMF, Tajikistan was again eligible for its next Poverty Reduction and Growth Facility award, which was granted in April 2009. This facility is designed to support Tajikistan's National Development Strategy and the Poverty Reduction Strategy for 2010–2012, in order to develop the country's hydroelectric sector, encourage agricultural diversification, and create an environment more conducive to private investment through further reform of land and property rights, improved state enterprise management, removing barriers to trade and investment, and increasing access to credit.[6] This strategy is a complement to the government's strategy for health, education, and food security for the same period. Labor remittances once again picked up in 2009, and showed a 25 percent increase between 2009 and 2010,[7] which translated into roughly a 5 percent increase in GDP.[8]

However, both the International Monetary Fund and World Bank remain concerned that unless Tajikistan accelerates its current pace of reforms, its economy will not continue to grow. The growing role of China in particular, and, also of other bilateral lenders such as Iran, Russia, and India (which stands eagerly in the wings), means that the international financial institutions may find it difficult to convince Tajikistan to accept the most unpopular aspects of their guidance.

Depicting the Tajik economy as "relatively undiversified and dependent on external capital flows—especially remittances,"[9] the IMF does not anticipate that the country will be able to return to its previous growth rates.[10] Although the growth rates of 2010 and 2011 exceeded expectations, Tajikistan remains at risk of being affected by feared global and regional slowdowns. The IMF projects a 6 percent increase in GDP in Tajikistan in 2012, assuming that there are no climatic or other natural disasters or unanticipated disruptions to regional trade.[11]

As the IMF noted in its June 2011 country report, much still remains to be done in the areas of competition policy, securities market development, the restructuring of state enterprises, privatization in general, and banking and infrastructure reform.[12] The conclusion of the risks section of the IMF's 2012 report was not much more positive:

> As a landlocked economy with very limited domestic resources, Tajikistan remains vulnerable to external shocks from a variety of sources. Developments with respect to global/regional growth, international food and fuel prices, regional trade disputes, and climatic conditions can make or break economic outcomes and likely represent the most pressing risks. Institutional capacity remains limited, and in this context the risk of policy missteps remains relatively high.[13]

A DEBTOR NATION

This reform program was funded through substantial borrowing by Tajikistan from the international financial institutions. Overall, Tajikistan's debt to multilaterals increased sixfold from 1996 to 2008,[14] and represented 61 percent of the country's external loan portfolio by the end of 2007 and 47 percent at the end of 2008, when the World Bank and the Asian Development Bank both decided to shift their activities from giving Tajikistan loans to providing it with grants. The shift between 2007 and 2008 reflects the disbursement of a $277 million loan from China.

Tajikistan's current account deficit also began widening, up from 2.8 percent of GDP in 2006 to 11.2 percent in 2007, which in large part reflected the Public Investment Program funded by the Export-Import Bank of China. This led to a widening trade deficit (as a share of GDP, from 35 percent in 2006 to 45 percent in 2007 and 40 percent in 2008), which was partly offset by a rise in remittances flowing into the country (which rose to 38 percent of GDP in 2007).[15]

Before the economic crisis of 2007–2008, Tajikistan had been benefiting from debt restructuring by the IMF and by its international creditors (most prominently Russia). This led the country's total external debt to decline from 84 percent of GDP to 42 percent in 2006,[16] and to 34.4

percent in 2010. The IMF expected it to remain at roughly that level through 2011.[17]

In April 2009, the Executive Board of the IMF approved the most recent three-year Poverty Reduction and Growth Facility for Tajikistan for 26 million Special Drawing Rights (SDR), or $38.7 million.[18] Even with the current program, Tajik authorities report that they will not be able to meet their planned spending goals, and that given revenue shortfalls they will be cutting back on planned increases in civil service wages and salaries (which will only increase by 10 percent, rather than the planned 15 percent) in order to keep fiscal deficits, planned at 0.4 percent of GDP for 2010, from increasing faster than planned.[19] This is likely to slow capacity building in the government sector.

The IMF noted that Tajikistan has found it hard to control its budget deficits, largely because of the country's generally low financial liquidity, its lack of access to international money markets, the near absence of a domestic debt market, no real stock market, the NBT's lack of capitalization, the need to increase social expenditures, and the government's continuing small and sometimes even shrinking tax base.[20] The IMF warned that deficits could increase to 1 percent of GDP in 2011, increasing the need for Tajikistan to adopt more prudent fiscal management. In fact, the Tajiks were able to keep the budget deficit at 0.5 percent of GDP that year. At the same time, the IMF urged the Tajik government to maintain a proactive stance toward social spending in the face of rising food and energy prices to prevent a sharp increase in the percentage of the population living below the poverty line.[21]

The Tajik budget for 2012 seeks to place more emphasis on wages and salaries, which the IMF warned should not be at the expense of building in buffers within the budget to protect the Tajiks against the risk of global slowdown or other exogenous shocks. The Tajik authorities generally agreed with the IMF, but they made the case for needing to increase social spending. Where the two clashed was on the questions of expenditures for what the Tajiks termed critical infrastructure projects, like Roghun.[22]

One of the challenges in discussing Tajikistan's economy, and its level of poverty, is the deficiencies in the statistical techniques that are used to collect national accounts and price statistics, and also to measure informal income. Although the IMF has routinely noted some improvements in this regard, as a result of the technical assistance that Tajikistan has received, it still regularly notes that the technical level of reporting in Tajikistan, though good enough for broad surveillance, remains inadequate.

This inadequacy has been a real challenge for both the IMF and the World Bank as they seek to prod and motivate the Tajik government to continue a reform process and goad it on to do better. As one IMF official once commented, off the record, the discussions in private tend to be much more pointed than the published accounts of Tajikistan's economic performance. This is true for both the IMF and the World Bank. Although the published evaluations by both the IMF and World Bank make clear that while there has been progress toward reform, it is still not sufficient to ensure that Tajikistan's postwar recovery will continue, or that the country is not at great risk of becoming a failed state.

Even in the "diplomatic speak" of international financial institutions, it is clear that this risk is a real one. Consider the following three examples, from a lengthy World Bank report on the completion of $40 million in grants from the Bank's concessional facility, the International Development Association (IDA), to improve government capacity; this excerpt is from the report's section on the assessment of risk to development outcomes:

> Both the government commitment to the overall reform agenda and its capacity to implement reforms are uneven. However, the global economic slowdown and the pressure it brings for sustainable fiscal and macroeconomic management has perhaps strengthened commitment to reform, because many of the structural rigidities responsible for a poor investment climate (for example, burdensome business regulation, an uncompetitive aviation sector) and subsidies of the past for favored industries, such as TALCO, are increasingly seen as no longer affordable. Government's decision to seek support from the IMF under the Poverty Reduction and Growth Facility also indicates a commitment to put into place sounder

practices of economic management. However, the Tajikistan's macroeconomic situation remains fragile, as a result both of recent imprudent central bank guarantees which have added to the government's debt burden and of the impact of the global financial crisis which has adversely affected the level of workers' remittances and prices of key exports, such as aluminum.[23]

As a result of the country's unreformed or partially reformed state-owned enterprises, the Tajik government has had a persistent problem— in both good and bad economic years—with tax arrears. Much of the money owed is the result of crosscutting arrears, in which the failure of one sector to pay taxes triggers nonpayment in another sector, leading to overall government underinvestment and underperformance. A lot of the problem directly or indirectly comes from the nonperforming nature of many of the loans in the Tajik cotton sector, but it is also the result of nonpayment by government-owned companies such as Barki Tojik.

And later in that same section of the World Bank report, in a comment made in relation to the risk to reform in the cotton, aviation, and energy sectors, the authors note that

> people who benefit from the current situation may resist reforms that threaten their interests. However, the government appears committed to continuing the reforms, due to the significant economic benefits that are likely to result from change and to support from development partners that has bolstered reforms and helped to build capacity for implementation.[24]

In its section on government performance, which is rated moderately satisfactory, the report observes:

> Government commitment to the overall reform program as laid out in the policy matrix of the PDPG [Programmatic Development Policy Grant] operation was strong, although it was stronger in some areas than in others.... However, the government's commitment to maintaining overall macroeconomic stability (and thus an enabling environment) was unsatisfactory, as demonstrated by the macroeconomic crisis brought about by the inappropriate involvement of the NBT

in guaranteeing cotton sector debt. One of the conditions for accessing funding under the PDPG operations is that the government maintains a stable macroeconomic environment. That it did not, resulted in a delay of nine months in the processing of PDPG 3. Although the government has taken decisive action to address the crisis, the inability of the authorities to maintain sound macroeconomic management throughout the implementation period results in an overall rating for government performance of moderately satisfactory.[25]

Finally, in the section justifying the rating for overall borrower performance, on which Tajikistan was also rated moderately satisfactory, the authors noted the following:

> The overall performance of the borrower was moderately satisfactory. The government demonstrated its commitment to the program, from identification of the reform program laid out in the policy matrix of the first operation to successful completion of each operation's prior actions. It facilitated the adoption of key policies, legislation, and regulations, and promoted their implementation. However, the government failed to manage the macroeconomic crisis that is still being resolved with the help of the IMF, the Bank, and other development partners.[26]

In its rejoinder to these observations by the World Bank, the Tajik government complains that the desired results have not been attained, in part because the expectations of the international financial institutions were likely too high. The Tajik government's rejoinder further complains that the government is expected to implement too many reform activities simultaneously, a demand that exceeds its technical and human capacity. In the government's defense, Tajikistan suffered a much greater "brain drain" after independence than any other country in the region, due to the prolonged fighting after independence. However, the Rahmon government has done little to try to attract back those who left; in contrast to Uzbekistan, Kazakhstan, and Kyrgyzstan (where an, albeit small, percentage of Russian speakers who had previously emigrated have returned), virtually no one has returned to Tajikistan. This is largely because bleak economic prospects are combined with an almost complete absence of the use of Russian in public life.

TAJIKISTAN'S BANKING SECTOR

Although still the least developed banking sector in the former Soviet Union, with the lowest share of foreign ownership, this sector has grown in recent years. The size of the total loans and deposits grew from 18 percent in 2005 to 31 percent in 2007, although when the cotton sector is excluded, total loans accounted for only 22 percent of the country's GDP.

The World Bank continues to hold out hope that through ongoing supervision and appropriate partnerships, the banking sector in Tajikistan can improve and meet international banking standards.[27] Although the Bank reports that the ratio of deposits to GDP averages about 30 percent for low-income countries (compared with 55 percent in middle-income and 85 percent in high-income countries), the ratio for Tajikistan was 11 percent in 2008. Tajikistan's ratio of loans to GDP is 28 percent, up from 18 percent in 2004, in large part because of the Law on Microfinance, which was enacted in 2004.

Although Tajikistan was not hard-hit by the global financial crisis, it did lead to a further deterioration of its financial sector, which had experienced some improvement in 2008, when Tajikistan's gross international reserves increased a little more than anticipated (to $199 million against a projected $169 million), still very low for a country with a population of its size. But even the global crisis led to corporate drawdowns, a drying up of trade credits, and a rise of nonperforming loans, all of which led to asset deterioration in 2009, and the deterioration of the somoni. As a result, Tajikistan's banks were forced to raise deposit rates and to toughen terms of credit, leading to further constraints on economic growth.[28]

Just as the global financial and economic crisis started in 2008, following several years of low inflation, inflation began to rise in 2007, with the Consumer Price Index rising at 27 percent year on year in August 2008, in large part because of rising food prices (reflecting the previous year's high oil and energy prices). Although inflationary pressures lessened somewhat as the crisis abated, inflation continues to be a concern for Tajikistan, which is vulnerable to both rising food and fuel prices, and starting in May 2011 the Tajiks became subject to Russian export taxes on refined fuel products. The IMF reports that headline inflation peaked at nearly 15 percent in May 2011, but declined to 12 percent by September 2011.[29]

This was all occurring at a time when the international financial institutions committed to a somewhat increased level of engagement in Tajikistan to provide assistance during the harsh winter of 2007–2008. However, as the following sections make clear, the economic reform process in Tajikistan has had something of a "push me/pull you" quality in recent years, with pressure from the international community being only partially successful, in large part because the rebukes were always mild and generally had few financial consequences for the Tajik government.

Although there is little chance of a major bank failure in Tajikistan, the country's banks still lack the capital and capacity to act as independent economic actors or play a major economic role in the country's economic development, save for direct intervention by the government, which uses them as an instrument (figure 4.1). As of mid-2008, the country had twelve commercial banks (of which one is the state-owned NBT and three are subsidiaries of foreign banks), seven credit unions, one nonbank financial institution, and 75 microcredit organizations.[30] Tajikistan's fledgling banking sector has had more than its share of bad publicity.

The largest private bank, Orienbank, has approximately 60 percent of the deposit market, and is headed by Hasan Sadulloev, President Rahmon's brother-in-law. It has been intimately tied to Tajik Aluminum, and its role described at length in chapter 6, which focuses on Tajikistan's industrial sector.

The Tajik banking system did not experience the kind of bank failure that occurred in stronger economies during the global financial and economic crisis of 2008–2009 because of its relative isolation from the global financial system, and because the state's dominating role in the sector prevented a bank failure in the traditional sense. But the NBT, which has some supervisory responsibility over the country's private banks, was itself still somewhat in turmoil in the wake of the leadership changes after the 2007 crisis over its use of international credits.

Consequently, the NBT was unable to respond proactively, and so the global crisis led to a substantial weakening of the country's banks and a sharp decline in private-sector credit. This said, Tajikistan did not fare as poorly as some of its neighbors during this crisis, as it did not suffer

FIGURE 4.1

CROSS-COUNTRY COMPARISON OF FINANCIAL INTERMEDIATION
(Percentage of Gross Domestic Product)

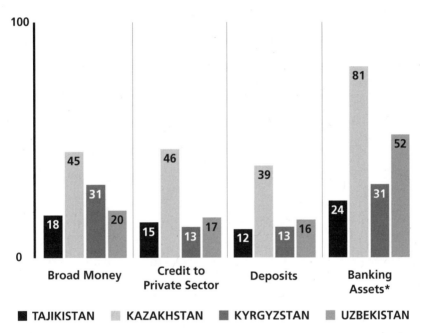

*Sum of net foreign assets of banks, credit to the private sector, credit to the government by banks, and other items net.

Source: International Monetary Fund, *Republic of Tajikistan: 2011 Article IV Consultation, Fourth Review Under the Three-Year Arrangement Under the Extended Credit Facility, Request for Waiver of Nonobservance for Performance Criteria and Modification of Performance Criterion—Staff Report; Staff Supplement; and Public Information Notice on the Executive Board Discussion, June 2011*, IMF Country Report 11/130 (Washington, D.C.: International Monetary Fund, 2011), 12, www.imf.org/external/pubs/cat/longres.aspx?sk=24915.0.

negative growth rates. And though the crisis led to the depreciation of Tajikistan's somoni (which went from an exchange rate of 3.43 somoni to $1 in January 2009 to 4.40 somoni to $1 in June 2009) many felt that this adjustment was necessary, and by 2010 the somoni was again considered to be slightly overvalued.

In its 2010 country report, the IMF noted that the commercial banks' return on equity and return on assets became negative in June 2010. General deterioration in the financial sector was reflected in problems with the country's two largest banks, the NBT and Orienbank; these banks are undercapitalized and have their loan portfolios overly tied, respectively, to the cotton and aluminum sectors. The IMF also noted that these two banks "most often were in violation of established prudential criteria" in their lending practices.[31] And it noted the country still has lax lending standards and the state is too directly involved in the internal operation of the country's largest banks. The NBT has not been able to effectively intervene to help bolster troubled private banks, and all the country's banks had their balance sheets adversely affected by the government's mandate that they become shareholders in the Roghun Dam project.

The NBT's functioning in supervising private banks has improved somewhat, especially as a result of the passage of the revised Law on Banking, but would benefit further from the planned adoption of legislation on bankruptcy.[32] The NBT, however, has not been diligent about trying to recover its debts from the cotton sector, which are to be repaid according to a 2010 presidential decree. Although the bank has signed agreements with many of the indebted investors, it has been lax about trying to collect the funds.[33] This will compound the financing problem in the cotton sector more generally, as the Tajik government announced in 2010 that because of the country's budgetary crisis, the only credit to be offered by the NBT in the agricultural sector would have to come from funds repaid to the bank during that year.[34]

However, it is unclear how the banks would fare in a subsequent crisis, and the IMF was concerned that the Tajik authorities would have trouble holding the fiscal deficit to 1 percent of GDP in 2011.[35] The level of 2011 reserves was partly the result of a $70 million loan from the Eurasian Economic Community's Anti-Crisis Fund.[36] The IMF defined the risks to its country program thus:

In addition, weaknesses in the banking sector may become more pronounced, requiring NBT intervention. In this context, the health of many state enterprises, as well as inter-enterprise and tax arrears[,] represent a drag on economic growth and the health of the financial system. They also represent contingent liabilities to the government—raising the level of fiscal risk. Institution capacity remains weak, despite significant improvements in recent years, and could constrain the speed and quality of reforms. Finally, a decrease in donor support—due either to constrained aid budgets, or concern over the pace of progress in such key areas as transparency, governance, and financial sector reform—remains a risk.[37]

In its reply to the IMF, the Tajik government made clear that it recognized that there are lingering problems with the NBT, but it argued for more time, as it maintained that much progress had been made since 2007:

A safeguards assessment update of the NBT was completed in mid-2010. The findings indicated that initial steps have been taken to address the risks identified by the special audit on cotton sector financing, but that considerable safeguards risks at the NBT remain. Both the accounting and the organization structure are still fragmented, and due to the weak internal audit function and an absence of any external independent oversight, access to broad and complete information has been restricted. Consequently, there is a need to further enhance data systems and the transparency of operational integrity. Restoring the credibility of the central bank and building the required capacity in key functions, such as internal audit and financial reporting[,] will require more time.[38]

The government acknowledged that other financial indicators continue to show weakness, and that a "small number of banks [are] consistently violating prudent rules." It noted that this occurred with regard to banks exposing themselves to disproportionate single-party risks and failing to meet reserve requirements. To try to address these problems, the

Ministry of Finance issued some $90 million in recapitalization bonds; "when resources permit," the government promises that there will be an effort to increase their value.[39] This was likely in response to the IMF's criticism of the undercapitalization and unsystematic way in which treasury bonds were being issued.[40]

In its 2012 country report, the IMF again offered advice similar to the concerns noted in the previous year, finding fault with the general pattern of financing for big state-initiated projects, and financing patterns for state-owned enterprises, warning again that Tajikistan would fail to achieve its financial-sector reform objectives if it did not provide tighter supervision:

> The persistence of such practices as directed lending, quasi-fiscal operations, insufficient financial discipline for large enterprises, and lack of coordination on macroeconomic policies between key agencies are problematic. NBT liquidity loans, Roghun spending, and continued arrears in state enterprises are key examples. Looking ahead, there are also risks to program targets and objectives given the convergence of (i) quasi-fiscal liabilities that have built up in the financial and state enterprise sectors, and (ii) increasing efforts to subject these sectors to real financial constraints and tighter supervision.[41]

The relatively undeveloped nature of Tajikistan's banking system has posed challenges for institutional lenders such as the EBRD, which Tajikistan joined in 1992. The EBRD did not begin supporting large investment projects in Tajikistan until 1996, but by the end of January 2012, the bank had signed 65 projects with a net cumulative business volume of €243 million ($319.6 million), and this includes €106 million ($139.4 million) for a cumulative trade facilitation program.[42]

The EBRD shares the concerns of the IMF with regard to Tajikistan's banking sector, which both consider to have shallow penetration; this is because its total banking system assets constitute about 25 percent of GDP, and because more than 60 percent of deposits are held in foreign currency, reflecting a lack of confidence in the local currency and continued fears of high inflation and exchange rate depreciation. They are also concerned about the virtue of capital markets. The EBRD concludes that

> there is potential to improve access to finance by increasing deposits, capturing a larger portion of remittances, strengthening the lending capacity of the microfinance industry and developing the nonbanking financial sector, including leasing. This, however, requires changes in tax policies and other legislative changes. Improved confidence in the banking system can induce keeping remittances in the banks and develop remittance-based finance to foster financial intermediation.[43]

Currently, 74 percent of the EBRD's lending goes to the private sector, both through support for small enterprises under the Tajik Micro and Small Enterprise Finance Facility and through the Tajik Agricultural Finance Framework, which is intended to help farmers recover from the bad loans that characterized the sector in the past, and by trying to establish better production chain relationships between farmers and agribusiness. But the EBRD complains that the lack of capacity in Tajikistan's banking sector has limited the amount of money that it has been able to distribute, and that more generally, the funding allocated has not been sufficient to meet Tajikistan's post-2008 crisis needs:[44]

> Against the backdrop of slow progress with reform that limits opportunities for bankable projects, the Bank will focus its policy dialogue with the Tajik authorities on the importance of structural and sectoral reforms to unlock opportunities for investment. For example, progress with banking sector reform would not only allow further Bank investment in commercial banks and MFIs [multilateral financial institutions] but would also increase the Bank's ability to provide credit lines for agriculture, MSMEs [micro-, small, and medium-sized enterprises], and energy efficiency. Improvements in the business environment and the tax system would create more bankable private enterprises that could benefit from EBRD and local commercial bank financing. Infrastructure and energy sector

reforms will help to create opportunities for investment in these sectors.[45]

The EBRD has worked with seven of Tajikistan's fourteen banks and with three microfinance institutions, setting for itself the task of enhancing the capacity of the sector more generally and of supervisory capacity and independence of the NBT as financial-sector regulator more specifically, with the aim of limiting state interference in the financial sector more generally, although it has financed public-sector projects for infrastructure and for improving clean water supplies.[46]

The EBRD's choice of partners in Tajikistan has been a source of criticism, because it is seen by some as further institutionalizing the dominant role of a handful of banks that are close to the president and his inner circle. For example, the EBRD acquired a 25-percent-plus-1-share stake (worth a roughly $12 million stake, and making it a minority stockholder with vested rights) in Agroinvestbank, Tajikistan's second-largest commercial bank in 2009. The EBRD had begun working with the bank in 2005, through its Micro and Small Enterprise Framework, and then through the EBRD Trade Facilitation Program, and EBRD's Tajik Agricultural Finance Framework as well. Despite complaints about the lack of transparency associated with it, Orienbank remains a major partner for the EBRD in Tajikistan.[47]

This just goes to emphasize the conundrum faced by the international financial institutions operating in Tajikistan. The twin desires of wanting to both increase the transparency of the banking sector and to also provide funding for major projects that are designed to spur economic growth often seem to conflict. The only banks able to handle the large sums of money involved in the major projects requiring international funding are the very actors that are the least interested in creating a transparent and independent banking structure, as it would undermine their privileged position. So the choice the international financial institutions face is withholding large-scale funding, or offering more money—sufficient to attract and sustain new and more independent actors to the banking sector.

PRIVATIZATION AND SMEs IN TAJIKISTAN

One of the goals of the international financial institutions active in Tajikistan has been to bolster the role of private ownership in the economy. The country has made considerable progress in small-scale privatization, which began in 1998; by 2007 some 90 percent of the economy had been privatized. But the 10 percent that remains in state hands (which includes TALCO, the Tajik Aluminum Company; and Barki Tojik, the national electricity company) makes a critical contribution to the country's GDP, and is generally viewed as nontransparent or only partially transparent.

The private sector accounted for 48 percent of Tajikistan's GDP in 2007, with 155,000 businesses that employed 1,076,000 people in 2007. This figure includes *dekhan* farms, which employed roughly two-thirds of all those working in the small and medium-sized enterprise sector. The majority of these were very small, as only 200 businesses had 200 or more employees.[48] Two out of every three private entrepreneurs operate their businesses under a patent regime, which provides a simplified tax regime for businesses with turnovers of less than 200,000 somoni, roughly $40,000. All others run their businesses on the basis of licensing certificates (with tax obligations set by profits, or through a simplified tax regime based on economic turnover).[49]

Tajikistan has liberalized prices, leaving few price supports in place save in the area of communal services and utilities, and it also has liberalized some of its terms of trade. Tajikistan began negotiations to join the World Trade Organization in 2001, and these have been advancing slowly. Tajikistan also accepted foreign exchange obligations under the IMF's Article VIII in 2004.[50]

The development of SMEs is critical for Tajikistan's continued economic growth. The country's private sector has been steadily expanding, but its capacity for growth is severely limited by the inadequately defined legal environment in which business operates, by the difficulty of securing financing, and by the pervasive atmosphere of corruption. All this serves to encourage Tajik businessmen to work outside the law, in Tajikistan's informal, or second, economy.

FIGURE 4.2

TAJIKISTAN'S RANKING FOR DOING BUSINESS COMPARED WITH THOSE OF OTHER COUNTRIES THAT BELONG TO THE COMMONWEALTH OF INDEPENDENT STATES

(Out of 183 Countries, Worst Performers Have Highest Ranks)

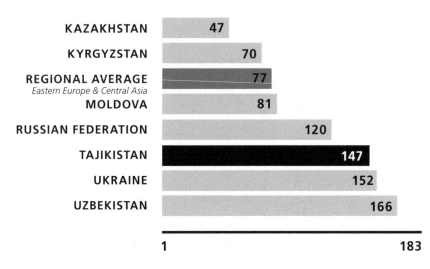

Source: International Financial Corporation, *Doing Business 2012: Doing Business in a More Transparent World—Comparative Regulation for Domestic Firms in 183 Countries* (Washington, D.C.: International Financial Corporation, 2011), 7, www.doingbusiness.org/~/media/FPDKM/Doing%20Business/Documents/Annual-Reports/English/DB12-FullReport.pdf.

These complaints notwithstanding, the World Bank's International Finance Corporation has reported some improvements in doing business in Tajikistan, which was ranked 147 of 187 countries in 2012.[51] Figure 4.2 compares its relative overall ranking with those of some other countries that belong to the Commonwealth of Independent States.

Tajikistan has clearly done better in some areas of improving its business climate than in others, doing well compared with some of its neighbors in terms of enforcing contracts and starting a business, and performing most poorly in terms of provision of electricity, taxation, and cross-border trade.

Tajikistan has made substantial gains occurring in the ratings that it received on protecting investors (going from 108 to 65) in a three-year period. But in a number of areas, it still ranked among the worst-performing countries, such as in paying taxes, where it ranked 168, worse than Kyrgyzstan, Uzbekistan, and Kazakhstan (which were ranked 162, 157, and 13, respectively),[52] and 177 in trading across borders, slightly better than Uzbekistan (ranked 183) and slightly worse than Kyrgyzstan and Kazakhstan (ranked 171 and 176, respectively), figures that demonstrate the overall difficulty of engaging in international trade throughout the region.[53]

In 2012, the cost in per capita income to start a business is higher in relative terms in Tajikistan, at 36.9 percent of per capita income, compared with 0.8 percent in Kazakhstan and 3.5 percent Kyrgyzstan.[54] Energy shortages are another serious problem for SMEs in Tajikistan. But difficult as it is for businesses in Tajikistan to acquire energy, the situation is worse in Kyrgyzstan, taking 337 days, versus Tajikistan's 238, while in Kazakhstan the process takes only 88 days. In 2012, the cost to obtain electricity was 1,297.9 percent of per capita income in Tajikistan, 2,545.6 percent in Kyrgyzstan, and 88.4 percent in Kazakhstan.[55] Costs to export goods were virtually identical for the three countries, but imports cost more in Tajikistan. In 2012, the costs per export container for Tajikistan, Kazakhstan, and Kyrgyzstan are, respectively, $3,850, $3,130, and $3,210, and to import a container, $4,550, $3,290, and $3,450.[56]

Since 2005, a variety of legislation has been introduced that is, at least on paper, designed to improve conditions for doing business. These include a law on movable assets, which took effect in stages in 2005 and 2006 (and was further refined by the law on state registration of immovable properties adopted in March 2008, which, taken collectively, provides for a modern system that allows movable property to serve as collateral to secure a broad range of obligations); a new law on joint stock companies adopted in 2007, which meets some international standards on shareholder rights but which the EBRD judged inadequate with regard to its requirements regarding disclosure and transparency of corporate government frameworks; a new law on foreign investments adopted in 2007 that offers guarantees regarding the right to repatriate investment profits; a new law on trade and service marks; a long-awaited Arbitration Law enacted in January 2008, which provides for the enforcement of domestic arbitration decisions (but Tajikistan has not yet ratified the 1958 New York Convention on the Recognition and Enforcement of Foreign Arbitral Awards); and, in April 2008, a new law on mortgages, which was designed to facilitate personal lending.[57] In 2010 legal changes were introduced to reduce the minimum capital required for business start-ups, in 2012 modifications were introduced to consolidate registration requirements for businesses with tax and other state authorities, and start-up businesses were given a full year of operation before all start-up capital requirements need be met.[58] Local authorities, however, are often slow to learn and enforce the legal changes that are designed to simplify business practices.

One of the areas in which there has been little improvement is in the operation of Tajikistan's securities market, which is governed by the Law on Securities and Securities Market, which was adopted in March 1992 and amended in March 2006. The country still lacks a functioning stock exchange, and it is not yet common practice for corporations to issue IPOs (initial public offerings) to meet their capital funding requirements. The existing legislation fails to provide for an independent authority to supervise the securities market, instead placing it under the authority of the Ministry of Finance, and giving the NBT supervisory responsibility over other banks and microfinance institutions. Following the law's amendment, in 2007, the EBRD's Securities Markets Legislation Assessment scored Tajikistan in "very low compliance" with the Objectives and Principles of Security Regulation published by the International Organization of Securities Commissions, and concluded that the securities sector was still in need of critical reform.[59]

Minority shareholder rights are not well protected, with few avenues available if they seek disclosure from the majority partners, and turning to the courts can be both time consuming and frustrating, because even if they secure a favorable judgment, there is no enforcement mechanism for the court's decision. The courts have little experience in this area, and no case law collections are made available.[60] Moreover, few businesses have confidence that the judicial process will give them a fair hearing, especially if they are going against a prominent person or even someone with more money (and hence someone who can offer large bribes).

Tajik enterprises still lack adequate bankruptcy protection. Insolvency is governed by the Law on Bankruptcy of Enterprises adopted in 2003 (which replaced a 1992 law), but which, according to the EBRD, is still in "very low compliance" with international standards.[61]

The EBRD's 2009 report presents a picture of a sector of the economy that has made some uneven improvement in the past five years but is still plagued with problems that undermine its long-term economic viability. And the EBRD's 2012 report paints much the same picture.[62] The overall profitability of this sector is still in question, which is reflected in the IFC's finding that the share of SMEs making investments in fixed assets has declined steeply, from 40 percent in 2002 to only 15 percent in 2007.[63]

Running small businesses in Tajikistan remains very challenging. Quite possibly because of this, the share of SMEs decreased by 1 percent between 2005 and 2007 (relative to individual entrepreneurs and private farmers), and their share of private-sector income dropped by 16 percent, which speaks to the general lack of profitability of what should be a mainstay force in private ownership.[64] The number of SMEs in Tajikistan is also growing quite slowly, with only 334 more SMEs reported in 2007 than in 2005. The average SME reported a profit of 14,707 somoni ($3,000) in 2007 versus 16,700 in 2005, despite a roughly 10 percent increase in the value of turnover in this sector. One of the reasons for this may well be that SMEs report paying 12 percent of their sales as "gifts" to various officials (versus 5 percent for individual entrepreneurs and 3 percent for *dekhan* farmers).[65]

During this same period (2005–2007), the average income of individual entrepreneurs increased by nearly a third, to 6,492 somoni (about $1,400), but during this same period their average turnover tripled,[66] again pointing to the increasingly challenging business environment they confront. Some of this increase is also a reflection of the increased penetration by individually owned businesses, as the profitability of enterprises in Dushanbe remained virtually constant (22 percent in 2005, and 23 percent in 2007).

The SMEs identify access to electricity, tax rates, and access to finance as the major obstacles that they face, with over half the farmers identifying finance as their key problem (with taxation and transportation in second and third place, respectively. As figure 4.3 shows, for SMEs in 2009, access to electricity was their first grievance (25 percent), with

FIGURE 4.3

SURVEY RESPONDENTS IDENTIFYING THE SINGLE BIGGEST OBSTACLE THEY FACE (Percentage of Respondents Identifying Each Obstacle)

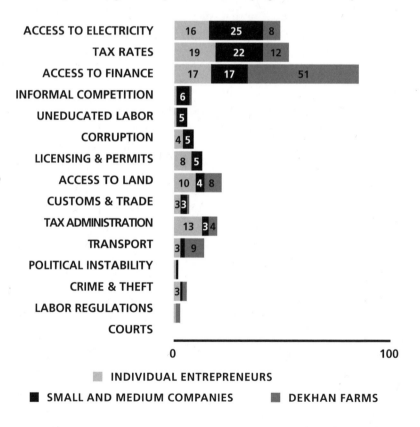

Source: International Finance Corporation, "Business Environment in Tajikistan as Seen by Small and Medium Enterprises," December 2009, www.ifc.org/ifcext/tajikistansme.nsf/ Content/Survey.

taxation slightly behind (22 percent). For individual entrepreneurs, the situation was just reversed, with 17 percent citing taxation and 16 percent access to electricity as their primary concerns.

The IFC report details both positive and negative developments. Its authors cite several improvements in the business environment in Tajikistan since 2002, relating to a reduction in the frequency of inspections, that a shorter time is now necessary to register a business, and that the average license is now valid for a longer period. The average SME still spends an average of 26.7 percent of its profits in direct costs for the four most common administrative procedures; and despite some improvements in the legal environment, companies paid more for registering their businesses in 2007 than in 2005.[67]

The cost of registration, however, has been steadily increasing, running about $300 on average for SMEs, $40 for individual entrepreneurs, and approximately $220 for *dekhan* farmers in 2007. Farmers also have a different registration procedure, which in 2007 averaged 45 days, down from 78 days in 2005.[68] There are also substantial regional variations in the cost of registration; for example, entrepreneurs in Sughd spent twice the amount, on average, as their counterparts in Dushanbe, while fully half those surveyed in Kulyab (Khatlon region) said that they had to make "unofficial payments" to get registered, compared with 10 percent in other parts of the country. And although the law does not specify their participation, those opening businesses must receive permission from the local *hukumat* (government). It can also be costly for new business owners to arrange to get their registration, because in Sughd and GBAO they must travel to the regional center, regardless of where in the region their business will be operating.[69]

Many businesses are also required to get licenses in order to operate. The average SME spent approximately 1,281 somoni ($300) to receive an average of 1.4 licenses (or 944 somoni or $198 per license), spending approximately a month on the licensing process. The licensing process is regulated by the law "On Licensing Certain Types of Activities," which was adopted in March 2004 and further modified in 2006. The 2004 law dropped the number of business categories requiring licenses from 1,000 to 115, and in 2006 this dropped to 65. This still is quite high for the region; for example, the IFC report notes that there are 22 separate licenses in the transportation sector in Tajikistan, while there are only two in Kazakhstan (one for hazardous cargo and the other for passenger transport). There are also many "unusual" activities that require licensing in Tajikistan, such as certification to provide electronic signatures, for technical protection of confidential materials, for the repair and maintenance of cargo-lifting devices, and for working in tourism, geodesy, and map-making—to name just a few. In addition, there are 23 different license granting agencies in Tajikistan.

In addition to licenses—which, as has already been noted, are covered by legislation—many businesses are also required to secure permits to operate, and these are covered by dozens of separate laws and regulations with no overarching legislation covering their issuance. The IFC reports that some $4 million was spent on permits in Tajikistan in 2007, and though the number of SMEs that had to obtain permits dropped to 37 percent in 2007 from 58 percent in 2005, the average number of permits per SME increased to 3.3 from 1.5. SMEs spent an average of 1,588 somoni (about $350) on permits in 2007—four times what they had spent in 2005—and the average cost of a permit increased more than tenfold (from 87 to 934 somoni or $18 to $196). *Dekhan* farmers reported paying five times more for permits (in 2007 they averaged 225 somoni or $47 each), and they also said that the time that they spent getting permits had increased from four to thirteen days. There were only moderate increases in the cost of permits that individual entrepreneurs had to get (these averaged 122 somoni or $26), and both they and SMEs experienced moderate decreases in the amount of time spent getting permits, from three to two days and from eight to seven days, respectively. The number of permits that Tajik businessmen must get is high for the region, and many of the permits are unnecessary, such as the need to get a permit to send advertisements going through the mail, which requires authorization from the Ministry of Transportation and Communication (from the Law on Advertisement, article 15), or the requirement that the design of financial accounting forms be approved by the Ministry of Finance (Law on Accounting, article 14).[70]

The lack of legal clarity regarding what permits are necessary and how to get them leaves Tajik businessmen at the whim of local authorities and increases the risk that "informal gifts" will have to be offered. Overall, SMEs engaging in tourism were most likely to need permits (88 percent of those interviewed from this sector said that they had received a permit in 2007), as did 85 percent of those working in the pharmaceutical industry and 73 percent of those engaged in medical services. Somewhat surprisingly, only 51 percent of those engaged in the construction industry said that they had gotten permits in 2007. There were also some differences based on the type of ownership; for example, 80 percent of individual entrepreneurs in the communications business said that they had needed to get permits, the most in any category.

Most permits are issued by local authorities; over 75 percent of individual entrepreneurs needing permits had to get one from them, but nearly 60 percent of those needing permits got one from the Sanitary and Epidemiological Service, and almost 50 percent from the fire authorities. For SMEs, among those who received at least one permit, close to 70 percent had to get a permit from fire officials, and just about the same number from local authorities, almost the same number from energy surveillance, and roughly 60 percent from the Sanitary and Epidemiological Service. *Dekhan* farmers needing permits most commonly (about 80 percent) got them from the local authorities, with the water authority being in second place, at about 45 percent.[71]

There is also a large amount of variation among regions regarding the frequency with which those owning SMEs reported having gotten permits, along with the reported costs of the permits. For many kinds of businesses, it is impossible to operate without the necessary permits, but the variance among regions of the country may well reflect the preference of those living far from regional centers to offer informal payments to cover missing permits as much as it does the overly bureaucratized nature of selected regional authorities.[72]

The IFC "Doing Business" indicators change from year to year, and the most thorough data are found in surveys done in 2007, and in the 2009 report. Analysts working for the IFC have admitted (when speaking off the record) that countries lobby hard for positive ratings, which might explain why the *Doing Business 2012* report no longer includes discussions of many of the categories described in the prior paragraphs.

The business registration process is the same for foreign citizens as it is for Tajik nationals. The introduction of the May 2009 law "On State Registration of Legal Entities and Individual Enterprises" led to a drop in the period necessary to register a firm, but the relative cost of registration nonetheless increased; in 2009, it took 49 days and 13 procedures costing 27.6 percent of per capita income, compared with 27 days, 8 procedures, and 36.9 percent of per capita income in 2011.[73]

Recent World Bank Enterprise Surveys, however, have found that the use of informal payments to circumvent or facilitate the permit process is decreasing, which strongly suggests that the permit process is becoming easier for SMEs to navigate. For the sector as a whole, the number of respondents reporting that they used "unofficial solutions" to obtain at least one permit dropped from 44 to 10 percent between 2002 and 2007. The greatest decline was for individual entrepreneurs, from 35 to 11 percent, and there was a significant drop in the use of "unofficial solutions" for *dekhan* farmers, from 54 to 18 percent from 2002 to 2005 (the question was not asked in 2007). But there was only the slightest change in this practice as reported by owners of SMEs (down to 38 percent from 45 percent), which suggests that a great deal of money or other gifts are still changing hands to run businesses of any size in Tajikistan.[74]

The situation with regard to construction project permits is particularly complicated, and any entrepreneur seeking to open a new business that requires construction could find himself or herself waiting a few years to see the project through from conception to the opening of the business. The World Bank and IFC's *Doing Business 2011* ranked Tajikistan 178th among 183 countries in the category "Dealing with Construction Permits." Building a warehouse requires 30 procedures (such as undergoing mandatory inspections, obtaining licenses and permits, and connecting to utilities), taking an average of 228 days at a cost of 996.1 percent of per capita income. In contrast, the averages for Eastern Europe and Central Asia, and for the countries that belong to the Organization for Economic Cooperation and Development (OECD), are, respectively, 22.2 and 15.8 procedures, 250.1 and 166.3 days, and 645.5 percent and 62.1 percent of income per capita. The World Bank report outlines the steps necessary to open a warehouse, which are summarized in figure 4.4.[75]

FIGURE 4.4

DEALING WITH CONSTRUCTION PERMITS: PROCEDURES REQUIRED TO BUILD A WAREHOUSE

STEP 1: Request and obtain:
- ❏ Location permit ---------------- **30 DAYS**

STEP 2: Request:
- ❏ Electricity connection------------- **1 DAY**
- ❏ Water services---------------------- **1 DAY**

STEP 3: Request and obtain approval from various authorities, including:
- ❏ Fire safety clearance—state anti-fire agency, Ministry of Domestic Affairs ------------------------------ **7 DAYS**
- ❏ Environmental approval*— Environmental Protection Agency (Environmental Protection Ministry) ------------------------ **45 DAYS**
- ❏ Sanitary Hygenic Service approval* —State Sanitary Hygenic Service, Ministry of Health ------------- **10 DAYS**
- ❏ Clearance from State Electric Agency*—Barki Tojik -------- **10 DAYS**
- ❏ Project clearance*—Water and Sewage Agency of Dushanbe ---------- **10 DAYS**
- ❏ Architecture planning assignment* ---------------------- **3 DAYS**
- ❏ Project clearance*—State Automobile Inspection Department of Domestic Affairs of Dushanbe city ----- **30 DAYS**
- ❏ Approval of project design drawings —State Department Expertise of Construction Projects ----- **30 DAYS**
- ❏ Final project clearance— Construction and Architecture Department --------------------- **20 DAYS**

STEP 4: Receive inspections from:
- ❏ Sanitary Hygenic Service
- ❏ Fire Safety Agency
- ❏ Electricity Inspection*
- ❏ Connect to electricity* --------- **13 DAYS**
- ❏ Water Services*
- ❏ Connect to water* ------------- **29 DAYS**
- ❏ Ministry of Environmental Protection
- ❏ State Architecture Inspection— Dushanbe city
- ❏ Prosecutor's Office
- ❏ Labor Authority
- ❏ Ministry of Transportation and Communications / State Body on Automobile Activity Management

STEP 5: Obtain final approvals:
- ❏ Request decision from Review Commission----------------------- **15 DAYS**
- ❏ Request decision from State Aceptance Commission------------------------- **1 DAY**
- ❏ Inspection by State Acceptance Commission------------------------- **1 DAY**
- ❏ Obtain decision ------------------ **30 DAYS**
- ❏ Inspection from Department of Project Adjustment and Technical Inspection of Dushanbe Telephone Service ------------------------------ **5 DAYS**
- ❏ Connect to telephone line
- ❏ Approval from Bureau of Technical Inventory (BTI) on acceptance of building and issuance of technical passport -------------------------- **15 DAYS**

STEP 6: Registration
- ❏ Of the right to the building------- **1 DAY**

*This step can take place simultaneously with another step.

Source: International Finance Corporation and World Bank, "Doing Business 2012. Economy Profile: Tajikistan," 2012, 31–37, www.doingbusiness.org/~/media/fpdkm/doing%20business/documents/profiles/country/TJK.pdf.

One area where there has been sharp improvement is in licensing procedures. The 2006 Inspections Law, which provides for a formal checklist system, created noticeable improvements in the inspections regime and saved the SME sector in Tajikistan $9.3 million in 2007 alone. Most strikingly, the average *dekhan* farm was inspected only twice in 2007, as opposed to ten times in 2002, and roughly half of all *dekhan* farmers interviewed by the IFC were not subject to any inspections at all. Although 87 percent of individual entrepreneurs reported that they were subject to inspections, the average entrepreneur spent only 91 somoni ($19) on inspections and the average *dekhan* farmer spent 12 somoni ($3). Although the burden of inspections on one level was reduced for SMEs—they underwent five inspections, on average, in 2007, in contrast to ten in 2005—the average amount spent on inspections doubled, rising to 2,500 somoni, about $530, although one-third of the SMEs underwent no inspections during 2007.

Nonetheless the cost of inspections is still a significant burden, especially for SMEs, which in 2007 were still paying 17 percent of their profits to inspection bodies (IFC figures for inspection costs reflect formal and informal payments taken together). In addition, many of the features of the new law are not being observed. There are supposed to be no inspections during the first three years of operation of an SME, yet over half the SMEs registered in 2006 reported that they were subject to inspections in 2007, according to the IFC survey. The new law also provides for advance notification of inspection, which was only infrequently observed. In July 2008, President Rahmon tried to improve the situation regarding inspections by calling for a two-year moratorium on inspections (to run through July 2010); but unfortunately, in not-atypical fashion, instructions were not issued to the affected agencies and ministries for nearly a year, until March 2009; even then, according to the IFC, there was no clear statement of exceptions, leaving the door opened to continued inspections.[76]

Financing remains a significant problem for most businesses. As already noted, Tajikistan has the most underdeveloped financial system of any country in the region, although microfinancing has expanded rapidly in the last decade in Tajikistan, growing more than 200 percent in 2006 and then another 120 percent in 2007; by 2008, the IFC reports that, according to the NBT's statistics from February 2009, there were some 150,000 borrowers in the country that had received 446 million somoni (roughly $95 million) in credits. At the same time, the IFC survey shows that some 70 percent of the SMEs have never had a relationship with a financial institution; only 86 percent of SMEs have a bank account (one of the smallest shares in the region), and only 22 percent of all *dekhan* farmers (down from 47 percent in 2002) and 7 percent of all individual entrepreneurs (20 percent of whom at some point have had a loan or a line of credit) had a bank account.[77]

Much of the microfinancing that is offered in Tajikistan is in dollar-denominated loans, and this is particularly true for individual businesses and SMEs. Many businesses had trouble operating in the aftermath of the financial crisis, first in 2009 and then again throughout 2010—in particular, when the Tajik somoni lost a quarter of its value during the first six months of that year.[78] There are no restrictions in Tajik law that disadvantage female borrowers; according to the IFC survey, female entrepreneurs (36 percent of the surveyed population) report better access to financing than do their male colleagues, as they are a target audience for many microloan programs. The Association of Microfinance Organizations of Tajikistan reports that over 62 percent of clients of microfinance organizations are women. At the same time, females engaged in the SME sector cite difficulty in access to financing as more of an obstacle to doing business than did their male colleagues (21 percent of females responded positively to this question versus 16 percent of male individual entrepreneurs, 25 percent and 24 percent respectively for SMEs, and 44 percent and 31 for *dekhan* farmers where the economic sector has been severely hampered by the shortage of capital).[79]

This conclusion is also borne out by the research in Jafar Olimov's 2007 study for the UNDP, in which many of his respondents in the SME sector reported that they were reluctant to seek financing because of high interest rates and collateral requirements (and insufficient collateral remains the major reason why loan requests are declined), preferring instead to arrange private financing from friends and relatives or to accumulate the capital themselves.

This study was based on two surveys done by the independent research center SHARQ in 2006. The first was a survey of 500 enterprise managers or accountants (of legally registered firms) drawn from the regions of Tajikistan in proportions that corresponded to each region's contribution to the nation's GDP. They reflected specialties that also corresponded to the distribution of enterprises by type nationwide, and was representative of nationwide trends of number of employees per enterprise as well. The second was a survey of 1,000 households covering the entire republic in a sample designed to reflect the geographical, urban/rural, and gender distribution of the country.

Jafar Olimov's study was very interesting as it sought to explore the strata of small businesses that generally fly below the IFC's radar, including unregistered businesses and other economic activities. Based on an econometric methodology devised by the author, the study estimated the size of the shadow (unregistered) portion of the economy (excluding organized crime) in 2005 to be 60.93 percent of GDP, with the size of the shadow economy as measured by avoiding the payment of taxes calculated to equal 32.98 percent of GDP. The study found that that portion of the shadow economy that was production for domestic consumption was 14.74 percent of GDP, and that home-produced goods accounted for 23.3 percent of the average household's income and were the sole form of income for 16.2 percent of the households surveyed. It also found that transactions in barter or other in-kind exchanges accounted for 13.1 percent of GDP. Although the study found that only 9.5 percent of all exchanges, overall, involved barter, 29.4 percent of all surveyed households received in-kind income.[80] This, of course, means that just over 70 percent of the country received cash salaries, creating traditional and modern sectors in the country, which are only partially overlapping.

The study found that, overall, firms spent as much on informal exchanges (bribes and gifts) as they would have if they had adhered to the letter of the law. But the preference for informal solutions was the product of complicated and burdensome legal procedures whose difficulty was magnified by the incompetent bureaucrats who supervised them.

The findings of this study reaffirmed the conclusions of the IFC survey on doing business in Tajikistan, as Olimov's respondents also noted that they often avoided paying taxes because of the difficulties inherent in the tax payment process, as well as the size of the taxes collected. The study found that, on average, firms underpaid taxes by 33 percent, and understated salaries by 34.92 percent. The share of tax inflows to GDP in 2005 was only 16.56 percent, the lowest in the region.[81]

The IFC survey also found that people, especially those in the SME sector, were confused about the tax system and how it operated at any given time. The Tajik government introduced a new tax code in 2005, which was amended nine times before the end of 2009, and the IFC considers that the end result, despite some positive changes, has become more complicated for those working in this sector of the economy. Many Tajik taxpayers remain angry over the changes that have been introduced, and there were brief demonstrations in Dushanbe in 2008 over this.[82]

The World Bank Group's *Doing Business 2011* and *Doing Business 2012* reports ranked Tajikistan 168 out of 183 countries on the ease of paying taxes, a measure that includes the administrative burdens involved (such as the number of payments made per year) and the amount of taxes businesses pay as a share of profits.[83] Tajikistan's tax system is still not sufficiently graduated, and includes various exemptions and privileges. Efforts to simplify the tax structure have not been especially successful, and the IFC considers the "simplified" tax regime for SMEs only marginally easier than the standard version, requiring 20 filings with tax authorities annually instead of 25.

Taxes in Tajikistan must be paid in person. So, in 2007, the average *dekhan* farmer and the average individual entrepreneur spent 4.6 working days annually simply filing or paying taxes, making five and seven trips to the tax authorities annually, respectively, while the average SME had to devote nine days to this process, and, on average, made ten trips to the tax authorities. In addition, businesses are subject to tax inspections, which for individual entrepreneurs declined from seven visits annually to five visits, between 2005 and 2007. The World Bank's *Doing Business 2012* report estimates that medium-sized companies in Tajikistan spend an average of 224 hours a year on preparing, filing, and paying taxes, including the corporate income tax, the value-added tax (VAT), and social security payments. This is lower than the regional average for Eastern Europe and Central Asia (302 hours annually) but higher than the OECD average (186 hours annually).[84]

But the members of the SME community are also partly to blame for the difficulties that they encounter, as the IFC survey reports that one-third of all respondents admitted that "firms like theirs" conceal part of their revenue from tax authorities, with some 25 percent of SME income concealed, on average. In addition, more than a third of all individual entrepreneurs interviewed said that they kept no financial or tax records in 2007,[85] a situation that obviously fosters the widespread "informal payment" system, and is certainly enough to drive any honest tax inspector (if in fact one exists in Tajikistan) crazy. The IFC survey reported that 69 percent of those who did not keep tax records did not do so because "I don't want to," with the others (22 percent) citing that they did not know how to keep financial records, and 10 percent simply claiming that it was "too complicated."[86]

For some kinds of businesses the structure of taxation is relatively simple, at least as written in the legislation. All but 1 percent of the *dekhan* farmers surveyed in the IFC study in 2009 paid the unified agricultural tax (which averaged 1,154 somoni or $242 per farmer). This should have exempted them from the land tax, the personal income tax, the road user's tax, the VAT, and the business tax, but 50 percent said that they paid land tax (for an average 1,022 somoni or $214, effectively doubling their tax burden) and 42 percent reported having to pay personal income tax (for an average of 434 somoni or $91). In addition, *dekhan* farmers are also required to pay social tax for any employees, which 83 percent reported paying (for an average of 1,055 somoni or $221). In total, this represents a significant tax burden for a cash-short sector of the economy.[87]

The problem is that those engaged in agroprocessing are subject to all these forms of taxation, and the law is very imprecise about what constitutes agricultural processing, giving tax inspectors a lot of leeway to charge farmers these additional taxes if they engage in any food processing (even for personal or family consumption). In addition to stimulating "informal payments" to tax inspectors, this provision has also created strong disincentives for the development of small-scale agribusiness in Tajikistan, denying the country's small landholders a potentially lucrative source of additional income.

The tax structure of Tajikistan was modified in April 2008, and what was intended to be a simplification of the tax system was seen by some as making it more burdensome. In June 2008, there was a demonstration of some 200 individual entrepreneurs and SME owners outside the

Tax Committee offices in Dushanbe. The protests largely focused on the new patent tax, which was levied on nonincorporated enterprises, and which, the protesters complained, effectively doubled their minimum tax burden.[88]

Individual entrepreneurs may pay a consolidated patent tax (if their turnover is less than 200,000 somoni or $41,915 per year), and 81 percent of those polled by the IFC in the 2009 survey chose this option (paying an average of 777 somoni or $163), but they are also subject to payment of retail sales tax (a local tax with an upward limit of 3 percent (which 50 percent reported paying, for an average of 752 somoni or $158), a social tax of 25 percent of each employee's salary (which 46 percent paid, for an average of 349 somoni or $73), and personal income tax (35 percent paid, for an average of 382 somoni or $80). In addition, they were subject to the road user's tax, real property tax, and the VAT (not to mention import and export fees for that small percentage of businesses that conducted foreign trade). Although only 9 percent of individual entrepreneurs reported paying the 18 percent VAT that applied in 2007, their average payment was 441 somoni or $92, making it a relatively large part of their total tax burden.

The tax regime for SMEs was even more complex. Those using the standard tax regime were subject to either a 25 percent profit tax (for banks, service industries, and those in the transportation and communication sector), while all other businesses had to pay 15 percent of their profits, with a minimum profit tax of 1 percent required of all businesses, as well as the road user's tax. Those filing under the simplified regime paid a turnover tax of 4 percent of annual turnover under 200,000 somoni ($41,915), and 5 percent for annual turnover over 200,000 somoni ($41,915) in lieu of the profit and road user's taxes. Both groups were subject to the VAT, social tax, and retail sales tax. The simplified tax regime offers just about as complicated a bookkeeping challenge as does the standard regime; turnover must be recorded, and given that no standard bookkeeping format is mandated, there are many grounds for arguments between business owners and tax collectors (and, presumably, much opportunity to offer unofficial payments to solve these problems). Just under half (49 percent) of those in the IFC's 2009 survey chose the simplified regime, which appears to reduce the tax burden of those operating in sectors with high profit margins, such as tourism and service industries, where over half the businessmen interviewed reported that they chose this tax option.[89]

Some of the taxes are particularly burdensome for low-margin businesses. This is a particular problem with the 2 percent road user's tax, which applies to all businesses with an annual turnover of 600,000 somoni (about $130,000), and is charged against presumed or reported expenditures.

The confusion over the tax structure is cited in Jafar Olimov's study as a major reason why Tajik entrepreneurs prefer to make informal payments rather than formal ones. This study details the systematic and deliberate underpayment of taxes in 2005, using a nationwide sample of both enterprises and households.[90]

Jafar Olimov's study was done before the tax system and licensing systems were modified. However, as with the IFC study, both profit (60.0 percent) and land tax (58.6 percent) were cited as the most considerable barrier for complete legalization of firms.[91] At the same time, the study shows that tax evasion is commonplace in Tajikistan. Only 7.6 percent of the firms interviewed admitted paying the VAT in full; 4.6 percent, the profit tax; and 11.2 percent, all the income tax that they owed. Likewise, only 17.4 percent paid the social tax in full, despite the fact that only 25.4 percent cited it as a barrier to legalization. In addition, 45.6 percent of the firms interviewed said that they avoided land tax payments; 39 percent, customs payments; and 44.8 percent, excise tax payments—with the latter two being the most underreported in terms of the total amount denied to the state treasury overall.[92]

In general, tax evasion was greatest (accounting for 45 percent of GDP) in Sughd Oblast (compared with the nationwide average of 32.98 percent) and lowest in Dushanbe, the Region of Republican Subordination (26.72), and Khatlon (24.95 percent), with the former accounting for far more of the country's trade turnover than the latter.[93] Agriculture reported the largest share of shadow economic activity (38.8 percent of GDP), with utilities and construction following slightly behind (37.66 and 33.56 percent, respectively). All three sectors are generally low-margin industries.[94]

The study generally found that while the informal economy may be playing a key role in providing employment and food security for a substantial portion of the Tajik population, it was also serving as a deterrent to the expansion of the size of businesses, through a spiral effect that was created by the underdeveloped nature of the Tajik financial sector. High interest rates and collateral requirements lead many entrepreneurs to seek private funding for business expansion, but the limited nature of private funding keeps businesses small. Moreover, few businesses are willing to engage in the degree of financial disclosure necessary to get funding, as this goes against the business culture that has come to dominate in the country's single owner–manager and small business environment.

The study also found that 46 percent of all those surveyed were employed in the informal sector (which is also consistent with other findings), either in agriculture on small family plots or in urban areas working for family members or self-employed. But these individuals did not pay taxes or social security and so were barred from collecting pensions.

Olimov reported that 86.4 percent of the enterprises studies received some or all of their start-up capital from private or family savings, and only 15.2 percent from a private or state bank, and this was for legally registered enterprises.[95] When entrepreneurs were asked why they did not seek a loan from a bank, 40.6 percent cited high interest, 22.0 percent mentioned the excessive costs of obtaining a loan, and another 17.4 percent noted the high risk of default (for what are typically dollar-denominated loans made in somoni). Interestingly enough, only 8 percent said that they lacked sufficient collateral and another 3 percent noted that they had an inadequate credit history.[96] The majority of those entrepreneurs surveyed made no use of the banking system in paying suppliers or expenses; only 40.86 percent said that they used the banking system, and 68.8 percent said that they paid suppliers through cash prepayment. The weakness of Tajikistan's banking sector seems to have pushed people into the informal banking sector, which makes them susceptible to all forms of pressure, both legal and illegal, along with higher interest rates.

Although the survey questionnaire allowed for multiple answers, virtually everyone—99.8 percent of those sampled—cited the inability to procure financial resources (from banks, 62.2 percent; from other financial sources, 37.6 percent) as a moderate or serious impediment to expansion and routine business operations; 57.2 percent cited shortages of electricity;[97] 75.0 percent cited inadequate transportation and/or communication; 53.4 percent cited restrictive customs and trade regulations; 73.2 percent cited licensing and authorization permits; and 86.4 percent cited taxes.[98]

Nonetheless, much like the IFC study, Jafar Olimov's survey also found that householders cited licensing and authorization requirements as a major reason why they chose to run their businesses in an "informal" way. Regardless, a very large proportion of those surveyed reported that they were in full compliance with the permits necessary to operate their business—a total of 64.5 percent of all entrepreneurs surveyed, although they did not say whether they received them legally or not.[99]

The IFC study also found that tax evasion seems to have increased since 2005. In the 2007 survey, 36 percent answered that "others like them" concealed revenue from the tax authorities, marginally down from the 32 percent in 2002, but a significant increase from the 24 percent figure recorded in the 2005 survey. Tax evasion appears least common among *dekhan* farmers than among any other part of the SME community (which again is probably a reflection of the cash-poor nature of this sector).

Tajikistan's import and export regimes are so complicated that they are a substantial disincentive for those in the SME sector to engage in foreign trade as part of their business. Only 2 percent of all *dekhan* farms, 14 percent of individual entrepreneurs, and 24 percent of SMEs in the IFC survey reported that they imported goods for their businesses, and only 3 percent of the SMEs engaged in the export trade, with only the largest SMEs (with an average annual turnover of 2.8 million somoni, about $600,000) likely to do so.

As already noted, Tajikistan is ranked 177 in the category of trading across borders.[100] Nonetheless, its volume of foreign trade has been increasing, accounting for $4.7 billion in 2007, or 126 percent of GDP.[101]

Tajikistan compares unfavorably with other countries in Europe and Central Asia, and also the OECD countries, on a number of measures, including the number of documents, the time, and the cost required for importing and exporting. For example, Tajikistan requires eleven documents to export goods and nine to import. In contrast, the numbers are seven documents for export and eight for import in Eastern Europe and Central Asia, on average, and four documents to export and five to import in the OECD countries. The difference in the times required for trade is even greater. It takes 82 days for export and 83 for import in Tajikistan; 27 and 29 days in Eastern Europe and Central Asia; and 4 and 5 in the OECD countries. These barriers are reflected in the differences in cost—$3,850 per container for export and $4,450 per container to import, versus, respectively, $1,774 and $1,990 in Eastern Europe and Central Asia, and $1,032 and $1,085 in the OECD countries.[102] In addition to the transportation challenges faced to get goods into and out of Tajikistan, the government's requirements regarding technical regulation, standardization, and compulsory certification introduce very high additional transaction costs. And Tajik businessmen are often forced to get certification for domestic trade. The existing customs code dates from 2004, and will require substantial improvement before Tajikistan has any real chance of accession to the World Trade Organization. There are still long waiting times for importing goods into Tajikistan, and corruption still seems to be rampant in the process; 69 percent of SMEs responding to the IFC survey that engage in importing activities reported that they were expected to offer gifts or other forms of unofficial payment to get their goods certified for import.[103]

As the section on foreign assistance details, substantial international attention is being directed toward improving Tajikistan's foreign trade regimes. Parliament passed a Law on Technical Regulation in April 2009, which took effect on January 1, 2010, that takes small steps toward improving technical regulation. Unfortunately, the new legislation does not provide a road map for modernizing the standardization and certification processes, nor does it address the multiplicity of actors in this sector, which is dominated by Tajikstandart, the primary but not exclusive regulating agency.

Similarly, like the IFC study, Jafar Olimov found that smaller firms spent a proportionately greater share of their turnover on gaining licenses and permits than did larger ones; 47 percent of firms with 50 to 100 employees spent 8 percent of their total sales on procuring them, while only 22.3 percent of the larger firms with between 100 and 499 employees spent the same percentage of their monthly sales. Moreover, firms reported that it was nearly three times faster to obtain licenses using informal means than by relying on official procedures.[104]

Similarly, the belief that personal access to senior governing officials was critical to business success made many business owners feel that they were too small to be able to use the legal and illegal levers to which larger and more influential businessmen had access. Most average-sized firms reported that they had no connections to major political figures, and so no real impact on drafting legislation affecting the business environment. Furthermore, most firms felt no confidence in the judicial system. Only one firm interviewed reported that that it had used the courts to successfully resolve a legal dispute, and 86.4 percent said that they had not sought relief from the judicial system at all.[105] So while many complained about the pernicious effect of corruption, they also felt disadvantaged if they lacked the access to use corruption to their benefit.

The priorities set in the EBRD's 2012 country program for Tajikistan for the next three years make clear all the lingering problems in this sector:

> The main policy dialogue in this area will be focused on improving the business environment. Special attention will be given to simplifying the tax system, eliminating areas of double taxation and improving tax administration so as to reduce the costs of tax compliance and giving firms incentives to become more transparent. Enhanced transparency in turn could enable the Bank to increase its lending to Tajik corporates and allow those firms to access more long-term credit at lower costs.[106]

MIGRATION

Given the weakness of SMEs described above, and the problems of agriculture depicted in the next chapter, it should not be surprising that upward of half the male population between the ages of 20 and 45 have sought employment outside the country, and in 2010 remittances made up 35 percent of Tajikistan's GDP—the largest share of GDP made up by remittances of any country in the world, according to World Bank statistics.[107]

Tajikistan faces a growing surplus labor problem of sufficient scale to make it a risk to social and political stability. During the past decade, the country's main means of addressing its labor surplus has been to encourage the working-age male population to take seasonal and even permanent employment outside of the country. Most go to Russia, and there is also a small migrant Tajik population working in Kazakhstan. The Federal Migration Service of Russia reports that 708,295 Tajiks were employed in the Russian Federation, including 77,770 women. This figure is just for citizens of Tajikistan; it does not include Tajiks who have managed to acquire Russian citizenship.[108]

This "brain drain" has taken many different forms—permanent resettlement in Russia of largely skilled and white-collar workers during the civil war, the further loss of a technically qualified workforce in the decade after reconciliation, and the seasonal outflow of unskilled labor to Russia and Kazakhstan during the growth spurts following the end of the 1998 financial meltdown in Russia.

Tajikistan's dependence upon remittances is greater than any country in the former Soviet Union; remittances accounted for $2,134,500,000 in 2008, up by 70 percent from the same period in the previous year.[109] The "trickle-down" effect of remittances is reflected in the structure of employment in Tajikistan's main cities, where 55 percent of the employed population works in commerce and the service sectors; in Dushanbe, 64 percent are employed in this sector.[110] These sectors of the economy have also served to absorb some of the drug income that flows through the country, but nonetheless this sector is still very small. On average, there is only one small business per 1,000 population, as compared with six in Russia and more than 30 in most countries belonging to the European Union.[111] So while remittances made an important contribution to Tajikistan's GDP, they were not sufficient to allow Tajikistan's private sector to reach the same level that it has achieved in some of the other countries in the region.

The population growth rate, combined with the declining quality of education, virtually guarantees negative repercussions for Tajikistan's economy and the competitiveness of its labor force. The structure of employment is complex in Tajikistan. The World Bank's 2007 Tajikistan Living Standards Survey (TLSS) reports that only half the total potential labor force (population age 15 to 64) is employed (table 4.1). However, Tajikistan's labor force participation rate, which dipped to 53 percent in 1997, has been rising in recent years; according to the 2009 World Bank Indicators, Tajikistan had a labor force participation rate of 67 percent, compared with 65 percent in Uzbekistan, 67 percent in Kyrgyzstan, 68 percent in Turkmenistan, and 71 percent in Kazakhstan.[112]

It is difficult to know how reliable these figures are, or what they are in fact measuring, although there can be no doubt that Tajikistan's

TABLE 4.1
TAJIKISTAN LABOR MARKET DATA, 2007

ASPECT OF LABOR MARKET	NUMBER OF PEOPLE
TOTAL POPULATION	7,016,518
TOTAL POPULATION, AGE 15–64	4,215,165
TOTAL LABOR FORCE	2,171,008
EMPLOYED	1,965,231
UNEMPLOYED	205,777
RETURN MIGRANTS*	99,349
OUT OF LABOR FORCE	2,043,653
STUDENTS	573,038
HOUSEWIVES	1,053,628
RETIRED	132,616

* Return migrants are a part of the domestic labor force if they are either employed or unemployed in Tajikistan.

Source: World Bank, *Tajikistan: Poverty Assessment*, December 3, 2009, 107.

population is seriously underemployed. They are self-reported data, and they show housewives as the principal sector of unemployed people. Although 17.5 percent of those interviewed claimed to be unpaid family employees, this figure is probably low. Many of these women are likely producing goods that are contributing to the unsalaried (or barter-based) income of the family. The same is also true of many students, and the labor force participation rate of fifteen- to twenty-four-year-olds is only 34.6.

Women are particularly disadvantaged in the labor market as a result of the evolving social conditions in the country. Though their levels of literacy are virtually identical to those of men, men are 2.4 times more likely to get specialized secondary, professional, and higher education than women, in a working environment where something as minimal as a three to five-month training program increases the likelihood of employment by 24 percent.[113] Moreover, women are also expected to bear the brunt of traditional economic pursuits—such as cooking, cleaning, and tending a household plot—all time-consuming activities (remembering that in many rural areas, even household water must be fetched, sometimes from a distant source) that can leave women of childbearing years in particular with no time for work.

These figures also likely underreport seasonal employees. According to the TLSS, the overall unemployment rate was 9.5 percent; however, this rate is defined as having not worked during the last 14 days, but having sought work during the previous 30 days, so it excludes the habitually unemployed.[114] Of the employed population, only 40 percent were "regular" employees, and 25 percent were compensated on a piecework basis.[115] These employees, along with most of the 11.4 percent who were listed as self-employed, do not participate in the social protection system (nor do those who are not employed). The portrait of employment that emerges from the TLSS is very similar to the data in Jafar Olimov's 2007 study, which found roughly a third of the population working "off-the-books" for relatives on farms or in shops and businesses in towns and cities (or 46 percent of the potentially employable population), with 3.5 percent as internal migrants within Tajikistan (mostly *mardikors*, or hired laborers, working on farms), and 10.6 percent as foreign labor migrants.[116] This does not include the portion of the Tajik population that works without a salary of any kind (estimated by Olimov to be 27.4 percent of the working-age population in 2006).[117]

Relations between employers and employees in Tajikistan are set forth by the Labor Code of May 1997, which was amended in 2006. It gives employees the right to join labor unions, which have failed to develop into any sort of strong public presence in the country. The country's largest labor union is the Federation of Trade Unions of Tajikistan, a refurbished version of the Soviet-era labor organization, which boasts some 1.3 million members (over 60 percent of the workforce), many of them state employees or workers at state-run enterprises who were effectively forced to join. Strikes at state-run enterprises are uncommon, although in 2009 some 400 workers went on strike for several days to protest unpaid wages, but returned to work as soon as they received their back pay. Three of the organizers of the strike, however, were reported to have been subsequently fired.[118]

In general, workers' protection is very limited, with severance pay set at a quarter of the monthly wage multiplied by the number of years of service. The code allows for the use of fixed-term contracts, and only one or two months' notice is required for contract termination. Tajiks can collect a maximum of three months of unemployment benefits, which, given that the country's minimum wage was under $1 a day (60 somoni, then $17, in July 2008), there is little incentive for people to register for benefits.[119] The law provides for a standard work week of 40 hours for those older than eighteen, with time and a half for the first two hours of overtime, and double-time salary after that. The Ministry of Finance is responsible for enforcing the financial aspects of the labor law, and the Agency of State Financial Control, which is attached to the presidential administration, is responsible for all other aspects of employment. Legal supervision of employment practices in Tajikistan is very lax.

Unemployment and poor economic conditions make offers of employment abroad more attractive, and people more vulnerable to exploitation. People with low levels of education and a lack of awareness of their rights are also more likely to become victims of human trafficking. Failure to regulate labor migration is also a concern, as workers who migrate illegally are especially vulnerable to exploitation and abuse.

THE ECONOMIC AND SOCIAL IMPACT OF MIGRATION

Since achieving independence, Tajikistan has been characterized by both internal and external migration, neither of which was typical during the Soviet period. In the Soviet Union, internal migration, within Tajikistan or anywhere in the USSR for that matter, was constrained by the *propiska*, or registration, system. All citizens were formally registered at their place of residence, and this registration was recorded in their internal passports (that is, passports for use exclusively within the USSR, which were a required form of identification), as was their place of employment.[120] Changing jobs required signing out from one employer and being registered by the new one, and changing residences required the point of relocation to be "open" to new settlers. In fact, in the 1970s and 1980s the Soviet government sought to get Central Asians to move to underpopulated regions in Russia, especially in Eastern Siberia, to take up jobs in the expanding industrial and support sectors for the natural resource extraction economies there. This was a harder sell during the Soviet period than it is today, when poorer or underemployed Tajiks still had the Soviet social welfare net extended to them. Now, having been denied virtually all social protection from the Tajik government, Tajik workers have a much stronger incentive to go to Russia.

There has been a great deal more movement of Tajikistan's population since the collapse of the USSR. The Tajik Migration Service, which was initially created in 1992 to deal with the flow of refugees created by the conditions of the country's civil war, has never been an equal partner of its Russian counterpart, the Federal Migration Service, in part because the latter had the full power of its host institution, the Ministry of Internal Affairs, at its disposal. The Tajik Migration Service was strengthened in 2004, when it was moved to Tajikistan's Ministry of Internal Affairs, and then again in 2011, when it became a free-standing agency under the government of Tajikistan.[121]

In the first years of independence, from 1991 through 1998, most of this migration was the result of the fighting in this period, as people sought to move from the war zones (in what are now known as Khatlon Oblast and the Region of Republican Subordination). The data on the movement of the population during this period are somewhat contradictory,[122] and many of the people who fled the country during this period (both ethnic Russians and ethnic Tajiks, most of them going to Russia) never returned. This was also true of those who moved around within Tajikistan; only those whose homes or farms had escaped serious damage returned to where they had lived previously, and this was a relatively infrequent occurrence, especially because most people moved to where they had family or some other form of support network.

During this period, seasonal migration from Tajikistan began to grow as well, because the country's economy had been all but destroyed during these years. Two nationwide surveys (combined with focus group analysis) done by Saodat Olimova of the independent research center SHARQ in February–March 2002 and January–February 2003 found that sizable numbers of Tajiks began to work abroad in 1998 and 1999.[123] Olimova's study found that even during this period, a time of crisis for the Russian economy, the overwhelming majority (86 percent) of Tajikistan's seasonal migrants went to the Russian Federation. In the early post-Soviet years, Tajiks traveled to anyplace where there was any possibility of employment; 3 percent of those surveyed said they went to Kyrgyzstan and 5 percent to Uzbekistan, both countries where they had relatively easy access to seasonal agricultural employment (Uzbekistan's borders not being firmly closed until 1999), and only 1 percent went to Kazakhstan (which in the late 1990s had yet to experience rapid economic growth).[124] Unlike later periods, when the overwhelming majority of migrant workers were in the twenty- to forty-year-old age cohort, in the late 1990s, according to Olimova's data, 40.7 percent of the hired labor came from the forty- to forty-nine-year-old group, whom Olimova termed "fathers." This age cohort, in her opinion, had better skill sets and more experience and so was more easily placed in what was a tough labor environment in Russia; while construction workers were more likely to be young (35 percent were from the eighteen- to twenty-nine-year-old cohort). In these years, shuttle traders,[125] who are a form of temporary migrants—at least according to the definitions of the International Organization for Migration—also played a considerable role in the Tajik economy, and formed the one sector in which women were a sizable minority (39 percent).[126]

There is no consensus on how to measure the total number of migrants who have left Tajikistan for Russia,[127] as many who work in Russia had some personal and direct ties to Russia before independence; others have Russian passports and in many cases are even "registered" in Russia rather than listed as Russian citizens living abroad. The International Crisis Group estimates that approximately 1.5 million Tajiks left the country to work in Russia and Kazakhstan from 2004 to 2008,[128] when the economic boom in both countries led to an acute shortage of workers, especially in the rapidly expanding construction sector. Other sources claim that this figure is around 2 million.[129]

The World Bank has criticized the methodology used in most studies that have attempted to estimate the size of the Tajik migrant population, maintaining that the surveys that have been conducted (with the exception of its household surveys) are too small to be fully representative. The TLSS for 2007 reported that some 350,000 people (or 5 percent of the population) were, or continued to be, abroad for at least one month between January and October 2007. Given that all these people are presumed to be employed (or they would not be temporary residents in Russia), these 350,000, 95 percent of whom are men, represent 20 percent of the current working population.[130] Based on the households surveyed, the World Bank concludes that 74 percent of currently absent household members working in Russia send home monetary remittances, with 18 percent sending home no money or goods at all.[131] In addition, the data from the TLSS suggest that approximately 100,000 laborers returned to Tajikistan during this same period. The labor migrants are relatively young, typically around thirty, and come disproportionately from rural and smaller families. According to the 2007 TLSS, over two-thirds of them had a high school education as their highest educational attainment. Fewer than 60 percent of the labor migrants had work permits in the host country. Russia remains the primary destination for workers from Tajikistan; according to the TLSS data, 96 percent go there. Some 1.5 percent go to Kazakhstan, 0.3 percent to other parts of the CIS, and 3.5 percent to non-CIS destinations (including Israel, the United States, Turkey, Iran, and the Gulf states). Of those who migrate to Russia, 51.4

percent go to Moscow, 6.6 percent to Saint Petersburg, 5.4 percent to Ekaterinburg, and 3.5 percent to Tyumen. For all migrants, the most important factor in the choice of destination was personal contacts (for 35 percent of all men and 41 percent of all women) or prior migration experiences (23 and 26 percent, respectively).[132]

Migration remains an activity dominated by those from poorer households. The 2007 TLSS reveals that 60 percent of the households in the lowest quintile by (preremittance) consumption had a member of their household work abroad at some point. By contrast, only 19.4 percent of the households in the second-lowest quintile had a family member living abroad at some point, and only 13 percent of the households in the other quintiles had migrant laborers in their families. Moreover, the economic contribution made by migrant workers was very significant for the lowest quintile of households, financing 56 percent of their consumption in rural households and 79 percent of consumption in urban households. In-kind payments and barter are more difficult in urban settings, because city dwellers are limited in the kinds of home-produced goods they can make, causing their households to rely more heavily on remittances to finance their consumption.

A study of migrants from Khatlon Oblast, supported by the International Organization for Migration and published in 2005, reported that 132,000, or more than a third, of the country's migrant cohort of 371,000 came from Khatlon. Migrants from Khatlon were primarily young males—two-thirds were between twenty and thirty-nine years of age, and 92 percent were men—and each remitted $1,296, on average, that year. The remittances helped support 35 percent of the population of the oblast (including both family and nonfamily members of those working abroad).[133]

There is relatively little legal protection awarded to the migrant laborers. In rather characteristic fashion, the government of Tajikistan has introduced a number of laws and regulations, sufficient in number for there to have been a compilation of the legislation published in 2006,[134] but which are basically declarative rather than remedial in intent.[135] The government sets forth a set of circumstances that it wished would describe reality, while offering few specific directions as to how these might be achieved, or providing consequences for those who fail to strive for them. This group of laws and decrees shows the Tajik government's strong support for labor migration as a means of eradicating poverty, as well as an impetus for the accumulation of capital for start-up businesses or the purchase of homes and farms.

The 2001 "External Labor Migration Concept" was intended to serve as a spur for improving the job-seeking environment encountered by Tajiks wanting to work abroad;[136] it called for the establishment of "private employment agencies" (which would be registered entities) that would facilitate the finding of jobs in Russia and Kazakhstan and presumably help to regulate the employment conditions that Tajik migrants encounter abroad. The main intent of the government, however, was to encourage labor migration as a way to alleviate social conditions in Tajikistan, by encouraging the potentially most politically active part of the population—those in the eighteen- to forty-five-year-old cohort—to find jobs outside the country, thus alleviating pressure on Tajikistan's own fragile and inadequate domestic labor market, bringing in foreign currency to the country through remittances that would stimulate job creation within Tajikistan, and simultaneously providing added stability to the Tajik somoni.[137]

The loss of professionals to Russia is of substantial consequence for Tajikistan's own economic development. In particular, Tajikistan is losing teachers of science, mathematics, and foreign languages, and doctors with specialized training, all of whom were already in short supply, because of the departure of Russians and other Europeans, along with Tajiks during the civil war years. This loss is further compounded by the fact that current standards of training in all these areas are substantially lower than they were during the years of Soviet rule. Some migration specialists worry that there is a further loss of expertise through migration, because, it is argued, over 90 percent of all migrant laborers change their specialties while working abroad, so that teachers, doctors, engineers, or agronomists who spend several years doing semiskilled or unskilled labor in Russia, albeit relatively well paid, are unable to work in their own fields because their knowledge has become obsolete by the time they are willing to return to permanent residence in Tajikistan.[138]

Table 4.2 makes clear the financial advantage accrued to migrants working abroad, with average monthly salaries, on average, six times higher than they are in Tajikistan and in a few sectors provide more than tenfold increases, such as housekeeping, which is largely done by women, and which earns Tajiks (overwhelmingly women) an average of $332.50 per month, with only drivers and professional employees earning more.

Obviously, not all the money earned by labor migrants returns to Tajikistan, but what does return to the country grew from two-thirds the size of national budgetary expenditures in 2002 to more than 200 percent of those expenditures in 2006. Over time, more and more of these remittances have entered Tajikistan via formal banking or wire transfers (Western Union being the most prominent, but several Russian firms operate in Tajikistan as well), once the state tax on monetary transfers (set at 30 percent) was eliminated in October 2006. Nonetheless, Khodjamakhmad Umarov, one of the authors of a 2006 study for the

TABLE 4.2
MIGRATION CHARACTERISTICS OF RETURN
MIGRANTS BY OCCUPATION ABROAD

	LEGAL WORK (%)	AVERAGE NET MONTHLY INCOME IN US$	MONTHS SPENT AWAY
CONSTRUCTION	52.2	323.9	9.1
UNSKILLED	45.2	270.6	8.5
PROFESSIONAL	86.5	405.7	10.3
DRIVER	76.6	385.8	14.6
SALE	61.4	308.5	11.0
AGRICULTURE	84.9	187.1	14.1

Source: World Bank, "Tajikistan: Poverty Assessment, December 3, 2009," 52, http://web. worldbank.org/external/default/main?pagePK=51187349&piPK=51189435&theSitePK=2587 44&menuPK=64187510&searchMenuPK=287276&theSitePK=258744&entityID=000333038 _20100118015430&searchMenuPK=287276&theSitePK=258744.

International Organization for Migration, claims that more than twice as much remittance money is still transferred informally than moves through formal channels (table 4.3).[139] Some of this money still moves through underground remittance systems (*perekidki*, from the term for throwing), which are trust-bound networks that, according to Olimova's 2003 study, were most highly developed in Dushanbe, Istaravshan, and Khujand. In these networks, which are much like those that have developed in Africa and throughout South Asia, one gives money to a trusted associate in Russia or where the migrant is working, and eventually receives money

TABLE 4.3
ESTIMATES OF REMITTANCES FROM EXTERNAL LABOR MIGRANTS, 2002–2005

	2002		2003		2004		2005	
	GOV'T (1)	UMAROV (2)	GOV'T	UMAROV	GOV'T	UMAROV	GOV'T	UMAROV
TOTAL REMITTANCES (US$ MIL)	131	195	422	635	722	1083	1000	1500
% NBE (3)	67.6	100.6	158.5	238.4	198.6	297.9	227.6	341.4
BANK TRANSFERS (US$ MIL) (4)	78.4	—	253.7	—	433.5	—	600	—
% Total	59.8	—	60.1	—	60	—	60	—
% NBE	40.4	—	95.3	—	119.2	—	136.5	—
UNOFFICIAL TRANSFERS (US$ MIL) (5)	52.6	116.6	168.3	381.3	288.5	649.5	400	900
% Total	40.2	59.8	39.9	60	40	60	40	60
% NBE	27.2	60.2	63.2	143.2	79.4	178.7	91.1	204.8

Note: NBEs = national budget expenditures.

Source: International Organization for Migration, *Perspectivy migratsii: Vostochnaya Evropa i Central'naya Aziya. Planirovaniye i upravleniye trudovoy migratsiey* (Vienna: International Organization for Migration, 2006), www.iom.lt/documents/Migr.Perspectives-Russ2006.pdf. 1) Official Estimates (National Bank of Tajikistan); 2) Estimates by K. Umarov; 3) Percent of National budget expenditures; 4) Official estimate of remittances transferred through banks (National Bank of Tajikistan); (5) Unofficial transfers = total remittances — bank transfers.

back from another acquaintance in his home village. Although banks and wire transfers have become increasingly common over time, several years ago the *perekidka* system was still being used to move large sums of money for which the sender was seeking to avoid tax liabilities.

Saodat Olimova argues that in recent years upward of 50 percent of the cash earned from remittances has moved into Tajikistan through the banking system. This is a result of increased efforts by the banks to attract this money (especially Russia-based bank transfer networks like Contact, Anelik, and Migom) because of the revenues earned from it. Some have gone so far as loaning migrant workers money for their plane fare in return for their agreeing to transfer their earnings back to Tajikistan exclusively through the bank loaning them the money. The risk that money smuggled back into the country will be confiscated en route has also increased.[140]

CHAPTER 5

REFORMING AGRICULTURE

T he challenge of agricultural reform remains one of the major tasks
facing the Tajik government. Following the National Bank of
Tajikistan scandal in 2007, significant steps were taken to reform
this sector, giving individual farmers more freedom to choose what crops
to grow and how to sell them. But when this occurred, it was already too
late for fast reversals in this sector. Much of the choice lands were already
in the hands of rich absentee landlords; small farmers had little capital
or collateral to use to receive the loans on offer; a substantial proportion
of the male workforce had left the fields for more lucrative employment
outside the country; and the Tajik agricultural sector had become seriously undermechanized and lacked the trained personnel to rectify this.
In addition, those working in the agricultural sector have faced competition for their land from real estate developers who have slowly chipped
away at the amount of land available near cities and other population
centers. Added to the equation is the legacy of more than a half century of
despoliation of the land through Soviet agricultural practices, damage that
has been compounded by the impact of climate change.

AN OVERVIEW OF THE COUNTRY'S AGRICULTURE

The challenge of developing Tajikistan's agricultural sector is exacerbated
by the environmental degradation that the country has suffered in recent
decades, much of which is already irreversible. The despoliation of the

country's land is the direct product of Soviet agricultural practices and poor land management more generally, along with the overuse of forests for fuel in recent years.

Overall, these conditions are worst in Tajikistan's mountain regions. This has led to soil erosion of rain-fed farmlands; degradation of pastureland and range land; degradation of forests and bushes, with the subsequent loss of biodiversity; irrigation-related land degradation (especially secondary salinity, waterlogging, and irrigation-related soil erosion); and further land degradation through natural disasters, particularly as the result of mudslides. In most respects, the land situation in Tajikistan is similar to that of other Central Asian countries, although generally more acute (table 5.1).[1]

Tajikistan has 14.3 million hectares of land, of which only about 0.74 million hectares are irrigated, of which 16 percent suffers from various degrees of salinity or related problems of waterlogging and soil erosion, contributing to the low yields of both food and cotton crops. In Tajikistan, 84 percent of the irrigated lands are of very low to low salinity, 2 percent slight salinity, 10 percent moderate salinity, and 3 percent high salinity. It is estimated that even low salinity reduces cotton yields by 20 to 30 percent, moderate salinity by 40 to 60 percent, and high salinity by more than 80 percent. There are even lower thresholds whereby salinity reduces yields for food crops (like pulses, maize, vegetables, and rice), upon which the food security of most Tajiks is increasingly based.[2]

In addition to issues with salinity, Tajikistan suffers from a substantial amount of soil erosion. The 2008 World Bank country environmental analysis for Tajikistan offered an elaborate analysis of soil erosion. In total, it found that 58.8 percent of all lands suffered from water erosion and 23.5 percent from wind erosion, with a total of 82.3 percent of all land in the country having suffered from some form of erosion (with 23.9 percent of the land considered to be seriously eroded). The report then broke down these findings by meadowlands, mountain lands, and alpine lands (and further by subcategory in each). It concluded that 49.7 percent of all meadowlands had suffered water erosion and 37.9 percent wind erosion, with 78.6 percent suffering some degree of erosion from either source (with 11.6 percent strongly eroded). Some 77.7 percent of all mountain lands suffered from water erosion, and 8.1 percent from

TABLE 5.1
EROSION IN CENTRAL ASIA, 1990-1999 AND 2000-2005

COUNTRY	TYPE OF EROSION	1990-1999		2000-2005	
		MILLION HECTARES	% OF TOTAL AREA	MILLION HECTARES	% OF TOTAL AREA
KAZAKHSTAN	Water	1.44	0.52	1.05	0.38
	Wind	1.47	0.53	0.6	0.22
KYRGYZSTAN	Wind erosion, water erosion, and pasturable erosion	5.4	27	5.7	28.5
UZBEKISTAN	Water	N.A.	N.A.	0.135	3.14
	Wind	N.A.	N.A.	0.365	8.48
TAJIKISTAN	Water	8.3	58	10.3	72
	Wind	3.7	26	3.7	26

Note: N.A. = not available.

State Committee on Land Management of the Republic of Tajikistan, "Natsional'nyy doklad Respubliki Tadzhikistan po osushchestvleniyu KBOOON" (National Report of the Republic of Tajikistan on the Implementation of the UNCCD), Dushanbe, 2006, 43, http://archive.unccd.int/cop/reports/asia/national/2006/tajikistan-rus.pdf.

Ministry of Environmental Protection of the Republic of Kazakhstan, "The Third National Report of the Republic of Kazakhstan on Implementation of the United Nations Convention to Combat Desertification," Astana, 2006, appendix 1, http://archive.unccd.int/cop/reports/asia/national/2006/kazakhstan-eng.pdf.

Center of the Hydrometeorological Service of the Cabinet of Ministers of the Republic of Uzbekistan, "Natsional'nyy doklad Respubliki Uzbekistan po osushchestvleniyu Konventsii Organizatsii ob"yedinennykh natsiy po bor'be s opustynivaniyem i zasukhoy (KBO)" (National Report of the Republic of Uzbekistan on the Implementation of the United Nations Convention to Combat Desertification (UNCCD)), Tashkent, 2006, 45, http://archive.unccd.int/cop/reports/asia/national/2006/uzbekistan-rus.pdf.

"Third National Report on United Nations Convention to Combat Desertification Implementation," Bishkek, 2006, 49, http://archive.unccd.int/cop/reports/asia/national/2006/kyrgyzstan-eng.pdf.

wind erosion, with 85.8 percent suffering some erosion (and 36.7 percent were severely eroded). For alpine lands, 85.0 percent suffered from water erosion, 11.3 percent from wind erosion, and 96.3 percent suffered from some form of erosion (with 52.6 percent severely eroded).[3]

There has also been an overuse of forests for fuel. The direct costs of deforestation include losses from nontimber products, fuel wood, tourism, and recreation, with the indirect costs including a loss of watershed protection. The World Bank reports an annual deforestation rate of between 6,000 and 7,000 hectares annually, with an estimated value of 15 million somoni ($3,144,000), or 0.2 percent of GDP in 2006.[4]

In 2008, the World Bank estimated that the total environmental damage to Tajikistan was about 690 million somoni, or $200.1 million, per year, or approximately 9.5 percent of GDP, with land degradation (including soil erosion) alone accounting for 3.8 percent of GDP (roughly 4.4 percent of GDP, when deforestation and rangeland degradation were included).[5] But though the environmental conditions necessary for agriculture are worsening, it remains a mainstay of the household economies of the majority of the population in Tajikistan, becoming the major economic pursuit of an increasing portion of the employed population while contributing an ever smaller percentage to the country's GDP.[6] In 1995, 59.0 percent of Tajikistan's working population was employed in the agricultural sector and contributed 36.7 percent to GDP. More than a decade later, in 2008, 66.7 percent of the employed population worked in the sector but contributed only 19.9 percent of GDP; see table 5.2. Agriculture accounted for between 20 and 30 percent of its exports and for roughly a third of the country's tax revenues.[7] This decline in the share of agriculture in the country's GDP (see table 5.3) speaks to the declining quality of the agricultural sector, largely because of the continuing crisis for those growing cotton, as more people are working in this sector, and the prices of agricultural products are increasing—especially as the balance between cotton and food crop production continues to shift to the latter.

Tajikistan can ill afford to waste its agricultural lands, given that it has only about 960,000 hectares of arable land, which is between 7 and 8 percent of the country's total surface area, and thus has only 0.12 to 0.15 hectares of irrigable land per person, and 0.2 hectares of arable land per

TABLE 5.2
POPULATION EMPLOYED IN AGRICULTURE, 1995–2008

ASPECT	1995	2000	2005	2008
TOTAL EMPLOYMENT (THOUSANDS)	1,853	1,745	2,112	2,168
AGRICULTURE (THOUSANDS)	1,095	1,135	1,424	1,447
AGRICULTURE SHARE IN TOTAL EMPLOYED (%)	59.1	65.0	67.4	66.7

Source: Agency on Statistics under President of the Republic of Tajikistan, "Employment by Sector of Economy," http://stat.tj/ru/analytical-tables/real-sector.

TABLE 5.3
AGRICULTURE AS A PERCENTAGE SHARE OF NOMINAL GROSS DOMESTIC PRODUCT, 1995–2008

MEASURE	1995	2000	2005	2008
NOMINAL GDP (MILLION SOMONI)	69.8	1,786.7	7,206.6	17,706.9
NET PRODUCT, AGRICULTURE (MILLION SOMONI)	25.6	448.9	1,527.2	3,517.9
AGRICULTURE SHARE IN NOMINAL GDP (%)	36.7	25.1	21.2	19.9

Source: Agency on Statistics under President of the Republic of Tajikistan, "Nominal GDP by Branches of Origin," http://stat.tj/en/analytical-tables/real-sector.

person in rural areas.[8] Two-thirds of the arable land is cultivated through irrigation, and almost a third of all agricultural lands (28.6 percent) are still devoted to cotton cultivation (see table 5.4).[9] This land covers about 50 percent of the food needs of the average population. In addition, 3.6 million hectares of land are used as pasturelands.

The presence of several large rivers that feed into both the Syr Darya and Amu Darya river systems, which serve the Caspian Sea Basin region and are replenished in part by vast glaciers, gives Tajikistan abundant

TABLE 5.4

ALLOCATION OF AGRICULTURAL LAND BY TYPES OF FARMS AND SELECTED CROPS, 2007

TYPE OF FARM OR CROP	TOTAL (HECTARES)	% OF TOTAL LAND	(% OF TOTAL)		
			STATE-OWNED FARMS	PRIVATE (DEKHAN) FARMS	HOUSEHOLD PLOTS
TOTAL	891,126	100.0	24.4	54.1	21.6
IRRIGATED LAND	595,980	66.9	26.9	55.4	17.7
COTTON	254,862	28.6	20.5	46.3	33.1
WINTER WHEAT	175,722	19.7	15.6	47.5	37.0
SPRING WHEAT	132,239	14.8	20.5	52.5	27.0
POTATOES	39,110	4.4	11.3	26.1	62.6
VEGETABLES	130,315	14.6	32.7	57.1	10.3

Source: Agency on Statistics under President of the Republic of Tajikistan, "Allocation of Agricultural Land," http://stat.tj/en/analytical-tables/real-sector.

sources of irrigation. The country has four well-defined valleys, where irrigated agriculture was steadily expanded under Soviet rule, with the amount of irrigated agriculture nearly doubling between 1960 and 1990. These are the Ferghana Valley, along the Syr Darya in Tajikistan's northern Sughd region to the Uzbek border; the Khatlon lowlands in the southwest, from Kulyab to the western border with Uzbekistan; the Hissar Valley, between Dushanbe and Tursunzade and then north to Khalton; and the narrow Zerafshan Valley, going east to west between the Ferghana and Hissar valleys. Each of these valleys has a slightly different balance between the production of cotton, cereals, livestock, and horticulture, as seen in figure 5.1. Tobacco is also grown in the Zerafshan Valley, where there is more abundant rainfall and the temperatures are

FIGURE 5.1
AREAS OF COTTON AND CEREAL CROP PRODUCTION

SOURCE: United Nations; CIA; Tajikistan Ministry of Agriculture

Source: Zvi Lerman and David Sedik, "The Economic Effects of Land Reform in Tajikistan," European Commission, EC/FAO Food Security Program, October 2008, 12, www.fao.org/fileadmin/user_upload/Europe/documents/Publications/Policy_Stdies/Tajikistan_en.pdf.

too low for cotton cultivation, while in the Gorno-Badakhshan region (which is overwhelmingly mountainous and only has very limited agriculture along the riverbeds), livestock breeding predominates, especially with flocks of sheep and goats. Khatlon produces the largest share of the country's gross agricultural output, as seen in table 5.5. Agriculture in Tajikistan has adjusted to geographic limitations—with flax, tobacco, and cereals grown on mountain slopes (in the Kulyab region, above 500 meters); fruit grown on the mountains at above 3,000 meters; and livestock grazed just about everywhere where crops are not planted.

The fighting after independence virtually destroyed the Soviet-era agricultural base, and though there has been a steady increase in the production of food crops, the cotton sector has never recovered. Figure 5.2 and table 5.4 above show this quite clearly. Throughout the war years, the structure of agriculture remained largely unchanged. And even after Rahmon's government began introducing agricultural reforms in the mid-1990s, local authorities continued to effectively force the cultivation of cotton, even on privately held and farmed lands, although farmers were also able to secure (through local land distribution and presidential land awards[10]) land for food crop cultivation.

TABLE 5.5
PERCENTAGE SHARE OF AGRICULTURE BY PROVINCE, 2006

PROVINCE	GAO	AGRICULTURAL LAND	SOWN AREA (ALL CROPS)	CATTLE	SHEEP
SUGHD	25	24	32	27	31
KHATLON	45	33	49	40	39
RRS	26	26	18	26	21
GBAO	4	17	1	7	8
TAJIKISTAN TOTAL	100	100	100	100	100

Note: GAO = Gross Agricultural Output.

Source: Zvi Lerman and David Sedik, "The Economic Effects of Land Reform in Tajikistan," European Commission, EC/FAO Food Security Program, October 2008, 13, www.fao.org/fileadmin/user_upload/Europe/documents/Publications/Policy_Stdies/Tajikistan_en.pdf.

FIGURE 5.2

AGRICULTURAL PRODUCTION BY CROP, 1985–2008 (Thousands of Tons)

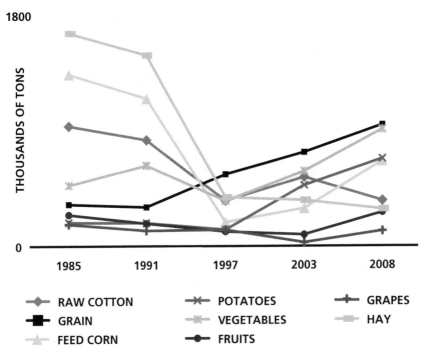

Source: Agency on Statistics under President of the Republic of Tajikistan, "Production and Yields of Major Agricultural Crops, 1985-2010," http://stat.tj/en/analytical-tables/real-sector.

THE AGRICULTURAL CRISIS OF 2007–2008: A TIME OF RECKONING

The Tajik government has repeatedly sought to raise agricultural productivity in the country. For example, the 2007–2009 Poverty Reduction Strategy called for raising productivity by 8.2 percent and agricultural output by 16.5 percent. Instead, the government found itself confronting a mounting debt crisis among farmers and alternating years of drought and cold in what were some of the worst winters in decades.

The winter of 2007–2008 posed a particular challenge for Tajikistan, given that an unusually dry summer and autumn were followed by the coldest weather in recent memory, which pointed up the failures of Tajikistan's agricultural reform programs in poignant and tragic fashion. Humans and animals perished from cold and hunger. The most affected oblasts were Khatlon, Sughd, and the Region of Republican Subordination.

A window on how the Tajik government handled this crisis is given in a March 2008 report done by the Food and Agricultural Organization of the United Nations (FAO). This emergency food assessment report, based on onsite observations in thirteen of the country's agricultural districts from February 8 through 15, 2008, evaluated the losses to agriculture caused by the harsh winter and sought to explain why the practice of agriculture had created such a degree of fragility for so many engaged in the sector. The FAO estimated the losses in wheat and potato production alone at approximately $75 million (not including the losses through seed freezing or through the consumption of potatoes that had been stored for spring planting); the losses in vegetable and fruit production were even higher, put at roughly $77 million. Much of these losses were of standing crops damaged in the field (including 15,000 metric tons of potatoes) or from the freezing of fields before winter crops could be planted.

The livestock sector, which is almost entirely in the hands of small *dekhan* farmers, lost an additional $40 million, roughly 10 percent of all livestock, not counting poultry, for which no loss estimates were available. Given the expected decrease in available fodder in upcoming months, the FAO estimated that livestock losses would increase still further, which is why an international relief program was launched. Farmers forced to sell off their herds were sometimes pushed to accept only 20 percent of the average sale price of the previous year, given how thin and sickly so many of the animals had become because of the shortage of fodder.[11] Moreover, every dead head of cattle represented a $500 loss for the affected household, and every dead sheep or goat meant an $80 loss. And the loss of lambs and calves was particularly painful, for they also meant a loss of income in the following year. Tajiks also lost about 2.6 percent of their stock of horses, creating a further burden for farmers, many of whom had lost their sole form of transportation.[12]

The loss of the wheat crop was particularly devastating. The average Tajik consumes some 180 to 190 kilograms of wheat per year, because it is the single most important staple in a typical diet (with potatoes being next in importance), and in various parts of Tajikistan wheat can be grown during three seasons of the year. Some 80 percent of the country's wheat is grown in autumn and winter, and so the wheat harvest was especially hard-hit. The FAO estimated that between 40 and 45 percent of the autumn 2007 crop (which accounts for between 60 and 65 percent of the total amount produced) and 100 percent of the winter crop (planted in January and February, which accounts for 25 to 30 percent of the annual crop) were damaged. Spring wheat is planted from March through May, but only at higher elevations, and that was the only growing season not affected by the unusually harsh winter. But the rise of global wheat prices by nearly 50 percent in 2007 meant that purchasing wheat was beyond the reach of the urban poor in addition to rural households used to depending upon the family's harvest for food. The areas most affected by the destruction of the wheat crop were Faizabad (in the Region of Republican Subordination) and Farkhor (Khatlon), where, respectively, 78 and 53 percent of the wheat was lost. According to the FAO, nearly 40 percent of the surveyed households that claimed to have sustained losses were judged to have been left vulnerable to food insecurity.[13] Many households reacted to this by taking measures that further increased the level of economic stress, including selling off their household possessions, while others borrowed money at very high interest rates.

The report found that those farmers who were dependent upon the production of potatoes were not as devastated as those dependent on wheat. Some 10 to 15 percent of the potato crop is produced during the autumn planting (which is done in late November and early December), of which 50 to 60 percent was lost. This was also true of the spring crop, which is planted from late February to early March and accounts for 30 to 35 percent of the annual product. During these months in the worst-hit areas, like Parkhor and Pyanj in Khatlon, between 75 and 100 percent of the newly planted potatoes froze in the field. Some 35 to 40 percent of the crop, grown mostly in mountain areas, is planted from April until June. For this reason, there was a real rush to get international assistance in the form of seed into the country. This helped ensure that some local potatoes were available for sale as well as for export, but large numbers of farmers throughout the low-lying areas lost virtually all their cash-producing surpluses, if not their basic diet.

Fruit production was also severely damaged during the winter of 2007–2008, and thus farmers lost yet another source of cash income. About 50 percent of the grapes and 50 percent of the spring vegetables (which now form a more important part of the typical Tajik diet) were lost, and 20 percent of all fruit trees were severely damaged.[14] All the damaged trees were used as fuel by farmers and their neighbors, but healthy trees were also cut down for the same purpose. In this way, the harsh winter exacerbated Tajikistan's growing problem of deforestation.

Other, more specialized areas of agriculture were also severely damaged, wiping out the savings of some poorer families. One of these was beekeeping, which provides a livelihood for some 120,000 families nationwide, many with very small landholdings, as keeping bees requires no land to speak of; 25 percent of these families had their beehives decimated by the cold, in most cases losing their only source of cash.[15]

A quick response from the international community saved Tajikistan from a major food security crisis. Tajikistan's Ministry of Agriculture supplied some 100 metric tons to the Kulyab region of Khatlon Oblast, 50 metric tons to the Kurgan Tyube region of the same oblast, and 20 metric tons to the grain-producing regions of Sughd Oblast. The FAO (in collaboration with the World Bank) supplied 1,264 metric tons of wheat seed to 70,000 households in nineteen districts (116 communities), and supplied additional seed to households through advertising done by the Ministry of Agriculture on television and in newspapers. The Tajik seed came from government and Agricultural Institute farms, while the FAO brought in seed with higher germination rates. As a result of the higher-quality of seed that was used in many areas, and because the spring conditions were highly conducive to planting wheat and other grains, the spring harvest was large enough to largely compensate for the losses from the winter.

Tajikistan's cotton crop did not fare as well, as heavy rains in spring meant that in some places cotton had to be replanted two or even three times, and in other places the rain was so heavy that it was never successfully planted. The low yields of cotton in the summer of 2008, combined with debt forgiveness, made it easier for farmers to abandon the crop entirely in their fall 2008 and winter 2009 plantings.

As a result, substantially more grain was produced in Tajikistan in 2008–2009 than in the previous growing season. Overall, 26 percent more wheat, a basic food staple, was produced; Sughd Oblast more than doubled its wheat production, almost everywhere else production increased by at least 13 percent, and in the Region of Republican Subordination it increased by 26 percent. The amount of barley grown increased by 44 percent and corn by 98 percent, largely because Khatlon Oblast almost tripled its crop.[16]

The international response in 2007–2008 was rapid, and helped the Tajik population avert a humanitarian crisis. It also demonstrated that the Tajik government could distribute humanitarian assistance in a rapid, and relatively corruption-free, fashion. At the same time, there is relatively little evidence to suggest that the crisis led Tajikistan's agricultural reform strategy to try to prevent the degree of climatic vulnerability that its agriculture had demonstrated.

THE TAJIK GOVERNMENT'S REFORM EFFORTS

Even before the winter of 2007–2008, there had been warnings that agricultural reforms in Tajikistan had not been performing sufficiently to safeguard the Tajik population. International development experts had long recognized that the country's agricultural reforms were slow and uneven. To quote a 2005 report from USAID,

> The beneficiaries of farm restructuring largely have been limited to a number of well-connected individuals. Access to land for these individuals is based on a system of political and family connections. The larger part of the rural population, who previously worked on the state collective farms, now work as landless laborers for these new "private" farmers.

The report goes on to note that according to a study published by the United Nations Development Fund for Women, only 5 percent of the rural population gained access to restructured (*dekhan*) agricultural farmland (not including leased land, household plots, and presidential land grants). The situation has improved somewhat since the USAID report was written, but USAID's observation that "in many instances a peasant's quality of life is measurably worse than it was before farm restructuring began" is still apropos.[17]

Tajikistan began its efforts at land reform in 1992, when it passed the "Law on Land Reform" and the "Law on Dekhan Farms," which were designed to transform the Soviet-era *kolkhozes* (collective farms) and *sovkhozes* (state farms) into privately held or *dekhan* farms. During the civil war, little was done to achieve this goal, until a government resolution in October 1995 mandated the restructuring of large, unprofitable Soviet-era enterprises into enterprises whose land was leased either to cooperatives or to individual *dekhan* farmers, and required that *sovkhozes* that were still operating at a profit be reorganized as cooperatives so that all the farmers could directly benefit.

The breakup of the collective and state farms was done in a way that maximized collective benefit over individual rights, as individual farmers could leave the collective farms if they wanted, but then they were required to accept as their share whatever parcel of land was offered to them by the farm management. So, in reality, either a collective farm was dissolved or its members were effectively forced to remain in a form of collective agriculture. Once the farm was reorganized as a collective *dekhan* farm, an individual or family could withdraw only with the permission of the chairman, the head of the district government, and the head of the local land committee.[18]

Recognizing that earlier measures had by no means provided adequately for the country's rural population, two presidential decrees were promulgated in 1995 and 1997 to augment this farmland, offering first 50,000 hectares of land and then an additional 25,000 hectares to be made available as household plots to landless or struggling farmers. The parcels that have been allocated under these decrees are known as "presidential lands."

To protect *dekhan* interests, a June 1998 presidential decree "On Ensuring the Right to Land Use" provided for the issuance of land use certificates and land passports. Two government resolutions designed to simplify the registration process were passed in 1999, but little came of them, particularly because the new measures worked against vested local interests, which were directing the crop selection process to profit from cotton cultivation.

The April 2001 "Law on Land Use Planning" was designed to further the process of land registration and the issuing of land titles by establishing procedures for surveying, mapping, and demarcating individual plots. However, even after this law's introduction, local officials were still able to intervene in the selection of crops through their rights to set priorities for land use. After this law was revised in 2008 (in a new "Law on Land Use Planning"), the state still retained the right to set priorities for intrafarm land use, a provision that effectively limits the rights of farmers to manage their own lands.[19]

In 2002, a new "Law on Dekhan Farms" was passed to replace the 1992 legislation, and this law distinguished between three types of *dekhan* farms: individual farms, family farms, and collective farms. Individual farms are those run by a nuclear family. Family farms are organized around *avlods* (the extended family units described in chapter 2), while collective farms can be established by any groups of farmers who seek to join together. By 2006, about 45 percent of all agricultural lands were found in individual households and family *dekhan* farms, combined, with the remainder in enterprises and collective *dekhan* farms.[20] The primary preoccupation of Tajik farmers is to ensure the food security of their families, which they are best able to realize through their household plots, rather than through their activities in the commercial agricultural sector.

The FAO report on the 2007–2008 economic crisis found that virtually every aspect of the government of Tajikistan's agricultural policy had been flawed in some way, either through the design of legislation or through the way that it was being applied, both of which contributed to the severity of the food crisis that Tajikistan was experiencing. The report criticized the work of the Land Reform Committee, which had been formed to help facilitate the agricultural reforms by providing advisory services to farmers, including legal advice and training. But this committee suffered from its own limited institutional capacity, and the FAO found that it was incapable of ensuring fair access to the land and had served the rural poor particularly inadequately. In particular, fair access was being impeded by the high costs and complex procedures necessary to obtain land use certificates. In addition, the FAO noted that there had been numerous violations during the process of land distribution, because of the flawed nature of the legislation itself, which did not specify clear procedures for the allocation of land; the absence of legal assistance made available to the rural population; and local farmers' lack of understanding of their rights. In addition, the process had been flawed by the transfer of debts from the state or collective farms that had previously existed to the *dekhan* farmers, who were given the land to use for private farms.[21] But most of the *dekhans* were effectively forced to join *dekhan* associations, which function much like the collective farms they replaced, with decisions about what crops to grow being made by the heads of these associations (who replaced the collective farm chairmen) through negotiations with local state representatives. They also continue to make most decisions about from whom to buy, to whom to sell, and what price to charge.

Not only is more of the arable land farmed by individual households and family farms, but the productivity of this land is better as well, as figure 5.3 makes clear. None of the reforms to date have recognized the right of private landownership. All land is still considered the property of the state. The 1997 "Land Codex" treats land usage as a form of ownership (*vladenie*). There are restrictions on construction on agricultural land, which is limited to 3 sotoks (30 percent of a hectare) and only to buildings that are linked to the agricultural enterprise (storage and processing).

Although *dekhan* farmers have the right to "transfer" control of their land, they are only able to transfer rights of land usage, and thus there has been no effort to create any sort of land sales market. There is no standard for land evaluation, so, for now at least, the right to transfer land usage through sale is more theoretical than actual. Land usage rights can be lost for unpaid debts, but for all intents and purposes the only way in which land is transferred is from fathers to sons, or within families. Nonetheless, a black market for land sales has developed, with the land committees of local governments selling land certificates

FIGURE 5.3
AGRICULTURAL PRODUCTION AND LAND PRODUCTIVITY, 1998–2006

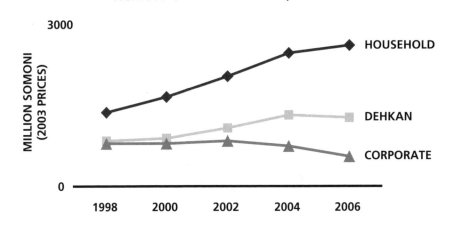

AGRICULTURAL PRODUCTION, 1998–2006

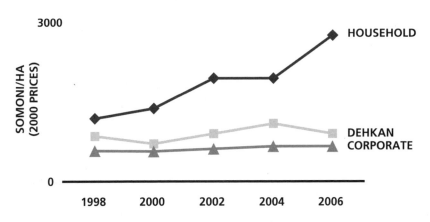

LAND PRODUCTIVITY, 1998–2006

Source: Zvi Lerman and David Sedik, "The Economic Effects of Land Reform in Tajikistan," European Commission, EC/FAO Food Security Program, October 2008, 28, 33, www.fao.org/fileadmin/user_upload/Europe/documents/Publications/Policy_Stdies/Tajikistan_en.pdf.

for usage for prices that reflect the relative quality of the land. Saodat Olimova reports that in Isfara in 2008, single hectare plots of agricultural land cost a minimum of $2,000 to $3,000, and hectare plots that lacked water and electricity cost roughly $1,000.[22]

It has been very difficult for farmers to actually obtain land use certificates that are designed to protect their land usage rights and to facilitate the transfer of land to one's heirs. These certificates (introduced in 1997) are to be issued by local land committees. They have been especially difficult to receive for collectively farmed lands, with frequent complaints of corruption, including requests for bribes when fathers try to transfer the right of land usage to their sons. The entire process of recording land use certificates, known as developing a land cadastre, has gone very poorly and has yet to provide most *dekhan* farmers and their heirs with the desired legal protection.

The World Bank has supported a Land Registration and Cadastre Project, which started in 2005 and runs through 2015, and USAID is funding projects in this area as well. From the start of this project through September 2008, only 509 land use certificates had been issued. The project was redesigned in September 2008 to reflect the technical and political challenges in getting privately held land plots registered, and the revised version was formally approved by the Bank in July 2009. The redesigned project issued an additional 1,979 certificates between late September 2008 and April 30, 2009. By 2012 the project had disbursed a total of $10.6 million, leaving half the funds still unexpended only three years before the program's projected end date.[23]

Moreover, even registered lands are not really the private property of the *dekhan* farmers, given the absence of legislation that fully provides for private landownership. Rather, the farmers have rights of land usage, and the presumed right to pass the lands under their control to their heirs. Because of this, lands that are not used for agriculture can revert to state control. As a result, farmers who default on their loans can lose their lands (and unused lands have not typically been systematically reassigned), but there is no formal process of bankruptcy, although the 2008 Law on Mortgages takes a step toward developing one. However, this law offers farmers little protection against creditors and does not provide for transparency in foreclosures of agricultural property, which can occur privately for unpaid loans or by the government for unpaid taxes. The current situation has prevented the development of a large landowning class, but it is anticipated that Tajikistan will develop its own form of agribusiness, as well as various kinds of tenant farming, after a clear law elaborating property rights is enacted.

The development of private agriculture in Tajikistan has also been negatively affected by the structure of taxation, which essentially treats privately held farmland as just another form of small business. There is an extensive discussion of the tax system in the section of chapter 4 on small business, and although the tax system was modified in 2008, most farmers still complain that even under the new system their tax obligations are excessive.[24]

Most Tajik farmers face the challenge of protecting what they have, which precludes them from taking any serious interest in expanding their holdings. A USAID report on a project on land reform and agricultural market development (that ended in 2009) highlighted many of the problems that farmers have faced in trying to exercise their land rights. It concluded that most in the countryside had little awareness of what legal protections they theoretically enjoy. Furthermore, when Tajik farmers do try to exercise their rights, they usually confront local governments that see their responsibility as protecting the interests of the central government rather than serving citizens with perceived grievances. To try and address farmers' legal concerns, the USAID project supported six legal aid centers in rural regions as well as 43 *tashabbuskors* (leaders, initiators), who were trained to be advocates for the rural population. This was just one of a number of international projects that have tried to enhance farmers' awareness of their legal rights.

To date, these projects have only touched a small percentage of the population. The USAID project in 2008–2009 provided assistance to just under 50,000 people, and also paid for the production of 29 national radio and 20 television broadcasts on farmers' rights, as well as publishing twelve issues of a Tajik-language newspaper (*Source of Wisdom*), which reached some 18,000 people. More strikingly, the legal aid centers it funded helped prepare 73 cases covering the grievances of 10,672 farmers (speaking to how many of the complaints existed in large farming communities), and in 39 cases the courts ruled in favor of the plaintiffs; the other 34 cases were either still pending or under appeal when the report was published. An additional 325 disputes were mediated without having to involve the courts. Also, as a result of legal advice received through this program, 1,561 farmers had 8 million somoni ($1,677,000) of debt canceled, and 10,341 farmers received subcertificates for their land and 153 full land use certificates.[25] The same project also worked with women (who were 87 percent of the fieldworkers in the regions where the project operated) to help them become farm managers or owners. USAID has committed more than $9 million to expand such activities between 2009 and 2012, but the Tajik government has not offered funding to extend these efforts to other parts of the country.

Since 2008, agriculture has been under the supervision of Deputy Prime Minister Murodali Alimardon, who was head of the National Bank of Tajikistan during the time when the IMF's funds were improperly used to finance private cotton intermediaries (including, the report strongly implies, Alimardon himself). But this longtime Rahmon supporter continues to maintain his innocence, claiming in an interview with *Asia-Plus* that he personally made no money from these unsecured loans and that "the scheme was aimed at supporting enhancement of the agrarian sector that experienced an acute shortage of funds" and that "problems of the whole agrarian sectors were being solved due to those funds."[26]

In early 2011, the Ministry of Agriculture (under the direction of Minister Alimardon) planned reforms for the period 2011–2020. One of the aspects of this reform is the creation of formal alliances between banks and associations of *dekhan* farmers to stimulate the development of agroprocessing businesses. The goods produced by these alliances are exempt from agricultural taxes for the period of the experiment, which is being introduced in Khatlon Oblast and in the Hissar Valley.[27]

Improving the profitability of Tajikistan's small household-directed farms is key to the revival of agriculture in the country. Zvi Lerman and David Sedik wrote a report on Tajik agriculture in 2008 for the World Bank, offering conclusions that are still relevant. They argue that whatever agricultural recovery Tajikistan has enjoyed has been fueled by the increase in productivity in household and privately held land. But overall, they argue, Tajik agriculture has achieved far less than other countries that belong to the Commonwealth of Independent States with more successful land reforms, for three reasons.

First, the recovery of agriculture is built on a relatively tiny base in terms of land resources. Unreformed enterprises and collective (*dehkan*) farms still account for over half of sown land in Tajikistan. If *dehkan* farms and agricultural enterprises had achieved the same level of productivity as household farms in 2006, agricultural production in the country would have been 114 percent higher. If they had achieved only half the productivity level as household farms, agricultural production in Tajikistan would still have been 37 percent higher. A further consequence of the incompleteness of land reform is the financial crisis in Tajik agriculture.

The second reason that land reform has not lived up to its potential in Tajikistan is that the government has retained a large role for administrative intervention in farm decisionmaking. Administrative controls on cotton-sown areas, as well as the monopolistic power yielded by "futurists" (as the Tajiks call the cotton factors or investors) who loan farmers money for seed, which is repaid through the sale of the harvest to the futurists at predetermined prices. The farmers' returns from raising cotton are lower than would be the case if alternative forms of financing were readily available. Limited returns are an important factor in the continued fall in cotton yields and production. Other crops without heavy administrative intervention, including wheat, have shown increasing yields in the past few years. Among the major crops, only cotton yields have fallen so dramatically.

The third and final reason agricultural performance has been disappointing is that the Tajik government has not addressed the longer-term needs of agriculture, rural development, and natural resource management.

Land reform is a basic first step toward the construction of a viable, sustainable agricultural sector that can be an adequate source of rural livelihoods in Tajikistan, though many further steps will be necessary. The failure to take the first and most basic step preserves an underperforming sector, keeping the rural population on the brink of food insecurity, given that agriculture is particularly susceptible to natural disasters and that the government lacks adequate tax revenues from the sector. The government's preeminent concern with emergencies and basic livelihoods is shared by the donor community in Tajikistan. Ultimately, the important role of land reform to provide a basis for agricultural growth and rural livelihoods remains unfulfilled in Tajikistan.[28]

THE COTTON SECTOR

The continued cultivation of cotton has taken a high toll on Tajik agriculture and on the country's economy more generally. Those who lived and worked on Soviet-era farms that cultivated cotton have found it difficult to break away from cotton growing. When land was privatized, there was only limited loan money available to help farmers switch the crops that they were cultivating. By contrast, cotton "futurists" quickly emerged; these were generally prominent individuals from the region with ties to the ruling elite. Many of them were militia commanders, and often provided the only semblance of both authority and source of potential funding in the immediate aftermath of the civil war. They "advanced" cotton seed free of charge to local farmers in return for purchase rights for the cotton crop at preset prices, providing many with the only prospect of holding onto their land. This system helped fund the creation of Tajikistan's new, post-independence elite.

This situation with the factors created a debt cycle. Many *dekhan* farmers started off with considerable debt, as they could only receive formal rights of land usage if they accepted a proportionate share of the debt of their disbanded collective farm—making it impossible for them to stop growing cotton, because they never fully paid off the debt for seed through the sale of their cotton crop, and thus obligating them to plant cotton three times each year, weather permitting. The only way out of this cycle was for the indebted farmer to turn over ownership of his land to the "futurist," something neither side wanted, for it cost the farmer his livelihood and forced the "futurist" to find someone to work the land to receive his profit.

In general, agriculture was in a state of decline in the last years of Soviet rule, and the situation dramatically worsened during Tajikistan's civil war. The share of cotton fiber in total exports exhibits a downward trend (figure 5.4), having declined from 25.7 percent of Tajikistan's total exports in 1993 to 7.7 percent in 2008, as shown in table 5.6.

FIGURE 5.4
COTTON FIBER EXPORTS AS A PERCENTAGE OF TOTAL EXPORTS, 1992–2010

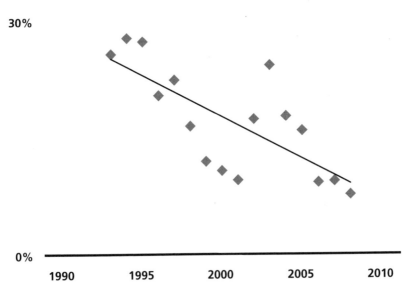

Note: Part of the variation in the percentage of total exports is the reflection of the challenges in the cotton sector—bad crops due to bad climatic conditions, and due to lower global prices for cotton—and part is a reflection of decreases in aluminum production in selected years.

Source: Agency on Statistics under President of the Republic of Tajikistan, "Exports by Product," http://stat.tj/en/analytical-tables/external-sector.

The drop in global cotton prices in 2009–2010 created substantial disincentives for continued cotton production, making it uneconomical for cotton factors to continue to finance cotton growing, as the industry had become only minimally profitable, even for those who owned factories that processed cotton. Saodat Olimova argues that this is one of the reasons why there were record harvests of grain as well as of fruits and vegetables, because now farmers were free to choose their crops and realize greater profits.[29]

This helped insulate the Tajik economy from feeling the full impact of the global rise in food prices and kept the country from having a food

TABLE 5.6

COTTON FIBER EXPORTS AS A PERCENTAGE OF TOTAL EXPORTS, 1993-2008

	TOTAL EXPORTS (MILLIONS OF DOLLARS)	COTTON FIBER EXPORTS (MILLIONS OF DOLLARS)	COTTON SHARE OF TOTAL (%)
1993	456	117	25.67
1994	559	155	27.73
1995	779	212	27.28
1996	769	157	20.38
1997	746	167	22.35
1998	597	98	16.42
1999	689	82	11.91
2000	784	84	10.71
2001	652	62	9.52
2002	739	128	17.32
2003	797	193	24.22
2004	915	162	17.70
2005	909	144	15.84
2006	1,399	129	9.22
2007	1,468	138	9.40
2008	1,409	108	7.67

Source: Agency on Statistics under President of the Republic of Tajikistan, "Exports by Product," http://stat.tj/en/analytical-tables/external-sector.

security crisis at that time. When cotton prices increased again in 2011, cotton factors sought to entice Tajik farmers to return to cotton production; many now had new incentives to do so given the legal changes that had liberalized the export process for cotton, and now allowed farmers to benefit from the sale of cotton according to international grading scales, as shown in table 5.6.

In an effort to address the sector's problems, in March 2007 President Rahmon issued Presidential Decree 111, "A Plan of Measures for Cotton Farm Debt Resolution for 2007–2009." This was followed by Presidential

Decree number 663 of 30 May 2009, which wiped out certain categories of agricultural debt but has not yet managed to jump-start agricultural reforms. The elimination of agricultural debt has given farmers more freedom to modify their crops. But although Presidential Decree 111 nominally provided for the full transferability of land user rights—which was supported by new legislation in January 2008 that, among other things, provided for amendment to the land code—this legislation still lacks clear procedures for establishing landownership and gives considerable ability to local authorities to determine land usage, although the intent of Decree 111 was allegedly to end government interference in the cotton sector.

The decree introduced the Universal Cotton Grading System in Tajikistan, making it the first country in the region to do so, and the decree also eliminated the licensing function of the Tajikistan Universal Goods Exchange. In addition, the decree also paved the way for reform of the tax structure in the cotton sector.[30]

The 2008 legislation was introduced during the period in which the National Bank of Tajikistan was being audited for its unauthorized lending of international credits in the cotton sector. At the same time, the Tajik authorities began trying to deal with the credit crisis that was crippling *dekhan* farmers, banning noncash loans by cotton financiers (who preferred to advance seed rather than cash) and providing $40 million worth of lands for small farmers. During the same year, there was an effort to liberalize cotton processing and marketing, through the introduction of policies that were designed to bring transparency in the ginning process.

While the cotton industry is a mainstay for certain elites in Tajikistan, it would be a mistake to overstate its importance for the economy as a whole. Cotton is of declining importance for the overall economy, and although it still produces the highest cash return per hectare planted, much of this money goes to those who finance the crop and never reaches the farmers themselves, which explains why most rural residents prefer instead to grow food crops.[31] As figure 5.5 demonstrates, the amounts of land sown with cotton and sown with food crops, which were relatively equal in 1991, have since diverged; food crops now account for a larger proportion of total land sown. As farmers are freed from agricultural debt

FIGURE 5.5

LAND SOWN WITH RAW COTTON VERSUS LAND SOWN WITH FOOD CROPS—HOW THE BALANCE IS CHANGING OVER TIME, 1991–2007

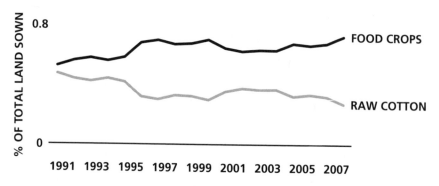

Author's calculations based on data from Agency on Statistics under President of the Republic of Tajikistan, "Production and Yields of Major Agricultural Crops," http://stat.tj/en/analytical-tables/real-sector.

created by loans from cotton factors, we are likely to see a further shift away from cotton to food crops.

Tajikistan has always been a relatively minor cotton producer on a global scale, especially when compared with Uzbekistan and Turkmenistan. And the conditions of the civil war introduced further burdens on what has been a beleaguered sector everywhere in the region, destroying irrigation canals and rendering agricultural lands useless without substantial reinvestment.

A study of the cotton economy in Sughd Oblast, done in 2006 by the Center for International Studies and Cooperation (Centre d'Étude et de Coopération Internationale, CECI), a Canadian center for international development, provides an interesting portrait of the uneven nature of land reform, the relative productivity of various kinds of *dekhan* farms, the prevalence of debt, and the general difficulty of making any sort of acceptable living by cotton farming (and farming more generally) in Sughd. The report noted how uneven the land reform process has been; for example, Matscha District has 586 collective *dekhan* farms, which produce 99 percent of the cotton harvested in the region, with only 1 percent produced by 52 independent and family farms combined. However, in Zafarad District there are only four collective farms, and 1,234 independent farms account for 78 percent of the cotton harvest.

The report describes how the idea of multiyear planning is still an alien concept for the vast majority of Tajik individual farms; only 34 percent of the farmers said that they engaged in it. It appeared to be even more alien for collective farms, just over half (56 percent) of which were run by former Soviet-era collective or state farm officials.

The CECI study also underscored the corrosive effect of rural debt, emphasizing how, regardless of the source of financing obtained, virtually all of Tajikistan's cotton farms have been burdened by debt obligations, some of them inherited with the land that they were awarded. "Futurists" provided financing for 80 percent of the collective *dekhan* farms surveyed, and 51 percent of the family farms and 31 percent of the individual farms. Most of this financing was obtained through a simple "business plan" listing how the money would be used that year. Some 35 percent of those surveyed said that they had ongoing debt (43 percent of the collective *dekhan* farms, 38 percent of the family farms, and 12 percent of the individual farms), and the average amount inherited from Soviet-era farms was roughly $16,000, which was paid out at a rate of approximately $800 per year.[32] In fact, until 2002 *dekhans* working former collective farms could not receive any credit unless the chairman of the farm authorized the granting of credit.[33]

The need for outside financing—common to virtually all farms, regardless of type—was the largest single impediment to "freedom of farming"; that is, farmers could not plant until financing was obtained, and this frequently was not available until sometime in April, causing them to delay planting and keeping them from maximizing the potential output from their land. Yet another problem, particularly for individual and family farms, was the challenge of gaining access to water, which was often unavailable when needed to support the newly planted crop, and there was often little forewarning when it would be available. Average holdings were also smaller for those with individual and family farms, although the lands on all three kinds of farms tended to be cultivated on a collective basis, either with other family members or those from adjoining plots. Again, for individual farmers this was almost inevitable, given the small size of their holdings, as those surveyed had an average of 4.5 hectares of land, four of which were irrigated and three of which were planted with cotton.[34] But although the cultivation of cotton is generally less lucrative than growing grain or other food crops, most farmers stay with it because there is a ready market that produces cash earnings, which inject funds into the household budget and also allow for the continued discharge of debt. The farmers' continued indebtedness and need for cash seem to have been at least as important as the pressure from local officials on collective farm managers and individual farmers to plant cotton, so that the government officials could meet the targets being set for them by district, regional, and national authorities. The net income from cotton, however, was very small: a maximum per household for collective farms in 2005 of about $60, and $25 for individual farmers. In that regard the CECI study, done before debt relief took effect, once again made a strong case for it. But the CECI study also showed that ready income from wheat growing, at least in Sughd, was still quite low—$40 or $50 per year—and the challenge of marketing was much harder.[35]

Saodat Olimova studied farms in the Shaaruz region, and blamed financing problems for why farmers continued to grow cotton. She found that farmers received 2.5 to 10 somoni per month (depending upon their technological qualifications), and they negotiated the preplanting purchase price of $236 per ton for first-quality cotton and $227.5 per ton for second-quality cotton. This was a firm offer, whereas independent financing subjected the farmer to 33 to 40 percent interest (in this local-ity at the time) and still needed to arrange for the supply of seed and to find a purchaser.[36]

A 2008 survey by the Asian Development Bank (ADB) saw pressure from local authorities and the difficulty of arranging independent financ-ing as the major reasons why cotton continued to dominate. This survey, done in Khatlon and Sughd oblasts, where much of Tajikistan's cotton is grown, found that, respectively, 66 and 72 percent of respondents said that the local government intervened in decisions about what crops they should grow. The study, however, showed that farmers were just as likely to grow cotton even without the intervention of the local government, which likely reflects the problem of debt as the driving force. In fact, 80 percent of the Khatlon residents who said that the *hukumat* had not intervened to influence their choice of crops grew cotton, as opposed to 76 percent who mentioned that they had experienced local government pressure, although in Sughd Oblast 65 percent of the respondents who had not experienced pressure grew cotton, as compared with 71 percent who had experienced pressure.[37]

In the 2008 ADB survey, 68 percent of the cotton farmers surveyed (all were from individual or family farms) said that they had received money from cotton factors (again, known as "futurists" in Tajikistan); and of the farmers who were dependent upon a single form of financing, 71 percent depended on futurists. This compared with, respectively, 14 and 8 percent for self-financing, and 12 and 15 percent said that they had made some or sole use of banks.[38] But the responses obtained to other questions in the survey make clear that farmers were using cotton futurists out of necessity rather than by choice. When asked about their expected sources of financing for the 2008 harvest, 37 percent of those surveyed said that they would seek funding from futurists, while 30 percent said that they would seek funding from banks, and the same percentage reported that they would finance the crop themselves.[39] This change in funding sources reflected the expectation that their debts were going to be wiped out through the promised legislation.

Similarly, the FAO report emphasized that agriculture has also been seriously handicapped by the lack of adequate credit being made available to those living in rural areas, a topic which is explored in greater length in the section on banking in chapter 4. But in early 2008, only 8 percent of those engaged in private farming had access to microfinance, while most farmers could not realistically expect to arrange financing through commercial banks, given the high interest rates and collateral requirements.[40]

The World Bank redesigned its Cotton Sector Recovery Project, initially approved in May 2007 and set to run until March 2013, to address the needs of farmers to obtain seasonal financing. This project was been designed to try to increase the freedom of choice of farmers regarding from whom to take funding, what crops to plant, and whom to have gin their cotton, if they chose to grow it—in other words to make them more capable of withstanding pressure from local officials.

At the project's beginning (in May 2007), some 70 percent of the farmers that it covered reported that they were free to choose their source of financing, 65 percent said that they were free to choose the gin for their cotton, and 52 percent said that they were free to choose how much land to allocate to different crops. There was virtually no change reported in April 2011, when $12 million of the planned $20 million had been spent. At that time, 72 percent reported that they were free to choose their source of financing, and there were no changes in the other two categories. This made it extremely unlikely that the project would meet its targets at its conclusion, which were that 90 percent of the farmers would report that they were free to choose their sources of financing, 80 percent would be free to choose their gin, and 75 percent would report that the local government does not influence the crops that they plant.[41]

FOOD CROPS AND LIVESTOCK

During the past twenty years, Tajik farmers have begun more intensive cultivation of food crops, making agriculture in Tajikistan (and in other cotton-producing countries in the region) more like what it was before the Russians introduced cotton—that is, geared toward the production of consumable crops. This pattern began in the last years of Soviet rule.

The government has repeatedly sought to raise agricultural productivity in the country. For example, the 2007–2009 Poverty Reduction Strategy called for raising productivity by 8.2 percent and agricultural output by 16.5 percent. Instead, the government found itself confronting a mounting debt crisis among farmers and alternating years of drought and cold.

The consensus of most observers who have studied Tajik agriculture is that if the Tajiks ever actually manage to fully reform their agricultural sector—providing proper financing, securing property rights, and setting up water users' associations on a nationwide basis that are capable of first repairing and then maintaining the irrigation canals—the country's farmers would be able to meet most of the food security needs of the entire nation. Food security, of course, is not the same thing as food self-sufficiency, but Tajik farmers no longer look at cotton production as a way to ensure the economic basis of their food self-sufficiency.

As it is, annual wheat production grew from 153,000 tons in 1991 to 640,000 tons in 2006, out of an annual requirement for the population of 1 million tons, while the annual production of grain in general

TABLE 5.7
LAND PRODUCTIVITY, 1991-2008

CROP	1991	1996	2001	2006	2008
RAW COTTON					
AREA (HECTARES)	299,275	228,777	253,073	257,647	226,282
THOUSANDS OF TONS	826	318	453	438	353
KILOGRAMS/HECTARE	2,760	1,390	1,790	1,700	1,560
KILOGRAMS/HECTARE, % CHANGE FROM PREVIOUS YEAR	—	−49.6	28.8	−5.0	−8.2
GRAIN					
AREA (HECTARES)	232,061	388,652	345,455	375,243	451,196
THOUSANDS OF TONS	304	548	494	773	943
KILOGRAMS/HECTARE	1,310	1,410	1,430	2,060	2,090
KILOGRAMS/HECTARE, % CHANGE FROM PREVIOUS YEAR	—	7.6	1.4	44.1	1.5
POTATOES					
AREA (HECTARES)	12,837	10,588	24,542	28,917	29,969
THOUSANDS OF TONS	181	108	308	574	680
KILOGRAMS/HECTARE	14,100	10,200	12,550	19,850	22,690
KILOGRAMS/HECTARE, % CHANGE FROM PREVIOUS YEAR	—	−27.7	23.0	58.2	14.3
VEGETABLES					
AREA (HECTARES)	32,539	24,658	33,903	40,663	45,674
THOUSANDS OF TONS	628	397	397	760	908
KILOGRAMS/HECTARE	19,300	16,100	11,710	18,690	19,880
KILOGRAMS/HECTARE, % CHANGE FROM PREVIOUS YEAR	—	−16.6	−27.3	59.6	6.4
FRUIT					
AREA (HECTARES)	55,140	64,615	57,831	67,203	74,221
THOUSANDS OF TONS	177	126	144	209	262
KILOGRAMS/HECTARE	3,210	1,950	2,490	3,110	3,530
KILOGRAMS/HECTARE, % CHANGE FROM PREVIOUS YEAR	—	−39.3	27.7	24.9	13.5

Author's calculations based on data from Agency on Statistics under President of the Republic of Tajikistan, "Production and Yields of Major Agricultural Crops," http://stat.tj/en/analytical-tables/real-sector.

grew from 304,000 tons in 1991 to 943,000 tons in 2008.[42] Potato, fruit, and vegetable production increased as well, as table 5.7 demonstrates. And most promising of all, agricultural yields for most food crops have increased significantly, even under the current less-than-ideal conditions, making it clear that with more thoroughgoing agricultural reforms, food security for the Tajik population should be a realizable goal.

Although the increased production might seem to belie this, in fact the infrastructure supporting agriculture in Tajikistan has been steadily deteriorating for the last twenty years. One of the major problems inhibiting the development of Tajik agriculture is the declining state of the country's previously highly developed irrigation system, which was maintained during Soviet times through annual state investment in its upkeep. Virtually no money was spent on its maintenance during the civil war years, and since 1996 the government has tried to fund its upkeep by levying water charges on the users of the system. But the fees collected fall far short of what is needed. Both the irrigation canals and the pumping stations that move the water from the two main rivers and their tributaries to distant farmlands have been deteriorating.

By 2002, some 16,000 hectares of irrigated land had been lost because water no longer reached then through the canal system.[43] During a 2010 drive through the southern part of Khatlon Oblast (in the territory of what used to be western Kurgan Tyube), this author saw miles of previously farmed lands that had reverted to semidesert, leaving whole communities bereft of their former livelihoods. In some places, water users' associations have been formed, and the efforts to organize them are discussed below, but in most parts of the country the ownership and management of the water irrigation networks remain unresolved.

The lack of adequate irrigation is one of the reasons for the decline in cotton production, but it has also seriously impeded the production of food crops and fodder for animals, contributing to the deterioration of livestock breeding and leading Tajiks to modify the kind of livestock that they maintain.

The practice of agriculture has reverted from its previously mechanized state to farming with hand tools and animals. For example, between 1991 and 2006, the number of tractors in use in Tajikistan fell from 37,000 to 19,000, the number of grain harvesters went from 1,600 to 900, and the number of cotton harvesters decreased from 3,000 to 600. According to

the FAO, these numbers had further fallen to 15,951 agricultural tractors and 757 combine harvesters-threshers by 2008.[44] Moreover, the Tajik
government has no real plans to help farmers reintroduce mechanization, while the farmers with their small landholdings have no realistic
possibility of borrowing money to mechanize on their own. The farmers
have also lacked the money to purchase fertilizers, which has helped limit
some of the soil and water pollution that was commonplace during the
Soviet period but has also made it more difficult to keep crops healthy
and gain high yields. Tajikistan has begun to introduce some natural
forms of pest resistance, by planting appropriate inhibiting crops.[45]

State seed farms have been degraded and pedigree livestock breeds and
poultry have been marked by disease and genetic degradation. Saodat
Olimova reports that farmers responding to the surveys she has conducted during the past decade have generally cited their leading problems
as linked to the inadequacy of technical support, from veterinarians,
livestock specialists, irrigation maintenance, and from those who repair
agricultural machinery, along with the difficulties of dealing with transportation agencies and trading companies specializing in agricultural
products. Many of these trading companies are connected with the same
cotton factors that issue credits for the purchase of seed.[46]

Agriculture has also been seriously affected by the near collapse of the
Soviet-era agricultural extension system, along with agricultural research
more generally, which has led to a deterioration of both the quality and
quantity of seed produced and has had also a detrimental impact on
livestock health. Tajikistan still has a number of higher educational institutions whose specialty is agriculture, including the Tajikistan Agrarian
University, and four agricultural colleges. The Agrarian University opened
in 1931, during the period of the collectivization of agriculture to train
specialists (eventually in 25 different specialties) to be employed in the
republic. It still graduates 600 to 700 students per year, more than half of
whom go directly to work in farming of one sort or another, with the rest
entering government service at the national or local levels. The university
also offers postgraduate courses and degrees. There has been some effort
made to maintain the quality of education at the institution by adjusting
the curriculum somewhat to meet the demands of privatized agriculture, including a department on agricultural business, which is run on a
fee-paying basis. But most of the faculty remains solely state employees

receiving low salaries, and delays in paying them basically force them to seek additional forms of employment to augment their jobs in the agrarian research sector. The FAO study also notes that most graduates of the university learn about how to use agricultural equipment that is far more sophisticated than what they will encounter when they graduate and go out to farm.[47] In addition, the four agricultural colleges (in Khujand, Tursunzade, Bokhtar, and Mastchoh) offer courses of up to three years in areas of vocational training related to agriculture.

The Tajik government, with international assistance, has also tried to develop some research capacity in the area of agriculture. The Academy of Agricultural Sciences was organized in 1994, to combine all the research institutes that work in the agricultural sector, and thus has eight institutes under its direction (institutes of crop research, horticulture, soil science, livestock breeding, veterinary medicine, mechanization, agricultural economics, and a special institute specializing in hoof-and-mouth disease). But here, too, the FAO reports that accomplishments on paper seem more significant than those in fact achieved. The total research staff for all these institutes combined was only 161, of which 20 were PhDs, and since the academy's formation, approximately half its research staff has left the country for higher-paying jobs abroad. This is not surprising, as average salaries were only $10 to $20 per month in 2008, and research budgets were largely nonexistent. There has been some limited international support for the activities of the academy through the Soil and Water Management Program supported by the International Center for Agricultural Research in the Dry Areas (ICARDA) with ADB and USAID funds, and through a wheat-and-seed production program in cooperation with the International Maize and Wheat Improvement Center (CIMMYT), which receives GTZ funding (GTZ has since been renamed GIZ, the German Society for International Cooperation).

Tajikistan's Crop Research Institute is the largest of the agricultural research institutions, and has branches in the Vakhsh Valley and Leninabad, maintaining experimental farms in these two communities and in Hissor, as well as three testing stations (in Dangara, Penjikent, and Kolkhobod, the latter two specialized establishments focusing on tobacco growing and silk, respectively). The farms and the other stations cover all of Tajikistan's other major crops, both food and cotton.[48]

Unfortunately, there is currently no effective system of relaying information about agricultural research to Tajikistan's farming population, as the agricultural advisory services that were previously made available at the regional and most local levels to state and collective farmers have now disappeared almost as completely as the formal farm structures themselves.

The Ministry of Agriculture does maintain a Department of Scientific Research and Dissemination, which has produced technical bulletins with small print runs since 1998, but which gave up publishing a more general monthly newsletter in 2000 due to a lack of funds. As of 2008, it still produced a 45-minute daily radio program on farm problems and a 30-minute weekly television broadcast.[49] The Ministry of Agriculture also continues to maintain *rayon* departments of agriculture staffed with eight to ten specialists (generally including agronomists, economists, animal husbandry specialists, a veterinarian, a farm planner, an irrigation specialist, and so on, depending upon the characteristics of the region). However, it is unclear how effective these local experts are; they are certainly underpaid, and that makes it more likely that they are suborned by local interests that seek to press farmers into planting cotton, if not in fact, then at least in the perception of those with small agricultural holdings.[50] The World Bank has also supported projects designed to enhance the work of *rayon* offices of the Ministry of Agriculture, funding work for the development of district-level project implementation offices, which are designed to strengthen the functioning of the *rayon* offices and to enhance the ministry's capacity more generally to provide much-needed agricultural extension services.

USAID has also begun to focus more on food security, following the harsh winter of 2007–2008. Since then, two large USAID projects have been introduced. The first is a $29 million project on family farming, slated to run from September 2010 through September 2014, that focuses on rural communities selected nationwide in which 30 to 50 percent of the residents lack food security (as measured by their daily caloric intakes). The second project, launched in September 2009, is on "productive agriculture, providing $9.5 million in food insecure areas of western Khatlon, Sughd, and near Dushanbe to provide technical assistance designed to achieve better agricultural yields, as well help them process and market agricultural surpluses."[51]

To date, these various efforts have not enabled Tajikistan to feed its own population, with the country set to import more grain for 2011–2012 (960,000 metric tons) to feed the population than Tajik farmers are expected to produce (679,000 metric tons). The expected harvest is anticipated to be 25 percent below that of the previous year, and 8 percent below the four-year average.[52]

Livestock breeding in Tajikistan began to get a boost in the late Soviet years, but it too went into serious decline during the war years, and has begun recovering from 1998 on (see figure 5.6). Approximately 90 percent of all livestock in Tajikistan is owned by individuals or family farms—in fact, households have been the driver of growth in cattle and small livestock breeding, while livestock breeding by large (previously state) farms has stagnated (figure 5.7) as animal husbandry becomes a mainstay of providing rural households with food, and something to trade or barter.

In a 2007 nationwide survey on the informal economy of Tajikistan (which included urban as well as rural households represented

FIGURE 5.6
LIVESTOCK HERDS, 1985–2009 (in thousands)

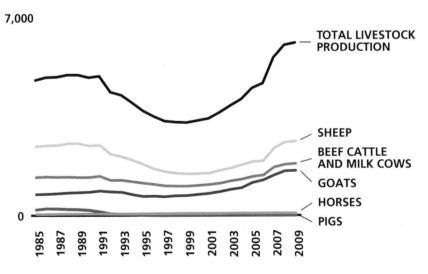

Source: Agency on Statistics under President of the Republic of Tajikistan, "Animal Husbandry," http://stat.tj/en/analytical-tables/real-sector.

FIGURE 5.7

LIVESTOCK RESOURCES IN TAJIKISTAN, 1990-2006

HEADS OF CATTLE

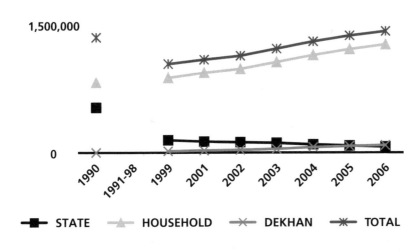

HEADS OF SMALL STOCK

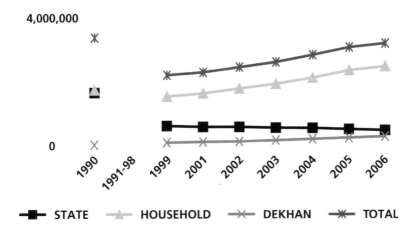

Source: FAO and Ministry of Agriculture and Nature Protection of the Republic of Tajikistan, "Report of the Tajikistan Emergency Agriculture and Livestock Rapid Assessment (February 8–15, 2008)," FAO Emergency Agriculture Rapid Assessment Report, Dushanbe, March 6, 2008, 12, http://reliefweb.int/sites/reliefweb.int/files/resources/D718D552F66477364925743C000FD263-Full_Report.pdf.

proportionately as they are in the country), researcher Jafar Olimov found that 41 percent of all households surveyed kept cattle for meat, 59 percent kept milk-producing cattle, 28.8 percent kept sheep and goats for meat, 7.4 percent kept sheep and goats for milk, and 3.3 percent kept draft animals. In addition, 50 percent of all households kept poultry for eggs, and 20 percent had poultry for meat. The total number of animals kept by households in Tajikistan has recovered to pre-1991 levels, although commercial livestock breeding is now less prevalent, as people are engaging in livestock breeding to meet their basic food needs. There are significant problems that need to be addressed in the livestock sector. The herds in Tajikistan are less healthy than previously because of the less frequent use of inoculations and the decrease in the amount of veterinary medical assistance available in most parts of the country. Tajikistan's cows have the lowest yields of milk in the entire

FIGURE 5.8
PRODUCTION OF FEED CORN, 1985–2009 (thousands of tons)

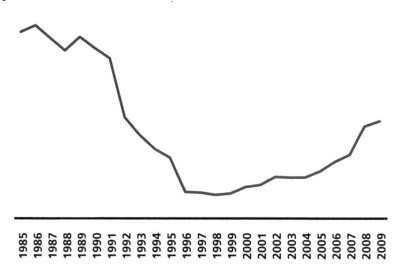

Source: Agency on Statistics under President of the Republic of Tajikistan, "Production and Yields of Major Agricultural Crops," http://stat.tj/en/analytical-tables/real-sector.

CIS, a statistic that reflects the animals' relative ill health, along with the difficulty of finding them suitable feed (as illustrated by the slow postwar recovery in feed corn production in figure 5.8). The production of fodder for animals has been impeded by the lack of adequate irrigation. The resulting shortage in animal feed has further contributed to the deterioration of livestock breeding.

The type of livestock breeding has also changed, with a shift to smaller herds with smaller animals that are privately owned and use limited grazing available close to their households and farms. There has also been a general decline in the quality and amount of pasturelands (now estimated at 3.6 million hectares), given their overuse and the shift of some pasturage to grain production.[53] This problem of erosion is especially severe in the mountainous and quasi-mountainous regions. The FAO itself has sought to play a leading role in advancing agricultural reform in Tajikistan and in seeking to enhance the chances that reforms will be executed in ways that may prove successful. It has sought to work closely with the Tajik government on projects related to animal health and production, on community-based land and water resource development, on giving policy advice on food security and on land tenure, and on questions about crops and how to market the products that are harvested. In fact, the FAO serves as something of an intermediary to design and supervise technical assistance projects in all these areas from international donors working in Tajikistan. For example, it has supported projects on enhancing livestock breeding and rehabilitating pastures in remote rural areas with funding from the European Commission.

The FAO used the Canadian International Development Agency (CIDA) funding to support the monitoring of food security in Tajikistan, but the Canadian government's focus in the region has now shifted almost exclusively to Afghanistan. CIDA also supported a project on land reform that focused on women farmers. Women are found doing field work more frequently than men now, largely because of the seasonal need for migrant labor in Russia, which attracts Tajik men, who go to Russia after doing the physically more demanding work of preparing the fields for planting in late February or early March. This continues a pattern established in the Soviet period, when men generally were in leadership positions in agriculture, or ran its mechanized aspects, while women tended the fields.

For Tajik farmers, who have long been used to working in collective structures and living within extended family units, like the *avlod*, the disruptions to both are creating additional stresses on the country's farming communities. However, to date, very few associations or institutions have been able to protect the interests of individual farmers. Most state and collective farms have had groups of *dekhan* farmers organized to allegedly represent the interests of those who formerly worked in the Soviet-era agricultural enterprises, but these have most typically become mechanisms for maintaining the interests of the Soviet-era agricultural management over those who formerly worked for them and now are, at least on paper, said to be independent farmers. This appears to be particularly true in the cotton-growing areas of Khatlon Oblast, and least as true in Gorno-Badakhshan, where the Aga Khan Foundation has funded a variety of projects that have enhanced community-level control of agriculture, with the FAO reporting that the situation in Sughd Oblast is somewhere between the two.[54] In some areas of the country, there are district *dekhan* associations that do in fact offer advice and opportunities for wholesale purchases to members who pay annual fees for the services that they receive; but this is more the exception than the rule, and the National Association of Dekhan Farmers is a formalistic organization, rather than one that represents the interests of small, private farmers.

USAID supported a Regional Agricultural Linkages (AgLinks) project through Winrock International, with a total budget of only $22.9 million over five countries, with $6.3 million being allocated for Tajikistan over a four-year period (through July 2008). The Tajik portion of the project cooperated with other USAID projects—such as the Farmer-to-Farmer Program, the Water Users' Association Support Program, and the Central Asia Microfinance Alliance—helping AgLinks leverage its resources. AgLinks also cooperated with the World Bank, GTZ (now GIZ), the Swedish International Development Cooperation Agency, and Helvetas, all of which were also engaging in agricultural projects of their own.[55] However, as the project's final report states, AgLinks experienced staffing problems (the largest linked to low salaries, which caused high turnover and the recruitment of staff members who often had less than ideal qualifications), and the efforts at collaboration across programs and agencies yielded little result.[56]

AgLinks was designed to take three agricultural "value" chains and try to revive them, and the U.S. agronomists chose apricots, Meyer (yellow) lemons, and grapes as three demonstration projects. But in each case there was a good reason why Tajik agricultural produce proved to be noncompetitive. Due to a lack of sanitation and no industrial standards for consistency in sizing, grading, and packaging, the Tajiks lost their regional market position to China, Iran, and Turkey. Tajikistan's Meyer-lemon-producing regions lack packing houses and cold storage facilities. Similarly, Tajikistan's grape-producing regions require extensive technical input for their vineyards to become productive (and although the AgLinks report did not mention it, the ownership of some of the potentially most attractive vineyards was also in question).

After failing to develop a clientele for the customized farming operation for the apricot industry that it developed, whereby an agricultural extension service would offer fee-for-service advice in marketing and project development to small and family farms, AgLinks eventually identified seven potential project partners, all medium-sized or larger enterprises, a restriction that was effectively introduced for them because of the difficulty that smaller farmers had in securing agricultural credit. In the end, AgLinks helped all three demonstration projects do the preparatory work necessary to seek further funding of up to $700,000 from the European Bank for Reconstruction and Development, but each had enough capital to develop its initial projects.[57] Two other demonstration projects—one for increasing yield of onions, another in the melon-growing sector—were also introduced, with expectations that both would eventually be expanded through other sources of agricultural assistance. Overall, the AgLinks results were quite meager for each developmental dollar spent.

However, while international assistance projects have picked at various problems within the agricultural sector to try and mediate, this piecemeal and pilot-project driven approach has yet to set a spark for an underfunded, overwhelmed, and still largely technically incompetent Tajik government to close the gap between reforms that exist mostly on paper and the challenges that Tajik farmers confront daily in their work life. Farmers in Tajikistan are much more socially isolated than they were in Soviet times, with collective farms broken up, and the Tajiks' traditional extended family structure is under real stress because of the growing trend of working-age Tajik males employed outside the republic. This means that more responsibility is being given to women, always a mainstay in agriculture, but who are now further handicapped by their inability to secure financial credit, something that was unnecessary in Soviet times, or to gain a leadership role commensurate with their economic responsibilities.

Much still remains to be done to introduce Tajik farmers to ideas of sustainable land management, which is attainable through crop diversification, especially if this is combined with better integration with water management. Irrigation and water management remain serious challenges for Tajikistan, and much more could be done through weed management along rivers and the introduction of widespread biodrainage techniques. Similarly, Tajikistan still needs to do much more to attain integrated livestock and range management, and especially to enhance the productivity of its mountainous regions, in part by developing and sustaining a diverse vegetative cover in these areas.

Finally, agriculture in Tajikistan will not be particularly profitable until far more attention is given to making farmers aware of the benefits of developing market value chains in their choice of crops, and the need to balance efforts to provide for personal food security with those to create the conditions for overall food security through farming for a profit.[58] It is hard to be optimistic, however, that even with goodwill, the Tajiks will be able to address these problems in anything like a reasonable time frame.

As a group of ADB consultants hired to help monitor projects designed to reduce farm debt noted in late 2008, it is becoming more and more difficult to find qualified Tajiks who can be hired to work on international assistance projects in senior or consultative capacities, given the increasing brain drain of qualified specialists from the country.[59] A vicious circle has been created, whereby it has become harder and harder to make a decent living in agriculture in Tajikistan (as also in many other sectors), leading more and more skilled and unskilled people alike to leave the country. And their leaving makes reforming these sectors increasingly difficult.

CHAPTER 6

TAJIKISTAN'S INDUSTRIAL SECTOR

As is true elsewhere in the economy, Tajikistan's industrial sector has had to absorb two different and equally paralyzing blows, in addition to being subject to the varying pressures of being part of an increasingly globalized economy. The first blow came from the abrupt end of the Soviet system of interrepublic economic linkages, and the second from the conditions of the civil war. As a result, in 1996 Tajikistan's industrial production was only 34.2 percent of what it had been in 1991, which was a period of poor economic performance in the Soviet context. By 2004, industrial production had risen to 63.6 percent of the 1991 level, in large part because of the revitalization of TadAZ (now TALCO), Tajikistan's aluminum plant, which accounts for roughly 40 percent of the country's industrial production (figure 6.1).[1]

Whole industrial sectors have effectively disappeared in Tajikistan during the past twenty years, but few new sectors are being developed to replace them (figure 6.2). For example, in 1990 the Republic of Tajikistan produced 2,054,000 kilowatt-hours (kWh) worth of high-capacity electrical transformers, compared with 27,900 kWh in 2008. It produced 1,067,300 tons of cement in 1990, compared with 190,400 tons in 2008; and it produced 1,067,000 cubic meters of reinforced concrete for construction in 1990, compared with 46,000 cubic meters in 2008. Other industries that have disappeared include forestry, fertilizer production, knitwear, shoes, hosiery, and cotton and silk fabric production. Refrigerators and freezers were also produced in Tajikistan during the Soviet period, and none are produced today.[2]

The challenges faced in trying to stimulate Tajikistan's industrial recovery are similar to those found in all sectors of the country's economy. The domestic economy is small, and the country's industrial base is predicated on old technology and aging equipment, and is generally still run according to Soviet-style management techniques. Labor productivity is also low (roughly half of what it is in Poland, India, or China, even by the Tajik government's own reckoning). In addition, most existing industrial firms face shortages of energy and frequently water as well, and this would pose a serious problem for any new start-ups, too.[3] Transportation into and out of the country is problematic, the trade and tariff regimes do not encourage either importing parts or exporting finished products, and most products shipped by rail still move through Uzbekistan, where rail links have been periodically closed down by the Uzbek government.[4] Finally, Tajikistan's industrial growth has also been slowed by declines in global commodity prices.[5]

The Poverty Reduction Strategy for 2007–2009 called for increasing industrial output by 25.6 percent, boosting labor productivity by 16 percent, expanding industrial exports by 18 percent, and raising the number of people employed by industry by 20.5 percent. But the advent of the world financial and economic crisis in 2008 made these goals highly unrealizable. In other areas, Tajikistan's traditional industries have lost market share because of their lack of competitiveness, and this includes light industries, food industries, and pharmaceuticals, where more than 60 percent of the domestic market is filled by imports.[6]

One of the major factors inhibiting the recovery of Tajikistan's industrial sector is the continued domination of state-owned enterprises, such as Tajik Aluminum, and the domination of state-owned utilities, which provide energy to industry for both state-owned and private enterprises (almost entirely microenterprises and small and medium-sized enterprises). The Tajik government has been most reluctant to accept advice from international financial institutions on privatizing such assets, and it has also been reluctant to introduce transparent supervision of them. A supervision unit for state-owned enterprises, organized with technical assistance from the European Commission and the International Monetary Fund, moved slowly toward becoming operational throughout 2010, although the Tajik government maintained that hiring and retaining qualified staff has been a problem.[7]

FIGURE 6.1

PERCENTAGE SHARES BY INDUSTRY OF TOTAL INDUSTRIAL OUTPUT, 2007

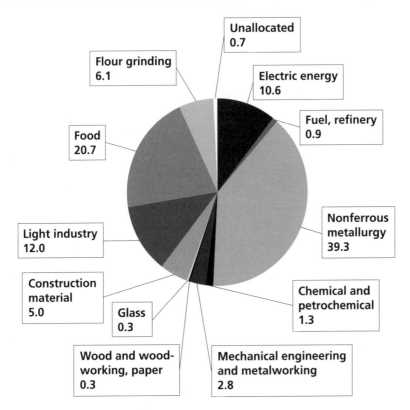

Source: State Statistical Committee, "Industrial Output by Sector in Constant Prices, 1980–2008," www.stat.tj/english/tables.htm.

FIGURE 6.2
PERCENTAGE SHARES BY INDUSTRY OF TOTAL INDUSTRIAL OUTPUT, 1980–2007

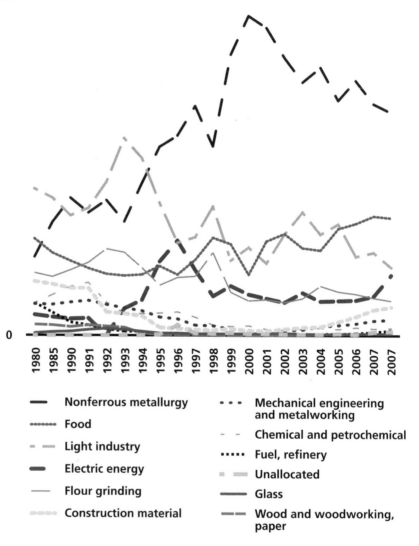

— Nonferrous metallurgy	• • • Mechanical engineering and metalworking
••••••• Food	– – Chemical and petrochemical
– – Light industry	••••• Fuel, refinery
— Electric energy	▪ ▬ Unallocated
— Flour grinding	— Glass
▭▭▭ Construction material	▬ ▬ Wood and woodworking, paper

Source: State Statistical Committee, "Industrial Output by Sector in Constant Prices, 1980–2008," www.stat.tj/english/tables.htm.

TAJIK ALUMINUM COMPANY

The history of Tajikistan's aluminum factory, potentially the country's major income-producing economic asset, is the subject for a compelling thriller—featuring Russian oligarchs, the Rahmon family, and prominent ethnic Uzbek families from Tajikistan's Communist Party elite. All vied for control, doing so most visibly in the London courts in what was one of the largest commercial litigations in UK history, with Tajik Aluminum's considerable share largely paid for by Tajikistan's taxpaying public.

Much of what we can learn about the history of the company since independence comes from these various court proceedings. After more than three years of preliminary hearings, the case, brought by the Government of Tajikistan through the vehicle of the Tajik Aluminum Plant against the plant's prior management and its partners, was formally heard in October and November 2008.[8] But in late November 2008, in the middle of the London trial, the Government of Tajikistan announced that it had reached an out-of-court settlement with the "TadAZ" defendants.

The Tajik Aluminum Company is a state-owned company, known since April 2007 as TALCO, and previously as TadAZ. It is one of the country's largest employers, with 10,170 people working in the enterprise in 2010.[9] The Tajik Aluminum Company is the country's single largest importer and its largest exporter, importing alumina and exporting aluminum. It accounts for over 50 percent of the country's exports.[10] Since 2004, Tajik Aluminum has been run as a tolling operation, with TALCO receiving a fee for processing the alumina that it converts to aluminum, paying the costs associated with the processing, and paying the ad valorem tax on the factory's production. Its major income stream goes to an offshore company, TALCO Management Ltd., which owns the alumina and aluminum that are processed in the factory. This company pays little in the way of taxes in Tajikistan and reputedly belongs to President Rahmon or his family members.

Tajik Aluminum is also the country's largest electricity user, and by its own account it used 30 percent of Barki Tojik's (the country's state-owned electricity provider) total electricity output in 2010.[11] Tajik Aluminum depends upon the preferential rates for electricity offered to industrial producers to maximize its profits. It is generally assumed that TadAZ's high usage rates have kept electricity tariffs low for industrial users, and TadAZ's slow payment history has also contributed to Barki Tojik's regular deficits.

As Tajikistan's electricity rates have risen more generally, Tajik Aluminum has been required to pay increasing amounts for its electricity, but the structure of a tolling operation turns the high costs of energy in Tajikistan over to Tajik Aluminum, while the holding company benefits from the higher sales price of aluminum. So while TALCO Management is rumored to have recorded untold millions in profits, in 2009 Tajik Aluminum registered a loss of 66.2 million somoni (approximately $16 million).[12]

Despite its "losses," Tajik Aluminum's potential value makes it an attractive object for privatization. Thus there was strong interest in the privatization of the plant from the early days of independence, particularly from global bauxite and aluminum producers. For several years, it was thought that RUSAL (Russian Aluminum) would be able to purchase the plant, which it effectively operated in 2005 and 2006. But the plant still remains a state-owned enterprise.[13]

RUSAL is reported to have had an interest in TadAZ going back to 2001, with the idea of incorporating the plant into a holding company that would have included assets in Guinea and the Nikolaevsk aluminum factory.[14] It also seems to have been the case that Viktor Vekselberg, another powerful Russian metals magnate, who owned RUSAL, also thought about trying to acquire the plant a few years later.[15]

Initially, the Tajik government promised that the plant would be privatized in 2007. But on February 25, 2009, the Tajik Parliament passed amendments to the Law on the Privatization of State Property that banned the privatization of the Tajik Aluminum Company, and also of the Roghun and Nurek hydroelectric stations. The Tajik authorities defended this decision as critical to protecting the country's national interests, but in reality very little money is actually transferred to the national budgets from these enterprises, and in some cases considerable costs are also involved. To be fair, each of these would be a complicated privatization project, but in the case of Tajik Aluminum it is also apparent that those who hold the management contracts for the company would lose a great deal of money if the company were privatized in a transparent fashion. By contrast, if Tajik Aluminum were privately owned and run to maximize its profits, it would be a source of substantial tax revenue for the Tajik state.

A HISTORY OF THE TAJIK ALUMINUM COMPANY

The history of the Tajik Aluminum Company over the past twenty years is a tale of who holds power in the country, showing the weakness of Emomali Rahmon in his early years in power, and demonstrating how he was able to first play Tajik interest groups against each other, as well as foreign actors, in order to consolidate his hold over this valuable asset and exercise his control, seemingly for his own personal benefit rather than that of his nation. The construction of the Tajik Aluminum plant was based on a project formally adopted by USSR economic planners in 1965, and modified in 1978, with construction beginning in 1974 and finally completed in 1989. The company achieved its maximum output between 1988 and 1990, producing 457,000 metric tons per year. Full capacity is 517,000 metric tons per year.

Avaz Nazarov and Abdukadir Ermatov took over the operation of the plant during the Tajik civil war, when Mikhail Sinani, the previous director, left Tajikistan. Some ties with Sinani remained, as his son was eventually employed by Ansol (a firm overseeing the management of Tajik Aluminum) in London. Avaz Nazarov, an ethnic Uzbek and a Kharkov Polytechnical Institute graduate, was from Tursunzade, Tajikistan, the site of the plant. Nazarov had a taste for business, and he found the financing—possibly from his father-in-law, who was said to have headed a refinery in Ufa, Russia; or possibly from powerful "families" in Uzbekistan. This financing allowed Nazarov and Ermatov to buy the raw materials necessary to run the Tajik Aluminum factory, and they seem to have found a way to make a profit as well as pay off the local military commanders (the region's "warlords,") who were competing with each other.[16]

Nazarov founded Ansol AG, a firm based in Switzerland that was given the management contract for Tajik Aluminum, and thus was responsible for financing Tajik Aluminum (providing circulating funds for thirty to forty-five days that paid the salaries and other expenses), providing the raw materials, and serving as the trading company for the sale of the aluminum on the London Metals Exchange. Initially, Ansol worked with Ashton Commodities, which was incorporated in 1997 for the purpose of obtaining raw materials for Ansol; and when Ansol entered into long-term purchase agreements with foreign providers, Ashton took on various "service" responsibilities, including helping to provide financing for the purchase of the aluminum. Ashton was owned by Aleksander Shushko, a British national of Belarusan origin. More recently, Ashton Commodities has listed its specialty as Islamic financing, suggesting that it has new business partners.[17]

In 1996, the government passed a decree that required prepayment for aluminum, making it difficult to find anyone that would be interested in taking over Tajikistan Aluminum's production and trade.[18] But at the same time, the factory was in an extreme state of disrepair; with half the electrolysis baths shut down and with production declining from 450,000 metric tons in 1990 to 188,850 metric tons in 1997. Moreover, the quality of the aluminum produced was much worse than in previous years, and there was an acute shortage of engineers at the factory, most having fled during the civil war.[19]

In the early years of independence, Tajik Aluminum used a number of different suppliers for its alumina (including Soviet-era partners like the Nikolaev and Ganja factories in, respectively, Ukraine and Azerbaijan), but when seeking a long-term supply agreement, it had to go through the Tajik government. Additionally, it toyed with joining forces with several different international companies.

An agreement between the Republic of Tajikistan and Alouette was adopted April 14, 1997. Allouette was a Greek firm controlled by the Vardinoyannis family, which was reported to have met Rahmon in Vienna in November 1997 to discuss the possible privatization of the Tajik Aluminum factory; the managers of the Nikolaev refinery were also interested in Tajik Aluminum's privatization, in their case offering a 25.1 percent share swap, in conjunction with Allouette (which presumably was interested in the Nikolaev factory as well). In both cases, the 100 percent privatization of Tajik Aluminum was envisioned. Murodali Alimardon, a deputy prime minister of Tajikistan who in 1997 served as the chairman of the National Bank of Tajikistan, also met with Allouette.

Nikolaev (Sibal) was Tajikistan's supplier of aluminum in 1998–1999; it wanted a guaranteed exclusivity of supply, and TadAZ broke with it in February 1999, paying the Ukrainians back for their initial investment.

Allouette was also pushed out and later brought charges against Nazarov and Ansol, which led to a worldwide freezing of orders against Nazarov (creating financial problems for him in 2003). It was the clash with Allouette that led Nazarov to enter a joint venture with Elleray (a RUSAL affiliate); this enabled Nazarov to settle financially with the Vardinoyannis family, which accepted a $15 million payment from Nazarov in 2003.

Norway's partially government-owned aluminum giant, Norsk Hydro ASA, which is Tajik Aluminum's current major supplier, had its first contact with the Tajik aluminum industry in 1993 (pre-Nazarov and Ansol), but it quickly lost interest in the project because the Tajik Aluminum plant was then producing aluminum that did not meet the standards of the London Metals Exchange. In 2000, however, Hydro made a new approach to Tajik Aluminum, offering it a long-term supply arrangement, which was agreed upon by the two parties on July 21. Also in July 2000, Hydro agreed to provide financing to support Ansol's management contract with Tajik Aluminum because Ansol had an existing relationship with the Saudi bank al Rahji. Initially, Hydro provided $33 million in financing to TadAZ; this sum reached $125 million annually in 2004.

But beginning in 2003, Hydro began to be edged out at Tajik Aluminum, a history that we are able to reconstruct as a result of the arbitration proceedings brought by Hydro against its former Tajik partners on February 3, 2005.[20]

On April 18, 2003, a protocol was signed in Moscow by Avaz Nazarov and Oleg Deripaska, the Russian aluminum magnate who founded RUSAL. This protocol called for Ansol to sell a 50 percent share in a new joint venture called Hamer, which in turn became the owner of Ansol's contracts with Tajik Aluminum; Ansol was reported to have sold this for $25 million. In addition, Ansol assigned its rights and obligations to supply raw materials and finished goods (which included contracts or agreements with Gerold Glencore, Hydro Aluminium, and Fondxel) to the joint venture, and the joint venture accepted its debts to Allouette, along with any other claims or obligations on the plant of up to $200 million. This agreement gave RUSAL the responsibility for the everyday management of the factory. The parties also agreed to jointly participate in any energy projects in Tajikistan as well as in the AzerAl (Ganja) project. In addition to the protocol, a confidentiality agreement between the two parties was signed on April 21, 2003.[21]

RUSAL maintains that the protocol was not a binding agreement.[22] Whatever the status of the joint venture, a framework agreement between Elleray Management and Ansol was definitely adopted on April 28, 2003, whereby Ansol transferred 50 percent of the shares of Hamer to Elleray Management—and thus effectively to RUSAL.[23]

RUSAL was clearly interested in playing a larger role in Tajikistan's aluminum industry and was pressing its case with strong support from the Russian government. In October 2004, Russian president Vladimir Putin made a visit to Tajikistan and signed fourteen separate agreements—including one for the establishment of a Russian military base (on the foundation of Russia's 201st Motorized Division, the Soviet-era Gatchina Division of the Red Army, regularizing its existence), an agreement whereby Russia transferred responsibilities for guarding the Tajik-Afghan border back to Tajikistan, an agreement on the write-off of Tajikistan's debt to Russia, an agreement on the construction of the Sangtuda hydroelectric station, and an agreement on long-term cooperation between RUSAL and the Government of Tajikistan.[24]

Now the story gets very complicated. On December 6, 2004, four days after Nazarov's long-term colleague Ermatov was removed as director of Tajik Aluminum, the factory stopped shipping aluminum to Hydro. It was this refusal to ship aluminum that served as the basis for Hydro's claim to international arbitration.

Tajik Aluminum claimed in court that an audit by Tajikistan's Committee for State Financial Control (known as the Act of Revision), which covered the period from June 1, 2002, to June 1, 2004, had discovered fraud in the price of alumina (which rose from $296 to $540 per metric ton in that period). The Government of Tajikistan maintained that this audit was done during the period from June 7 to October 29, 2004.[25]

The allegation of fraud created the basis for an investigation by the General Prosecutor's Office of Tajikistan, and supposedly explains the "desire to resign" of Ermatov and chief accountant Kucharov, and Nazarov's own interest in leaving the joint venture. The Government of Tajikistan's position was also that TadAZ did not give sufficient information to Rahmon or the Tajik government for them to have been aware of the fraud and mismanagement before the Act of Revision, and that this was deliberate.[26]

The actual ouster of Hydro in fact appears to have not occurred until January 2005, given that Sharipov continued negotiating with Hydro as late as December 23, 2004.[27] All the December documents canceling the agreement with Hydro were handwritten letters, and there were no computer-generated or typewritten supportive materials. Sharipov claimed that both he and his secretary were computer illiterate.[28]

While all this was going on, RUSAL was negotiating with representatives of the Rahmon family to create the promised joint venture. There was a meeting in Dubai on January 13–15, 2005, allegedly at the behest of the president of Tajikistan, to try to reach an agreement between all the parties that the existing barter agreement should be suspended and replaced by a tolling operation. There appear to be tapes of some of the conversations made at this meeting (made without the consent of at least some of the participants).[29]

The first agreements were between RUSAL (represented by Chantell Developments, with Deripaska as signator) and a hitherto-unknown company representing the Tajik side called Amatola SA (USA), which offered Orienbank as its signatory on the Tajik side. Amatola listed its office as at the same address as Orienbank (a privately held bank with some government holding at the time of the trial), and Amatola's memorandum of association identifies Orienbank as the founder. Sheralisho Kabirov, soon to be deployed from Orienbank to Tajik Aluminum as deputy director for finance and commerce, and Hasan Sadulloev, the president's brother-in-law and head of Orienbank, were the signatories for Orienbank.[30] This new joint venture was called CDH, which was listed as a nonresident company (paying $23 million in profit tax in 2005), and it reputedly had a nonexistent office in Latvia, with checks paid to the company first going to the Latvian bank and then being forwarded to Orienbank in Tajikistan.[31] RUSAL's shares were transferred to Amatola at the end of 2005.

In a written statement submitted to the court, Sadulloev claimed that he had no idea what he signed; that a document was put in front of him and he signed it without knowing what was in it. This is certainly a strange admission to come from the head of a bank. Orienbank signed the Amatola documents in the name of the Closed Joint Stock Holding Company Ismoili Somoni—Twenty-First Century, another mysterious business that appears to have ties to President Rahmon's family. Sadulloev admitted to chairing Ismoili Somoni; but in his witness statement to the court, he stated that he owns no shares in it. He argued in that statement that he offered to sign as chairman of the board of Ismoili Somoni because he could not secure the formal agreement of the Board of Directors of Orienbank to agree to the establishment of the joint venture quickly enough, implying that Orienbank, not Ismoili Somoni, was the Tajik owner. For his part, Kabirov stated that he had no idea what he was signing.[32]

There is real confusion over the role of Orienbank in this transaction, and also in others related to Tajik Aluminum, because Orienbank maintains that it cannot own shares of other companies, and none were listed at the time on its website, so presumably its participation in this and other transactions was as a guardian for those that in actuality held the shares.

Hydro was certainly aware of the developments by January 16, 2005, when it learned that it would no longer be receiving aluminum from Tajikistan. And on January 19, 2005, Hydro sent a letter to TadAZ informing it that Hydro considered the Tajik firm to be in default of its agreement, and demanded the $125 million that it was owed, which it stated it would go to arbitration to obtain if necessary.

Hydro was granted its first arbitration hearing before the London Court of International Arbitration in February 2005, and the arbitration tribunal found for Hydro in a November 4, 2005, decision, which was then challenged by Tajik Aluminum.[33] This resulted in an arbitration review by a tribunal of the Commercial Court, headed by Justice Morrison, on April 26 and 27, 2006, and a judgment that was publicly issued on May 18, 2006.[34] The accounts of the 2006 review provide the best window into the "Hydro Affair."

The tribunal found for Hydro. Concluding that whatever corruption may have existed in the practices of Nazarov and Ermatov and the former's treatment of the latter, there was no evidence to suggest that it had any bearing on the relationship of Ansol or Tajik Aluminum to Hydro. In effect, the tribunal effectively argued that Tajik Aluminum, not Ansol, was responsible for perpetrating a fraud.

The tribunal reaffirmed the earlier award, and added compound daily interest from its original date:

- $127,658,289.67 as damages for breach of the Barter Agreement for nondelivery of 71,383,090 metric tons of aluminum;

- $16,896,377.40 for damages relating to detained aluminum;

- $2,600,825.15 for interest up to September 15, 2005, with $16,024.88 of additional interest to be compounded daily; and

- £1,740,119.00 toward Hydro's court costs in the arbitration.[35]

Beginning in June 2006, the Government of Tajikistan began actively negotiating with Hydro in order to find a way to meet the terms of the settlement, and meet it in a way that would not cost the Tajik side any money. Having effectively used up its options in the UK legal system regarding the situation, TadAZ then negotiated a settlement directly with Hydro, and did this in a way that ended any prospect of further legal proceedings between Hydro and the Tajik government and effectively pitted Hydro against RUSAL.

According to John Helmer, it was the Tajik government that reached out to Hydro, inviting it to a series of "secret" meetings in Dushanbe in June 2006.[36] Whether the Tajiks sought out the Norwegians or this was a European-led initiative is unclear, but Helmer offers convincing evidence that a June 2006 visit by Norwegian diplomats and business leaders paved the way to Hydro's formal invitation to return as a supplier for Tajik Aluminum, which occurred in December 2006.

The terms of the December 20, 2006, agreement were that TadAZ would pay $70 million to Hydro and that TadAZ would either deliver 800,000 metric tons of aluminum at a discounted rate over four years or deliver 480,000 metric tons of aluminum to Hydro at a discounted rate plus $24 million additionally over four years, and that Hydro would sell up to 450,000 metric tons of alumina to TadAZ over three years at an agreed-on price.[37] Hydro was also reported to have agreed to help the new Tajik management with its litigation against the former manager, Avaz Nazarov, and in return would take $57.5 million from the proceeds of successful litigation. Moreover, it has been reported that the EBRD helped Hydro, in which the Norwegian government has the controlling stake,[38] negotiate with the Tajik government, so that the contract would go to a European company, a not surprising position for the EBRD to take given how much financing it was providing in the country.[39]

The Hydro settlement contract set up the requirement that there be a third-party agreement by December 25, 2006, which would entail purchasing the 320,000 metric tons of finished aluminum from TadAZ between January 1, 2007, and December 31, 2010.

Tajik Aluminum's agreement with Hydro effectively made RUSAL superfluous, but to eliminate the Russian company's role required finding a way for the Tajik side to end its agreement with CDH, because CDH had provided the raw materials to the factory (supplied by RUSAL).

Some of the details of how this occurred came out in the arbitration hearings before Justice Tomlinson between Tajik Aluminum (by then known as TALCO) against the Nazarov-era management (including individuals tied to RUSAL) that were held in 2008. TadAZ's strategy for eliminating RUSAL was to have a worldwide tender for a new tolling partner. The tender was organized with virtually no publicity and no forewarning as the call for the tender appeared on December 22, with bids to be submitted by December 29 at 5 p.m. Dushanbe time, with the Christmas holiday intervening. The winning bidder would be required to accept the terms of the tolling agreement reached with Hydro.[40]

The only bidders were TALCO Management (BVI), Alaska Metals (BVI), and Noble Resources (Hong Kong). Alaska Metals is controlled by Akhbar Mahdavi, an Iranian metals dealer with an opaque past.[41]

The three "new" bids were virtually identical in their conditions, which the respondent in the 2008 Tomlinson hearing (the Nazarov-era management) maintained demonstrated that they had been prepared by the same group of people. Effectively, the only difference was the sum offered—CDH offered $408 as a tolling fee; Alaska, $410; Noble, $412; and TALCO Management, $415.[42] The respondent further maintained that TALCO was itself a creation of the Tajiks who were part of CDH, citing a copy of a letter sent to Jamshed Murtazakulov, a nominee director of CDH, by a company whose job it was to organize and license new companies.[43]

As part of their agreement with Hydro, the Tajiks agreed to the Norwegian firm's demand that any third party (that is, management firm) to the contract had to be at least 70 percent beneficially owned by the Tajik government, with the remaining shares beneficially owned by persons at arm's length from the Tajik government. Although CDH did not meet this requirement, TALCO Management was designed to meet it (although the company was not required to be subject to independent auditing).

The shareholders in TALCO Management are Vostochnyy Kombinat Redkikh Metallov, Barki Tojik, Ismatullo Hayoev, Jamshed Abdulov, and Maruf Orifov; this is courtesy of an email to Hydro reproduced at the November 3 arbitration proceedings presided over by Justice Tomlinson.[44]

Moreover, the Tajik authorities founded their new working arrangement with Hydro on effectively making the latter a party to the Tajik government for the various legal cases in which it was engaged that were related to the aluminum industry. Hydro agreed to take on no legal undertakings against Hamer or RUSAL, as long as Tajik Aluminum was fulfilling the terms of the December 2006 settlement, and to cooperate with Tajik Aluminum in resisting any legal claims by these parties, as well as to cooperate with Tajik Aluminum in any fraud actions by Tajik Aluminum against these parties. This is clearly stated in provisions that effectively require Hydro to turn against its former business partners and to help Tajik Aluminum recover any claims that are found in TadAZ's benefit against them. This confidential settlement was circulated by John

Helmer on his website, and its legitimacy has never been questioned by any of the parties involved.[45]

In February 2007, the agreement between Tajik Aluminum and CDH—in effect, the Tajik government's agreement with RUSAL—was terminated. (One month later, in March, Rahmonov changed his name to Rahmon, as if to make a public statement of his break with Russians and with Russianness.)

In June 2007, the Tajik government filed suit against RUSAL in London for "fraudulent behavior" in 2003 and 2004, when TadAZ was supplied through a barter arrangement.

There are some ironies in Hydro taking a leading role in Tajikistan's metallurgy sector in partnership with CDH, given the Norwegian company's well-publicized "integrity" program in the area of corruption and human rights, such as the provision in the program's handbook under "fraud" that a "red flag" should be noted when "a business relation... requires that payment be made to a third party or in a country which has no connection to the transaction or operations, including tax havens."[46]

The relaunching of TadAZ as TALCO and the creation of TALCO Management allowed Hydro to be in formal compliance with this provision. But Hydro must have had some suspicions as to who was really profiting from the new tolling scheme, given the personal roles that President Rahmon and those close to him had played in the negotiations with Hydro and the publicity that the TALCO cases were getting.

Eventually, on April 27, 2007, RUSAL settled out of court with Nazarov and Ansol, and the details of the settlement were not made public.[47] Almost immediately after this, those defendants who were RUSAL employees were removed as parties in the Ansol suit.

In response, Tajik Aluminum sought to include RUSAL in its suit against Ansol (the Nazarov-era management), but a June 27, 2007, ruling by Justice David Steel in the High Court in London refused their application.[48] After this occurred, the Tajiks brought suit against RUSAL in the British Virgin Islands, to seek compensation for the same "harm" cited in the London case,[49] while RUSAL filed a $312 million countersuit against TALCO in the Zurich Arbitration Court claiming its nonfulfillment of contract terms.[50]

THE LONDON COURT CASES

The various trial proceedings in the complaints launched by Tajik Aluminum against the Nazarov-era management of the company (which included some of the Russian partners) provide a wealth of material from which to study the operation of the company. Hearings are of course by definition presentations of multiple versions of reality, but the reactions of the presiding judges over these various hearings give us a neutral voice to use in trying to orient ourselves. None of these men were shy about expressing their incredulity at various points in the proceedings, usually with witnesses for the complainant (Tajik Aluminum) but also with the witnesses for the respondent (defendant) on a number of occasions.

Many of the documents relating to the case are available through the UK court reporting system, or can be obtained through successful application to the lawyers involved. But thousands and thousands of pages of supporting documents to these proceedings have yet to be made publicly available, although the contents of many of these are apparent from discussions in the public proceedings.

The timetable for the proceedings was as follows. Commercial trials or arbitration efforts take years from the filing of the original papers to a final decision by the court. A complaint was filed by TadAZ in the Chancery Division on May 13, 2005, alleging that the earlier management (Nazarov-era) had engaged in practices that denied the Tajik Aluminum Company its rightful profits, while for its part Ansol (the Nazarov-era management) sought 50 percent of the anticipated profits that Hamer would have made under a 2005 extension of its contract and future contracts that were expected to be concluded in 2006 and 2007.

Although the complaint was brought by the Tajik Aluminum Company (TadAZ), it was effectively a complaint by the Tajik government, which owned the company and which needed to be able to show convincingly that the prices set by the management were designed for its personal enrichment and to deny funds to the State Treasury. In an effort to demonstrate this, TadAZ sought and obtained a freezing order against the defendants of the main action and an order for Ansol to divulge its worldwide assets. The search-and-seizure order led to some 2,000 bundles of documents being put together by the defendants, which were held by their solicitors but were not turned over pending appeal. On May 23, the defendants applied to set aside the freezing order; and on October 21, 2005, it was in fact set aside (effectively annulled).[51] These documents would have been of potential benefit to the Tajik government in its arbitration proceedings with Hydro, and the broadness of the request by the Tajik government's side was one of the reasons why access to them was eventually denied by the court in the review process.

Justice Blackburne, who considered the appeal to set aside the freezing orders, saw no reason, however, that the case should not move forward, noting that the prices set by Ansol provided the potential basis for a claim, but that its claims with regard to the pricing of aluminum or that Nazarov got control of the aluminum factory through bribery were not "proven" by the arguments presented in their brief (their "skeletons"). To quote Justice Blackburne:

> Although I see the force of much of what has been urged on the defendants' behalf about the extent to which the cost to Ansol of sourcing Tadaz's alumina requirements enters into the computation, in particular the need to finance Tadaz's activities as well as to supply on a continuous basis its raw material requirements, the need to do so by recourse to barter arrangements, the logistical difficulties presented by the plant's remote location and the political context (a newly independent country emerging from a prolonged civil war, an authoritarian system of government and so forth), the fact is that for many years Ansol has been for all practical purposes Tadaz's exclusive alumina supplier and recipient of the finished aluminum. It is equally the fact that Ansol, whose business appears to have been very largely devoted to its relationship with Tadaz, has over the years made very considerable profits from its dealings with Tadaz. It also seems likely, although to what extent is very much in dispute, that the prices charged to Tadaz by Ansol (and later Hamer) for the alumina supplies, even when allowance is made for transportation costs and the like, exceeded what Tadaz could arguably have been expected to pay if it had

been able to source its requirements on the open market. I accept, of course, that whether Tadaz was so able is very much a matter of dispute. It is also the fact that Mr. Nazarov, in circumstances which he has not explained, was exceedingly generous in 1999 when making a gift to Mr. Ermatov or to his son (it does not to my mind matter at this stage which it was) of a £300,000 flat in London and that he has provided generously for Cherzod Ermatov's education and other living expenses while in London. As Mr. Rosen observed, these matters call for an explanation.[52]

For that reason, Judge Blackburne said that there is an arguable case against Ansol, Ermatov, and Nazarov.

At the same time, Justice Blackburne argued that Ansol had a serious counterclaim that RUSAL had breached the joint venture agreement, which included charges that RUSAL was working with the Tajik government to set up a tolling arrangement in advance of the abrogation of the 2003 barter agreement.[53] It may well be that Justice Blackburne's argument was one of the reasons that RUSAL and Ansol agreed to an out-of-court settlement before the full case was presented in court in October 2007.

Justice Blackburne strongly implied that the Tajiks did not act in good faith with their foreign partners when he turned the attention of the court to a letter of December 13, 2004, from TadAZ (after the Nazarov-era management was removed) to Hamer (the joint venture that included both Hydro and RUSAL) claiming that it was in default of its obligation to make various payments on TadAZ's behalf. He noted that this letter makes no reference to the 2003 barter arrangement being a fraud, despite the fact that the Tajik authorities later claimed that they had launched a criminal investigation against Hydro for committing fraud on December 7 of that same year. Though not saying so directly, Justice Blackburne raised the possibility that the Tajik authorities had postdated documents to drum up charges after the fact. He drew further attention to Sharipov's handwritten letter of December 7, which only turned up during the hearings for the first time, as Blackburne wrote:

Not the least of the curiosities of this episode is that Mr.
Sharipov's handwritten letter only emerged in the course of
TadAZ's reply evidence notwithstanding that four months of
investigation (including an interview with Mr. Sharipov in
the course of April 2005) had preceded the launching of these
proceedings during which it might have been thought that a
letter of such significance would have surfaced so as to appear
in the very voluminous evidence that was before the court on
12–13 May. On any view, Mr. Sharipov's appointment on 6
December, his handwritten letter the following day and the
decision to prosecute (based on having "established" a conspiracy) taken on the day after that display remarkable speed
on the part of Mr. Sharipov and the Prosecutor General. The
defendants take an altogether more cynical view of events:
they say that they have been concocted (in the case of Mr.
Sharipov's letter much after the supposed event) as part of the
conspiracy to discredit them and are inherently implausible.[54]

Moreover, Blackburne found evidence that Orienbank was controlled by
close members or associates of President Rahmon's family, and

> it is common ground that there was no kind of tender
> process for the award of the contract [to CDH]. In these
> circumstances, it is difficult to view those who are said ulti-
> mately to control CDH as being independent of those who
> control TadAZ. On any view RUSAL was closely involved in
> these events.[55]

Blackburne further brought out how the Government of Tajikistan used
its legal powers to favor CDH.[56]

This set the stage for the actual hearing of the case in London in
October and November 2008, under Justice Tomlinson, which was
adjourned before it was completed as a result of an out-of-court settlement between the two parties.

The respondent's case (that of Ansol, the Nazarov-era management)
maintained that the Government of Tajikistan already was well aware of
the barter agreement with Hydro but wanted to get rid of Hydro (through

breaking the contract with Hamer) and substitute a tolling arrangement for the barter arrangement, and to use Orienbank, which was run by Rahmon's brother-in-law, rather than Ansol as the Tajik facilitator.[57]

Most of the evidence on the Tajik side was provided by those who had replaced the Nazarov-Ermatov team, Sharipov and Kabirov, who were brought into TALCO in December 2005. Iskandar Mirzoev, the deputy head of the Department of General Supervision of the General Procurator's Office, who was responsible for issuing the investigation against Hamer in December 2005, also gave critical testimony. At the time of the trial, Mirzoev served as the prosecutor of the city of Tursunzade.

The government alleged that Tajikistan's financial crisis was so severe then that it feared instability in the country if the operation of the plant were not quickly righted. The Tajik government based this argument on a claim that TadAZ was paying too much for alumina that the plant then made into aluminum. Justice Tomlinson delved into the whole question of aluminum pricing, and through his questions it was made clear that the claim, that the Tajik government maintained, that Nazarov and company could have paid "spot prices" was difficult to sustain because unlike in the oil industry, or as is true with some other commodities—including aluminum—there is no real spot market in alumina given how limited its sourcing is. There is a market price, but that also reflects shipment costs put on top. Most aluminum-producing plants are supplied through long-term contracts to ensure supply, rather than to depend on picking up some excess alumina on a temporary "spot" market created by overproduction at a particular alumina plant. The suit alleged that Ermatov and Nazarov extorted millions of dollars from the Tajik government in profits illegally taken from the plant, with the "proof" offered largely centered on property owned by Ermatov, who fled Tajikistan in December 2005, and the members of his family.[58] For their part, the respondents in their case pointed out that Tajik Aluminum never had any substantial profit under the tolling agreement that was introduced after its management contracts were terminated.

Although the wrongs and rights of both sides were never finally addressed by the court, as no judgment was ever reached in this case, the court proceedings detail how much money "leaked" from the plant during the period starting from Ansol's control through December 2005. Testimony was offered about the large sums of money paid out by Nazarov to those who were working closely with him, and to their families. In his testimony, he claimed that these were Tajik "cultural practices," and he stated that the sums of $100,000 a month he paid out in 1999 and 2000 were to maintain 100 families dislocated by the civil war, while the Tajik government maintained that this money went to support Nazarov's own personal lifestyle and that of his family and friends.[59]

Such "cultural practices" also were offered as an explanation by Nazarov for why he provided $48 million to President Rahmon and his family, in the form of cash, gifts, and jewelry for him and other high-ranking officials and their wives; and that the tens of millions of dollars paid out in a service agreement signed with Pakhtoi Shakhritus constituted a similar kind of transaction as no services were performed.[60]

In the supporting documents submitted with the defense case, Bulygin, then the chief executive of RUSAL, noted that Hamer, the joint venture of which RUSAL was a part, was expected to provide $1 million per month to help support the Presidential Guard. Presumably this was a "voluntary" contribution, such as businesses are asked to make in much of Central Asia.[61] Neither the claimant nor the respondents were willing to call such payments bribes. As the Ansol respondents maintained,

> Such payments are not "unlawful" in Tajikistan, nor were they made with the intention of influencing the recipients, including Mr. Ermatov, to do or not do anything. They were made because that is the way Tajikistan is run: Ansol was simply required to make these payments.[62]

The following payments were reported (in the amended revised defense in the 2006 hearing before Justice Cresswell) for presidential trips, which included large delegations and family members of Emomali Rahmon as well (the following reference numbers are to trial paragraphs):

- 48.1. Presidential trip to Geneva in June 2000.
- 48.2. Presidential trip to Tokyo in May 2001 (with a large delegation).
- 48.3. Presidential trip to Paris and Washington in December 2002.

- 48.4. Presidential trip to Geneva in June 2003.

And added to this:

49.1. Such payments were made with the full knowledge and consent of the Government of Tajikistan, including the President and the Prosecutor General Bobohonov, who were themselves the beneficiaries of such payments (see Schedule 3 hereto[63]) and were demanded of Ansol whenever such officials travelled. For example, in Geneva in June 2003 Mr. Alimardonov requested Mr. Sushko (via Mr. Ermatov) to ask Mr. Nazarov to arrange payment in Kerdanian jewellery store to pay for jewellery for the President in the sum of $768,000 (approximately 482,000 pounds sterling). Similarly, in May 2001 Mr. Shusko was required by Mr. Alimardonov via Mr. Ermatov and Mr. Nazarov to fly to Tokyo to pay a shopping bill from the Mikimoto store for pearls for the President totaling 61,911.27 pounds sterling and also bills from other stores (see Schedule 3 hereto [unavailable]). Furthermore in April 2004 Mr. Sadulloev told Mr. Shushko that he needed to buy some jewelry for the President's wife (his sister) and Ansol was required by Mr. Sadulloev to pay for the jewelry, which it did, to the sum of $755,000. All such payments were made by Mr. Shushko on behalf of Ansol and at Mr. Nazarov's direction.

49.2. In addition, the President's representatives (including Mr. Alimardonov) demanded that payments be made by Mr. Nazarov to Ansol for the president's personal benefit as the price of continuing to do business with TadAZ. In particular, in 2003, a demand was made for a monthly fee of $1 million per month to be paid to the President. The consequence of not complying with this demand would have been the loss of the business and all the money that Ansol had invested in Tadas. Mr. Nazarov requested that such payments be formalized in a written agreement. On 27 August 2003 an agreement for consulting services was entered into between JSC Pakhti Shakritus (represented by R. A. Sadulloev) and Ansol.

The agreement provided for a monthly fee of $1 million to
be paid in the account of Pakhtai Shakhritus at Orienbank in
Dushanbe. No services were rendered under the agreement.
The President was the ultimate beneficiary of the payments
made under the agreement. Such payments were not repaid by
TadAZ in aluminium.[64]

The Tajik government's side granted that payments were made to
a certain Pakhtoi Shakhritus, but insisted that these were not bribes.
"Pakhtoi shakhritus" literally means the cotton of Sharuuz District. So
that there is no confusion over the spurious nature of the agreement,
it is enough to note that Pakhtoi Shakhritus was represented by R. A.
(Rakhmattulah Assidulaevich) Sadulloev, a brother of Rahmon's brother-
in-law, Hasan Sadulloev. But in his statement to the court, Sadulloev
maintained that it was some other R. A. Sadulloev, as he was sure that his
brother was not a director of Pakhtoi Shakhritus.[65] In a country as small
as Tajikistan, such a claim was just not plausible.

This led to a remarkable exchange between Justice Tomlinson and Mr.
Rosen, Tajik Aluminum's lawyer:

> Tomlinson: "Well, here is an allegation being made by you,
> a state entity, that there has been widespread bribery and
> corruption by an individual in order to secure control of the
> state industry, and yet at the same time the allegation is that
> the state has also received large sums of money from the same
> source over the same period."

And then Mr. Rosen's response:

> Rosen: "If the state has received it then it is not bribery. The
> state is the owner of the Tajik Aluminum Plant."

And again Judge Tomlinson's response:

> "No, but there is room for the suggestion—and it is early
> days, I say no more, but there is room for the suggestion that
> the inference to be drawn from the receipt of the large pay-
> ments is that there was at any rate acquiescence in what was
> going on.... That is the case against you as I understand it."[66]

However, while Nazarov clearly did not want to admit that he had bribed the president, his testimony all but said he did—a point that the lawyers for the government tried to use to their advantage, quoting from Nazarov's pretrial witness statement:

> Rosen (quoting Nazarov): "I did not say that such payments were bribes. The basis upon which the demands were put to me by the President himself and by Mr. Alimardonov, and subsequently, Mr. Sadulloev [and your Lordship knows those two gentlemen as proposed witnesses] on behalf of the President was that the President needed money for solving various problems in Tajikistan. I had no option but to comply as and when I could do so."[67]

The Government of Tajikistan argued that the sums of money paid to the president and the members of his family were not bribes but funds that went toward solving Tajikistan's problems. And in the following paragraph (cited in Justice Blackburne's 2005 decision), the lawyers for Ansol detailed the increasing consolidation of power in Rahmon's hands, and the promotion of relatives of Rahmon:

> He [Ermatov] is a victim of this process because not only has the President persecuted those whom he regards as his political rivals but he has also sought to place under his personal control key sectors of the Tajik economy by appointing to important positions those who are his relatives or come from his place of birth rather than appoint competent professionals. An example is the President's brother-in-law, a Mr. Sadulloev, who now controls a significant proportion of the country's cotton industry and is head of Orienbank which is Tajikistan's largest commercial bank. In late 2003 he (Mr. Ermatov) was pressured by the head of Tajikistan's National Bank, acting on the President's instructions, to transfer Tadaz's accounts to Orienbank. Mr. Sadulloev attends on behalf of the President all important commercial and intergovernmental talks taking place in Tajikistan. Through friends and family members the President and his brother-in-law now own 76% of that bank's

issued share capital. One of the President's daughters controls all imports of sugar to Tajikistan; her husband is Deputy Director of Dushanbe Airport and as such is in control of fuel purchases and air ticket sales [which are mostly done through travel agents at jacked-up prices], while his other son-in-law is head of Tajikistan's Commodity Exchange. A wish by the President to take for himself and his close associates the benefit of Tadaz's trading lies behind his removal from the directorship of Tadaz, the refusal to permit further supplies of aluminium to Hydro, the denial of the existence of any indebtedness to that company, the replacement of Hamer with CDH and the extraction by CDH of $23 million worth of aluminium in the first two weeks following the making of the tolling agreement between Tadaz and CDH. In addition CDH has seized cargoes of alumina and other raw materials which were being acquired for Tadaz under the former barter arrangements.[68]

Judge Tomlinson, however, even in these opening days, noted that if these claims were true, the claim and the counterclaim would both be difficult to defend:

I have by no means thought it all through and through and it is very early days, but it seems to me that if the allegation that is made in paragraph 208, if it is both maintained and provided, then I see difficulties in both the claim and the counterclaim.[69]

Subsequent comments make clear that what Tomlinson meant here is that the possibility existed that it would be proved both that Rahmon took bribes and that Rahmon knew that Nazarov was giving bribes to Ermatov. The complainants maintained that Nazarov should have informed the Tajik law enforcement officials that bribes were being required of him—something that in the context of Tajikistan would be blatantly ridiculous.

The case was adjourned right before the Tajik government was supposed to put forward its key witnesses, including Murodali Alimardon, then the country's deputy prime minister, and the key figure in the National Bank of Tajikistan cotton scandal. He was present at the opening day of the trial, but he had to return home for "pressing business" before he could testify. (It also adjourned before testimony by Sadulloev, who was being required by the court to testify in person, despite his "ill health" after having been shot by his nephew—that is, Rahmon's son.)

The court proceedings strongly suggest that if the case had continued, even more compromising details would have revealed how the Rahmon government operated, or that key officials and possibly President Rahmon himself would have been forced by the court to testify or refuse to testify and hence have been in contempt of court. The necessity for them to testify was foreordained by the decisions made by the lawyers for Tajik Aluminum—that is, the Government of Tajikistan—as to how they were going to argue their case.

They effectively boxed the Government of Tajikistan into a corner through the arguments they chose, and what the witnesses presented while testifying, because commercial court cases in the United Kingdom in particular accord the presiding justice a great deal of discretionary power to question witnesses at length. The continuation of the trial put the Government of Tajikistan at substantial risk of becoming internationally discredited. The size of the settlement made to end the trial was not made public, but the Ansol respondents are rumored to at minimum have had their considerable court costs reimbursed by the Tajik government,[70] and presumably there was also an agreement that there would be no further claims made against them by the Tajik government.

TAJIK ALUMINUM UNDER TALCO: LITTLE PROGRESS TOWARD REFORM

Tajik Aluminum under TALCO has made very little progress toward implementing promised reforms. The company is not profitable. It is not audited in a timely fashion. It makes no real effort to achieve public accountability, and it is still being run by the same management that took over in December 2004. As was true then, in 2012 TALCO remained 70 percent government owned, and the ownership of the other 30 percent has never been fully disclosed.

The amount of aluminum being produced by Tajik Aluminum also dropped when the factory went over to a tolling agreement, at least through the first nine months of 2010, which are the most recent data TALCO had published by April 2012. TALCO is reported to have produced 419,000 metric tons of aluminum in 2007.[71] And, during the first nine months of 2009, TALCO produced 265,000 tons of aluminum, down 135,000 from the previous year.[72] This was partially a reflection of the severe winter and the electricity shortages it produced. But the next year, in 2010, when the weather was milder, TALCO worked to 87.71 percent of capacity but still had a 10.5 percent drop in production from 2009. Although the drop in world demand can help explain the latter, it has no reflection on the former. The company's lack of profitability does not mean that TALCO Management fails to make a profit, for its income is based on the difference between the purchase price of alumina and the sale price of aluminum, minus transportation and tolling costs. TALCO Management's profits would nonetheless have increased substantially given that aluminum traded at 127 percent of its 2009 price on the London commodities market.

In 2010, Tajik Aluminum paid only 186.2 million somoni (approximately $42.5 million) in taxes or in other funds payable to the state budget. It is still considered Tajikistan's most valuable industrial asset. TALCO Management Ltd., which actually owns and sells the aluminum processed in the Tajik Aluminum smelters, is not required by Tajik law to disclose its income, and it does not. Its ownership structure also remains opaque.

TALCO Management blamed most of the disappointing performance of the factory in recent years on the global economic crisis, and on its website the company made sure to praise the country's president for showing strong leadership to prevent the economic decline from being worse, lauding him for creating opportunities to diversify production and decrease transportation costs.[73] And in the same corporate briefing statement for 2010, the management also boasts of having introduced an "integrated system of management" that provides for quality, ecological, and health controls.[74] In fact, Hydro, which signed a protocol on protecting the environment and ensuring workplace safety as part of a strategic partnership agreement covering the period 2010–2013 that was signed on May 14, 2009, between Tajik Aluminum (TALCO GUP) and Hydro Aluminum, appears to bear much of the cost of meeting improved ecological standards.[75]

But criticisms of TALCO have not led to any management changes. As noted above, the same team that was put in after Nazarov, headed by Sadriddin Sharipov, remains running the company at the time this book went to press in July 2012.

The International Monetary Fund has remained a prod pushing TALCO toward greater transparency. But the IMF's use of carrots rather than sticks has not conveyed any sense of immediacy to the Tajik government, which continues to own and to effectively operate the plant, as the director and deputy director report directly to the government. For instance, it took more than two years to get the company to publish the results of the international audit to which TALCO agreed under pressure from the IMF to provide after the scandalous behavior of the National Bank of Tajikistan in the cotton sector was revealed.

When these data appeared, late, they were posted in a way that precluded printing a copy. The company has also been delinquent about publishing audits for 2009, 2010, or 2011, none of which had been published by May 2012. The website of Tajik Aluminum (talco.com.tj) is poorly maintained; despite its being designed for international readers, when accessed in April 2012, the English-language page was still reporting news from 2007 in its lead.

But TALCO seeks to project itself as an "award-winning" company; the banner on its website boasted that it had received the "Best Enterprises of Europe" award,[76] given by the Europe Business Assembly in Oxford, a private organization of undisclosed funding that seems to specialize in giving awards to former Soviet bloc countries and their enterprises.[77]

In a move nominally aimed at achieving greater transparency, TALCO created a board of directors to work with its director, but the board does not consist of independent figures; rather, it is drawn from the company's department heads, people appointed by the director or deputy director.[78] So there is still no independent check on management's performance or independent body able to offer advice on the company's operations.

The Tajik government's management of TALCO, along with other state-owned companies, has come under World Bank criticism for its accounting standards. Tajik Aluminum issued its first financial statements that met international accounting standards in 2000. Then the first group of international auditors was dismissed by Tajik Aluminum because of "unsatisfactory performance."[79] The audit firm then chosen by Tajik Aluminum was not on the list of World Bank–approved auditors, and the Bank found the fiscal year 2000 and 2001 audits unacceptable.

Tajik Aluminum's published audits for 2007 and 2008 clearly show that it has not thrived under the new arrangement. It registered a loss of $3,215,000 in December 2007, as opposed to a profit of $12,983,000 the previous December.[80] This loss occurred even though there was a slight increase in production (from 413,800 to 419,000 metric tons). The main reason for this is that the tolling fees were kept very low.

The losses were still higher in 2008, $25,998,000 after taxation,[81] but the taxes Tajik Aluminum paid were minimal, even though they represented the sole profit that accrued to the Republic of Tajikistan from this large state-owned enterprise. In 2008, the company paid only $2,239,000 in profit tax, down from $8,545,000 the previous year. One of the reasons for its reduced profitability was its $50,946,000 investment in plant improvements, improvements that would be of at least equal benefit to TALCO Management Ltd., rather than to the plant, for the plant only benefits from the tolling fee, and the income from the sale of aluminum remains with TALCO Management, which has worked hard to keep down the costs of tolling.

In 2008, the plant paid nearly twice the electricity tariffs as the previous year, $93,016,000 instead of $57,411,000, and the tolling fee was raised to $493 per metric ton from $411 the previous year, but the amount of aluminum produced also declined. Tajik Aluminum also had to pay the law firm Herbert Smith CIS LLP's legal fees, the amount of which was not indicated in the audit.

Tajik Aluminum was required to raise its borrowing ceiling, and it did this through an upward valuation of its fixed assets, which nearly doubled in worth, despite the fact that the only change was the small investment in improved production already noted above.[82] The company continues to maintain that its success is the result of the farsighted leadership of TALCO Management Ltd., which is guiding it to a program of diversified production and increased profitability, and that the future of Tajik Aluminum is intertwined with that of TALCO Management.[83] But the cost of investing in improving the quality of production is met by Tajik Aluminum and not by TALCO Management.

According to this arrangement, the costs of the company's imports and the value of its exports are assigned to Tajik Aluminum on its ledger sheets, but the alumina belongs to TALCO Management, and so, too, does the aluminum that is produced. TALCO Management sets the prices of all goods provided to or bought from Tajik Aluminum, and Tajik Aluminum receives its profit solely through the tolling fee that it "negotiates" with TALCO. Tajik Aluminum is also responsible for all the other costs associated with the operation—including the costs of importing any other materials necessary for processing the alumina. And it also pays for all the energy supplied to the plant, both electricity and fuel.

When the Hydro agreement was ending in late 2010, TALCO continued to use Hydro as its principal supplier of alumina. By then, it was also securing metals from Glencore, as well as the Noble Group and Alaska Metals.[84] Glencore is an internationally known leader in the field, and the Noble Group is a major Hong Kong–based commodity trader.[85] Alaska Metals is privately owned, having been formed in 2006 and based in Zurich. Its website provides no information about its ownership or management, and its homepage features a picture of the Presidential Lyceum it supports in Tursunzade, the home to Tajik Aluminum.[86] Alaska Metals also bid in the tender that TALCO won, and it looks very much as if it was created solely for this purpose.

THE UZBEK CONNECTION

The development of Tajik Aluminum has regularly become intertwined with Tajik-Uzbek relations for several reasons: because of the proximity of the plant to the Tajik-Uzbek border near Surkhan Darya Oblast, which, the Uzbek authorities have consistently claimed, suffers ecological damage from the plant; because any increase in hydroelectric power to fuel the expansion of the plant is perceived by the Uzbek authorities as creating a risk to Uzbekistan's water supply given that it requires investment in upstream reservoirs and hydropower plants; because all freight to and from Tursunzade, where the plant is located, must pass through Uzbek territory; and finally, because during the Nazarov-Ermatov era the plant was run by ethnic Uzbeks with close ties to powerful Uzbeks in Tashkent and to pro-Uzbek forces in the Tajik civil war.

The Uzbek authorities stress that the plant should be operated in accordance with a 1994 intergovernmental agreement relating to the joint management of the ecological challenges associated with the plant.[87] The Tajik authorities maintain that the operation of the plant is in accordance with all ecological requirements, and that its operation is an exercise of Tajik sovereignty.

During the civil war, Tursunzade was first under Tajik government control, but then came under the control of General Gaffor Mirzoev (who presumably received some "tribute" from the plant). He had some 3,000 men under his control in a "presidential guard," and he also supplied the plant with protection. He later headed the Anti-Drug Agency and was arrested and sentenced to life in prison in 2006. In the trial against him and Democratic Party leader Mahmadruzi Iskandarov, it was alleged that Avaz Nazarov and RUSAL were using Ansol money to support a coup d'état planned by these men for February 2004 (although this does not appear to have come up in the later UK court hearings).[88]

In addition, Nazarov was said to have been under the protection of Rafur Rakhimov, a powerful and rather mysterious Tashkent businessman who traded in petrochemicals, natural gas, and light industry, and was a benefactor of international boxing and the International Olympic Movement in Uzbekistan, as well as Salim Abduvaliev (known as Salimboi).[89] Abduvaliev was the son of a powerful Soviet-era collective farm chairman from the Ferghana Valley who was reported to have had business ties with Michael Chernoy in the aluminum industry between 1990 and 2000.[90] Whether there was a financial relationship between

Nazarov and these two powerful Uzbek figures is hard to know, but it does help explain why Rahmon felt that he had less than full control of TadAZ during the Nazarov-Ermatov period.

It would be a mistake, however, to presume that the relationship between Nazarov and two of Uzbekistan's powerful families somehow shaped Oleg Deripaska and RUSAL's involvement in the project, as some Tajik journalists have speculated.[91] After the announcement of RUSAL's partnership with Tajikistan, Deripaska traveled to Tashkent to try and reassure the authorities there that he would be sensitive to Uzbek ecological concerns in the development of the aluminum plant. Uzbek press reports following Deripaska's December 16, 2005, visit emphasized Uzbek president Islam Karimov's conviction that an ecologically sensitive solution to running and further developing Tajik Aluminum could be found.[92] But in much the same way that it would be impossible to imagine such a demonstration as devoid of influence from the Uzbek authorities, it is difficult to consider Deripaska's trip and the promises he made while in Tashkent as not at least partially reflecting Moscow's agenda. Given the very public endorsement by the Russian government of the RUSAL projects in Tajikistan, the interests of the Kremlin rather than those of powerful Uzbek "family" leaders seem a far more likely explanation for the Russian aluminum magnate's behavior.

The Uzbek authorities have repeatedly made their objections known to plans to build the Roghun hydroelectric station based on plans that call for a 335-meter dam. And when the Tajik government began collecting money for the construction of Roghun based on a dam of this height, the Uzbek ecology movement began once more "becoming active" with protests in Termez against higher-than-average rates of pulmonary and digestive diseases, along with blood disorders in the Surkhan Darya region, said to be the result of pollution from the plant. The March 2010 protest came during a period of escalating tensions between the Uzbeks and the Tajiks over the dam, with some thousand rail cars bound for Tajikistan being held up on the Uzbek side of the border. Although the Uzbeks may be exaggerating the environmental risks associated with the factories, it is also obviously the case that Soviet planners paid little attention to environmental risks to neighboring communities when they decided on factory locations, choosing them instead for how they facilitated various aspects of the production cycle.[93]

CHINA AND INDIA COME COURTING

India, with substantial reserves of bauxite, has regularly expressed interest in helping Tajikistan develop its aluminum smelting capacity. A high-level Tajik delegation traveled to New Delhi in August 2006 at India's invitation to discuss the issue.[94] In July 2008 Nalco, the National Aluminum Company of India, was reported to have unsuccessfully tried to buy a majority stake in TALCO.[95] India's president, Pratibha Patil, even went to Tajikistan in 2009 in an attempt to deepen economic ties between the two countries. But while India continues to play a strategic role in Tajikistan's security relations, its economic influence has been difficult to strengthen, in large part because New Delhi often finds itself in unsuccessful head-to-head competition with Beijing.[96]

China seems to almost always win out, as its firms are willing to overpay for Tajik assets, as well as provide more development assistance and better loan terms. China also shares a border with Tajikistan, which still faces huge hurdles in getting goods to and from India. In the last several years, Chinese partners have been inching their way into what could become a dominant position in Tajikistan's aluminum sector. In May 2008, China's National Heavy Machine Corporation signed an agreement with TALCO to support the creation of the Tajik Chemical Metallurgic Corporation under TALCO's control.[97] The project calls for the construction of two aluminum fluoride- and cryolite-producing facilities. Plans were expanded to include China's Tianchen Engineering Corporation in 2010,[98] which is constructing a plant that will annually produce 100,000 tons of the sulfuric acid that is necessary for the shift to domestic production of alumina.[99] Sulfuric acid is also used in processing gold, and Tajikistan is also interested in reviving its gold-mining and -processing industry.

In April 2011, TALCO announced that the construction of the sulfuric acid plant would begin within the year, and that within five years the company would be able to shift to domestic supply for 60 percent of its

raw materials.[100] TALCO has allocated $30 million for plant construc-
tion. Transportation fees for bauxite, reported at some $250 million per
year, are sharply cutting into TALCO Management's profits. In the short
term, the company is also trying to get more favorable tariffs for Tajik rail
to move bauxite through Ukraine. The Tajiks estimate that some 10,000
to 15,000 new jobs will be created when the project is completed.[101]

This was a project that RUSAL had planned as part of its investment
in TadAZ, but it is now being realized with the help of the Chinese government and corporate interests.[102]

One wonders where Tajikistan will get the bauxite rock to process into alumina. China is a major bauxite producer with substantial
bauxite reserves, but its appetite for aluminum created serious challenges for its domestic production capacity. And with further economic
growth, the Chinese demand for aluminum is certain to grow.[103] The
China Aluminum International Engineering Company, better known as
CHALIECO, has agreed to work with Tajik Aluminum and GU (State
Entity, the Scientific Research Institute of Metallurgy) and Guangxi
Aluminum Institute, on scientific and technical cooperation necessary to
complete this project.

TAJIKISTAN'S URANIUM INDUSTRY

Tajikistan was a uranium producer and processor during the Soviet
period, with worked deposits found in three *rayons* of Sughd Oblast.
The first "yellowcake" in the Soviet Union was produced in Tajikistan,
where an experimental uranium mine began operating in the area of the
town of Gafurov in 1945, and a hydrometallurgical plant was opened
in the same year in Taboshar to process the ore. The Gafurov mine was
closed in the 1950s when the center of uranium mining shifted first to
deposits near Adrasman (which was worked in the 1940s and 1950s) and
then to the right bank of the Khujand River (near Mogoltau Mountain,
in the 1970s and 1980s). The Taboshar processing plant closed in the
early 1970s. Roughly 90 percent of the uranium mined in Tajikistan
was processed outside the country, and Soviet planners largely used
uranium-processing facilities in Tajikistan to work uranium deposits from

neighboring republics. Vostokredmet (Vostochnyy Rare Metal Industrial Association) was organized in 1945, and during the Soviet period it was known as the Leninabad Mining and Chemical Combine; it was renamed Vostokredmet in 1992.[104]

During the Soviet era, Vostokredmet was a major facility—processing uranium from deposits in Tajikistan, Kyrgyzstan, and Uzbekistan—and was the principal source of yellowcake for the USSR's various defense facilities. It continues its operations to the present day, and is located in the city of Chkalov in Sughd Oblast. In addition to uranium processing, it also served as the processing point for the Zerafshan gold fields, with the processing of gold serving as the plant's mainstay since independence.

Initially it had been assumed that Tajikistan's uranium reserves had been largely depleted by Soviet metallurgists, but in a speech to Parliament in April 2008, President Rahmon claimed that Tajikistan still had approximately 14 percent of the world's uranium reserves and recommended that Parliament amend existing legislation to allow foreign companies to gain ownership stakes in the development of these assets.[105] The reserves are said to be found in the Mogoltau-Karamzar, Gissaro-Karategin, and Pamir regions.[106]

Until that time, most of the press coverage about this sector was restricted to safety issues concerning tailing dumps dating from the Soviet period that are found in northern Tajikistan, a topic discussed at further length in the section on ecology. Even with the call for foreign investment in this sector, the Tajik government has continued to insist that it lacks the money to clean up these problems on its own. The country's neighbors have also complained about the continuing pollution from Tajikistan's tailings, and have objected to the damage to regional ecosystems if Vostokredmet expands its operations. Uzbekistan, too, is against the operation of this factory, and especially plans to work the tailings in order to extract salable uranium. This will further increase the ecological risks associated with the tailings themselves, and will mean that the uranium will need to be transported across Uzbekistan to a port for shipment, further increasing the ecological risks for Tajikistan's unhappy neighbor.[107] One can understand Uzbekistan's displeasure, because in 1999, when Vostokredmet once again resumed processing small amounts of uranium (it was closed in 1994 during the country's civil war), a study done by the Center for International Trade and Security at the University of Georgia found that Tajikistan's export control system was only 8 percent compliant with international standards.[108]

Not surprisingly, Tajikistan's nuclear potential has attracted considerable international interest. In September 2009, Indian president Pratibha Patil traveled to Tajikistan to secure access to the latter's uranium supply, and signed an agreement with President Rahmon on the development of Tajikistan's uranium industry to their respective countries' mutual benefit.[109] President Patil touted the accomplishments of the Uranium Corporation of India Ltd. during her visit, although at the time of this writing, there had still been no further developments to report.

Russia, which has been able to develop a parity relationship with Kazakhstan's globally significant uranium sector in recent years, has also been pushing for an enhanced role in Tajikistan's uranium industry. Russian president Dmitry Medvedev raised the prospect of enhanced cooperation between the two countries in both the uranium and natural gas industries during bilateral consultations between the two presidents in August 2008. In late 2009, Russia's state-owned Rosatom began a series of high-level negotiations to try to convince the Tajik authorities to form a partnership with them.[110] Russia's hope is that Vostokredmet could once again work in concert with the joint Kazakh and Russian nuclear program. Russia renewed its offers again in 2011.

While the Tajik government is mulling over the Russian bid, China continues to press its cause. As early as 2000, the head of Hai-Yu, China's uranium company, began pressing the Tajik authorities for a 49 percent share in Vostokredmet, as well as to loan the Tajik government the money necessary to pay for its share of retooling the factory.[111] In 2008, China's Guangdong Corporation also pressed for a role in the development of Tajikistan's nuclear sector.[112]

The Iranians have been the most interested of all, for Tajikistan's uranium would be a tremendous boost to Tehran's plans to develop nuclear energy, and of course they are rumored to have other interests in the nuclear field. The Tajik government continues to report that there are no plans to sell Iran any of Tajikistan's uranium, despite regular Iranian press leaks to the contrary. There is no reason, however, to accept the Iranian claims as true.

Tajikistan's principal nuclear-processing plant, Vostokredmet, which has been discussed above, has also recently been in the news. This factory is one of the "owners" of the state share in TALCO Management Ltd., which makes questions of its control of vital interest to the Rahmon government, despite the fact that its production level is only a small fraction of what it was during the Soviet period.

Since Tajik independence was achieved, Vostokredmet's main function has been to process gold, and it holds the licensing rights to some of Tajikistan's gold deposits. Through the operation of this state-owned enterprise, the Tajik government is able to control the extraction, the smelting of gold, and the export of the proceeds of the country's gold industry. Vostokredmet is one of the companies that the International Monetary Fund and the World Bank have urged Tajikistan's government to make more transparent, in part through its partial privatization.[113] It currently provides virtually no information about its activities or financing.

In June 2009, there was a shakeup of the management of the Vostokredmet factory, when the managing director, Shavkat Bobodzhonov, an employee of the plant for nearly forty years, was arrested for "spying for a foreign power"—that is, Uzbekistan—and was sent to prison for ten years.[114] This arrest of an ethnic Uzbek sparked fears in the local community, because, according to press accounts, the state provided no compelling evidence of Bobodzhonov's treachery, raising concern that it was a case of "guilt by ethnicity." Fergana.ru reported that local residents were shocked, and some five hundred signed a petition to President Rahmon protesting Bobodzhonov's arrest, noting that there was not a more honest individual to be found, as Bobodzhonov still lived in his Soviet-era apartment and did not even own a car, not to mention more expensive luxury items.[115]

TAJIKISTAN'S GOLD INDUSTRY

Tajikistan had a well-developed gold-mining sector during the Soviet period, although most of the gold deposits that were easiest to develop were already substantially depleted by the time of independence. There are still deposits in northern and central Tajikistan, as well as in the southern Pamirs, with dense deposits in the Djilau-Taror and Turkestan-Chorin regions of Central Tajikistan. This was the area of the Anzob metallurgical factory (*kombinat*), which was a major producer of antimony during the Soviet period and now has scant production and operates as a joint venture with a U.S. firm.[116] However, there are reports that this U.S. firm (Comsap) is in fact controlled by President Rahmon's brother-in-law, Hasan Sadulloev, who is the dominant figure behind Orienbank, and that Sadulloev also holds Tajikistan's antimony concession.[117]

China's Zijin Mining has been working with metallurgists from Tajikistan to revitalize that country's gold industry.[118] Tajikistan developed a gold extraction industry while under Soviet rule. Zijin Mining began working Tajikistan's gold fields in 2007, when it took over the 75 percent stake of Commonwealth and British Mineral Ltd. in the Zerafshan JV, formed in 2004.[119] The JV, operated through Avocet mining, a Commonwealth and British subsidiary, had mining and exploration rights over a 300,000-hectare area near Penjikent, and sold the subsidiary to Zijin Mining for $55 million.[120]

Although Tajikistan is the smallest gold producer of the four Central Asian states with gold reserves (the others being Uzbekistan, Kyrgyzstan, and Kazakhstan), it nonetheless produces 1.3 to 1.5 tons of gold annually, and its gold industry was boosted by the announcement in January 2011 of two new gold fields, the first in the central part of the country, with an estimated 177 tons of gold reserves, and the other in the northern part, with 79 tons.[121] Chinese business interests (the China Global New Technology Export and Import Company) also have a dominant role in Tajikistan, having taken over the Altyn-Topkan mining complex in Sughd, which is expected to produce 1 million tons of lead-zinc per year when its restoration and expansion plans are complete.[122]

CONCLUSION

During the past twenty years, the Tajik government has not done a very good job of realizing the country's industrial potential, and there is no strong evidence to suggest that the situation will improve in the immediate future. The conditions of the civil war dealt a death blow to most of the country's industrial enterprises, which would have faced serious stress even under the best of circumstances because the collapse of the Soviet Union meant the end of the interrepublic supply chain that sustained them.

In his first years in power, President Rahmon lacked the power to introduce systematic reforms in the industrial sector, given that it would have pitted him against powerful interest groups, such as the Tajiks who took over control of the Tajik Aluminum plant during the civil war years. But as the detailed examination of the history of this factory has shown, when Rahmon gained the power, he lacked the will to substitute a market-based economy predicated on transparent business practices for the rent-seeking that had previously prevailed.

Moreover, as the trial proceedings in London relating to Tajik Aluminum strongly intimate, Rahmon chose to use his power and influence to gain a strong foothold for his own family as the dominant rent-seekers. The strongest evidence of this is that the Tajik government halted the lawsuit (which it had brought itself, and which cost untold millions of dollars to present) against the civil war–era management of Tajik Aluminum when the revelations it could have produced would have forced Rahmon's brother-in-law and perhaps even the president himself to give testimony.

There are few signs that Tajikistan's industrial policy will be changed by its current government leaders, who seem content to take the slowest path possible to the reforms for which the International Monetary Fund and other international financial institutions are pressing, such as the introduction of international accounting standards, public audits, and appointing independent directors to enterprise boards. And because President Rahmon seems to be seeking Chinese, Iranian, and Indian investment in his potentially very valuable metallurgical sector, he seems even less likely to want to heed the largely Western-dominated voices of the international financial institutions.

CHAPTER 7

TAJIKISTAN'S INFRASTRUCTURE AND ENERGY CRISIS

ajikistan's infrastructure was badly damaged during the civil war, exacerbating the country's transportation and communication challenges and handicapping its ability to trade internationally, as Soviet-era links were developed to further interconnectivity among the various parts of the Soviet Union, with no eye to Tajikistan ever becoming an independent country. As figure 7.1 shows, highways were built to avoid mountain ranges, so that regions like Sughd (Khujand) were linked to the rest of the USSR, through Uzbekistan, and Tajikistan was connected to the Soviet rail system through Uzbekistan as well, with little connectivity across the republic, and mountainous regions like Jirgatal and Murghab were accessed from Kyrgyzstan.

The Soviet authorities made an enormous investment in Tajikistan by almost completely electrifying the republic. This was something of a principle under communist rule; the slogan "Communism is Soviet Power Plus Electrification of the Entire Country" was posted throughout much of the USSR. However, on most other infrastructure indicators, which are listed in table 7.1, Tajikistan does very poorly compared with the other early transition countries, as categorized by the European Bank for Reconstruction and Development (EBRD).[1]

FIGURE 7.1

TRANSPORT INFRASTRUCTURE: CAREC CORRIDORS, ROADS, AND RAILROADS

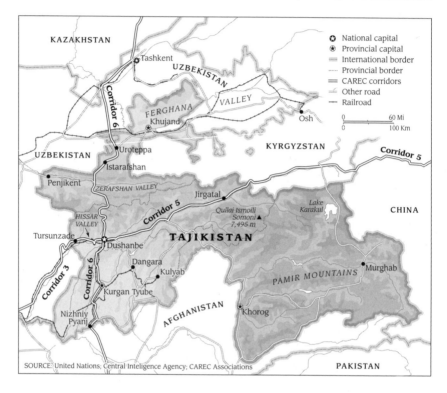

SOURCE: United Nations; Central Intelligence Agency; CAREC Associations

TABLE 7.1
ACCESS TO UTILITIES (PERCENTAGE OF HOUSEHOLDS)

ASPECT OF UTILITIES	TAJIKISTAN	OTHER EARLY TRANSITION COUNTRIES
ELECTRICITY FROM THE PUBLIC GRID	99	99
PUBLIC (PIPELINE) CENTRAL HEATING	2	13
PIPELINE GAS	15	43
PIPELINE TAP WATER	30	56
PUBLIC SEWAGE SYSTEM	13	37
FIXED TELEPHONE LINE	17	45

Sources: European Bank for Reconstruction and Development, *Strategy for Tajikistan*, January 26, 2009, 29, www.ebrd.com/downloads/country/strategy/tajikistan.pdf; European Bank for Reconstruction and Development and World Bank, Life in Transition Survey, 2006.

The Soviet-era grid was designed not to supply independent countries with their electricity needs, but rather to service a common, export-driven economy in which the weaker links were subsidized by the center. Utilities were made available to domestic consumers at virtually no cost, although industrial users were given priority. Given this established infrastructure, Tajikistan, much like its neighbor Kyrgyzstan, has fared very badly since the collapse of the USSR and the subsequent breakdown of the regional energy-sharing arrangements that had carried over from Soviet days. As table 7.1 shows, the government has found it virtually impossible to provide adequate supplies of utilities, particularly electricity, to meet the basic needs of the country's domestic consumers. The situation is similar for large industrial users: Although TALCO (Tajik Aluminum) uses about 40 percent of the electricity output produced by Barki Tojik (the country's main and nationally owned electric company), neither TALCO's needs nor those of the country's other large industrial users are fully met.

Various international financial institutions have made a great deal of effort to improve Tajikistan's infrastructure and to restructure the country's utilities to operate on commercial principles. Tariffs for electricity, water, and other utilities have increased sharply. But with the exception of those parts of the country served by Pamir Electric, all other electricity tariffs and most water usage fees remain below cost-recovery levels, and multiple tariffs are still applied to reduce the costs for "privileged" (generally industrial) users.[2] Pamir Electric is a public–private partnership that has been supported by the International Finance Corporation and the Aga Khan Development Network.

Beginning in 1998, and acting in coordination with the IMF and the World Bank, the Asian Development Bank (ADB) offered Tajikistan a Post Conflict Infrastructure Loan, which was designed to fund the development of a comprehensive set of reforms that would reorganize the energy and transportation sectors along market-based principles. This initiative notwithstanding, Tajikistan's infrastructure development has progressed in a relatively patchwork fashion, with the Tajiks taking money when and where available and never getting international assistance to fully correspond with the Rahmon government's own priorities in this sector.

In general, Tajikistan's energy sector is one of the least reformed in the former Soviet Union. While estimates vary, its energy transmission and distribution networks still lose roughly 20 percent of all energy generated each year, a loss that is ill-afforded in an electricity-short country.[3] There is no third-party access to its transmission networks, and a very limited independent regulatory presence, with electricity tariffs remaining below generation and transmission costs.

WATER USAGE AND CLEAN WATER

Tajikistan is a water-rich state, home to 83 percent of the headwaters of the Amu Darya River system and one percent of the Syr Darya River system. Yet the country has shortages of potable water, and has not managed to replace Soviet-era water distribution systems with a comprehensive national plan that speaks to the country's clean water, irrigation, and hydroelectric needs.[4]

It is impossible to separate out the issue of water from any discussion of utilities more generally. Water is a utility, paid for by the country's domestic consumers. Water is a prerequisite for irrigation; without it, Tajikistan's agricultural productivity would be restricted to its mountain regions and to the lands directly adjacent to its major rivers and their tributaries. Water is also the source of Tajikistan's hydroelectric potential (see figure 7.2).

FIGURE 7.2
WATER RESOURCES AND HYDROELECTRIC STATIONS

SOURCE: United Nations; Central Intelligence Agency; Republic of Tajikistan Environmental And Social Impact Assessment Study

President Rahmon's plans for using the country's hydroelectric potential have increasingly left the Tajik government at odds with the Uzbeks. Each side maintains that the other is the one at fault. The Uzbeks assert that the Tajiks must be bound by consultation when making decisions involving the Amu Darya River, as it is a transboundary waterway, while the Tajiks cite the de facto Uzbek approval for the completion of Soviet-era hydroelectric stations, based on documents that were signed in 1992 and 1993.[5] President Islam Karimov and Uzbekistan's other leading government officials have long and vocally opposed Tajikistan's running its hydroelectric stations in winter (departing from the Soviet-era "irrigation" design for these projects[6]), and have been infuriated by the Tajik government's plans to build the Roghun hydroelectric station, whose giant reservoir could serve as something of an "on and off" switch for much of the water that flows west to support Uzbekistan's own irrigated agriculture, depending upon the height of the reservoir. More than 50 percent of all the irrigated agriculture found in Central Asia is in Uzbekistan.

The Tajiks maintain that if the Uzbeks used water more efficiently, there would be enough water for everyone. But nowhere in the region is water used efficiently. Turkmenistan has the highest per capita consumption of water in the region (and one of the highest in the world), at 5,324 cubic meters per year. This is over twice Uzbekistan's per capita usage of 2,292 cubic meters; Turkmenistan is further downstream and also vulnerable to both Kyrgyz and Tajik plans in the hydroelectric sector. The Tajiks use only slightly less water per capita than the Uzbeks do, consuming 1,983 cubic meters per capita on average during the period 1998 through 2007. This compares with 528 and 485 cubic meters per capita in Russia and China, respectively, and 291 cubic meters in Israel (which has made enormous strides in using drip irrigation and other types of low-water-usage technology in its agriculture). Moreover, due to accelerating glacial melt, the Tien Shan Mountains, of which Tajikistan's ranges are a part, lost between 25 and 35 percent of their glacier volume during the course of the twentieth century. This creates a pressing reason for addressing water usage patterns, and adds more complications (and a sense of urgency) to plans to build big hydroelectric stations in Tajikistan and Kyrgyzstan. In today's world, even so-called renewable resources are not infinitely renewable.[7]

Access to clean drinking water is another real challenge in Tajikistan, a problem that dates back to the Soviet period, when providing clean drinking water and modern sanitation was much less of a priority than introducing electricity. According to the World Bank's 2007 Tajikistan Living Standards Survey, 38 percent of all Tajiks depend upon drinking water that comes from a lake, stream, river, or unprotected well, all of which are highly susceptible to contamination.[8] As a result, gastric illnesses and waterborne diseases such as typhoid and cholera remain a real and ever-present danger in Tajikistan, especially in rural areas, where rich and poor alike have trouble accessing safe water sources.

Tajikistan has also had a serious problem with contamination of urban water supplies. Even in the capital city of Dushanbe, the quality of drinking water was woefully inadequate during the Soviet period, and water purification systems fell into further disrepair during the civil war. The situation grew so bad that in 1994 there was a typhus epidemic in the city.

Tajikistan's water resources are jointly managed by the State Inspectorate for Water Resources and local water service agencies. Yet most Tajik municipalities experience real difficulty simply maintaining their existing water systems, given that user fees generally cover only the basic operating costs of these combined water and sewage systems, and leave no additional funds available for improving water quality or financing new meters. According to a 2007 Oxfam report, water usage tariffs range from 2.0 to 45.0 dirams per cubic meter for potable water (roughly $0.006 to $0.13 per cubic meter), and from 0.78 to 1.3 dirams per cubic meter for irrigation water (approximately $0.002 to $0.004).[9] (Traditionally, agricultural users were exempt from paying for the water that they took on schedule from irrigation canals, but now farmers do pay for irrigation canal maintenance.) The report estimates that then-current tariffs reflected just ten percent of the costs of providing water.[10] To make matters worse, household, industrial, and agricultural users are given limited financial incentives to conserve water by the district water supply agencies performing housing and communal services, and collecting usage fees.

The World Bank's 2005 Multiple Indicator Cluster Survey found that only 93 percent of the urban population and 63 percent of the rural population had access to a source of improved drinking water (which included piped water, public tap water, borehole or tube well water, and protected well water or protected spring water or rainwater).[11] Access to water also varies significantly by region: for instance, only 52 to 55 percent of the population in GBAO and Khatlon Oblast has access to such water.[12]

The donor community has been working with the Tajik government to try to improve this situation. The World Bank supported a program to improve the water quality in Dushanbe[13] from 2002 through 2010, with approximately $24 million of some $29 million disbursed by August 2009.[14] This program has resulted in some 75 percent of the population of the city now having access to safe and reliable water supplies 24 hours a day (as compared with 52 percent in 2003). At the same time, a higher percentage of water usage fees are being collected, increasing from 21 to 65 percent for the first nine months of 2008.

The EBRD has also worked to mobilize donor grant co-financing (in order to meet IMF requirements), and thus, Tajikistan received support from the Swiss for its two modernization projects for the Khujand Water Supply Project (a total of €7.4 million, or $9.1 million), from the Netherlands (€3.7 million, or $4.6 million) for the Dushanbe Solid Waste Project, and from Sweden (€800,000, or $986,640) for its Southern Cities Water Supply Project.[15]

The Khujand Water Supply Project, which began in 2004, has been designed to increase the capacity of the Khujand Water Company, which supplies the capital city of the northern region of Tajikistan with its water. The first phase of the project introduced water meters (purchased from a Swiss company) in a third of the city's households, and the second phase (2008–2012) has been focusing on improving the financial performance of the water authority, using Estonian technical expertise. Along with financial improvements, the project will introduce water meters to all the households in the city by the end of 2012.[16] The project is twinned with one being implemented by the EBRD at the same time in Lithuania, which the EBRD says has enhanced the success of the Tajik project. Yet, the EBRD report also implies that there was substantial local resistance to the idea of introducing water meters in individual households as residents feared it would increase the costs of water, but water meters are critical to the commercial viability of municipal water systems.[17] The success of this and other water projects is critical if Tajikistan is to solve its pressing need to supply safe drinking water to its population.

In February 2010, the EBRD also signed an agreement with Tajikistan's Ministry of Finance and its communal services agency (the State Unitary Enterprise Khojagli Manzilyu Kommunal), for a $4.2 million project to support improvements to the water supply in southern Tajikistan, most particularly in the cities of Dangara (Rahmon's hometown), Kulyab, and Kurgan Tyube.

The challenge of providing safe drinking water to towns and villages, both those with and those without municipal water systems, is very complex and is at best only being partially met. In these areas, drinking water, whether from wells or (less frequently) from underground pipes, is being drawn from the same network as irrigation water, and this system of canals and pipes has not been kept in good repair, leading to substantial transmission losses. Tajik communities have had difficulty coming up with funds for routine maintenance, and the national government lacks the money for a comprehensive repair and rebuilding program. Moreover, the Tajiks themselves have never internalized any water conservation habits. Those who come from rural regions are used to Soviet-era practices and think of water as a free public good of which they are entitled to unlimited use, and this attitude carries over to village, town, and urban dwellers who make use of drinking water to tend their gardens and private plots.[18]

In addition to its struggle to provide safe drinking water, Tajikistan has also made little progress in introducing healthy hygiene facilities (either indoor plumbing or proper outdoor plumbing). A total of 34.3 percent of its people—roughly 25 percent in urban areas, and close to 40 percent in rural areas—lack access to proper facilities in their households (see table 7.2),[19] with little differentiation of access by income.[20] This is a particular problem for Tajikistan's schools; a survey done by the United Nations Development Program during the 2007–2008 food and energy crisis found that 64 percent of the schools surveyed lacked a working water supply.[21]

TABLE 7.2

THE TAJIK POPULATION'S ACCESS TO FACILITIES, 2000–2008
(percentage of urban, rural, or total population)

ACCESS TO IMPROVED FACILITIES OR SOURCES BY POPULATION SEGMENT	2000	2005	2008
SANITATION FACILITIES			
TOTAL POPULATION	90	93	94
RURAL POPULATION	89	92	94
URBAN POPULATION	99	95	95
WATER SOURCES			
TOTAL POPULATION	60	67	70
RURAL POPULATION	49	57	61
URBAN POPULATION	92	93	94

Source: World Bank data, http://data.worldbank.org.

OIL, NATURAL GAS, AND COAL

Tajikistan is estimated to have some 1,033 million metric tons of standard fuels (oil, natural gas, and natural gas condensate), in eighteen proven deposits.[22] The principal deposits and facilities include: for natural gas, sixteen oil-gas deposits currently under exploration, including the Ayritanskoye, Madaniyatskoye, and Ravatskoye deposits in the Ferghana depression; and for petroleum, the Beshtentyakskoye, Kichik-Belskoye, Shaambary, and Uzunkhorskoye deposits in the Southern Tajik depression.[23] Tajikistan used some 26,850 tons of oil products in 2007, with 70 percent of them coming from Uzbekistan, 27 percent from Turkmenistan, and the remaining three percent largely from domestic sources. Tajikistan also has roughly 40 deposits of coal, totaling 4.5 billion metric tons. Coal production has declined since independence; just 100,000 metric tons were extracted in 2005. The cost of extracting coal, and the apparent low quality of the coal, is such that historically it has not been viewed as a cost-efficient source of energy for industry.[24]

Tajikistan's gas sector suffers from the same lack of transparency that is characteristic of its utilities in general; the IMF presses for international audits of the sector as a condition for continued funding of structural reforms, and Tajik authorities continue to do everything possible to slow down this process while trying not to jeopardize the country's continued funding. Tajikistan's consumers still buy their gas from a state-run monopoly, Tojikgaz, which is not fully transparent in its operations.

Tajikistan is heavily dependent upon gas sales from Uzbekistan for heating in winter, and gas prices have increased more than threefold in recent years. There is a great deal of discussion of how to achieve greater energy security and efficiency, in terms of both hot water and heating supplies, which the EBRD in particular is exploring with the Tajiks, who are also interested in developing their coal industry and increasing the use of coal-fired power production. Tajikistan is also seeking (and already securing some) investment to develop its own natural gas reserves.

While Tajik leaders hold out hope that the development of untapped gas reserves will lead to greater energy self-sufficiency,[25] Gazprom (through its Zarubezhneft subsidiary) has bought rights to develop the Sarykamysh and Sargazon fields.[26] For now, and likely for the foreseeable future, most of the gas used in Tajikistan comes from Uzbekistan, and Tojikgaz has frequently been in debt to its Uzbek provider, UzTransGas. At the same time, Tojikgaz is usually owed money by its largest users, including the electricity monopoly Barki Tojik and the Tajik Cement Company, whose officials complain that they cannot pay their bills due to rising electricity tariffs. But tariffs for electricity users are increasing far more slowly than the price of gas paid by Tajikistan. In 2008, gas went from the 2007 price of $100 per 1,000 cubic meters to $145, and then jumped to $245. In 2010, Tajikistan paid on average $240 for every 1,000 cubic meters (24 cents per cubic meter); by the third quarter of 2011, it was paying $284.33 per 1,000 cubic meters (28 cents per cubic meter).[27] This number rose to $264 per 1,000 cubic meters in 2012.

These prices reflected the higher prices that Uzbekistan was getting in gas sales to Russia. Furthermore, Uzbekistan requires prepayment for its gas shipments, and cuts off gas supplies if these are not received or if there is a break in time between contract extensions, such as occurred in April 2012, when there was a fifteen-day stretch in which Tajikistan received no gas.[28] Most of the gas goes to industrial users.

Tajikistan suffers from a substantial gas shortage in winter as well, for the utility company finds public resistance to its efforts to pass on the purchase price for gas from Uzbekistan to the country's consumers. There is also a subsequent knock-off effect, because commercial and domestic users' unpaid electricity bills leave the electricity company unable to make its payments to the gas company. For example, in the winter of 2009–2010, customers in Sughd Oblast (outside Khujand city) received gas only from 4 until 7 p.m. starting on December 23, having had no gas at all since sometime in October. The gas cutoff occurred because Sughd-gas owed TajikTransGaz more than $1 million, and the gas supply was reconnected when $700,000 of this was received. As noted above, the Uzbek authorities demand prepayment for gas, a practice that TajikTransGaz is trying to get its customers to accept as well. Although this practice is being successfully instilled in Khujand city, where gas is generally available 24 hours a day, provincial customers have proven more reluctant. Sughd consumers pay five cents per cubic meter.[29]

The World Bank has reported that the collection rates of Barki Tojik and Tojikgaz were 85 percent and 90 percent, respectively—lower than anticipated, but higher than most independent observers maintain (because of what they claim are hidden mechanisms that allow for energy to be removed from the system without being easily able to be traced).[30] The World Bank has been working with Tajikistan to reduce commercial losses of gas and electricity, and to reform pricing in the energy sector. In 2009, the annual weighted average of the posted tariff equaled $.0174 per kilowatt-hour (kWh), after two tariff increases. Prices are supposed to be reviewed quarterly. Gas tariffs were also increased that year, but pricing in both sectors suffered from the drop in value of the Tajik somoni, upon which both tariffs were based.

As with many other projects in this sector, the goal of pilot projects was to enhance the technical capacity of the Tajik agency involved, and to lead to enough increased liquidity so the Tajiks would be able to fund the nationwide application of the reform themselves.

The World Bank does report reductions in losses of energy through transmission by both Barki Tojik and Tojikgaz, and improved collection of tariffs by both companies as well, in both cases using figures provided by the companies themselves. Tojikgaz reports a difficult-to-believe increase of 105.6 percent of customer billings recovered in 2009, up from 95.3 percent in 2005, and Barki Tojik reports 71.8 percent of customer billings received, as opposed to 21.9 percent. The total loss of electricity generated went from 18.7 to 13.7 percent, and gas from 21.9 to 14.6 percent.[31]

There have also been slow but steady efforts to introduce gas and electricity meters into individual households. The World Bank has also been helping Barki Tojik install electric meters. While this task has been largely accomplished for those who buy their utilities through Pamir Electric, Tojikgaz has had trouble getting even 60,000 new meters installed annually, having been hindered in part by its own financial difficulties, and by the inability of the Tajik government to secure international financing for a nationwide project.

REFORMING THE ELECTRICITY SECTOR AND ENHANCING ELECTRICITY GENERATION

Tajikistan has an acute energy shortage, and is seeking help from both large and small users to address and alleviate it. The government's Poverty Reduction Strategy for 2007–2009 called for extending daily electricity availability from 16 to 20 hours per day (on an average calculated yearly), but instead the country found itself confronting worse electricity shortages in these years than it had experienced previously.

After the acute electricity shortages in the winter of 2007–2008, the situation eased somewhat for the next few years, both because of some increases in supply but also because the next few winters were less severe. But during the unusually cold winter of 2011–2012, the country once again experienced severe shortages of electricity, with rationing starting earlier in the autumn and lasting later into the spring than in the previous two years.[32]

There is a sad irony to this, because Tajikistan has a hydroelectric potential of some 40,000 megawatts (MW), with an annual energy content of 527 terawatt-hours (TWh), of which only roughly ten percent is currently being developed.[33] Tajik officials believe that with the construction of new hydroelectric dams the country's export potential could rise to 12 TWh (12 billion kWh) in 2015.[34]

Tajikistan's electrical system is the product of the interdependencies that existed between the Central Asian republics during Soviet times, when electrical grids were set up to link large energy consumers to the closest energy producers in a way that paid no heed to republic boundaries, and existed primarily for administrative and economic planning purposes, rather than denoting any sort of meaningful political or economic autonomy. The grids were also designed to respect geographical impediments, like mountains, and not make what were then viewed as unnecessary expenditures to traverse them.

Until late 2009, Tajikistan (with the exception of GBAO) was part of the Central Asian electricity grid—which effectively ceased to exist as a unified system when both Uzbekistan (where many of the central relays were) and Kazakhstan withdrew from it. The Uzbeks complained of poor repayment by the Tajiks, while the Kazakhs maintained that the Tajiks were "stealing" (illegally diverting) electricity slated for southern Kazakhstan. The grid had functioned by means of an automated relay system which had linked the electricity grids of southern Kazakhstan with those of the other four Central Asian countries. It has been replaced by national relay systems, with cross-border transfers of electricity no longer occurring automatically, but through regularly negotiated inter-republic agreements and subject to cut-offs within each country.

Tajikistan has three separate grids—a northern grid, for the Sughd region; a southern grid, for Khatlon, Dushanbe, and beyond; and an eastern grid for Gorno-Badakhshan. The eastern grid is connected to the southern grid through a long 35 kilovolt (kV) line that has limited capacity, and has been made effectively redundant by the 2002 decision to split off Gorno-Badakhshan from Barki Tojik and have it instead serviced by Pamir Electric. The northern grid is supplied by electricity generated in Tajikistan when water is discharged from the Vakhsh River dams to support irrigated agriculture in Tajikistan and further downstream during the growing season, but requires electricity and gas purchases from

Uzbekistan, or electricity relayed via Uzbekistan from Turkmenistan, during the rest of the year.

Because of the high cost of Uzbek gas and electricity, the Tajiks built a new line to link the northern part of the country with the southern electricity grids and new hydroelectric stations. Initially planned in the Soviet period, the first part of the project opened in late 2009.[35] Central to this are three 220 kV power transmission lines that link a 500 kV power grid bringing electricity from the southern part of the country to its north.

In 2007 Tajikistan received $604 million in loans (in the form of credit from the U.S. Export-Import Bank) from China to support this project, among other things. Tajikistan received an additional $200 million loan from China in September 2008 to cover the construction of a new hydroelectric plant, although this project was subsequently put on hold.[36] Although the line connecting the north and south will dramatically change Tajikistan's ability to supply its northern regions, it has still not provided substantial relief in the north, because of both power generation challenges in the south and more general transmission issues in the north. The amount of electricity generated from June to August 2010 increased just one percent compared with the same period in 2009.[37]

The severe winter of 2007–2008 furthered the Tajik government's conviction that the country needed to develop a range of projects to alleviate its electricity shortage, including relaunching the Roghun hydroelectric station, which not only involves building the world's largest reservoir, but also including some 50 small hydroelectric stations (mostly run-of-the-river projects) slated to be developed with international funds. Originally, these projects were scheduled to be completed in 2009, and though Tajikistan spent much of that year in active negotiations with a number of foreign partners (including the Czech Republic, Russia, China, and Iran), the projects remained on the drawing board in early 2010.[38] The Tajik government also signed an agreement with a Malaysian company to build a power plant fueled with food waste.[39] Furthermore, Iran has also partnered with Tajikistan on the Sangtuda 2 Plant, and has announced plans for the construction of the 150 MW Ayni Power Plant on the Zerafshan River,[40] and a small 22 MW hydropower plant on the Iskandarya River, which is a tributary of the Zerafshan.

Despite these recent plans, however, Tajikistan has been slow to reverse the drop in electricity generation that occurred between 1990 and 1998, at the conclusion of the civil war. Numerous factors accounted for the loss of capacity, including the reduction of capacity of the Nurek Hydroelectric Station due to silting, along with a real crisis of maintenance and the lack of spare parts that were characteristic of the country's entire electricity-generating system. The latter was largely the result of a shortage of funds, but was aggravated by increasingly more incompetent management. As such, crises with regard to independent electricity generation have been more serious in Tajikistan than in any of the neighboring Central Asian countries (see table 7.3).

TABLE 7.3
ELECTRICITY OUTPUT AND CONSUMPTION 1980–2010 (in billion kW/h)

	1980	1985	1990	1995	2000	2005	2010
TOTAL OUTPUT	13.6	15.7	18.2	14.8	14.3	17.1	16.4
HYDROPOWER AS SOURCE	12.6	14.4	16.9	14.6	14.1	17.0	16.4
TOTAL DOMESTIC CONSUMPTION	9.7	15.3	19.4	15.4	15.6	17.3	16.6
INDUSTRY CONSUMPTION	4.6	8.7	11.1	6.6	5.8	7.5	7.3
AGRICULTURE CONSUMPTION	2.7	3.5	4.2	4.6	4.3	3.9	3.6
HOUSEHOLDS CONSUMPTION	0.7	1.0	1.3	2.0	2.8	2.7	2.9
LOSSES OF DOMESTIC CONSUMPTION	0.9	1.1	1.6	1.8	2.2	2.7	2.3

Source: Agency on Statistics Under President of the Republic of Tajikistan, "Electricity output, sale and consumption, 1980–2010," www.stat.tj/en/analytical-tables/real-sector/.

The reform of Tajikistan's electricity sector has also gone more slowly than that of the electricity sectors in either Kyrgyzstan or Uzbekistan. Barki Tojik is a state holding company—in other words, a government-run monopoly—which still controls electricity production, transmission, and sales, and the Tajik government has not made the overhaul of the energy sector any sort of priority. As illustrated above it is instead concentrating on increasing generating capacity through new giant hydroelectric projects and piecemeal enhancement of the existing capacity; this puts any sort of major institutional reform, privatization, or commercialization of energy in a very distant second place.

Every aspect of the existing electrical system's infrastructure—from dam maintenance through the generation of electricity, to transmission and distribution to regions, enterprises, and households—either needs attention or could have its productivity enhanced. But these efforts alone will not be enough to ensure the development of a sustainable economy in Tajikistan.

The biggest challenges that Tajikistan faces in its electricity sector are interrelated. The first is to raise the prices of electricity so that there is cost recovery in the sector, a challenge that will continue to increase with the commissioning of Sangtuda, and even more so if Roghun is commissioned. Tajikistan has kept the lowest electricity prices in the region and has maintained the lowest cost recovery ratio as well (recovering only 24 percent of the cost in 2003, as compared to 94 percent in Kazakhstan).[41] The World Bank's 2004 trade diagnostic study of Tajikistan (still the most recent such survey) recommended that electricity prices be raised to 3.8 cents per kWh for export parity; only then would the country's strategy of developing export markets make any sense, as this would cut down domestic usage and raise money to build transmission lines.

In December 2009, Tajikistan sold electricity to domestic users for 7.5 dirams (approximately $0.017) per kWh. The rates in 2010 were 9 dirams ($0.020) for domestic users, 21.3 dirams ($0.048) for industrial users, and 8.2 dirams ($0.019) for TALCO, which has a rate distinct from that of other industrial users.[42] In April 2012, the electricity price was raised to 11 dirams ($0.022) for domestic consumers and 28 dirams ($0.058) for industrial users.[43]

The average tariff collection rate remains unsatisfactory, and declined to 62 percent in 2009, down from 65 percent in 2007.[44] Each price increase creates angry ripples throughout the population, as do efforts to improve collection rates. Ordinary Tajiks are clearly unhappy about these increases, even though they would benefit economically in the long run by having reliable electricity.[45]

Electricity prices need to be raised, and in addition collection rates must be improved and transmission losses reduced. The low prices and low collection rates have led to asset deterioration, especially of transformers, and keep electricity demand high (even if there is not the generating capacity to fill this demand in winter).[46] In other words, consumers are not facing the full costs of electricity.

Raising electricity prices would change patterns of domestic use, encouraging less waste but allowing consumers to have dependable access to electricity when they want to use it, would create even more of an electricity surplus to export, and could create the income stream necessary to pay for the construction of power lines to transmit the energy to Afghanistan and beyond, or to China. But neither the World Bank nor anyone else studying Tajikistan would minimize the challenge involved in raising electricity prices.[47] Having seen the violent ouster of President Kurmanbek Bakiyev of Kyrgyzstan in April 2010 following a sharp increase in utilities, the Tajik authorities will certainly not move more rapidly to raise domestic rates for electricity. Vested interests in the aluminum industry in particular will continue to press for reduced rates for their product. And given the alleged ties of President Rahmon's own family to the aluminum industry, it is hard to believe that the Tajik government will push rapidly to get industrial rates raised, either.

Moreover, Tajikistan must also reform its electricity monopoly, Barki Tojik, which is another very deeply vested interest. But reforming the entire sector would be easier if Barki Tojik would be able to come closer to recovering the costs of electricity production.

The World Bank argues against "lifeline tariffs," a term used for setting lower utility tariffs for lower-income households, and urges instead that cash subsidies be offered to such families. This latter option gives them the incentive to reduce electricity usage in favor of putting the funds toward other needs, something that is of potential benefit to the environment and a way to further stimulate the economy. However, the government has instead chosen a solution that benefits Barki Tojik, shifting income to it as direct compensation for a portion of the cost of electricity sold to poorer households—based on estimated usage figures provided by Barki Tojik rather than by the designated households.

The Asian Development Bank (ADB) gave Tajikistan a technical assistance grant in 2006 for a consultant to do a full audit and evaluate the operation of Barki Tojik and to recommend reforms for the company's method of operation. The firm Corporate Solutions was hired to prepare this report, and its findings were made publicly available in 2009.[48] The agreed-upon timetable for implementation is a very long one, with the last proposed reforms not being slated for introduction until 2018. What the report does not reveal is how much pressure was exerted by the Tajik side to get nearly a decade to introduce reforms to one of the country's most important state-owned entities, or how hard the ADB pushed to get a more rapid timetable of reform.

The impetus for this technical review was the failure of the Tajik government to make timely improvements in the operation of Barki Tojik on the basis of earlier and smaller technical assistance projects. At the time of the report, the annual value of hydroelectric output was just under five percent of the country's gross domestic product (4.7 percent). The end result was the much larger, and much more public, critical evaluation of Barki Tojik's performance, which was the prelude to what was effectively a donor-mandated restructuring of the company because of its seven major failings:

- The failure of the company to implement recommendations of earlier audits.

- Serious weaknesses in the company's accounting procedures.

- A lack of control over financial and business operations of the company.

- No internal audit department.

- Inadequate automation of accounting operations.

- The absence of a development strategy or a long-term plan.

- An organizational structure that was inconsistent with the scale of its operations.[49]

The report established a nine-year reform program for Barki Tojik, divided into three phases—commercialization, 2009–2012; competition, 2013–2015; and divestment, 2016–2018. This timetable means that the Tajik government is advocating plans for the development of massive new hydroelectric generating stations to be run by a largely unreformed government monopoly (that is, Barki Tojik). What's more, the major reforms and divestiture are designed to come before the most serious reforms have been implemented. And this timetable has not been contested by the international financial institutions that are expected to finance these projects.

The goals in the program's first phase were to create an organizational structure that divided the company by its three main functions (transmission, distribution, and generation); improve financial reporting and introduce reforms to the tariff charged and the legal foundation of the company; and improve the regulatory environment governing the electricity sector more generally.

In the program's second phase, Barki Tojik is to be reorganized, if the government considers it appropriate, into several state-owned but functionally independent enterprises, with links between these enterprises to be solely through supply contracts that will be monitored by a functioning regulatory system. And in the final phase, the government is supposed to seriously consider the prospect of privatizing the generation and distribution systems, with transmission to remain state-owned, but accessible to other interested players.[50]

To date, the management of Barki Tojik has focused on the restructuring of tariffs, and very little has been done to introduce systematic reforms in the administration of the company. An independent board of directors has not yet been appointed; furthermore, although the organizational schema now clearly lists the company by its three separate functions, functional accountability still rests with the company's director (whose functions have not changed appreciably since the end of the Soviet era).[51] No substantial changes have been made to the regulatory framework governing Tajikistan's energy sector, and Barki Tojik had until the end of 2011 to introduce Western accounting standards (unless of course it asked for and was granted an extension). It is unclear whether this goal has been achieved, because the most recent news on the Barki

Tojik website is from 2008–2009 (in English); the Russian language version of the site also still includes the 2008 audit but nothing more recent than that—although it does have various news items from 2012.[52]

The unreformed, or at best partly reformed, nature of Barki Tojik has made it far more difficult to successfully execute the piecemeal enhancements of the electric system that it has put forward as critical (some 20 projects in all).[53] These projects, for which funding is being sought from foreign investors, are in addition to electricity-sector modernization efforts already being supported through international loans and grants.

The World Bank has put considerable attention into trying to upgrade basic utility services for the Tajik population in general and for the poor in particular, with a number of projects specific to the electricity sector and many grouped under an Energy Loss Reduction Project. Here, too, in large part because of the scale of funding, a piecemeal approach has been applied. Much the same is true of funding by the ADB, which financed this sector through a Power Rehabilitation Project loan of $34 million in 2000.

EXPORTING ELECTRICITY FROM TAJIKISTAN

The development model that is being pursued by the Rahmon government is predicated on Tajikistan developing into a major electricity exporter. The country has placed great hopes on the CASA-1000 (CASA, standing for Central Asia South Asia) project, which is designed to take surplus electricity from Tajikistan and Kyrgyzstan and sell it in Afghanistan and Pakistan. Much of the funding for CASA-1000 will come from the ADB, which had hoped to have a new regional energy market fully functioning by 2016.[54] (This goal seems increasingly less realistic, as the major intergovernmental agreements have yet to be negotiated.) In the Tajik case, this would mean upgrading the Nurek hydroelectric station, getting Sangtuda 2 up to full capacity, and preventing the increase in the sedimentation that is found in the Nurek reservoir.

To date, these activities have yet to materialize, although Tajikistan is already providing some electricity to Afghanistan, including from a 220 kV line supplied by Sangtuda 1. Afghanistan has contracted for

Tajikistan's electricity at 2 cents per kWh, but for now Tajikistan only has surplus electricity to supply its neighbor in summers.[55] In the opinion of the World Bank, it will be impossible for Tajikistan to repay the loans for Sangtuda and Roghun (assuming it is built) without developing an export capacity. Without this, "the planned Sangtuda and Roghun projects could quickly lead to financial disaster."[56] It would be ideal, in their opinion, for Tajikistan to get firm guarantees from importing countries willing to buy electricity at the Tajik border. Moreover, the World Bank notes, that it would be ideal for Tajikistan to persuade Uzbekistan to take a stake in the planned investments, so that cheaper transit fees could be obtained.

It has been hard for Tajikistan to sell electricity to its Central Asian neighbors. Uzbekistan has not been buying from Tajikistan, and has put in large transit costs for relays of electricity across its territory. Kazakhstan has preferred to buy from Kyrgyzstan (which is closer, for one thing); furthermore a swap deal arranged with Tajikistan and Russia—through which the Tajiks would have "sold" electricity to Russia in return for debt relief (meaning Tajikistan would have supplied southern Kazakhstan with energy and Kazakhstan would have sent electricity from northern Kazakhstan into Russia)—fell apart because the Tajiks could not arrange access to the electricity grid going into southern Kazakhstan.

In the case of Tajikistan, the ADB has provided $21.5 million in loan money through the Tajikistan-Afghanistan Power Transmission Interconnection Project approved in 2006 (which funds the construction of a 220 kV double-circuit transmission line to link hydropower stations along the Tajik side of the Vakhsh River to Afghanistan through a grid that will cross at the border town of Sherkhan Bandar, and then further down to Kunduz and beyond).

Given the lack of security in Afghanistan and the challenges of nation-building there, plans for creating a unified regional electricity market to serve both Central Asia and South Asia are moving forward very slowly. The international financial institutions have begun focusing on rehabilitating Tajikistan's existing energy network and supplementing it with the development of small hydropower plants (which the EBRD is supporting).[57] A variety of solar and wind energy projects are also being experimented with, and the number of these projects seems certain to increase because Tajikistan is one of the countries included in a project by the ADB that is designed to support the development of renewable energy.

The legal environment to support renewable energy still needs strengthening, and is likely to await the restructuring of Barki Tojik, which opposes the right of communities to sell excess energy generated by renewable energy sources, even after Tajikistan's legislature passed a law on renewable energy in late 2009 that is designed to stimulate energy generation from renewables. From 2009 through 2011 the Tajik government has received financing to support feasibility studies and the eventual construction of 20 small hydropower plants and two medium-sized plants with capacities of 10 MW and 30 MW, respectively.

TAJIKISTAN'S GIANT DAMS

Central to the Tajik government's approach to solving the country's electricity problem are the completion of two Soviet-era hydroelectric plant projects and the expansion of the capacity of the country's third and longest-operating large hydroelectric plant. Some 95 percent of the hydroelectric power generated in Tajikistan comes from plants located on the Vakhsh River (which, along with the Pyanj River, serves as a tributary for the Amu Darya River). Soviet planners designed hydroelectric projects along the river to serve what they understood to be the mutually reinforcing needs of irrigation and electricity generation, using water released in summer for irrigation to generate electricity. More hydroelectric dams meant more irrigated land and more electricity for industrial projects, as well as electricity to support the pumps that drove the irrigation system. In all, three giant dams—Nurek, Sangtuda (consisting of two parts), and Roghun—were planned, as well as several smaller ones, which helped regulate the flow of the Vakhsh as much as providing more electricity.[58] Tajikistan also has the Kayrakkum reservoir on the Syr Darya River near the city of Khujand that generates electricity in summer, to provide for irrigation just beyond.

During the Soviet period, there was a common electric grid that encompassed southern Kazakhstan, Turkmenistan, Tajikistan, and Uzbekistan, which generated electricity seasonally by hydropower, gas, and coal, and fed into the grid from various electricity-generating stations throughout the region. All of this was centrally regulated though all-union Soviet ministries and individual republics had no real say in how much electricity they would generate each season and from what generating station. All drew from what was in effect a common electricity pool. Although the common grid was maintained at least in part for more than fifteen years, the control over which generating stations would produce how much electricity eventually fell to the countries themselves—who in turn struggled to make decisions on how to do this in concert.

When all the Tajik hydroelectric stations operate in summer, the country produces surplus electricity, which used to be "exported" to Uzbekistan, and now Tajikistan would like to sell it to foreign customers. In the past, the Uzbeks would swap the Tajik electricity and, in effect, irrigation water (which they used in the summer) for electricity sent to Tajikistan in the winter. But now Tashkent prefers to meet the country's electricity needs by itself. Less electricity is currently used, and Tashkent makes more money selling electricity and gas to the Tajiks.

Tajikistan signed an agreement with Turkmenistan in 2008, only to discover in January 2009 that the Uzbek government would not allow this electricity to be transported across Uzbekistan (through a series of swaps), and neither the Turkmen nor the Tajiks were willing to pay Uzbekistan transit fees for its relay. This created further pressures on the Nurek hydroelectric station (which serves northern Tajikistan), leading the Tajiks to generate some winter electricity, pushing down water levels nearest to the "dead" zone (that is, so low that electricity could no longer be generated), and forcing tighter electricity rationing for Sughd Oblast in January 2009. This effectively meant that industrial production in all but a handful of "strategic enterprises" ground to a halt for most of the first quarter of 2009.

Nurek

The Nurek hydroelectric station is the oldest major dam project on the Vakhsh River. Before the commission of Sangtuda 1, Nurek (along with the rest of the Nurek Baipaza hydropower cascade) produced 90 percent of Tajikistan's electrical energy. It is a large, earth-fill, 300-meter dam with a capacity of 3,000 MW (3 million kWh)—currently the largest in Central Asia. It has a reservoir of 10.5 million cubic meters, although there are estimates that up to 17 percent of its capacity has been lost through the accumulation of silt, which is also reducing its life expectancy by nearly thirty years.[59] The reservoir is designed to operate from a minimum level of 857 meters above sea level, with a normal pool level of 910 meters above sea level. The regulation storage of the conservation pool is 4,000 cubic kilometers.[60]

The project was proposed in 1959 and construction began in 1961, when the Soviet leadership was starting to look seriously at the economic potential of what was then still an economically underdeveloped region. Nurek helped spur Tajikistan's industrial development; among other things, it led to the opening of the country's aluminum factory and a new, large chemical factory, and created new possibilities for expanding irrigated agriculture. The hydroelectric station also seems to have operated at a profit, even in Soviet times, with the cost of the upkeep being about $60 million per year, and $150 million credited to the hydroelectric station as earned income for the electricity generated.[61]

In the post-Soviet period, it has become more difficult for the Nurek GES (hydroelectric station) to operate profitably. The Tajik Aluminum factory has been an undependable partner, producing far less aluminum than it did in the Soviet era—when the supply of raw materials for the factory was assured, transportation in and out of the republic was fully dependable, and electricity was available year-round (coming from Uzbekistan when Nurek was close to idle in the winter months). Today, the aluminum factory must wait for shipments of alumina to arrive (and getting it in by rail from Uzbekistan is not always easy), and then seek a sufficient supply of electricity from Barki Tojik for winter. In 2003, the cost of producing electricity was 0.3 cents per kWh, excluding transmission, while the average domestic retail price was 0.5 cents per kWh. But if Nurek has trouble generating profits, then all the newer hydroelectric projects will face much bigger challenges—given that they will have considerable construction costs that profits will need to offset.

Funding has been designated to rehabilitate the giant Nurek power station and to enhance its capacity. In fact, Nurek Dam is a potential moneymaker for the Tajik government, because the sunk costs of the investment were incurred during Soviet times. But Sangtuda (which is currently unfinished) needs pricing and demand that are higher than current levels to make a profit.[62]

In 2008, the ADB approved a $54.77 million grant to rehabilitate Nurek's 500 kV switchyard. Nurek GES could become something of a cash cow for Tajikistan, if electricity prices were raised and the company was reorganized as a free-standing, state-owned entity (rather than one that is fully subordinate to Barki Tojik). It is the judgment of the World Bank that Nurek's profits would best serve Tajikistan's interests if the money went directly into the state budget (rather than going toward Barki Tojik), where it just compensates the company for other losses. The World Bank argues that this money could go toward projects designed to help alleviate poverty or support infrastructure development, or could simply go toward enhancing the country's human capital.[63]

Sangtuda

The largest foreign direct investment project in Tajikistan to date is the Sangtuda 1 hydroelectric plant, a run-of-the-river project downstream of Nurek on the Vakhsh River that uses water released from the Nurek reservoir that flows through the Baipaz cascade. The installed capacity of the project is 670 MW, with an annual generating capacity of 2,700 gigawatt-hours. The project dates from 1986, when the USSR Ministry of Energy ordered a feasibility study, and a plan for the hydroelectric station prepared by the Hydroproject Institute in Tashkent was approved in 1988. Work on this project had not gone far when it was abandoned after the collapse of the Soviet Union; its completion requires an additional $483 million. Russia's RAO UES spent over $250 million, and the Russian Federation secured a further share in the project by agreeing to write off $299 million of Tajikistan's sovereign debt. For their part, the Tajiks contributed some construction material and labor.[64] Sangtuda also benefits from its location, in a relatively densely settled part of the Vakhsh River Valley (in contrast to Roghun), which has meant that a great deal of the infrastructure necessary for the project was already available. The average incremental cost of electricity for the project is $0.0197 per kWh, making it the most cost-efficient new hydroelectric project in not only Tajikistan, but in all of Central Asia.[65] But though cost-efficient in relationship to Roghun, or Kambarata in Kyrgyzstan, it is not priced at a recoverable cost basis.

The first three generating units of Sangtuda 1 were commissioned in 2008, and the fourth and final unit in May 2009. In the winter of 2008–2009, the opening of Sangtuda 1 meant that there was enough available electricity to provide one more hour per day to restricted areas, meaning that electricity was available from 6 to 9 a.m. and then again from 5:30 to 9:30 p.m. It is rather eerie to drive down rural roads and watch the countryside suddenly go dark; yet, most households do not have auxiliary electricity systems (such as gasoline power generators, or less frequently, solar panels) to draw upon.

The plan is for Sangtuda's energy to feed into the 500 kV line being constructed to reach the northern part of the country, as well as a 500–725 kV line that Tajikistan would like to construct to cross the Pyanj River into Afghanistan and then into Pakistan. So far, the latter plan is confined to the drawing boards.

The functioning of Sangtuda 1 has also been affected by unpaid debts in the electricity sector; in November 2009, the company had an operating deficit of 42 million somoni (nearly $10 million).[66] This bears out the judgment made by the World Bank in 2004, that the project would not be viable without substantial raises in the cost of electricity.

Construction of Sangtuda 2 hydroelectric station began in 2006 and was officially launched in September 2011, at a ceremony in which the presidents of both Iran and Tajikistan participated. While Sangtuda 2 will eventually be able to produce 1 billion kW of electricity (220 MW per year), at the time of launching it was able to only produce half of its ultimate capacity. The bulk of the funding for the project ($180 million) was provided by Iran, and $40 million by Tajikistan, which will not receive any revenues from the project for 12.5 years, until the cost of the project is repaid.[67]

Roghun

The Roghun Dam is to be built on a site 70 kilometers upstream from Nurek. Plans for the development of a giant hydroelectric station at Roghun date from the 1960s, and if constructed in the way that the Tajik government would like, it would be the tallest dam in the world—topping out at 335 meters (1,099 feet)—and would have a maximum potential generating capacity of 3,600 MW. The development of the Roghun project is expected to improve the functioning of Nurek as well, allowing it to generate more electricity (400 gigawatt-hours during the first stage of Roghun alone) and last longer, as it will reduce the speed with which silt builds up in the lower dam. Yet unlike Nurek (and Sangtuda, which is even further downstream), the size and location of Roghun's reservoir should allow year-round water flows and so would permit year-round electricity generation without disrupting irrigation further downstream.

The original project, based on a study done by Soviet engineers from 1965 to 1972, was endorsed by Gosplan (the State Planning Board of the USSR) in 1974, and finally approved by the Soviet Ministry of Energy in 1976. The Hydroproject Institute in Tashkent did the project design and construction plan. Construction went on throughout most of the 1980s, although work was halted at the end of the decade, after a 45 meter upstream embankment coffer dam and the diversion tunnels had already been built, because the project was deemed too expensive.[68] In 1993, the diversion tunnels were blocked by flooding and the embankment dam collapsed. What was left were several underground works; some temporary as well as some permanent roads; some power, water, and sewage systems; about 14 cubic meters of stockpiled construction materials; and the preparatory work for the reservoir.

The original project called for the development of a 335-meter clay core embankment dam, with a reservoir with a volume of 13.3 cubic kilometers with a spillway that consisted of an intake shaft, a tunnel, and an open chute as well as an underground power house with six turbines of 600 MW each, as well as an outdoor switchyard with a 500 kV transmission system. The project was initially intended to have a life span of fifty years, and was intended by Soviet planners to provide for unmet electricity demand of 10 billion kWh per year in Kazakhstan as well as 4.0 billion kWh in the northern part of Tajikistan (then Leninabad Oblast), as well as to meet energy needs in Afghanistan, with the intent of supplying a copper mine in Ainak that Soviet planners hoped to develop. In addition, Soviet planners expected the development of

Roghun to provide irrigation for 350,000 hectares of non-arable land in Uzbekistan and Turkmenistan.

In October 2004, RUSAL (Russian Aluminum) reached an agreement with the government of Tajikistan on plans for the construction of the Roghun hydroelectric station, in which RUSAL was to relaunch the Roghun project with a minimum of a $560 million investment (in return for shares in Roghun GES).[69] The expectation was that RUSAL would use the electricity from Roghun in the Tajikistan Aluminum plant (then known as TadAz), and expand production through the construction of a second plant alongside the first. The announcement was part of a deepening of the Tajik-Russian relationship, which was celebrated during joint press conferences of Russian president Vladimir Putin and Tajikistan's Emomali Rahmon, and which also involved Russia's RAO UES finishing the Sangtuda project.

RUSAL then hired Lahmeyer International of Germany to carry out a feasibility study of the project, which was completed in December 2006. One of the challenges that the Lahmeyer team had to confront is that the dam site is on a seismically active region, and the site itself is framed by two (third-order) faults—the Ionakhsh fault (which is found upstream of the site) and the Gulizindan fault (which is located downstream of the site). Both are reverse faults and create the risk of cumulative displacements. This is one of the reasons that the Lahmeyer group recommended that Roghun be built with an underground power house on the left bank of the river using the cavern left from the original project, as well as adding a 175 meter start-up dam that is integrated with the main dam and facilitates starting up three years sooner than in the original plan. The 2006 version of the project also calls for the building of tailrace tunnels, which were not a feature of the Soviet-era plan. These new features, as well as a redesigned spillway, are intended to give the Roghun Dam an enhanced capacity to manage flooding, which if unchecked, puts the stability of the embankment dam at risk. The geology of Roghun's site makes the construction of adequate spillways quite challenging. The Lahmeyer version of the project assumes the same need to resettle 715 families as in the original Soviet era project, with the simultaneous loss of the agricultural lands that they worked and grazed livestock on.

The Lahmeyer group recommended that the project be built follow-ing the example of Nurek, which is located in a geographically similar area to Roghun, as a rock-fill embankment dam. The seismological risk at Roghun, however, may be somewhat greater, as that is where the Ionakhsh fault crosses the reservoir and is submerged, and the study admits that the risk of earthquakes up to 6.6 on the Richter scale must be considered a real one.[70] Roland Schmidt, the senior project engineer, wrote:

> Taking into account the heterogeneous bedrock with hori-zons of low shear strength and in view of the present active faults, a conservatively designed embankment dam with clay core was identified as the preferred option, as this involves the least amount of uncertainties in design and construction. Embankment dams have a high resilience to foundation defor-mations and are therefore better suited than a brittle concrete dam or a CFRD [concrete-faced rock-fill dam].[71]

The Lahmeyer report says that the optimal installed capacity for Roghun is 2,400 MW, to be obtained through three (Francis) turbines to be installed during stage one (when the lower dam is to be completed), and a final turbine at stage two—for a total of four rather than six turbines, as called for in the original Soviet plans. Most importantly the dam is projected to be only 235 meters at stage one, rising to a maximum height of 285 meters, as the project engineers in the Lahmeyer project argued that constructing a higher dam would yield only a marginal increase in profit for the eventual hydroelectric station but would cost a great deal more to construct.

The choice of a rock-fill embankment entails the highest construction costs, leading to unit costs of $0.039 per kWh (with a discounted rate of 8.5 percent) for stage one and $0.025 per kWh when stages one and two are combined, with an economic internal rate of return that goes from 11 percent for stage one to 16 percent if both stages are completed.[72] Stage one calls for a dam with a height of 225 meters, with a total reservoir volume of 2.78 cubic kilometers, a live storage capacity of 1.92 cubic kilometers, and an energy output of 5.6 TWh. Stage two would have a reservoir volume of 6.78 cubic kilometers and a live storage capacity of 3.98 cubic kilometers. Construction at the third stage, up to 335 meters, which the original plan called for (and the Tajik government still wants), would create a reservoir with a volume of 13.3 cubic kilometers and a live storage capacity of 10.3 kilometers. This reservoir would effectively control the entire flow of the Vakhsh River, whereas constructing the dam to a height of 285 meters would leave 40 percent of the mean annual flow of the river uncontrolled. It is impossible to imagine a scenario in which the Uzbek government would consent to such a situation; the 285-meter dam would likely be more acceptable to Uzbek authorities, as the Vakhsh River only accounts for 25 percent of the total flow of the Amu Darya, so roughly only 15 percent of the Amu Darya's flow would be restricted; see figure 7.3.[73]

FIGURE 7.3
ROGHUN HEIGHTS

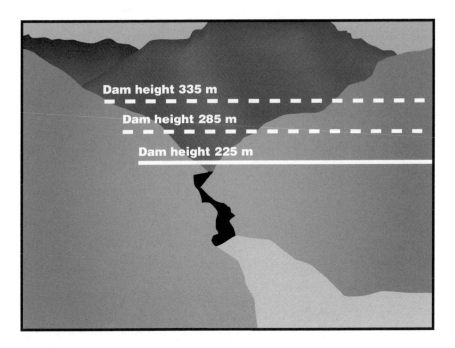

Roland Schmidt, "Prodolzheniye stroitel'stva Rogunskoy GES v Tadzhikistane: otsenka osushchestvimosti proekta," *Gidrosooruzheniya,* 2008: 1, 22.

Roland Schmidt also clearly states that Lahmeyer's understanding was that permission of the neighboring states must be sought for this project:

> According to definitions by international financing institutions, the Vakhsh River as a tributary of the Amu Darya is a transboundary river, and as such, is beyond exclusive control by a single party. In line with regional and international interstate agreements on the use of water resources, Tajikistan should notify and consult with the downstream states before modifying the Vakhsh River's hydrology. The successful initiation of such a notification process is a prerequisite for safeguarding financing of the project and its implementation.[74]

RUSAL (through the agency of Rusal Servis) began a season (2006–2007) of preparatory work at the site of the Roghun Dam in 2006, only to be formally notified by Barki Tojik in October 2006 that it was to cease all work on the project. Relations between Tajikistan and RUSAL continued to sour throughout that year, and on August 29, 2007, the Office of the President of Tajikistan informed RUSAL that the agreement for long-term cooperation with the company had been annulled.

A number of issues separated the Tajik government from RUSAL. The most public of these issues was the dispute over the height of the dam, which RUSAL said could be brought up to 335 meters if the Tajik government wanted to pay for the difference in project costs. Others included the construction design and materials (RUSAL wanted to build a concrete dam, despite Lahmeyer's recommendation of rock and clay), and the future ownership of the Roghun hydroelectric station (of which the government of Tajikistan apparently wanted a 50 percent share, as opposed to the 10 percent share said to be RUSAL's offer).[75]

After RUSAL was told to stop working on the project, the Tajik government announced in October 2006 that it planned to move forward with the development of the Roghun hydroelectric station on its own—including raising the $1.37 billion for the project's construction. But in 2007, Tajikistan said that it would accept World Bank funding for the environmental and technical feasibility studies related to the project, triggering a set of international consultations with all the riparian states on the Amu Darya River that continues to this day.

In an effort to save both the project and peace in the region, the World Bank has made an unprecedented effort at consultation with all the states that could potentially have an impact on the project—with particular effort to respond to the Uzbek government's concerns, which were expressed in a series of bilateral and multilateral consultations on the project in 2008 (the content of which has been publicized).[76]

In March 2010, the World Bank's terms of reference for the two feasibility studies were accepted by the various countries affected by the project, with Tajikistan nonetheless pressing for an additional, broader environmental study to examine water usage patterns in the region more generally.[77] This is not likely to occur under the terms of the current project being tendered—particularly since the World Bank has already funded two different feasibility studies.

The first of these studies is a techno-economic assessment being carried out by Coyne et Bellier. The second is an environmental assessment that relates specifically to the risks associated with the Roghun project (but not with water usage patterns more generally) by Poyry Energy Ltd. The work of each will be reviewed by an independent board of experts (all with international reputations) that will evaluate the final findings, which are expected in late 2012. There are regular meetings to review interim results, to which all the riparian states are invited. These results are also being made available on the World Bank's website.[78]

The Tajik government has engaged with the World Bank in its efforts, but it has not backed off its plan to use Tajik expertise and a modification of the Soviet-era plan to build the project on its own if international assistance is not forthcoming. The Tajik plans have seriously harmed the country's relationship with Uzbekistan, leading to "unrelated" rail stoppages that have made trading with and by Tajikistan very difficult.

This became a priority in 2009, when a national campaign was launched to facilitate the sale of shares in the project to the population of the country, which anecdotal information strongly suggests was effectively a program of compulsory purchase. The Tajik government maintains that it can construct the first phase of Roghun for $1.4 billion, or 24 percent of the 2010 gross domestic product, of which $600 million would need to be spent on imports. Its intent is to fund this through the establishment of the Roghun OJSC (Open Joint Stock Company), 75 percent of whose shares would be held by the government and 25 percent (1.5 billion somoni or $315 million) through the public "offering," of which 800 million somoni ($168 million) had already been collected by March 2010.[79] By that time, the funds were formally being supervised by a board headed by the prime minister, government officials, and representatives of other equity shareholders. Initially, the collected funds were simply turned over to the government to be accounted for in the same manner as all other income. The nationwide collection campaign, which was discontinued in April 2010, targeted all sectors for specific contributions; school and hospital directors were asked to get their employees to contribute between 500 and 5,000 somoni apiece, depending upon their monthly salary, and there were reports of government employees who refused to donate being fired from their jobs.[80]

The International Monetary Fund complained that this nationwide campaign of stock purchases would decrease the country's economic growth rate by up to one percent for each year collected, including declines in household consumption and corporate investment.[81] Some 45 million somoni ($9.45 million) per month were alleged to have been spent on the project in 2009. In its May 2010 country report, the IMF urged Tajikistan to set a ceiling on equity sales and contributions to Roghun OJSC.[82]

There is still no reliable estimate of the Roghun project's cost, which will depend upon the final design and the cost of materials. But the Tajik government is already spending money on the project, albeit less money than has been collected; the government budgeted approximately $148 million (650 million somoni) for 2010, half the money that was collected, and half of this had been spent by mid-year. The public campaign to collect money for Roghun was largely suspended in April 2010, with some 25 million somoni ($5.25 million) being collected in the four months following the suspension.[83] When the 2010 data for Roghun were eventually published (later than required by the World Bank's terms[84]), it revealed that of the roughly 1.46 billion somoni ($330 million) collected, over 567 million somoni ($121 million) was collected from the population, over 41 million somoni ($8.7 million) from banks, and 185 million somoni ($39.4 million) from enterprises buying shares in Roghun.

There were also data provided on how the money was spent, listing which companies were paid for tasks that were allegedly related to Roghun, but no data that met international accounting norms.[85]

It is hard to believe that Tajikistan can undertake the Roghun project on its own, particularly when it comes to raising all the needed funds—estimated at $2.1 billion by the World Bank in 2004, more than the country's gross domestic product that year—without going to international financial institutions.[86] Yet these institutions will only grant funds for a project whose costs are recoverable over an acceptable loan period, and that is developed and implemented according to international norms, which would mean addressing the transboundary water issues.

Nonetheless, Tajikistan's government continues to make plans to proceed with the Roghun project on a timetable of its own choosing. It has announced plans to start operating the first two turbines by 2012–2013, and to use the money it would raise to complete the remaining four turbine generators.[87] The key element contributing to the accomplishment of this timing is the first diversion of the rivers necessary to build the dam. This has been delayed several times, but the Tajik government has warned the World Bank that it had initially planned to start the process in November 2011, roughly a year before the feasibility study on environmental impact was likely to be completed.[88]

Tajik plans for the Roghun project were met with a strong rebuff from the World Bank, whose experts warned that the construction of the first stage (the 120-meter dam) should not begin until the final dam project is approved; aside from being uneconomical, the current high level of sedimentary materials in the Vakhsh River needs to be addressed in the final project.[89] The World Bank reported that Tajik officials agreed to accept this recommendation, as well as that no further communities would be relocated from the Tajik government's proposed project path until a final decision about the dam was made.[90] The Tajik press, however, reported demands from Tajik experts that the project should move forward along the government's own schedule, providing evidence of Tajik government displeasure.[91] The World Bank's December 2011 announcement related to the Roghun project made clear that no decision had been made about the dam's final height and that all options remained under consideration by the international experts.[92] The Tajik authorities are also threatening that they will begin construction themselves if there are delays in the release of the expert reports.

The release of the reports is likely to present difficult choices for Tajikistan, and quite likely for Uzbekistan as well. If the World Bank–funded technical reports lead to the formation of an international consortium to move the project forward, then Uzbekistan's concerns are likely to be at least partially mollified by World Bank–supported development projects designed to mitigate the negative effect on the Uzbek economy (that changes to water flows linked to the dam's construction and operation might possibly bring). The challenge will be if the Tajiks move forward with the development of Roghun before a technical report is issued, or outside the guidelines that it might provide.

Many believe that the Tajiks lack the expertise to move forward with the Roghun project in a manner that would permit its construction according to international norms, and in ways that would not put the environment at risk. Such critics note that the Soviet-era dam project was being built by technical elites who came from the entire USSR, and that since the collapse of the Soviet Union, Tajikistan has suffered one of the worst brain drains in the region.[93] And the Uzbek authorities have made clear that the version of the project that the Tajik government has proposed will have a detrimental effect on the Uzbek economy, even under its more positive scenarios.[94]

TELECOMMUNICATIONS

Yet the energy sector is not alone in its lack of infrastructure. Tajikistan's economic development is also hampered by a lack of reform in the area of telecommunications, which is covered by the 2002 Law on Electric Communications. The sector is still formally regulated by the State Service on Supervision and Regulation in Communications and Information (SSRCI) (which is subordinated to the Ministry of Transportation), and thus lacks the independence that the legislation envisioned. In addition to the SSRCI, the telecommunications sector is also subject to the State Committee on Radio Frequencies and the Antimonopoly Agency, which has some responsibility for setting and supervising tariffs. Tajiktelekom is the state-owned (90 percent state, 10 percent employee held) operator of local, long-distance, and international telephone and Internet services; yet, as figure 7.4 shows, penetration of Tajikistan by fixed telephone service is quite low.[95] By contrast, the mobile phone subsector—which is served by several independent providers (all of which are part of joint ventures—is increasing in size, with over 1 million subscribers reported in 2009.[96] Unlike Tajiktelekom's landlines, mobile phones provide access even in remote areas, and prices are more affordable—due to competition among service providers.

FIGURE 7.4
MOBILE CELLULAR SUBSCRIPTIONS, INTERNET USERS, AND TELEPHONE LINES

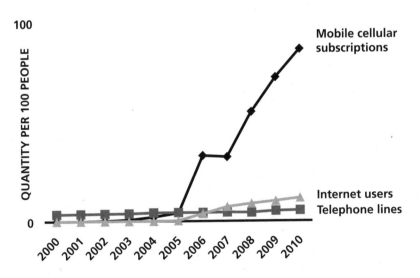

Source: World Bank Data, http://data.worldbank.org/country/tajikistan?display=default.

TRANSPORTATION

The country's transportation sector has also faced its share of changes since independence. Moving around Tajikistan has gotten easier in the past few years, especially by road and by air; the Central Asia Regional Economic Cooperation (CAREC), the ADB's subunit that works on enhancing economic cooperation among the region's states, has ambitious plans for Tajikistan as it develops its seven major transit corridors to more readily link this part of the world with Europe and Asia. Tajikistan has received substantial international assistance in the reconstruction of its road and highway system, and if the CAREC program is fully realized, there will be much more, as shown in figure 7.1.

Under the CAREC program, Tajikistan is slated for transportation improvements in Corridor 3, which includes a strengthened road link from Herat across to Hairiston (in Afghanistan), into Uzbekistan, and then to Tajikistan, crossing the country and going on to Kyrgyzstan, then from Kazakhstan to the Chinese border. Corridor 5 calls for a strengthened road link from Torkham, Afghanistan, to the Tajik border at Nizhniy Pyanj and across Tajikistan to China to join the Chinese railway system at Kashi, China. (China has announced long-term plans to extend the reach of its rail links across Kyrgyzstan, Tajikistan, Afghanistan, and on to Iran.)[97] The road at Torkham connects to the Pakistan highway system and eventually goes to the port of Karachi. Corridor 6 also begins at Torkham, and into Tajikistan at Nizhniy Pyanj, crossing Tajikistan and entering Kyrgyzstan just beyond Jirgatal, then through Kyrgyzstan and Kazakhstan to link with the Russian road and rail system.[98]

Tajikistan currently has some 30,000 kilometers of roads, and even the newly reconstructed roadways still would not be considered highways by any sort of European or U.S. standard. The ADB awarded the government of Tajikistan some $20 million in 2000 for a Road Rehabilitation Project, which was designed to address the roads most damaged by the civil war, including the road from Dushanbe to Kulyab—which in 2010 was still not fully rehabilitated (although enormous improvements were evident along much of the route).

The ADB has also supported substantial reforms of the country's transportation network—including the Tajikistan–Kyrgyzstan Border

Road Rehabilitation Project, allocating $15 million to the first phase in 2005 and an additional $30 million to the route in 2005. This project receives additional funds from China, as it is designed to improve Tajikistan's transportation links with Kyrgyzstan and China, as well as further north to Kazakhstan and on to Russia. The impulse for the latter project is largely the result of the difficulty of moving goods from Tajikistan through Uzbekistan (via Khujand to Tashkent and then north to Shymkent, Kazakhstan. But as figure 7.1 makes clear, the high elevations of these routes makes them non-optimal for heavy freight, and multi-ton cargo trucks further have accelerated their normal weather-related deterioration.

The EBRD has estimated that Tajikistan is losing some $50 million in road assets annually due to poor maintenance and weather conditions that cause mountain roads in particular to wash away during annual mudslides.[99] It is hard to describe just how bad Tajikistan's roads are, but journeys of eight or more hours to go up toward the Kyrgyz border, 12 to 16 hours between Dushanbe and Khorog (Gorno-Badakhshan) (272 km as the crow flies, and 1014 km by road) up to 14 hours between Dushanbe and Khujand (759 km) are the norm. The timelines required for these trips will be cut by about a third when the new tunnels (completed in 2009, but by 2010 already under repair) are finally reopened. The international financial institutions and bilateral donors are supporting a number of major infrastructure projects. These include the Khujand–Dushanbe road, which has been rebuilt by a number of donors, including Iran and China. One wonders, however, given the corruption that seems rampant in some of these road works, whether the new highways will last more than a few years at their most difficult passage points (the experience of the Khujand–Dushanbe road is indicative of this). This author has traveled a new highway being built between Garm and Jirgatal, along a section that was being financed through Chinese assistance; the asphalt was being laid on dirt roadbed, without crushed rock or any other sort of stabilizer—which ironically even the Soviet-era road that it is replacing had.

Although road maintenance requires regular attention in any country, the challenge of keeping Tajikistan's highways in good working order seems likely to continue to overwhelm the Tajik government. In addition to normal wear and tear, exacerbated by poor construction quality, Tajikistan has also faced a series of environmental disasters (fortunately, in recent years, these have generally been quite localized), which have also created transportation challenges and have forced the government to increase the country's loan burden to try to meet them. For example, in October 2007 the ADB approved a $2 million Japan Fund Poverty Reduction Grant to reconstruct a bridge in northeast Tajikistan that had been washed away due to flooding in 2006; the lack of said bridge had left a number of rural communities without any modern road connections to the rest of the country.

Beyond roadways, Tajikistan has approximately 480 kilometers of railroad track, made up of separate southern and northern lines, both of which cross Uzbekistan, but do not intersect; see figure 7.1. The railroad system, too, is beset by problems, and in mid-November 2011 the southern line was shut down, possibly permanently, after an explosion on the Uzbek side of the tracks. There is speculation that the Uzbeks were themselves the source of this alleged terrorist act, as it gave them an excuse to permanently cut off this rail spur.[100] Other concerns are caused by the generally problematic state of Uzbek-Tajik relations, as Tajikistan's international freight goes through Uzbekistan—which has periodically halted freight traffic into the country. This has been a particular problem since the opening of the Northern Distribution Network to transport goods from the Baltic Sea ports by rail to near the Afghan border.

Overall, between 1995 and 2002 the railway's productivity declined by 60 percent, largely as a result of a 50 percent decline in shipments at the same time that there was a 20 percent increase in personnel. But the decline in freight traffic is also a reflection of the sad state of the Tajik rail system, which urgently requires investment in both repairs and modernization.[101]

The Tajiks hope that their rail transportation issues will be solved by Chinese investment in a new transcontinental rail link through Kyrgyzstan, Tajikistan, and Afghanistan to Iran, and the construction of a projected rail line across Afghanistan that would link their country with Turkmenistan's railroad lines, giving them an additional link to Europe that would bypass Uzbekistan.

The Tajik air transportation system presents an even bigger problem—largely the result of the government's refusal to engage in serious negotiations with most international providers, preferring that the income from air travel go almost exclusively to Tajik Air (formerly a state-owned company) and Somoni Air (a private company that is rumored to be owned by leading Tajik officials or their families). Over the past few years, Somoni Air has become the virtual monopolist of Tajik international travel, introducing six Boeing aircraft and new routes. Turkish Airlines has twice-weekly flights into Dushanbe Airport, which is also served by some minor Russian private air companies (UTair and S 7) and by Kazakhstan's Air Astana. Yet, a major increase in air travel to the country is also dependent upon the much-needed and frequently delayed reform of Dushanbe Airport—a project initially planned to proceed with funding from the government of France, which was using the airport's runways to support its NATO operations in Afghanistan. Now, however, French forces no longer use the airport.

Most air freight coming into the country goes through the Tajik Air State Unitary Aviation Enterprise (of which Tajik Air is a part), which has an aging air fleet and substandard auxiliary services both for system maintenance and equipment repair, and for training of personnel. The country's air traffic control system and ground facilities are also outdated. Tajik Air's freight and passenger lines charge high rates for cargo and tickets, respectively, and are generally the highest-priced in the region. With respect to passenger travel, the privately owned Somoni Air has taken over some of Tajik Air's routes, using leased equipment and flight attendants from a private South Korean company. Migrant workers are a lucrative and vulnerable market. As a result of what is an effectively captive market, getting airline tickets in Tajikistan is frequently a costly and time-consuming process, as many high-demand routes sell out mysteriously on the day of issue, tickets can only be obtained from private travel agents who can charge up to two or three times the face value.

The Tajik government set very modest goals for its rail and air transportation sector, seeking to increase freight passenger traffic by 12.6 and 4.7 percent, respectively, in its Poverty Reduction Strategy for 2007–2009.[102] Despite the modest nature of the goals, the reforms in the air transportation sector have been viewed by the World Bank as very successful, because it is virtually the only instance in which a vertically integrated state monopoly has been broken up; Tajik Air has been divided into six separate firms with different functional responsibilities. Most importantly, the airport, the airline, and air traffic control were all separated. The Ministry of Transportation informed the World Bank in 2010 that all the new firms were servicing their debt and paying dividends to the government in a timely fashion, and were generally able to offer higher salaries as well.[103] In addition to the division of Tajik Air, the World Bank provided technical assistance to introduce more modern technical regulations in the air transportation sector and to improve accident investigation.[104] There was also a nearly threefold increase in the number of flights per week served by Dushanbe Airport, and a similar increase in the number of passengers traveling through the airport; despite the increases, however, in 2010 there were still only 175 flights per week passing through Dushanbe Airport.[105] (This is a strikingly low figure if one recalls that air travel is the primary means of connection between Dushanbe and the country's second-largest city, Khujand, as well as between Dushanbe and Khorog). All successes aside, the World Bank's concern that Tajikistan's government still places significant restrictions on foreign carriers in order to assure the dominance of the country's two airlines continues. The EBRD has sought to support the development of new infrastructure for this sector, targeting civil aviation—including air navigation, airports, and air carriers—but has had only limited success in its efforts to rehabilitate and modernize the sector in order to make it financially viable—with each subsector becoming financially independent. It has had some success in contributing to the commercial viability of Khujand Airport—which was a minor facility in Soviet times, but does offer local residents some international services and regular connections to Dushanbe. Until 2010, Khujand residents faced a 12- to 16-hour drive to Dushanbe to get international air service, as the visa regime with Uzbekistan made the Tashkent airport (approximately 2 hours away by road) effectively unavailable.

The EBRD has additionally helped fund the modernization of the civil navigation system, but has had far more limited success in unbundling Tajik Air State Unitary Aviation Enterprise, which continues to have a role in all three sectors. The EBRD had initially planned to support a Tajik State Air Fleet Modernization Project—which was signed in 2005, but canceled in 2007—but backed away because of the inability to get Tajik State Air to unbundle its holdings.

CONCLUSION

For now at least, Tajikistan's economic plans far outstrip its infrastructural capacity, as well as the international funding available to improve it. Critical to many of these plans is Tajikistan's desire to develop new export markets to be served by its vast hydroelectric potential. But the most important of these projects, the construction of the Roghun hydroelectric station (with the world's highest dam at 335 meters, if the Tajik government gets its way), is still pending the results of international studies organized by the World Bank, which are to report on the optimal size of this project and its economic and environmental feasibility.

The number of smaller projects designed to alleviate Tajikistan's own chronic energy shortages are also to be funded by various international agencies. But their ultimate success will depend upon the willingness of the Tajik government to reform the country's electricity monopolist, Barki Tojik, which is still a very non-transparent government-run and -owned company.

Tajikistan's transportation system is slowly being improved, but the prevalence of graft and corruption that has been characteristic of many of the new construction projects is sufficient to call into question how long many of these projects will be viable without substantial additional investment. It is hard to see, however, whether this investment will be forthcoming without a substantial increase in trade both in and through Tajikistan; this increase in turn will partly depend upon the success of new infrastructure projects, and the reform of the energy sector more generally. Because Tajikistan's infrastructure is potentially of importance to Afghanistan and Pakistan, increasing security and economic prosperity in these two neighboring countries would spark new investments in Tajikistan. But lacking this, only those international actors with a direct financial interest such as China (if it continues to develop natural resources in and around Tajikistan) will be willing to make substantial investments to upgrade Tajikistan's relevant infrastructure.

CHAPTER 8

WOMEN, CHILDREN, FOOD, AND SOCIAL SAFETY

T he Tajik government has found it increasingly more difficult to maintain Soviet-era social safety nets, such as free education, free health care, adequate pensions, and help for the country's non-able bodied population. Tajikistan's already-strained social services and support networks were stretched beyond capacity during the harsh winter of 2007–2008 and further put to the test by the global financial and economic crisis that followed shortly after, when the country's industrial output dropped by 13 percent in the first half of 2009, largely due to the drop in the price of aluminum, one of its principal exports.

The international community has only been willing and able to go part way toward helping Tajikistan meet its burgeoning social needs. Although the country was the subject of an international appeal in 2007–2008, competition for international grant support and foreign assistance has since increased, and revelations of the misappropriation of funds by the National Bank of Tajikistan have made some potential donors wary and prone to look for more worthy candidates.

The global crisis has made it harder for the Tajik government to maintain and increase its social protection programs, such as those that are designed to provide financial relief to poorer households faced with rising utility costs or help low-income households keep their children in school.[1] The 30 percent decline in remittances (compared to 2007), led the World Bank to project that the poverty headcount in Tajikistan would increase.[2]

At the same time, Tajikistan's position on the United Nations Human Development Index has continued to drop, from 103 (of 162 countries ranked) in 2001 to 122 in 2006, but then increased to 112 (of 169) by 2010.[3] The World Bank's 2007 Tajikistan Living Standards Survey—for which data were first issued in 2009—reports that the country experienced a per capita consumption growth rate at the national level of 7.5 percent for the period of 2003–2007 (between the two surveys), with faster growth rates in urban areas (9.9 percent) than in rural areas (6.6 percent). The highest growth rates were in Gorno-Badakhshan Autonomous Oblast, at 22.8 percent (but this underpopulated region only accounts for 3 percent of the country's total population, and is the recipient of the Aga Khan's beneficence), and Khatlon (President Rahmon's home region), with 13.4 percent. In contrast, Dushanbe and the Region of Republican Subordination surrounding it grew by only 5.3 and 3.4 percent, respectively, and Sughd (in northern Tajikistan, which adjoins Uzbekistan's Ferghana Valley) grew by 5.9 percent.[4] This improvement in the standard of living is reflected in the fact that 55 percent of the households surveyed in 2007 reported that their financial situation had improved over the past three years.[5]

This growth (which preceded the economic crisis of 2008–2009) benefited the poorer sections of the population disproportionately, because the poverty headcount (as measured by those living on less than $2.15 per day, at purchasing power parity) dropped from 64 percent in 2003 to 41 percent in 2007, with 1.3 million people (including 1 million in rural areas) "escaping" poverty in this period, and this despite an increase in population of roughly 0.4 million. This still left a rural poverty headcount of 54 percent in 2007 (down from 72 percent in 2003).[6] There was also a substantial decrease in the percentage of the population living in extreme poverty during this same period, overall from 41.5 to 17.1 percent (dropping in urban areas from 39.4 to 18.9 percent, and in rural areas from 42.3 to 16.4 percent). In fact, 73.7 percent of the country's total population lives in rural areas, and 75.7 percent of its poor people live in rural areas, indicating that the rural population is slightly poorer than the urban population (in terms of income). However, the rural lifestyle tends to be substantially harsher, with far less access to government and social services in general (quality social services, in particular). Sughd had the highest incidence of poverty in the country, with 38.1 percent of the poor population, and 29.1 percent of the overall population. Khatlon was the next poorest region,[7] with 31.5 percent of all poor people and 35.7 percent of the overall population.[8] In Sughd, the rural population was poorer than the urban population (with poverty headcount rates of 74.0 and 53.6 percent, respectively), whereas in Khatlon and the RRS the poverty headcount rates were higher among the urban population than among the rural population (respectively, 52.5 percent compared with 46.2 percent; and 56.8 percent compared with 47.6 percent).[9] The percentage of the population that was "dissatisfied with their financial situation" in the 2007 TLSS was 56.9 percent, very close to the proportion (53.5 percent) of "consumption poor" in the national poverty assessment.[10]

The World Bank defined the poverty line as an income of 139 somoni per month per person,[11] or $46 in 2007 values,[12] and extreme poverty as 89 somoni ($30) per month, which was seen as the cost of the typical food basket necessary for a diet of 2,250 calories per day. This latter figure is just below the median monthly income in the agricultural sector from 2007 (which was 80 somoni, or $27), and is more than 30 percent higher than the median 54 somoni ($18) per month earned in in-kind or barter payments by unpaid family workers.[13] Median monthly salaries in the state-owned enterprises were 139 somoni ($46) (just at the poverty level); for those in the public sector more generally, 172 somoni ($57); and in the private sector, 178 somoni ($59).[14]

The difference between the figures for poverty and extreme poverty was $16, and it goes without saying that few readers would want to live on the food value of 2,250 calories that this amount of money buys. In-kind contributions obviously play an important role in helping fill the food baskets of all Tajiks, which is why extreme poverty is slightly more prevalent in urban areas, where the poor must purchase a larger portion of their food. The mean per capita consumption in Tajikistan was 157 somoni per month (or $52) in 2007.[15]

The World Bank has done simulations to estimate the impact of the global financial crisis on poverty rates in Tajikistan, using two separate models—one based on straight declines of remittance rates, and the other on the loss of remittance rates being partially offset by people seeking increased employment locally. Using the first model, the World Bank finds that overall poverty will increase from 53.1 to 57.9 percent, with a 30 percent drop in remittances, which is in fact approximately the loss in income that Tajikistan's population experienced in the aftermath of the 2007 crisis. With the second simulation model, the total poverty rate was estimated to be 55.7 percent. The urban/rural poverty ratios based on the models were 52.6 and 59.7, and 51.1 and 57.3, respectively. With a 30 percent drop in remittances, the Gini coefficient (the measure of income inequality) would increase from 32.1 to 35.1 percent.[16] The poorest population in the GBAO tended to be those living in villages above 2,000 meters in elevation.

Most disturbing is the fact that 58 percent of the poor are from families in which the head of household is employed, with wage earners in the agricultural sector faring the poorest. Some 58.3 percent of the nation's poor come from this category of family, as do 16.3 percent of those living in extreme poverty. Among those employed in industries other than agriculture, 47.8 percent were living in poverty and 13.2 percent in extreme poverty. Among those who claimed to be unemployed, 60.4 percent were living in poverty and 21.0 percent in extreme poverty. Self-employed individuals working in agriculture appeared to fare only slightly better, with 52.7 and 18.9 percent respectively living in poverty and extreme poverty. Among the self-employed outside of agriculture, 44.8 percent were living in poverty and 13.7 percent in extreme poverty.[17] The presence of labor migrants in a family seems to only begin to mitigate poverty if those working outside the country contribute more than 20 percent of the total household earnings; otherwise, their contributions are generally not large enough to create a poverty profile that is different from that of the general population.[18]

According to 2007 poverty indicators collected by the Tajik government, approximately 53 percent of the total population was still living in poverty (49.3 percent in urban areas, and 54.4 percent in rural areas, with the overall 53 percent figure reflecting the rural nature of Tajikistan's population)—of whom more than 17 percent were living in extreme poverty (18.9 percent in urban areas, and 16.9 percent in rural areas), and this was before the impact of the global economic crisis of 2007–2008 was felt. As table 8.1 demonstrates, the proportion on the population said to be living in poverty can change substantially based on the level at which the poverty line is set. The situation was worst in Sughd (formerly Khujand) Oblast, where 69.4 percent of the total population (74.3 percent of the rural population) lived in poverty and 31.8 percent (34.3 percent of the rural population) lived in extreme poverty.[19] Not surprisingly, Sughd is one of the areas where a significant portion of the population has left to work in other countries. The 2007 TLSS concluded that wages accounted for 44 percent of a household's income on average; home-produced goods, 27 percent; and income from working abroad, 17 percent (table 8.2). 55 percent of the "income" of households in the two poorest income quintiles came from home production.[20]

TABLE 8.1
VARIATION IN POVERTY INCIDENCE CORRESPONDING TO CHANGES IN THE POVERTY LINE

CHANGE IN THE POVERTY LINE (%)	POPULATION LIVING IN POVERTY (%)	POPULATION LIVING IN EXTREME POVERTY (%)
−20	33.8	7.4
−10	44.5	12.0
−5	49.0	14.4
Current poverty line	53.5	17.1
+5	58.6	20.2
+10	62.6	23.3
+20	69.4	29.7

Source: World Bank, *Tajikistan: Poverty Assessment*, December 3, 2009, 5.

TABLE 8.2

BREAKDOWN OF HOUSEHOLD DISPOSABLE INCOME (percent)

SOURCE OF INCOME	RURAL	URBAN	TOTAL
WAGES	39.4	56.2	43.7
SOCIAL ASSISTANCE	2.4	3.5	2.6
PRIVATE TRANSFERS	1.1	2.7	1.5
CONSUMPTION OF OWN PRODUCE	30.0	17.4	26.8
NET INCOME FROM AGRICULTURE	6.8	1.2	5.4
INCOME FROM WORKING ABROAD	17.9	14.8	17.1
OTHER INCOME	2.4	4.1	2.9
TOTAL	100	100	100

Source: World Bank, *Tajikistan: Poverty Assessment*, December 3, 2009, 30.

Pensions and Other Social Assistance Programs

Barely one percent of the poorest quintile of Tajikistan's population is adequately covered by social assistance programs. This compares with roughly 30 percent in both Georgia and Kyrgyzstan, both considered very poor countries.[21] The government has repeatedly pressed for additional international assistance in this area, after having reported that it was only able to support 34.71 percent of the most basic needs in this sector under the Poverty Reduction Strategy for 2007–2009.[22] However, Tajikistan's high indebtedness and general lack of a track record in the sphere of social assistance (in part because of the low level of technical capacity of many in the appropriate government bureaucracies) has left much of the mandate in this sector unfunded.

Tajikistan's social protection system is based on a pay-as-you-go pension system, with benefits that are so low that it creates a strong incentive for evasion of social welfare payments by those earning any sort of decent wages. Limited disability payments are provided, along with some financial benefits to poorer schoolchildren. Electricity and gas compensation for the poor, at best, exists on paper, and at worst, is designed as a way to shift revenues to the state-owned utilities, which then provide free service to those qualifying households that apply for them.[23] Tajikistan spends only 0.5 percent of its gross domestic product on social protection, by far the smallest amount spent on social assistance anywhere in the former Soviet Union or Eastern Europe. Moreover, more households were receiving old-age pensions in 2007 than in 2003 (33.3 percent of households in 2007, up from 27.2 percent in 2003), because certain other payments were scaled down between 2003 and 2007 (including secondary school stipends and survivor benefits) and disability pensions became harder to receive; thus, fewer households overall were receiving some kind of social protection funding in 2007 (34.4 percent) than in 2003 (38.7 percent).[24] The social protection system does very little to alleviate poverty in the country, with the World Bank estimating (based on 2007 TLSS data) that these transfers reduced the poverty headcount from 54.8 to 53.1 percent of the population.[25] Table 8.3 examines social protection transfers in 2007.

The government of Tajikistan has had great difficulty maintaining the social safety net provisions to which the country's population grew accustomed during the Soviet era. Funding for schools and hospitals, especially in the more remote rural areas, became increasingly more problematic in the last years of Soviet rule, and the existing physical plant was substantially damaged during the civil war.

Old-age pensions in particular have been sorely inadequate, although they improved somewhat in August 2008, after the TLSS was conducted in 2007. Most households with potential retirees (women fifty-eight years and older, men sixty-three years and older) do receive them (86.8 percent). At the time of the survey, one-third of retirees received the minimum pension of 36 somoni per month (approximately $11). Disability pensions were 26 somoni ($5.46) per month. About 28 percent of the old-age pensions go to the poorest quintile of the population, and 49.4 percent to the two poorest quintiles, which does little to alleviate their poverty. Old-age pensions constituted just 5.5 percent of

TABLE 8.3
SOCIAL PROTECTION TRANSFERS, 2007
(by share of households receiving transfers)

QUINTILE OR TYPE OF HOUSEHOLD	OLD-AGE BENEFIT	DISABILITY BENEFIT	OTHER BENEFITS	ALL BENEFITS
QUINTILE (PRETRANSFER)				
1	39.8	8.7	0.9	41.6
2	35.1	5.7	0.4	36.2
3	31.2	3.5	0.2	32.0
4	28.2	3.9	0.2	29.1
5	20.8	2.3	0.2	21.2
LOCATION				
URBAN	24.8	4.4	0.2	26.1
RURAL	33.9	5.0	0.5	34.8
TOTAL HOUSEHOLDS	33.3	5.2	0.4	34.4

Source: World Bank, *Tajikistan: Poverty Assessment*, December 3, 2009, 59.

the average household income for those receiving them in 2007, and 8.1 percent of the household income of those in the poorest quintile. This compares with 6.6 percent and 11.8 percent in 2003. Recipients of disability payments were able to cover about 3.6 percent of their average household expenditures.

Of course, these figures depend on the definition of "household expenditure"; if the elderly live with their families, then it is understandable that pensions will make up a small percentage of household income. More telling is the comparison of pensions to what would be termed a "living wage." Estimates of what would be an appropriate "living wage" vary widely; and in reality, to be more accurate they must be determined by region rather than being uniform countrywide. In 2009, estimates of the price of food included in the consumer basket ranged from about 100 to 200 somoni ($21–$42) per person per month. Another complication is that the country does not have a standardized means of calculating the living wage, and poverty rate estimates can therefore vary widely. In April 2009, Tajikistan's Parliament adopted a law on the living wage meant to address the discrepancy between the cost of living and pensions. The law, which defines how the government should set the subsistence level to determine assistance to the poor, established a consumer basket whose cost would fluctuate with market prices.[26] Furthermore, the government is supposed to update the subsistence level every quarter, although it does not always meet this goal.[27]

Yet another further stress on the pension system is that migrant workers expect to receive pensions, despite the fact that they have made no contributions to the pension system for any of the years of their employment outside the country. However, on a positive note, there are few accounts of the government being in arrears in its pension payments.[28]

The existing system is considered by the World Bank to be administered by staff that is neither competent nor trained to target assistance, to deliver it properly, and to handle complaints from potential and targeted recipients.[29] There is hope, however, that coordinated donor assistance could improve this situation—with the World Bank focusing on pension reform and financing a functional review of the social protection system more generally, the European Union offering a €5 million ($6.3 million) budget to do a policy matrix covering social assistance, social services, and a labor market strategy, and to collect poverty statistics (that is, everything but pensions), and UNICEF focusing on disability and social worker training.

Health Care

Tajikistan's health sector is also in a state of crisis, with government reform efforts underfunded and insufficient. In 2010, Tajikistan's government was spending 1.6 percent of the country's GDP on health care, or 6 percent of total government expenditures—the lowest proportion spent by any of the Central Asian countries.[30] Tajikistan also had the lowest total health care expenditures per capita, at $49 in 2010.[31] Total health expenditures constituted 6.0 percent of Tajikistan's GDP in 2010.[32] The

Tajik government, however, noted in its Poverty Reduction Strategy for 2007–2009 that it was only about to meet 21.17 percent of its high-priority needs in this sector.

At 73.3 percent of total health care expenditures, private spending on health care is higher than in any other country in the region.[33] Of course, none of this money goes toward reforming the health care sector. This makes it highly unlikely that Tajikistan will meet the UN Millennium Development Goals of spending $3.6 billion between 2005 and 2015 in order to meet unmet targets for reducing child mortality, improving maternal health, reducing tuberculosis, better treatment of HIV/AIDS, and improving access to safe water (as tainted water is a leading source of morbidity and mortality of children).

This said, the country made some modest progress in meeting its Country Partnership Strategy Goals for the 2007–2009 period (as prepared by the World Bank's International Development Association and International Finance Corporation), including the reduction of infant mortality and maternal death rates, and the development of fifteen pilot regions for a case-based health care delivery system in hospitals.

Nonetheless, the health care system currently serves the rich far better than it does the poor—from birth, through childhood, adulthood, and old age. Richer people make more visits to doctors than poorer people do, for while Tajikistan's Constitution provides free health care for its citizens, in reality public spending comes nowhere close to meeting the cost of health care for the country's citizens.[34] According to 2010 data, only 26.7 percent of total health care spending in Tajikistan was public spending, compared with 56.2 percent in Kyrgyzstan, 59.4 percent in Kazakhstan, 62.1 percent in Russia, 47.5 percent in Uzbekistan, and 59.4 percent in Turkmenistan.[35] Foreign assistance makes an important contribution to the health of Tajikistan's citizens, by funding technical assistance for the government trying to speed up the pace of reforms, and by funding the activities of nongovernmental organizations designed to increase public awareness of the importance of good nutrition and preventive health care, as well as free or low-cost clinics and paying for childhood immunizations. Most of the burden of paying for health care, however, rests firmly with the Tajiks themselves.

For the poorer segments of Tajikistan's population, the choice often boils down to either becoming poorer by paying for health care or going without it and suffering the consequences. The TLSS from 2007 reports that 45 percent of the poorest households said that they found it either impossible or very difficult to pay for medical care, compared with 29 percent of the rich, but at the same time the share of the population saying that they did not receive medical care because they could not afford it dropped from 50 percent in 2003 to 33 percent in 2007.[36] The majority of those who were in this category came from the poorest quintile living in rural areas; 76 percent of those who said that they or a member of their family did not follow through with medical care when referred to a hospital for treatment came from either Khatlon Oblast or the Region of Republican Subordination.[37]

However, when difficult choices about spending money must be made, Tajiks still seem strongly inclined to get health care for their children, although either boys get sick more frequently or Tajiks are simply more inclined to seek treatment for their sons. In the 2003 TLSS, 7 percent of boys and 5 percent of girls under eighteen were reported to have received medical treatment in the previous month. Eighty percent of them saw a state doctor, but 40 percent were treated at home, which almost always entails private payment. The most common causes for treatment were respiratory infections (30 percent), diarrhea (15 percent), and malaria (10 percent). The presence of malaria in Tajikistan at such a rate is also a very troubling sign of the deterioration of conditions in rural areas. During the course of treatment, 87 percent received prescriptions for drugs, of which 90 percent were filled, with the remainder going unfilled because of cost. More than 90 percent of these households reported that they paid for hospital charges for their children, more than 80 percent said that they paid for medicine, 75 percent for other medical supplies, and 67 percent paid for fees for physicians or other medical staff. This lack of access to affordable and good-quality health care has an impact on life expectancy starting at birth; Tajikistan's infant, child, and maternal mortality rates remain high.

The Tajik government also does little to maximize the quality of the contribution that public funds make in advancing the good health of its citizens. The country's health care system comes under the Ministry of

Health, which is responsible for developing health policy, supervising disease control, and managing all the federal-level health institutes and training institutions for physicians and other health care professionals. Federal health guidelines are set in coordination with the Ministry of Finance, which has even more responsibility for setting regional and local budgets by sector, including for health care. Oblast health officials are charged with working with both the Ministry of Health and their oblast-level financial officials. The health care for each district is under the supervision of the chief physician of the central *rayon* hospital, but each health care facility ultimately is responsible for its own budget. Moreover, despite pressure from the World Bank and its affiliated institutions in particular to have Tajikistan achieve this, there has been little effort to clarify the division of labor between central authorities and local governments.

Only 23 percent of the public funding for health care comes from the national government, with the remainder coming from the regions. This partially decentralized funding system has led to substantial differences in the quality of health care available in different parts of the country, which reflect both differing allocations by local governments and differences in local populations' willingness and ability to pay for care. For the nation as a whole, public funding per capita for health care was $6 in 2007. In GBAO, where the population density is lowest, it was $10.5, and 76 percent of public expenditures went toward keeping hospitals operating that are disbursed throughout the region. Per capita public expenditures for health care in Dushanbe are $7 per person, and here 47 percent goes for hospitals, but 37 percent goes for clinics, the highest proportion in the country. In both Khatlon and the Region of Republican Subordination, $3.3 per capita was allocated for health care expenditures; in Sughd, $4.5; and in all three cases, roughly two-thirds or more of the funding went to hospitals.

Most of the government money allocated to the sector goes to keeping its facilities running, rather than improving the care and treatment of patients. Tajikistan's health care system is large, and still organized much as it was in the Soviet period, with the first priority in budgeting going to maintaining infrastructure and paying salaries. The philosophy of medical treatment continues to be inpatient treatment rather than preventive care, and ensuring that the system reaches not just to the oblast level but also to the district level, even in the country's remotest parts. Largely because of this, only 10 percent of Tajikistan's people reported that they did not seek medical care because it was too far away.[38]

The system has 2,300 public health care facilities, including 335 hospitals for "specialized" treatment. In addition, the system employs approximately 14,000 physicians and 30,000 other medical personnel.[39] The number of hospital beds increased in the immediate aftermath of the civil war as the government restored facilities damaged during the conflict, but now has begun to decline slightly, a trend that is true for the Central Asian region as a whole. Tajikistan has a relatively high ratio of hospital beds per 1,000 people, but the lowest ratio of physicians per 1000 people in the region.[40]

About 65 percent of total public health care expenditures go to maintaining the hospitals, even though the current demand for inpatient treatment does not justify maintaining the current number of beds. In 2005, 16 percent of all facilities surveyed by the World Bank reported receiving no government funds beyond payroll or in-kind contributions and 39 percent reported receiving no drugs, while only 50 percent had any stores of drugs at the time of the survey.

One of the problems that Tajikistan needs to confront is that it has no domestic pharmaceutical industry to speak of, so that the government-run clinics must purchase imported medications (which are obviously quite expensive by local Tajik standards). The government of Tajikistan has made the development of a national pharmaceutical industry based on local raw materials something of a priority, at least as far as getting it listed in its national development plans, but there does not seem to have been substantial progress made toward this goal.

Many of Tajikistan's health care facilities are in poor repair, lacking modern equipment and often even electricity or adequate sanitation (table 8.4). The physicians and administrative staff running the health care system generally lack the training for the kinds of administrative tasks that they now confront, not to mention declining skills in their medical specialties.

TABLE 8.4

HEALTH FACILITIES: ACCESS TO ELECTRICITY, HEATING, PIPED WATER, COMMUNICATIONS, AND TRANSPORTATION VEHICLES

TYPE OF FACILITY AND ACCESS	URBAN	RURAL	TAJIKISTAN
	AVERAGE NUMBER OF HOURS PER DAY		
ELECTRICITY AVAILABILITY IN THE WINTER	19	6	9
HEATING AVAILABILITY IN THE WINTER	12	4	5
	PERCENTAGE OF FACILITIES WITH ACCESS		
ACCESS TO PIPED WATER	95	29	41
ACCESS TO COMMUNICATIONS (TELEPHONE OR RADIO)	85	9	23
ACCESS TO TRANSPORTATION VEHICLES	48	12	19

Source: World Bank, *Tajikistan: Poverty Assessment*, December 3, 2009, 92.

The money allocated by the government is not sufficient to keep medical equipment in working order or to pay adequate salaries to physicians and other health care employees. This means that doctors and nurses must moonlight outside official working hours and expect payments from patients on the side, while ordinary Tajik citizens are expected to bear most of the financial burden for health care. The 2007 TLSS reported that Tajik citizens paid 59 percent of the actual costs of their hospital treatment, 89 percent of their ambulatory care costs, 89 percent of the costs of the drugs they received while in the hospital, and 98 percent of the costs of the drugs that they received through ambulatory care.[41]

Certainly most health facilities in Tajikistan come nowhere close to conforming to Western standards of medical treatment. As table 8.4 details, these facilities generally lack round-the-clock access to electricity and heating in winter, rural health facilities normally lack access to running water (and consequently have no indoor plumbing, either), most appear to have no means of communications, and many have no way to collect or transport the sick.

Physicians and nurses receive very low salaries. Those who are government employees (the vast majority) receive 119 somoni ($25) if they are primary health care staff and 78 somoni ($16.39) if they are secondary health care workers, and a World Bank study reports that 18.5 percent of them hold informal jobs (at least half-time), in addition to those in their hospitals and clinics.[42] They also generally levy informal charges on their patients, with 46 percent of them admitting to such practices, which are most commonplace in Dushanbe and least common in GBAO. In fact, a World Bank study reports that doctors in Dushanbe make 1.8 times their salaries in unofficial payments.[43]

Many Tajiks are reluctant to pay for what used to be free, and the "informal" costs that they were used to paying have gone up considerably, along with "gifts" for physicians and the cost of drugs. In an attempt to address the informal payment system, the Ministry of Health introduced an experimental Basic Benefits Package in four *rayons*, with a formal copayment system for all but the poorest in the communities. However, early reports from the project suggest that the fee structure is still set too low to cover actual costs and what physicians and nurses perceive to be a reasonable salary, so the practice of giving "informal gifts" persists even in the pilot hospitals.[44]

The current generation of children appear to be in worse health than their parents were in childhood, and a substantial proportion seem certain to develop serious health problems in adulthood. Roughly 42 percent of all children in rural areas have moderately or severely stunted growth, as compared with 31 percent in urban areas, with children in Dushanbe the least likely to be severely stunted (at 30 percent) and those in Khatlon Oblast the most likely (43 percent).[45]

Children's health is seriously compromised by the absence of clean water; 18 percent of the children in the poorest quintile (and 11.6 percent in the richest) reported that they had suffered from diarrhea in the two weeks before the administration of the 2007 TLSS.

Yet another looming problem is narcotics addiction, and the related crisis of HIV/AIDs, whose numbers of cases in Tajikistan increased fourfold (from 2,500 to approximately 10,000) from 2001 to 2007.[46]

At the same time, the Ministry of Health is reported to have registered only 2,204 cases of HIV/AIDS for the period from 1991 through July 1, 2010, of whom 79.4 percent were age 20 to 39, and 54.5 percent were said to have been users of narcotics. There was also a marked increase in HIV/AIDS cases among women, rising from 14 percent of registered narcotics users in 2000 to 20.7 percent in 2010. And the number of cases that resulted from sexual transmission also increased, from 8.2 percent in 2003 to 28.1 percent in 2010.[47]

Opiate usage in Tajikistan is estimated at 0.5 percent, with the overwhelming majority being heroin users. This is the lowest prevalence of drug addiction in Central Asia; opiate usage in Kazakhstan is estimated at 1 percent, and at 0.8 percent in Uzbekistan and Kyrgyzstan,[48] a discrepancy that may call into question the reliability of the Tajik statistics.[49] The population with HIV/AIDS is almost exclusively drawn from opiate users.

Women and Children

Women remain underrepresented in Tajikistan's political life, making lobbying the government on issues pertaining to them more difficult. Women held 17.5 percent of the seats in the Parliament that sat from 2005 to 2010, and will hold fewer seats in the current Parliament. Only 21 percent of candidates on the party lists were women, and most were given slots toward the bottom of the list, virtually ensuring that they would not be seated; only 12 percent of the candidates (16 of 129) for single-mandate districts were women. Women are also underrepresented in the electoral administration; 3 of the 15 members of the Central Commission for Elections and Referendums, and only 4 of 41 heads of the district election commissions, are women.[50]

Tajikistan's birthrate remains high, with the population growing by roughly 2.2 percent each year. Approximately 45.7 percent of Tajikistan's population is under the age of nineteen, making it the youngest population in Central Asia.[51] The country had a mean age of 20.5 and a median age of 20.8 in 2007, according to its Statistical Committee, with the poverty assessment reporting a mean age that is now approximately 20 and is projected to increase to 26 by 2025.[52] The hardship of the civil war notwithstanding, there was a 34.4 percent increase in the number of children aged 5 to 19 between 1990 and 2005. Although the birthrate in Tajikistan has been slowly declining, the population in the five- to nineteen-year-old age cohort is expected to remain relatively steady in the near future, with a projected increase of 4.1 percent between 2005 and 2030, at which time it is projected to begin declining.[53] The high birthrates are not evenly distributed across the country: birthrates remain highest in GBAO, in Kulyab, and in the more remote parts of Sughd and the RRS.

Large family size appears to be a contributing cause of poverty in the country. According to the 2007 TLSS, households with three or more children accounted for 53.2 percent of the total population, but 62.2 percent of the total poor, whereas childless households only had a 31.9 percent poverty rate (this figure included the elderly).[54]

Tajikistan's child mortality rate remains relatively high; according to the Multiple Cluster Indicator Survey from 2005, the under-5 mortality rate was 79 per 1,000 live births, down from 126 from the 2000 survey, but still an unreliable statistic because only 88.5 percent of all births in Tajikistan are registered.[55] Child mortality rates vary across the country, with some parts of the country exceeding 130 deaths per 1,000.[56] Morality is also likely linked to income; child mortality rates were 100 per 1,000 for the poorest 60 percent of the population versus 74 per 1,000 for the richest 40 percent, both unacceptably high. According to the World Bank, the high level of infant and child mortality is largely the result of avoidable causes, such as premature delivery, low birth weight, meningitis, and diarrhea.[57]

In addition to high child mortality, Tajikistan also has one of the highest maternal mortality rates in the region,[58] and the highest percentage of low-birth-weight babies in the region, with 10 percent of all newborn babies being classified as such.[59] These statistics are at least partially indicative of many Tajik women's lack of access to prenatal care.[60]

The Tajik government set the goal of cutting the maternal death rate by nearly one-third, as well as reducing the rates of infant and child mortality, between 2005 and 2009, but with little realistic guidance on how this target could be achieved.[61] Because of underreporting and misclassification (for instance, failing to record a maternal death if there was not a live birth), the situation painted by government statistics may be more positive than the reality. Moreover, with misleading government data, it is hard to translate government targets into ones that the international community can use as a yardstick for evaluating progress.

In 2009, Tajikistan also had the worst performance in the region with regard to immunizing children against childhood diseases; 93 percent of children age 12 to 23 months received diphtheria immunizations,[62] and 89 percent (down slightly from 2005 and 2006 but up from 2007 and 2008) were immunized against the measles.[63] In 2009, the Japanese government stepped in with a grant to help Tajikistan's government pay for children's immunizations. In the spring and summer of 2010, the country experienced a polio outbreak, another reflection of the lack of routine access to standard immunizations among Tajikistan's children.

Diarrhea, caused by poor water quality and unsanitary living conditions, is one of the major causes of Tajikistan's high infant and child mortality rate. At the time of the 2007 National Development Strategy, only 23 percent of the urban population and 5 percent of the rural population lived where there were sewers; and of 699 centralized water supply systems in the country, 113 were inoperable and 358 did not meet sanitary requirements.[64] Approximately 34 percent of all children under five years of age living in Tajikistan have no access to improved water sources; 21 percent have access to piped water in their dwellings. An additional 13 percent of children have access to piped water in their yards, but 21 percent must rely on water from a public tap.[65] The situation is worst in Khatlon and GBAO, where only 50 percent of children have access to improved sources of drinking water, as compared with 95 percent in Dushanbe and 70 percent in the Region of Republican Subordination.[66]

In addition to a high infant and child mortality rate and lack of access to common childhood immunizations and safe drinking water, Tajik children also suffer from various forms of developmental challenges stemming from malnutrition. Although chronic malnutrition has declined since the end of the civil war, in 2007, according to UNICEF's data, 27 percent of all Tajik children suffered from chronic malnutrition; 27 percent of children under five were stunted (that is, short for their age), 17 percent were underweight (for their age), and 7 percent were wasted (low weight for their height). Ten percent of Tajik children were found to be both stunted and underweight, while 1.4 percent were stunted, underweight, and wasted.[67] Diarrhea was second only to the common cold as a cause for why children were reported to have sought medical care for an acute condition in the past four weeks in the 2003 TLSS, when a quarter of all boys from ages three to ten were said to suffer from acute diarrhea.[68] The poor quality of Tajikistan's water is a major contributing factor to these conditions, as children with diarrhea have trouble gaining and maintaining weight. The relatively low incidence of breast feeding by Tajik mothers is also believed to be a contributing factor to the abnormally low height and weight patterns in Tajikistan.[69] In addition, 35 percent of the population (including both children and adults) was iodine deficient, which leads to goiters, but also to intellectual retardation, a major concern with children.[70] A UNICEF study cited the 2003 National Micronutrient Status Survey, which found that 57 percent of women of reproductive age and 64 percent of children had low urinary iodine excretion (the principal method to determine iodine deficiency).[71]

A UNICEF study of 398 children divided into two focus groups (consisting of six- to twelve-year-olds, and twelve- to sixteen-year-olds), funded by UNICEF after the 2003 TLSS was made public, speaks to the severe challenges often facing Tajikistan's children. A total of 36 meetings were conducted in eighteen communities spread across nine districts and cities (four each); the focus groups included boys and girls and were held in urban as well as rural settings.

The percentage of children living in poverty in Tajikistan is higher than the overall poverty levels. According to the 2007 TLSS, 57.6 percent of all children were living in poverty, versus 51.3 percent of the adult population, and 19.2 percent of children were living in extreme poverty, as opposed to 15.9 percent of the adult population.[72] There were substantial regional disparities with regard to poverty, with higher-than-average incidences of child poverty found in both Khatlon and GBAO regions. Chronic child malnutrition is also worst in these regions. Acute malnutrition is also high in Dushanbe, as the urban poor in the nation's capital are rarely the subject of the kind of international attention and programming that is designed for the poorer regions of the country.

The children in the UNICEF study were asked to describe what they considered poverty to be, and they responded that poverty was a lack of jobs for the older generation, a lack of enough food, a shortage of warm clothing and footwear, and not being able to afford school supplies. Many children (in both groups) answered that you could tell whether a person was poor or not from how his or her house looked, if it was not renovated, had no windows, or lacked heating. Many children answered that poverty was when parents had to leave their children and go to Russia to work, and that poverty hit mothers more than fathers, as they were more frequently left behind. Others responded that "poor people were shy and kept their heads down" because they were embarrassed by how they looked.[73]

When asked the cause of poverty, the children responded that it was caused by the civil war, by a lack of steady jobs and low salaries, by a lack of education, and by having too many children. Some younger children noted that poverty was caused by parents who gambled or drank. Others mentioned that poverty was the result of spending too much money on weddings and funerals, speaking to the support for restrictions on the size of religious celebrations.[74]

Child labor in Tajikistan remains a significant problem. According to the Tajik authorities, 2.4 percent of all children aged twelve to fourteen work full time, and these are figures offered by a government that has systematically understated the extent of the country's social problems. And these figures do not include children working in their own households or on family farms. If anything, child labor is a bigger problem than in Uzbekistan, the importing of whose cotton has been banned by certain nations that belong to the European Union.

UNICEF's *Children's Voices: A Qualitative Study of Poverty in Tajikistan* documented how children in poor families are often the principal breadwinners, working in markets in big cities and in district centers, where boys pull carts, unload trucks, and sell fruit and vegetables. In Tajikistan's largest cities, children work as conductors on buses and trolleys. Older boys are sometimes hired to work at construction sites, while younger boys wash cars or sell small items like cigarettes, chewing gum, or even plastic satchels. Girls sell fruit, bread, pastries, or herbs in markets, and in rural areas girls collect and peddle milk. Older girls work as nursemaids or servants in rich people's homes, or work as dishwashers, waitresses, or bar maids. Some do sewing or make handicrafts. Rural youth work as farm laborers, in family holdings, and as *mardikors*, and virtually every child from a rural area reported that he or she had been involved in some form of agricultural activity, from planting to harvesting, to making fuel from dung, or making food crops edible.[75]

According to a UNICEF-commissioned study done in 2007, some 200,000 children aged five to fourteen are working (excluding non-intensive household chores, in which the vast majority of children engage[76]), and approximately 65,000 are engaged in paid work.[77] Older children are more likely to work than younger children; 25.3 percent of children aged twelve to fourteen were reported working, as compared with 6 percent of children aged five to eleven.[78] The share of children under fourteen who work varies considerably from oblast to oblast, with the highest proportion found in GBAO (28 percent) and the lowest in Dushanbe (5 percent).[79]

There do seem to be some government efforts, if not to eliminate, then at least to reduce the use of school children in harvesting.

Notwithstanding a presidential decree of 2006 banning the use of child labor on cotton farms and a similar decree from the Ministry of Education, Tajikistan does not meet the International Labor Organization's conventions restricting child labor (including Convention 138 on the Minimum Age and Convention 182 on the Worst Forms of Child Labor). The country's minimum age for employment is sixteen, although fifteen-year-olds may be employed with permission from local trade unions. This requirement formally meets the International Labor Organization's minimum age for employment. In reality, the use of child labor remains commonplace in agriculture, in household employment, and in various urban settings. Children as young as seven may work in the household and in family farms, and are considered as providing unpaid "family assistance."

Daily reality often takes precedence over official pronouncements against child labor. Cotton remains an important agricultural product for Tajikistan, and the labor-intensive nature of the cotton harvest, which stems from the de-mechanization of cotton harvesting after independence, means that a large proportion of the rural population is involved. A 2010 School of Oriental and African Studies report on child labor in cotton fields, based on data from the 2009 harvest, concluded that Tajikistan has made little progress on curbing child labor in cotton fields.

Children aged fourteen to eighteen are regularly used in cotton harvests to fill the need for additional cheap labor, which has become more acute with growing adult labor migration. Children under fourteen are sometimes illegally used as well. Schools are central to mobilizing children for work in cotton fields, which occurs with the knowledge, and often direct involvement, of local governments.[80] Moreover, much of the use of child labor outside the household is in fact legally sanctioned because of a loophole inserted into the Tajik labor law:

> To prepare young people for production labour, it is allowed to take pupils from schools, [and] students [out] of professional colleges for carrying out light work, which will not cause damage to their health and education. Work should be performed during free time after reaching [the] age of 14 and with the approval of a parent guardian.[81]

The U.S. Department of State's 2009 human rights report for Tajikistan, however, indicates that this practice by school officials is becoming less common. It further notes that in 2008, prosecutors in Khatlon Oblast charged two school officials with exerting unlawful pressure on students to participate in the harvest. At the same time, the report concludes that there has not been a concerted effort by Ministry of Labor officials to deploy inspectors to catch school officials engaging in this practice, and Ministry of Education officials are also generally loath to discipline teachers or administrators who are complicit in it.[82]

There are also accounts of children being sent to Russia effectively as forced laborers to help with harvests there, but no data are available on the frequency of such occurrences. The following is an account from a nine-year-old child from Shahristan District in Sughd Oblast:

> The whole group of older schoolchildren was brought to Russia to the city of Volgograd to work in the agricultural sector and pick watermelons. They worked hard, but as a result no money has been paid to them yet.[83]

Unfortunately, Tajikistan's child labor problem appears to be growing worse over time, given the labor shortages, particularly in rural regions, that have been created by the departure of many young men (in the twenty- to forty-year-old age cohorts) to work in Russia or in Kazakhstan. This means that more children are being forced to work at agricultural planting and harvesting times, and it has also led to more "fatherless" households, forcing children out to work, especially if remittances are not sent home, or the mother and adult children in the household do not provide financial support in lieu of the missing head of the household.

In addition, there is the problem of street children, unattended orphans, and runaways, whose numbers are difficult to estimate accurately. The Society and Children's Rights (Tajik) nongovernmental organization reported that there were some 3,000 such children living on the streets of Dushanbe in 2002.[84]

For all their complaints, almost all the children interviewed by UNICEF noted that life had gotten better in recent years, and that schools were improving, with teachers returning to work because they were receiving better wages, with new textbooks, and with some children studying in schools that had recently been repaired. Some of the girls noted that conditions had improved enough so that they were able to return to school. Children living in former combat zones spoke of the sustained peace as a cause, and those with parents in Russia claimed remittances were the cause, and this was a very commonly cited factor. Some of the older children living in rural areas spoke of the presidential decree that had provided land for their parents.[85]

Women remain in a disadvantageous social position. Violence against women remains commonplace. Rape is punishable by twenty years imprisonment, but very few women bring instances of rape to the attention of the police, and the law includes no provision against spousal rape—which is something that simply does not exist, at least according to the country's legal system. At the same time, however, Amnesty International estimates that a third to a half of all Tajik women have been subjected to physical, sexual, or psychological violence by their husbands or other family members.[86] Many wives also lack legal protection, because while they had religious ceremonies, their marriages were never registered with the civil authorities. Sometimes this is because the bride is entering into a polygamous arrangement, but frequently it is because the bride is younger than the official minimum marriage age of seventeen; other times it is done to save the ten days' minimum wage that is levied as the registration fee.

Women whose marriages are based solely on religious law and not recorded in civil proceedings appear to be most vulnerable to abuse, and they enjoy absolutely no legal protection if they are divorced by their husbands in accordance with religious law (through the declaration "I divorce thee, I divorce thee, I divorce thee" made in front of two witnesses). Most of Tajikistan's 44 nongovernmental organization crisis centers (three of which operate out of government-donated premises) tend to be seriously underfunded, and there are no laws specifically dealing with domestic abuse; a draft law on domestic violence has been in the works for several years, but no law had been passed as of early 2012.[87] Moreover, when cases of domestic violence are reported to the authorities, they are not always properly investigated; often, the authorities may ignore domestic abuse, classifying it as a private family matter or favoring a reconciliation-and-mediation approach over pressing criminal charges against the perpetrator.[88] To date, little information has been collected by the government authorities about domestic violence, and virtually no public relations efforts have been made to try to prevent its spread. The Tajik government has also given very little attention to female suicides, which, according to the Amnesty International study cited above, are frequently caused by domestic abuse.

Migration is also creating new social pressures on women, many of whom are discovering that their spouses have "second" wives in Russia (and less frequently in Kazakhstan) who are receiving a share of the family income. Women are also being forced to do harder physical labor than previously, especially those living on farms, where now frequently there are no able-bodied men to help with the harvest.

Violence against children is also relatively frequent. The UNICEF study reports that 50 percent of children were subjected to some sort of physical discipline, and that in the 2003 TLSS 7 percent of the children reported that they had been beaten with a hard object during the previous month, with 4 percent reporting that they had been "hit over and over as hard as one could"; but 44 percent said that they would suffer in silence because parents "have the authority and right to use violence to punish them."[89] Worse yet, violent behavior is also tolerated in other settings: Between a quarter and a half of teenagers said that they had suffered physical or psychological abuse at school from either teachers or classmates.[90]

Food Security

According to Goskomstat Tajikistan, the average Tajik spends $21 a month on food, while a "rational"—and by that one presumes "healthy"—food basket would cost $42 a person, far below international standards (as reported by the Tajiks, $70 for an adult and $90 for a child; but in fact, international formulas are more complicated). But most Tajiks find it difficult to feed their families even at the level of Tajik government standards, because government salaries, which can be as low as $60 per month, barely feed one person at this level, let alone a family.[91] One of the consequences of such low wages is that Tajiks appear to be eating fewer meals per day, going from three meals a day to just two.[92] The Tajik government reports that it was able to meet 47.13 percent of its high-priority needs in the food security and agricultural sectors combined.

Tajikistan has the highest rate of undernourishment in Central Asia, with 30 percent of the population being reported as undernourished, according to the UN Food and Agriculture Organization's food security indicators, in contrast to 11 percent in Uzbekistan, 6 percent in Turkmenistan, 8 percent in Kazakhstan, and 10 percent in Kyrgyzstan.[93] Similarly, malnutrition among children, as reflected in both height and weight, was also the highest reported in Tajikistan, according to the World Bank's data for height, at 33.1 percent of all children under five, versus 19.6 percent in Uzbekistan, 18.1 percent in the Kyrgyz Republic, and 17.4 percent in Kazakhstan. For malnourished and underweight children, the data reported 14.9 percent for Tajikistan, and 3.5 percent for Kazakhstan, 4.4 percent for Uzbekistan, and 2.7 percent for Kyrgyzstan.[94]

The composition of the minimal food basket by item (figure 8.1) shows just how unhealthy and seriously compromised the typical Tajik diet is. Moreover, Tajiks' diets have become considerably more unhealthy in recent years than they were even at the time of the collapse of the USSR, a period of relative deprivation compared with that of the previous decade or two.

According to the 2007 TLSS, 24 percent of participants reported living in households with inadequate food consumption, with 32 percent of the consumption poor and 15 percent of the consumption nonpoor making this claim, as did 44 percent of the population in the bottom quintile by consumption. In general, the highest incidence of

FIGURE 8.1

THE COMPOSITION OF THE COST OF A MINIMUM FOOD BASKET

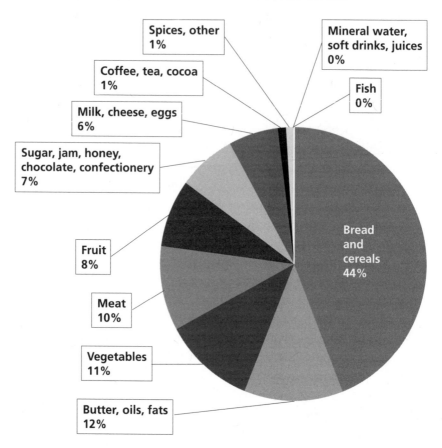

Source: World Bank, *Tajikistan: Poverty Assessment*, December 3, 2009, 107.

food insecurity was reported during the winter and early spring, when up to 75 percent of the extremely poor report that they were food insecure, a problem that is much more severe in rural than in urban areas.[95] The TLSS found that the poorest 20 percent of the population consumed fewer than 2,000 calories per person per day, with the poorest consumption quintile consuming only 1,550 calories, while the richest decile consumes nearly 4,000 calories. The consumption patterns of the Tajiks have led to long-term food deprivation for many children.[96] The Tajiks are the most undernourished nation in Central Asia, with 26 percent of the population reported as undernourished in 2006–2008, as compared with 11 percent in Uzbekistan, 8 percent in Kazakhstan (in 2000–2002), 11 percent in Kyrgyzstan, and a reported 7 percent in Turkmenistan.[97]

A study by the United Nations Development Program of 2,500 residents of Sughd Oblast's poverty-stricken Zerafshan Valley illustrates just how limited and unhealthy the average Tajik diet is in the poorer parts of the country. For most people in this region, the basic diet is bread and tea; 90 percent said that they eat them one or more times daily, with 70 to 80 percent of those surveyed adding that they eat sugar, oil, and salt daily as well, and most of the remaining respondents saying that they eat these things several times a week. Between 29 and 50 percent (the data were collated by district within the Zerafshan Valley; hence the variation) said that they eat potatoes, carrots, and onions daily, and a majority of those sampled in all the districts said that they ate these foods several times a week. These food items are the mainstay of the typical diet in the region. Only 9 to 14.7 percent reported consuming meat or milk products daily; 30 to 45 percent said that they ate them two to three times per week, and 19 to 23 percent said that they ate them rarely. When asked if they consumed tomatoes, cucumbers, processed vegetables, or fresh fruit, 41 to 63 percent answered that they never ate them, and 23 to 29 percent said that they ate them rarely. The respondents reported that their diets improved somewhat in the fall, after the harvest and when animals that could not be fed through the winter were slaughtered.[98]

The situation with regard to food security further deteriorated after these surveys were done. According to an assessment done by the World Food Program to identify the country's emergency needs in the spring of 2008 following an unusually harsh winter, roughly a third of the urban population were chronically food insecure, and 15 percent were severely food insecure. Moreover, they judged the situation as especially severe in the cities of Khujand and Taboshar (Sughd Oblast) and in Kurgan Tyube and Sarband (Khatlon Oblast). The proportion of severe food insecurity was highest among the elderly and the infirm. The same study found that 34 percent of the rural population faced food insecurity, and 11 percent were severely insecure. In all, 1.9 million Tajiks were judged food insecure, of whom 977,000 were severely food insecure.[99]

Education

By Soviet standards, the level of educational achievement of the Tajik population was relatively low, and the quality of the education that the population has been receiving has certainly deteriorated since independence, with access to specialized education having also declined. Nevertheless, when compared with the populations of other countries with similar income levels, the Tajik population remains a well-educated one. Literacy remains close to universal, with reasonably good skill levels in both reading and writing. The 2007 TLSS reported that 90 percent of Tajiks said that they could easily both read and write, as compared with 4.3 percent saying that they could not.[100] This attests to the fact that even in Soviet times, a small percentage of the Tajik population never received any education at all. Although there has been very little research on this, a study supported by the United Nations Development Program in the Zerafshan Valley found that nearly 4 percent of the adult respondents said that they had never had formal education.[101]

Tajikistan's high literacy rates mask a deteriorating education system. Faced with low salaries, many teachers have switched to more lucrative fields or have emmigrated, leaving the country with a shortage of qualified teaching personnel. The consistent lack of funding has resulted in outdated educational materials and supplies, and weak infrastructure—some school buildings are not only in need of repair but also often lack reliable access to electricity and running water. As a result, today's students are receiving a lower-quality education compared with their parents' generation.[102]

The Tajik government has repeatedly pledged to increase spending for education as part of its poverty reduction strategies and efforts to meet the Millennium Development Goals. However, as with many other aspects of its policy, the Tajik authorities have found it much easier to say the right thing about the need to reform education than to devise and fund policies that lead to substantial reforms within the country's educational system. For example, between 2004 and 2009 the government introduced ten programs, five national plans, and a series of projects in the field of education.[103]

This would be a very ambitious schedule of reforms for any country, even one replete with talent in the field of educational innovation. The woeful state of the country's educational system, and the Tajik government's relatively limited financial resources, should have dictated a modest, step-by-step approach to educational reform. But the approach that was chosen instead emphasized issuing a series of increasingly more ambitious declarative statements. Moreover, the intent of some of these programs and projects has been to increase the ideological content of education, to create citizens loyal to the current political system and to its president. Saodat Olimova reports that this process has been pursued at the expense of education in the sciences and languages.

Although state expenditures on education have increased in recent years in both real and relative terms, the Tajik government devotes a much lower proportion of its GDP to education today—3.7 percent in 2008[104]—than it did in 1991, when it spent 8.9 percent. Moreover, there is a growing gender gap in school attendance, especially for grades nine to eleven.[105]

The Tajik government acknowledges the existence of very serious problems in the education sector. The following comes from Tajikistan's Poverty Reduction Strategy for 2007–2009:

> The quality of education has declined as a result of: the low wages paid to teachers at general education schools; a shortage of teachers in rural areas; outdated subject matter, teaching materials and methods; educational institutions with a physical infrastructure that is in very poor condition and does not have the capacity to meet demand; a shortage of instructional materials and textbooks in certain subjects. There are problems with access to education for children from poor and socially vulnerable segments of the population and the secondary education coverage for girls is inadequate.

The report also notes that limited electricity availability means that basic computer training courses cannot be offered, but it makes no other comment about how the absence of electricity and heat creates serious problems for the education of children more generally.[106] In somewhat typical fashion, the Tajik government has set the goal of introducing modular and interactive instruction techniques in all schools, and of having 50 percent of all schools connected to the Internet. But connectivity is being introduced with no real attention to how likely the school is to have daytime access to electricity.

The National Development Strategy for 2007–2015 echoes many of these words, adding that

> the quality of instruction and training and the knowledge and skill levels achieved by students fall significantly short of contemporary demands. Scientifically based curricula and study plans have not yet been developed for all levels of instruction. The shortage of up-to-date textbooks, teaching aids, and scientific and methodological materials make it all the more difficult to conduct classes and to master the assigned curriculum. There is a shortage of textbooks in the Tajik, Russian, Uzbek, and Turkmen languages.
>
> The situation is aggravated by the shortage of schoolteachers and by their poor qualifications, which can be attributed, among other things, to the low wages paid in the profession. This has an adverse effect on morale and on the sense of commitment among teachers, including those at higher education institutions, and it creates opportunities for corruption.[107]

All these projects are hampered by serious shortages of funds. The Poverty Reduction Strategy estimates priority needs in the educational sector to require $44.2 million, of which Tajik officials say they are short 79.83 percent.

Although the Tajik government has begun saying the right things about educational reforms, its efforts at actual reform have been hampered by the laws regarding education and the lack of capacity of state officials and of the educational establishment itself. In its National Development Strategy, the government hides behind methodological jargon to explain the country's education problems, complaining that the sector has been plagued by "inadequate statistics and ineffective methods of [performance evaluation]." The report goes on to say that the current situation is partly the result of the "poor organization of the instructional process at educational institutions," adding that "as a consequence, primary, secondary, and higher vocational and professional educational institutions both within the country and abroad are providing training in occupations that are not always in demand, while there is a shortage of workers with specialized training in other fields."[108] This is accurate—overall, the number of people receiving technical and professional education has declined, both in absolute and relative terms, and this is true for both specialized secondary and higher education. Today, 14.64 percent of the economically active population has received higher education, another 16.44 percent has received technical or professional education, 49.5 percent of the economically active population has received secondary education, and 15.1 percent has received incomplete secondary education.[109]

The Ministry of Education also remains sensitive to various forms of political pressure, and it in turn places pressure on the institutions of higher education in particular to only employ individuals (especially in positions of responsibility) who are publicly identified with supporting the president and the programs of his administration. Pressure is also exerted against private institutions. For example, in 2009 the Tajikistan Institute of Innovation Technology and Communication was closed for three months, formally for technical reasons—but many believed because many members of the faculty were associated with the country's political opposition.[110] In 2010, this institute was permanently closed.[111]

Private and public education are under the supervision of the Ministry of Education. Private education has been permitted in the country since 1994, although it is of limited influence. Only 11 percent of preschool-age children attend private school, 1 percent of Tajikistan's pupils attend private primary schools, 3 percent private secondary schools, and 2 percent private institutions of higher education. Private secondary schools are somewhat elite institutions, but Tajikistan State University and the government's Technical Institute are still considered by most to be the most prestigious in the country. The Ministry of Education tries to scrutinize what is going on in the country's private schools, and it is reported to only be willing to allow one of them to open when it feels confident that the institution will be able to be maintained under its full control, a situation that helps explain the slow growth of private education in Tajikistan.

Saodat Olimova reports that in 2011 there were 53 private general educational establishments financed through private sources, 41 of which were offering some form of secondary education (including 14 lycées and 27 gymnasiums); of the rest, 7 were general schools and 3 were primary schools.[112]

However, public education is only partly funded by the government of Tajikistan. Households finance roughly half the cost of educating their children; according to the 2007 TLSS, this amounts to about 145 somoni ($42) for primary education and 345 somoni ($100) for specialized education, about what the government spends per student. Families pay for tuition in private schools, uniforms, textbooks, stationery, and meals and lodging for children who board for secondary education. They are also assessed part of the costs of school repairs. Although the Tajik Constitution guarantees free education for grades 1 through 9 (which is compulsory) and for general secondary education (grades 10 and 11), public schools in Tajikistan have been levying tuition payments on families to try to cover the actual costs of running their schools. Overall, the World Bank reports that 13 percent of general education (grades 1–9) students pay tuition (including 49 percent in Dushanbe), as do 23 percent of secondary school students and 50 percent of students in institutions of higher education.[113] Poorer students were less likely to pay tuition than richer students, reflecting both their higher dropout rates and the fact that levies are more likely at the better schools.[114] Moreover, the Tajik government is pushing for an expansion of private education in the country, which will further differentiate the life chances of rich and poor children.

Higher education costs, on average, 836 somoni ($243) per year. Family expenditures on education are reported to have increased from 2.4 percent of overall household expenditures in 1999 to 4.3 percent in 2007, with urban households placing more priority on education than do rural ones. The 2007 TLSS shows urban households spending $4.4 per month on education (5.2 percent of total expenditures), as opposed to $2.3 a month (3.9 percent) in rural households.[115] Given that rural households are more likely to live further away from secondary schools than do urban ones, and to need to pay room and board for that reason, this would help to explain the rural dropout rate of secondary school students. These payments exclude any "informal" costs to get favor for their children that are not included in the World Bank's figures. The admission process for higher education in particular has been especially prone to corruption, which is one reason why Tajikistan has moved toward a standard entrance examination system.

The cost of higher education is largely borne by the students, and the state scholarships offered are based on merit rather than need, so they wind up going disproportionately to children from more affluent homes, because they are the most likely to have attended the better schools. Wealthier families are also more likely to be able to be able to afford payments for tutors and bribes to get into the better specialized and higher educational institutions. The data from the 2007 TLSS suggest that 72 percent of students in institutions of higher education come from the top two quintiles by income, and only 5 percent come from the lowest quintile (table 8.5). Predictably, the upper quintile is overrepresented in all but the most basic forms of education.

TABLE 8.5
DISTRIBUTION OF ENROLLED STUDENTS ACROSS INCOME QUINTILES, 2007

EDUCATION LEVEL	RICHEST	RICH	MIDDLE	POOR	POOREST
PREPRIMARY	32	22	8	19	20
PRIMARY	18	19	21	22	21
BASIC	20	20	21	20	19
SECONDARY, GENERAL	29	23	21	16	12
SECONDARY, SPECIALIZED	23	31	16	19	12
HIGHER EDUCATION	50	22	15	8	5

Source: World Bank, *Tajikistan: Poverty Assessment*, December 3, 2009, 72.

The government, however, has steadily increased its spending for education, which increased to 22 percent of its expenditures by 2007 ($12 per capita), up from 12 percent ($5 per capita) in 2003, but then declined to 19.3 percent in 2008, as the impact of the global financial and economic crisis began to hit. Nonetheless, educational expenditures still fall far short of the World Bank's recommendation and the government's own stated goal in its Poverty Reduction Strategy of 6 percent of GDP.

In 2007, 81 percent of educational funding came from districts and municipalities, which collectively financed 81 percent of its cost. The local governments are solely responsible for preprimary education (which enrolled only 9.1 percent of eligible children in 2007) and provide 97 percent of the funds for general education schools, while the national government pays for most of the cost of specialized secondary and higher education. But there are substantial differences between the quality levels of schools, given how much discretionary authority local governments have with regard to allocating funds. As a result, the poorer regions spent one-seventh the amount of money that the most affluent ones did. The government does provide additional funds for "special needs" schools, but even their allocation is at the discretion of the regional authorities where the schools are based.[116]

The government attempted to balance regional expenditures on schools through a 2007 decree setting norms for financing for general education schools. This decree set guidelines for local authorities and school directors to follow in drawing up budgets for their schools and instructed them to be engaged in fund-raising and commercial projects with local businesses to muster the necessary monies to meet these norms. Training was intended to be provided to school directors and accountants in various management techniques, but the funding to conduct this program does not appear to have been found.[117]

Part of the problem is that the government must spend more money just to stay even, given that the school-aged population (children aged five to nineteen) increased by 27.5 percent from 1990 to 2000, and another 5.4 percent between 2000 and 2006. At the same time, the average level of educational attainment in Tajikistan has been declining since the end of Soviet rule, as table 8.6, which represents educational attainment by age cohort, makes clear. The higher educational attainments of the fifty- to sixty-year-old cohort reflect Soviet-era access to free primary and secondary education and higher institutions that was supported by a well-developed system of state stipends, and the lower educational attainments of fifteen- to twenty-five-year-olds were a product of the civil war years. Although enrollment figures remain substantially below those of the Soviet period, they improved somewhat between 2003 and 2007—primary school enrollment increased from 96 to 97 percent, secondary school enrollment from 71 to 80 percent, and higher educational enrollment from 14 to 18 percent.

TABLE 8.6
EDUCATION ATTAINMENT: PERCENTAGE DISTRIBUTION BY AGE

AGE (YEARS)	EDUCATIONAL ATTAINMENT					
	NONE	PRIMARY	BASIC	SECONDARY GENERAL	SECONDARY SPECIALIZED	HIGHER EDUCATION
16–20	1	6	36	54	2	1
21–25	1	4	22	59	7	7
26–30	0	2	19	58	10	11
31–35	< 1	1	9	61	15	12
36–40	0	1	10	59	18	12
41–45	0	2	10	57	17	14
46–50	1	2	12	53	21	11
51–55	1	4	20	40	19	16
56–60	2	7	22	32	20	17
61–66	0	16	24	32	12	16
TOTAL	< 1	4	19	54	13	10

Note: This is the highest degree obtained for those no longer studying.

Source: World Bank, *Tajikistan: Poverty Assessment*, December 3, 2009, 74.

The Tajik government has also lacked the funds to address vocational-technical education in the country, something that it recognizes is also a pressing problem, especially as it tries to prepare Tajik youth for an evolving employment market both at home and, especially, in markets like Russia, where there is a demand for skilled labor but an inadequate labor supply. The 2007 National Development Strategy talks about how the existing standards for vocational training are not at all reflective of demands that are found in the contemporary workplace, and that there are no funds available to refit or build new vocational-educational centers with modern technology. It also notes that there does not seem to be a way to get Tajikistan's private sector involved in this effort.[118] Training offered in the existing vocational training network is still largely focused on the country's Soviet-era industries, which no longer offer much opportunity for employment in Tajikistan. As a result, fewer students were enrolled in these institutions in 2009 than in 1992, when the country was in the middle of its civil war.[119] And this was at a time when overall enrollment in higher educational institutions in Tajikistan was increasing, as it was a way for young men to avoid military service.

Moreover, even if funding were available for creating a more modern vocational-technical system, virtually no one in Tajikistan would be capable of teaching in it, leading to the need for even further funds. To date, only the Aga Khan Foundation has shown a strong interest in the development of this sector, which it will serve through its expanding University of Central Asia (which has a campus in Khorog). Other donors—in particular, the European Union, which has focused on higher education—have only been interested in working in preprofessional sectors or in general education. At the same time, multilateral donors like the World Bank and Asian Development Bank and bilateral donors like the U.S. Agency for International Development have focused on schools' physical plant and on curriculum reform in general education.

At the other end of the education ladder, enrollment in preprimary education in Tajikistan (at 11 percent) is quite low relative to the other countries of the former Soviet Union, and even for countries with similar GDP levels; this is especially true for rural areas, where only 3 percent of the eligible children attend preschools. The Tajik government has set a target of 40 percent of the preschool-age population being covered by preprimary education, but right now this is a seriously underfunded mandate. And although 18 percent of the children attend preschools in urban areas, these schools are much more available in urban communities than in rural ones, and a much higher proportion (54 percent) of those interviewed in the 2007 TLSS said that they did not send their children because they preferred to keep them at home than did their rural counterparts (18 percent). Cost did not seem to be a significant factor in parents' decisions, as only 8 percent of urban parents and 2 percent of rural parents cited it.[120] What seems more important are cultural factors, the deeply rooted belief that children are better off being kept at home, that they remain healthier and better cared for, and concerns that the quality of most preschool education is so low that it makes little or no contribution to a child's future educational success.

Tajikistan has the strongest gender inequalities in education of any post-Soviet country (figure 8.2), and these are not improving over time, although both boys and girls drop out of school as they get older, with a substantial drop-off starting at age fifteen for boys but thirteen for girls. By the age of sixteen, only 74 percent of all girls are enrolled in school, compared with 89 percent of boys. At seventeen, 52 percent of girls are still in school, versus 81 percent of boys. And at eighteen, only 24 percent of girls are still enrolled, as compared to 37 percent of boys.[121] The Tajik government's Poverty Reduction Strategy for 2007–2009 set the goal of getting a minimum of 91 percent of children to stay in school through the age of fifteen, and to achieve an equal gender balance among schoolchildren in this age group.[122] The strategy also set a target of 99 percent of all school-age children getting an education.

The differential education levels between boys and girls are very troubling, because they bode ill for the educational chances of the next generation of Tajiks, both male and female. Poorly educated mothers do a much worse job of supervising their children's performance in school than do their better-educated female counterparts. The fact that such a high percentage of Tajik households have "absent males" is sure to further exacerbate this problem, because the women in these families are also more frequently working out of the home as wage earners, further diminishing their capacity for supervision.

FIGURE 8.2
GENDER INEQUALITY IN EDUCATION

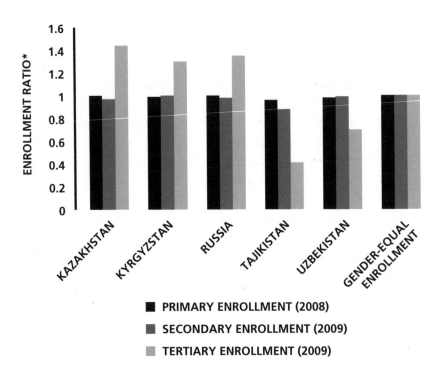

PRIMARY ENROLLMENT (2008)

SECONDARY ENROLLMENT (2009)

TERTIARY ENROLLMENT (2009)

*Ratio of female-to-male enrollment in tertiary education; a ratio of 1 represents gender-equal enrollment.

Source: World Bank, Education Indicators, http://data.worldbank.org/topic/education.

Financial conditions play a major role in the decisionmaking process.[123] The World Bank reports that the highest dropout rates occur in communities where students are expected to pay tuition. And in Dushanbe, where roughly half the students pay tuition, 17 percent of the respondents cited financial reasons for why they left school early, compared with 11 percent in other urban areas and 6 percent in rural areas.[124] The gender biases are smallest in Sughd, partly because they are also smaller among the Uzbek population than among the Tajiks, and also in GBAO.[125] For rural youth in particular, the long distances that children have to travel can represent a major hardship. This is especially true for those living in remote areas in GBAO and in the Zerafshan region in Sughd (which consists of the Gornaya Matcha, Penjikent, and Ayni districts). In a United Nations Development Program survey published in 2007, some 69.9 percent of those surveyed said that there was no transportation available to get their children to school. When asked about continuing education, some 96.4 percent of respondents from Gornaya Matcha said that they would send their children more than 100 kilometers away after they received incomplete secondary education close to home; 25.3 percent gave the same answer in Penjikent, and 19.6 percent in Ayni.[126]

Tajik schools are also in terrible physical condition, although the government has been putting increased resources into trying to improve their physical plant as well as increase the number of teachers and the quality of the curriculum. Much of this comes through support from the World Bank.

Improving the physical condition of schools has been a priority of the Tajik government in recent years, including a renewed commitment to repair or replace operating schools that are in derelict condition, upgrade school water systems, improve heating, and install separate sanitary facilities for boys and girls.[127] USAID has provided some emergency relief in this area, and more substantial funding is coming from the World Bank. The intent is to build 450 new schools nationwide.

The World Bank has programs that support 416 schools (75 percent of them primary) for the development of parent–teacher associations and extracurricular activities and for improving school enrollment and completion. The Bank is also providing 100 rehabilitation grants to improve school infrastructure, to do the large-scale rehabilitation of seven district school offices and 100 schools, and to support curriculum development at the Ministry of Education.[128] These activities are all under a grant of approximately $24 million that covers the period from May 2003 until July 31, 2013.

One big challenge with all these school construction and repair projects is to keep the money from falling into the wrong hands, as the enabling legislation calls for homes, railroad wagons, and administrative buildings to be reconstructed as necessary to meet the critical shortage. This builds in a temptation to find the "right" buildings and give contracts for their reconstruction to the "right" companies, creating a situation in which more attention seems to go into finding the right people to benefit from the process than to achieving the outcome itself.[129]

A 2006 report from the International Monetary Fund showed that 45.1 percent of all schools still lacked sufficient desks (and many schools ran two separate sessions each day), 36.5 percent lacked blackboards, and 71.7 percent still lacked heating fuel. The situation in rural schools is somewhat worse than in urban ones.[130] The claim to adequate heating fuels must also be viewed with some skepticism, for it means that children are educated in rooms with heating in winter, but these (as this author saw herself) can be located in trailer-like structures supplied with heat from primitive dung- or wood-burning furnaces. Overall, however, there appears to have been some significant improvement, as reported by 65 percent of the communities in the 2007 TLSS, including 57 percent improvement in the supply of tables, chairs, and blackboards. But only 48 percent reported improvement in classroom heating, and 17 percent reported that the physical conditions in their schools had deteriorated.[131] There is also a serious problem of maintenance—even new and renovated schools are often in poor condition. For example, in March 2010 this author visited the new school (erected on the site of the earlier one) in President Rahmon's home town, Dangara, which had been open only five years, and already the septic system (for outdoor plumbing) was not functioning, leading the school director to confide that people were keeping their daughters home because of this (presumably, the boys just quietly used the school grounds to take care of their needs).

Tajik schools also continue to close in the winter because of inadequate heat (operating without electricity in winter, however, is the norm). They also close in the spring and fall, to allow students to help with planting and with the harvest, or with other communal tasks when extra labor is needed. The latter practice seems to be on the initiative of local authorities, which neither consult on nor report school closures. This appeared to have been the case when this author observed the entire citizenry of Dangara set to work to finish a giant teahouse that was to be the meeting place when President Emomali Rahmon celebrated Navruz in his hometown with Turkmen president Gurbanguly Berdymukhamedov. The 2007 TLSS reported that 20 percent of the schools were closed for at least a week during the 2006–2007 school year, with as many as 40 percent reporting such a closure, and only 2 percent in Dushanbe.[132]

Getting to school, especially in inclement weather, is a challenge for rural students in particular; although 95 percent of all students live within 5 kilometers of their general education schools, that can be a considerable distance to cover for younger children in rural areas where there is no public transportation and many families lack their own means of transportation. Nonetheless, only 4 percent of all parents reported that their children did not attend school for this reason. This does call into question the accuracy of school attendance figures as reported in the 2007 TLSS, in which 20 percent of students reported missing at least one week of school, and only 6 percent said that they had missed more than two weeks. The distances that need to be traveled to reach specialized secondary education and higher education are much longer; respectively, only 63 and 55 percent of the communities are within 5 kilometers of them, which is why expenses for room and board become such a financial challenge for so many families.[133]

Students may also need to skip school in order to help their families during the planting and harvesting seasons, or because they must work to help their families financially. Absenteeism can be much higher in certain localities, especially in poorer districts that grow cotton. For example, a 2007 UNICEF-commissioned study reported that students in Zafarabod District in Sughd Oblast missed up to one-third of all classroom instruction because they were out working in the fields.[134] The same study reported that some 200,000 children aged five to fourteen were engaged in some sort of work (excluding nonintensive household chores, in which the vast majority of children engage[135]).

Surprisingly, only about 20 percent of the child laborers surveyed by UNICEF dropped out of school. School dropouts are rarer in rural areas (7 percent of all working children) than in urban areas (26 percent of all children),[136] reflecting the seasonal nature of agricultural labor. However, there is no question that the prevalence of child labor seriously diminishes the quality of life for children who are forced to work, and that by making it harder for them to perform well in school, it also likely substantially diminishes their chances for economic betterment during their adult years. To quote a twelve-year-old boy from Khamadoni District in Khatlon Oblast, and a thirteen-year-old from Roghun District in the Region of Republican Subordination, respectively,

> Once we get back from school and do all [the] housework there is no time left. In the cotton season we pick cotton till late at night.... However, everybody likes to play, and I work so hard during the day that coming back home I am so tired that I cannot do my homework[;] sleep hangs on my eyelids.[137]

Tajikistan's education system has suffered from the loss of the most experienced teachers, especially in the sciences and foreign languages, to migration or career changes. Only 61 percent of the teachers working in 2008 and 2009 had completed higher education.[138] Part of this problem is also derived from the nature of the educational curriculum, which still has dozens of mandated subjects, all of which require special certification to teach. One of the products of this is that Tajikistan has relatively low faculty/student ratios, of 22.5 and 16.5 for primary and secondary education, respectively—and these ratios are especially low considering the country's low GDP.[139]

Tajikistan's higher education system has been charged with producing a new generation of teachers, graduating them (under conditions of questionable supervision) in large numbers, and sending them to schools with vacancies. School salaries have gone up, but not sufficiently to make the profession attractive. The government also seems quite far from meeting its goal of sending 20 to 25 percent of all teachers for professional retraining.

There has also been attention to curriculum reform. But this is still at the earliest stages. The National Development Plan from 2007 sets as a goal that

> a number of programs will be implemented focusing on the introduction of a unified educational management system; connecting educational institutions to the Internet; setting up a higher education loan program; ensuring that students are better informed about human rights, public health, hygiene, and a healthy lifestyle.

But the report then goes on to note that these will be accomplished "as financial resources allow." And these resources have not proven adequate to even attempt most of these goals, including creating a system of higher educational loans or of giving scholarships to girls from poor families, something that the document advocates as a "social goal."[140]

Partly in recognition of the poor state of higher education in the country, the government of Tajikistan maintains a quota of students who can pursue their education outside the country at state expense—including about 3,000 young people between 2004 and 2009 (for up to six years of instruction), at the behest of "presidential funds." The overwhelming majority of these young people go to school in Russia.[141]

The entire Central Asian region has been struggling, largely unsuccessfully, to maintain Soviet-era educational standards, which were themselves in decline in the years leading up to the USSR's collapse. But Tajikistan has had a harder task than most trying to do this, given the brain drain during and even after its civil war and the shortage of resources. The failings of the educational system and the slow pace at which reform is proceeding are likely to have more subsequent effects than in any other social service sector. This situation has led to reduced economic opportunities for Tajiks seeking employment both at home and abroad, and has made the country a less attractive place for foreign investment. Yet even if the pace of educational reform increases, a full generation of the workforce will be marked by the substandard education that they received, and the country will need to face the exacerbated social problems to which this is likely to lead.

Labor Migration and Forced Labor

Human trafficking for forced labor and sexual exploitation is a major concern for both Tajikistan and its neighboring countries. Tajik men are trafficked to countries like Russia for labor in construction and agriculture. The trafficking of men appears to be a far more severe problem than the trafficking of women as sex workers, given the continued the pervasiveness of traditional values in much of Tajikistan (one partial exception is Sughd Oblast). In recent years, Tajik women, including young girls, have been trafficked to the United Arab Emirates, Russia, India, Turkey, and Iran, although it has been difficult to assess the severity of this threat. As an indicator of the problem's extent, the International Organization for Migration has reported that 300 girls and women were lured from Tajikistan in 2000 to the Emirates with promises of respectable jobs but were forced to work in the sex trade instead.[142] In Sughd Oblast, there were twelve cases reported of minors trafficked abroad in the sex trade in 2010, primarily to the Emirates and Turkey.[143]

Evaluations of Tajikistan's efforts to combat human trafficking are mixed. The government is taking steps against trafficking; among other efforts, it created an antitrafficking unit at the Ministry of the Interior, has implemented antitrafficking legislation, and is cooperating with organizations like the Organization for Security and Cooperation in Europe and the International Labor Organization. For instance, as part of the OSCE-organized Dialogue on Human Trafficking, the OSCE has been working with the Tajik government to implement measures like the country's National Anti-Trafficking Action Plan.[144] Conversely, some of the Tajik initiatives, such as the Ministry of the Interior's antitrafficking unit, are plagued by inefficiency and a lack of funding, the relevant authorities can lack training on dealing with victims of human trafficking, and the country continues to rely on internationally funded shelters and nongovernmental organizations for much of the work being done with awareness-raising campaigns and victims of human trafficking.[145]

Trafficking of persons is covered by Article 130.1 of Tajikistan's Criminal Code, which prohibits both sexual exploitation and forced labor, and provides a sentence ranging from five to fifteen years (a maximum incarceration term that is five years less than for rape, for example) for offenses in this category. In the first six months of 2009, Tajikistan's Commission on Human Trafficking reported only 22 complaints involving trafficking in persons, and during the first nine months of 2009, one person was prosecuted under Article 130.1, three people under Article 132 (deceptive recruiting), and nine people under Article 9 (trade in underage persons).[146] Tajikistan remains a "tier 2" country for human trafficking, according to the U.S. State Department's reports on forced labor and trafficking in persons. This status means that the government of Tajikistan has failed to pursue sufficiently rigorous standards (including providing adequate legislation and follow-up) in its efforts to combat human trafficking.

Moreover, the government has not put any serious effort into finding jobs for the potential migrant laborers. Instead, many Tajiks find work through job fairs organized by labor brokers from Russia, who come to particular towns or regions (with permission from, and presumably to the pecuniary advantage of, local leaders) to sign up workers. Immigration specialists point out that the workers are often sent to towns different from, and generally more remote than, those for which they originally sign up, and that their conditions of employment often resemble incarceration more than voluntary employment. In many cases, workers are almost completely dependent on their employers for transportation to work sites and back. Sometimes, these workers have their passports taken from them when they arrive, and do not get them back until their contracts are finished, making it impossible for them to "escape." There are also many reports of cases where workers do not receive their wages, or receive reduced wages, or are compelled to work 16 to 18 hours a day, along with reported instances of "foremen" physically abusing those working for them.[147] Furthermore, with long working hours and in some cases, no transportation or passports, workers have no means of independently accessing basic services like those given by Russian government agencies and banks.

Tajik migrant workers also generally have little understanding of their legal rights, and even those who are better informed often have a difficult time successfully asserting them. In Olimova's 2003 study, 67.6 percent of the labor migrants reported paying for registration, even though it was supposed to be provided free of charge. In part, this was because the migrant workers could not afford to make repeated visits to government offices to obtain registration, either because they would lose much work time or because they were physically unable to leave, and so it was easier to simply pay bribes to get the registration.[148]

The creation of the State Migration Service (in the Ministry of Labor and Social Protection) was intended to address the employment conditions encountered by Tajiks, and to ensure that there are agreements between private employment agencies and employers to provide some protection to Tajiks who go abroad without guaranteed health or disability insurance, and to pay for their transport home in the event of disability or death. There are bilateral agreements between Tajikistan and the Russian Federation on the protection of the rights of Tajik nationals in

Russia and of Russian nationals in Tajikistan (signed in 2004), and there is an intergovernmental agreement between Tajikistan and Kazakhstan (adopted in 2006), which calls for bilateral working groups on the regulation of external labor migration. These agreements provide for the mutual recognition of degrees and professional qualifications, and the agreement with Kazakhstan in particular stipulates that these workers have the rights of social protection afforded by the operative legislation of the receiving country, including specifically employer-provided health care. But there is no evidence that either side has followed through to ensure compliance by those who employ Tajik migrant labor. Tajik laborers in Kazakhstan must technically be issued an identity card granting them free movement in the country. In reality, it appears that very little is actually done to make sure that this occurs, despite the introduction of a program called Registration of Labor Migration of Tajik Nationals (established in June 2003), which is supposed to enable issuing Tajik nationals working abroad an external registration card (effective January 2004) that is to be processed by the State Migration Service.

Tajik migrant workers can now stay in Russia for up to 90 days without registration.[149] Inconsistencies in Russia's migration law create a special set of issues for the children of migrants, especially in areas like access to education.[150] Although there are many complaints about the treatment of Tajik migrants in Russia, there is no evidence that the ill treatment of Tajiks is the result of any Russian government policy designed to limit migration of seasonal laborers from Central Asia. There is, however, some evidence of Russia's Federal Migration Service (FMS) using its authority as a bargaining chip to gain the upper hand in disputes between Russia and Tajikistan. In November 2011, Tajikistan jailed two pilots, one of them a Russian citizen, who stopped to refuel in the country on their way from Afghanistan. The men were sentenced to eight years in prison on charges of smuggling and illegal border crossing. Russia contested the charges, and the dispute escalated. Seemingly in retaliation, the Russian authorities began rounding up Tajik migrants, ultimately deporting more than 300, although the authorities denied that the deportations were tied to the pilots' case and instead cited them as part of an effort to address illegal immigration. Meanwhile, Russia's chief public health official and head of Rospotrebnadzor, Gennady Onishchenko, suggested a temporary ban on Tajik labor migration, citing health concerns that included the high rates of tuberculosis and HIV among Tajik laborers.[151] In a move that was most likely a response to Russian pressure, Tajikistan freed both pilots later that month.[152]

Violence against migrants does seem to be stimulated by certain Russian nationalist groups. In the first nine months of 2009, 48 Tajiks were reported to have been killed in racially inspired incidents, a drop from 97 deaths in 2008 (with 525 injuries),[153] and a decline that probably reflects the fact that fewer Tajiks were working in Russia during the crisis period, rather than a decline in xenophobia. If anything, nationalist xenophobia has increased as a result of Russia's declining economic fortunes. The events following December 15, 2010, when ethnic clashes erupted in Moscow and hundreds were arrested in an attempt to prevent further violence, demonstrated that although largely limited to nationalist fringe groups, violent racism and xenophobia persist in Russia. This will have growing implications as Russia comes to increasingly rely on migrant labor in the years to come.

In addition to ethnic violence and discrimination, Tajik (and other) migrants are subjected to abuse at the hands of corrupt law enforcement officials, both in Russia and as they transit home, who try to extort money from migrant laborers, sometimes even arresting them on falsified charges. Those who are able to afford and obtain airline tickets (which are themselves the object of racketeering because there is such a strong demand for them) try to avoid the roads and rails. But this is not always possible, especially for Tajiks working in relatively remote locations in Russia and Kazakhstan.

The following quotation from a focus group interview in the 2003 Olimova study is presented by the author as a description of a not-infrequent occurrence, and as an illustration that brutality toward migrants is by no means a trait particular to ethnic Russians. The respondent, a fifty-two-year-old from Dushanbe, reported:

> Recently we were on our way back from a commercial trip
> to Bishkek and passed through Osh [both in Kyrgyzstan].
> Traveling with us were some young guys returning home
> from working in Russia. They were afraid of everybody. They
> paid the sum "for travel" demanded by the driver of the van,

but unlike the other passengers, who were seated inside the van, they were forced to sit in with the baggage. When I tried to protest, the driver told me, "And you shut up or I'll kick you out of the van and you'll be worse off than they are." Whenever the van stopped at a police post or at the border, the driver said to the officers, "I have Tajiks in the van who are coming back from Russia and they've got loads of money on them. At each post the guys were required to pay a lot of money. The poor guys were so scared they agreed to pay. On the way we stopped off at the driver's home. The owners of the house took away all the gifts the guys were bringing home for their relatives. When we approached the Uzbek border, they were asked again to pay for crossing the border. At the last post, the guys were asked to hand over their last remaining money. They refused and were beaten up, badly injured, and allowed to go home.[154]

The Russian government's policy has been to attempt to manage labor migration through the FMS, which in its current form was created in 2004 and falls under the umbrella of the Interior Ministry. It is in charge of migration-related law enforcement, control, and supervision, and provides government services in the sphere of migration. There is even some evidence that the Russian Federation is trying to get migrant workers to settle permanently in Russia, rather than to have to continue to monitor and regulate a constantly arriving and departing seasonal workforce; some even claim that this is one reason why the formal labor quotas for migrant workers from Tajikistan and Kyrgyzstan have been cut by the Russian authorities.[155] It is difficult to know how much credence to put on these reports, as the Russian government terminated its expedited service for obtaining Russian citizenship in July 2009, when the International Crisis Group (ICG) reports that the service was "facilitated" by a $3,000 bribe. Expedited citizenship was a process designed for citizens of the former Soviet Union who arrived in Russia from a former Soviet republic, and who were registered in the Russian Federation by July 1, 2002, or had a temporary or permanent residence permit but did not have Russian citizenship. Under these circumstances, persons wishing to obtain Russian citizenship could do so without having fulfilled the requirements for minimum residency (five years), proof of Russian language proficiency, and proof of legal income. The expedited citizenship program was renewed multiple times, eventually ending on July 1, 2009. It remains in effect for other categories of migrants—for instance, for family reunification.

The FMS has argued that the migrants who wanted to file for expedited citizenship had enough time to do so. Moreover, the expedited citizenship option had the unintended consequence of attracting applicants who wanted Russian citizenship without intending to settle in Russia permanently, because being a citizen makes working in the country much easier. Opponents of the decision say that terminating the expedited option effectively denies a path to citizenship for citizens of countries of the former Soviet Union who have lived in Russia legally for many years and will now be forced to deal with a complex bureaucratic process.

Even as early as 2005, the number of Tajiks opting not to return home was increasing by 8 percent per year, during the period from 1997 through the first nine months of 2005.[156] But according to the same ICG report, only 79,000 Tajiks have received Russian citizenship since independence, and not all of them have done so because of a desire to have an easily available "escape" route in case the political and or economic situation in Tajikistan deteriorates further.[157] The International Organization for Migration's report, however, shows that a total of "1,213,855.5" people from Tajikistan chose to remain in Russia from 1993 through September 2005, using data from the FMS—and offering no explanation for what that "0.5 person" constituted.[158]

Most of those returning home did not do so because they lacked a residence permit (5.5 percent of males, 3.8 percent of females) or work permits (5.2 and 7.2 percent) or because their permits expired (3.5 and 5.6 percent), or because their work was seasonal (6.8 and 2.5 percent, remembering that these data are from 2007, before the crisis), but for family reasons (18.3 and 20.5 percent) or because they were homesick (27.7 and 32.4 percent).

Although migrant households are somewhat better provided with durable goods, such as cars and other vehicles, and various electrical appliances, increases in quality of life are relatively marginal. Remittances sent from abroad provide for family subsistence and somewhat improved family living conditions, but households do not as a general rule become affluent. To quote from Olimova's conclusions in her 2003 study:

> Despite the increase in purchasing power, labour migration clearly does not produce wealth. Even migrants who improved their families' financial position are just relatively better off. The only real estate that they own is the flat or house where they live, and they have neither accumulated substantial capital nor created means of production. Migrant earnings have not had a significant effect on small business development.[159]

The rate at which return migrants are employed in Tajikistan is slightly lower than the national average (50.0 percent of male returning migrants were employed, versus 58.5 percent of the entire male population), suggesting that many migrants are content to not seek work when they are back in Tajikistan because they are anticipating a return abroad when they need to earn money again. And they do return, despite the fact that there are also substantial social dislocations associated with migration, including what many experts feel to be a substantial diminishing of family values. There are reports that up to 30 percent of single migrants find spouses while living abroad; even more worrisome are reports that up to 50 percent of those migrants with families at home enter into legally unsanctioned marriage arrangements while living abroad, something that men in particular find easy to justify given Islam's purported tolerance of polygamy.[160] For the families left behind in such cases, obtaining child support is next to impossible, particularly if there has been no official divorce or if the parents had been married in a religious ceremony without registering the marriage with the state. The burden of supporting the family then falls on the mothers, many of whom are poorly educated, rural women not accustomed to working outside the home.[161] However, there have been some encouraging developments on the part of the state. Amid a wave of cases where migrant laborers divorce their wives with a mobile phone text message or call, the State Religious Committee announced that the Council of Ulema was set to issue a fatwa banning "SMS divorce" (that is, a divorce done via text message).[162]

Migration has also reinforced patriarchal values, as where family units combine to try to preserve a male head of household. Olimova's 2003 study reports that 28.8 percent of the households in her study consisted of two or more households living together, and that households headed by females, which increase in number through migration, are likely to be poorer than those headed by men (even multigenerational households).[163] Households headed by women also seem to have higher incidences of social problems, given that children are often left unsupervised for long periods when their mothers are working. A variety of health concerns are associated with returning migrants, whose more traditional sexual mores are challenged in Russia, which frequently means that they bring back sexually transmitted diseases—including, less frequently, HIV/AIDS.[164] Migrants' health can also deteriorate because of their working conditions.

The recent economic crisis has had a significant effect on labor migration. The crisis caused a slowdown in Russia's and Kazakhstan's construction sectors, important sources of employment for Tajik labor migrants; caused remittances to Tajikistan to drop by an estimated 30 percent in 2009; and resulted in harsher regulations for labor migrants and a disruption of the seasonal migration cycle.[165] The Olimov study reports that fewer migrants returned to Tajikistan in the winter of 2008–2009 because they could not afford the journey. A total of 40.3 percent of labor migrants surveyed reported a salary drop, and 23.6 percent reported working fewer hours and firings. For some, these hardships resulted in a deterioration of living conditions and a decrease in money transferred home. At the same time, host countries adopted lower quotas, deportations rose, and migrants reported a worsening relationship with law enforcement.

The crisis has also had several domestic implications for Tajikistan. First, as the ICG report points out, increased domestic unemployment resulting from the return of migrants from Russia and other host countries has been a potential source of unrest. The 2009 fall in remittances has also been significant for a country so reliant on them—in 2008, remittances accounted for up to 49 percent of Tajikistan's GDP.[166] The ICG report estimates that it may be two or three years before Russia's demand for migrant labor returns to precrisis levels.[167]

For migrants returning to Tajikistan, reintegrating into Tajik society can be challenging. On the one hand, some who return start their own businesses and generally fare better in finding work—unemployment is almost 1.5 times lower among returning migrants than the population as a whole. At the same time, after spending years abroad, returning workers may find themselves socially marginalized. Family conflicts also arise. As the Olimov report observes, women naturally come to play a more important role when the head of the household is absent, and many are reluctant to give up their new freedom and influence when their husbands return; so the clash between traditional gender roles and women's new independence leads to conflict.

CHAPTER 9

LOOKING AHEAD

Twenty years after independence, Tajikistan is still a country that is very much at risk. It began this period with a devastating civil war, which dramatically exacerbated the economic challenges of having to build a nation-state from the fragments of the unitary Soviet economy that Tajikistan's leaders had inherited. These challenges have only been partially resolved. Tajikistan has introduced a semiconvertible national currency, created a legislative foundation for small and medium-sized private enterprises, and introduced some agricultural reforms. Yet its economy remains dominated by large, state-owned enterprises that are only minimally transparent, and even more important, the economy cannot support a substantial minority of the working-age population, as more than 50 percent of men aged twenty to forty-five years are said to work outside the country. Future efforts at economic recovery will need to take better account of Tajikistan's deteriorating environment if they wish to be successful.

The process of political institution building that began with the negotiation of the National Reconciliation Agreement has been effectively frozen over time. The Parliament is now less representative than it was in the late 1990s, the media are less free, and independent political and religious groups are more hampered in their functioning. All important decisions must be made in consultation with the president, whose family also provides most of the country's economic leaders. No viable political institutions have developed to promote an orderly political transition.

President Rahmon has sought to use international institutions and interested foreign powers to try to increase Tajikistan's economic opportunities, more or less taking whatever funds are available—even if it commits him to reforms that he either will not seriously attempt or lacks the technical expertise to successfully introduce, creates a lack of coherence in his economy, and sets up competitive relationships between powerful countries (each of which might someday decide to disengage with Tajikistan).

In many ways, it is most surprising that Rahmon has been able to keep up this juggling act for as long as he has, continuing in office as much because of public apathy as his political cunning. But as the years go on, the problems seem likely to mount. And they could increase quite rapidly because NATO's drawdown from Afghanistan could increase the security threats Tajikistan faces and mean less international assistance for the entire Central Asian region.

TAJIKISTAN'S CIRCUMSCRIBED WORLD

The civil war and the process of reconciliation that followed meant that Tajikistan began its state-building process roughly five years later than all the other former Soviet republics in Central Asia. In many ways, it never really "caught up," because by the time Emomali Rahmon had sufficiently consolidated his power to be able to govern, the other four Central Asian countries had more or less carved out their paths. This left the Tajik leader to try and figure out how to advance his own and his country's interests in the space left to him. In doing so, he faced hostile and potentially hostile neighbors, and great powers offering restricted kinds of protection that frequently seemed to the Tajiks to better serve the agendas of the protectors than of the "protectee."

Most of Tajikistan's electricity lines and other links to the outside world went through Uzbekistan, which had already staked its claim to be a regional power and defined Tajikistan as a risk to its domestic stability, seeking to reduce Tajiks' access to Uzbekistan by maintaining tight border controls and even introducing a visa regime for citizens of Tajikistan.[1] For the Tajiks, these restrictions were particularly burdensome, because their long-distance trucks did not meet European continental standards (under the TIR system), so freight from Tajikistan was never handled as through freight but instead needed to pass arduous inspections that increased the cost of shipping out of the country.[2] Shipping through Kyrgyzstan was little better, as the mountainous roads were not always passable in winter, but this did open up shipping opportunities onward through Kazakhstan both across to Russia and Europe and out through China.

Tajikistan's long border with Afghanistan has also been a constant source of challenges. Tajikistan was pressed to take sides during the fighting that followed the Soviet withdrawal, given Afghanistan's large ethnic Tajik population. Tajikistan's trade prospects have been affected by the destruction of Afghanistan's highway system and the continued security risks associated with using them. As a result even the opening up of new bridges between Tajikistan and Afghanistan has done little to improve the overall trading environment of either country. Tajikistan still confronts the insecurity of Afghanistan's highways as it seeks to access Afghanistan's ports, and Afghanistan can access Tajikistan's markets, but still is confronted with the difficulties of getting long-distance freight across Uzbekistan into Tajikistan.

Moreover, as Tajikistan moves toward membership in the Customs Union with Russia, Kazakhstan, and Belarus (which will almost definitely also include Kyrgyzstan), Tajikistan's trade with Afghanistan will need to conform to the terms of trade that have been established for the Customs Union as a whole, and Tajikistan will no longer be free to set preferential trading standards directly with Afghanistan.

Russia was initially almost an exclusive trading partner with Tajikistan, but in recent years (see figure 9.1), Moscow's advantage has begun to decrease, especially as Tajikistan's increasing engagement with the international financial institutions has helped Tajik economists and financial planners think of better ways to try to manage the trade deficit that the country had accumulated to Russian enterprises.

At the same time that Tajikistan has been moving toward closer economic integration with Russia and the other members of the Customs Union, the country has begun paying more attention to its trade-and-tariffs regime, as part of an effort to increase its economy's global reach. In March 2004, Tajikistan began the process of accession to the World Trade Organization, which at the time of this writing is far from complete. In the early years of the accession process, Tajikistan was hampered by its

FIGURE 9.1

TAJIKISTAN'S IMPORT AND EXPORT PARTNERS, 2001–2010

IMPORT PARTNERS

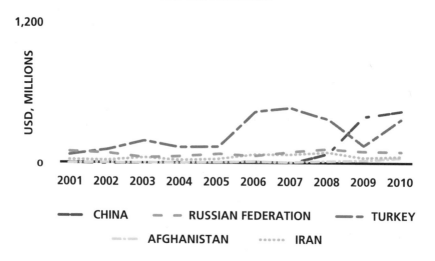

EXPORT PARTNERS

Source: International Monetary Fund, Direction of Trade Statistics, Yearbook 2011, 2011.

desire to ensure that its trade-and-tariff policies stayed roughly in sync with those of Russia and the other members of the Eurasian Economic Community.[3] But over time, that organization has effectively been supplanted by the Customs Union of Russia, Belarus, and Kazakhstan, and Tajikistan has been able to pursue its negotiations on a more exclusively national track.[4] Nonetheless, there are still many obstacles before Tajikistan will be in ready to join the World Trade Organization.

It is not clear how Tajikistan's moves toward Russia and the Customs Union will affect its relations with China, which is quickly becoming an important trading partner, or for its other significant partners, such as Iran, as is shown in figure 9.1.

RISKS OF ENVIRONMENTAL DESPOLIATION AND CLIMATE CHANGE

Tajikistan's future economic growth and the welfare of its citizens will be adversely affected if it does not begin to better address the environmental degradation of recent decades. There is little reason for optimism that the country will be able to successfully do so.

Added to this are the growing risks associated with climate change, and the increasing incidence of weather-related and other environmentally generated natural disasters. Taken collectively, their potentially devastating effects are so great that the United Nations Development Program is placing a real priority on developing an early warning system to better anticipate future disasters.

In 2008, the World Bank estimated that the total environmental damage to Tajikistan was about 690 million somoni, or $200.1 million, per year, or approximately 9.5 percent of the country's gross domestic product, with land degradation (including soil erosion) alone costing 3.8 percent of GDP (rising to 4.4 percent if deforestation and rangeland degradation were included).[5] Environmental degradation caused by natural disasters, including landslides and mudflows, led to an annual loss of approximately 1.6 percent of GDP. Other forms of environmental degradation included indoor and outdoor air pollution (increasingly linked to the growing number of automobiles);[6] the degradation of the water supply (which has an impact on hygiene and sanitation); and over exposure to lead.[7] In addition to having a negative impact on Tajikistan's economy, environmental degradation has a strong negative impact on the health of the population, with 2 percent of adult mortality attributed to air pollution (both indoor and outdoor, taken collectively) and 17 percent of child mortality (under five years of age) linked to the country's inadequate water supply, which affects virtually all its rural population.[8]

As in so many other areas, Tajikistan has taken a formalist approach to addressing its environment. The country's Constitution, as adopted in 1994 and amended in 1999 and 2003, commits the state to ensure a healthier environment for its citizens and establishes state ownership of mineral resources, water, and air, pledging the state to use these to the benefit of its citizens.[9]

The Constitution has been supplemented by the 1993 Law on the Protection of Nature, which established the responsibility of the various government departments and agencies to supervise the environment and which was amended in 1996 and in 2002 to reflect structural reorganizations of the government. There was also a Law on Specially Protected Territories, setting up the system of nature reserves and national parks, all of which are recorded in a Cadastre of Specially Protected Territories, and a 2003 Law on Radiation.[10]

These laws have been supplemented by a large number of laws and action plans that are intended to improve, prevent, and mediate the country's environmental risks. These include a State Program on Environmental Education, adopted in 1996, which called for the development of education programs designed for enterprise managers in particular, to reduce the negative impact that their factories were having on the environment (with particular emphasis on the need for recycling and the gradual shift to closed-cycle production), but which the government did little to implement, in part because of lack of donor interest in funding it.

There was also a State Environment Program for 1998–2008, adopted in 1997, which surveyed the state of the environment in each oblast and listed what activities were necessary to either restore or to maintain a proper ecological balance. The plan also listed a set of practical measures that could be taken to prevent further land erosion, and it allocated land for planting highly productive crops. It offered plans for reforestation (in densely populated areas in particular) and for the protection of sensitive areas, as well as making recommendations for actions that could restore air and water quality. Recommendations were also made for how local industries could use environmentally friendly raw materials and production techniques. In addition, the appropriate government agencies were supposed to report annually on the progress made toward fulfilling the program's goals.[11] Over time, the protected territories have been expanded to include roughly 20 percent of the country, and reforestation projects in the Hissar Valley and the Dushanbe region.

Saodat Olimova, however, argues that the reforestation projects are underfunded, and though many engaged in them lack the necessary scientific background, these projects are strongly supported by their local communities, which often donate much time and energy to them.[12]

Other projects, like the biogas plant at a sewage collection facility in Khujand, which would have removed a major source of water pollution in Sughd Oblast and further downstream, was abandoned in the early stages of production because oblast environmental protection would not (or could not) produce the necessary funding.[13]

In 2001, the Tajik government also adopted a National Action Program to Combat Desertification. It called for the chair of the State Committee for Land Administration to coordinate the development of a national action plan to combat desertification, to classify all the land in the country as to its degree of soil degradation and erosion, and to recommend new legislation or modifications to existing legislation that would elaborate new strategies for combating desertification, as well as to encourage increased activities by public and nongovernmental organizations to achieve these goals.

In 2003, the government adopted a National Strategy and Action Plan on Conservation and Sustainable Use of Biodiversity (in genotypes of plants and animals, as well as in communities and ecosystems). To supervise the initiative's implementation, the government also established the National Biodiversity and Biosafety Center. That same year, it adopted a National Action Plan for Mitigation of Climate Change. And two years later, in 2005, a Center for Environmental Policy and Information was established with funding from the Asian Development Bank to provide a database and to help with the coordination of Tajikistan's policies related to the environmental challenges it is facing.[14] This was also supported by a National Environment Action Plan, which was established in 2006 to monitor both Tajikistan's meteorological services and the implementation of its environmental obligations, such as the Stockholm Convention on Persistent Organic Pollutants.[15]

But the Tajik government reports that it was only able to meet 26.11 percent of its priority needs in the area of promoting environmental sustainability as part of its Poverty Reduction Strategy for 2007–2009. And this was the situation despite the fact that the government's goals with regard to implementing improvements in environmental protection, as described in the Poverty Reduction Strategy, were quite modest, including calling for a 5 percent increase in the area of land covered by forests, a 3 percent increase in the land set aside for biological diversity, a 5 percent reduction in the area of degraded land and pastureland, a reduction of 7 to 9 percent in the discharge of polluted wastewater in groundwater and surface water sources, and a 4 percent reduction in the release of point and nonpoint air pollution. In addition, it called for household solid waste disposal sites, garbage dumps, and tailing ponds to be brought into conformity with the requirements of environmental legislation, and for the restoration and further expansion of the environmental monitoring system.[16] But again, no specific direction was offered as to how this would occur. It was simply a call to heightened duty by the existing environmental agencies.

In addition to the problems that Tajikistan's legislation was designed to at least partly redress, the country faces serious environmental issues from its industry, particularly from TALCO, Tajikistan's aluminum plant, which has created a severe air pollution problem in the city of Tursunzade where the plant is located, accounting for over 75 percent of stationary air pollution there in 2004, when the plant was working at less than 75 percent capacity. The plant also releases fluoride compounds, which then contaminate the local water supply.

A World Bank report notes that the daily intake of inhabitants in Jamoat Karatag (Karatag village) in the Tursunzade region is 2.8 milligrams of fluoride; health risks begin to be a factor at 0.2 to 0.3 milligrams per kilogram of body weight, not to mention the cumulative impact of consuming that much fluoride on a daily basis for years at a time. Overconsumption of fluoride can lead to various gastric conditions (including chronic diarrhea), to immune system impairment, and, at its most severe, to organ failure.[17] Moreover, the pollution from TALCO also affects Uzbekistan, and has exacerbated the tension between the two countries.

TALCO, however, is not the country's only major industrial polluter. The Anzob Integrated Mining and Concentrate Plant in the Aininsk District of Sughd Oblast releases antimony and mercury; the Integrated Mining and Concentrate Plant in Adrasman, Sughd, releases lead, zinc, and gold; and Vostokredmet in Penjikent, Sughd, releases uranium and vanadium. Overall, Tajik enterprises annually generate about 1,000 tons of galvanized toxic waste, which is first stored at the enterprises and then dumped in landfills. Tajikistan has no centralized sanitary facilities for storing hazardous wastes, nor any specialized treatment facilities, not to mention plants that recycle hazardous materials for secondary use. A 2009 expert assessment found ten tailing sites in Tajikistan with a combined total of 170 million tons of waste mass (55 million tons of radioactive waste mass and 115 million tons of rocks and low-grade ores, spread over 3.0 square kilometers).[18] Of these, approximately 64 million tons of radioactive tailings (mainly in Sughd[19] and the Faizabad District) are left from Soviet-era uranium production and are found within 6 kilometers of residential communities.[20]

The deteriorating quality of Tajikistan's groundwater is linked to municipal discharges (including poorly maintained sanitation systems), industrial pollution, agricultural pollution (created by the long-term use of fertilizers and other pesticides), and poor drainage on irrigated lands.

Overall, the World Bank notes that Tajikistan's 2002 State of the Environment Report estimates that 22 to 25 million metric tons of solid waste, 20 million cubic meters of liquid industrial waste, and 200 million metric tons of mining waste have accumulated in the country. Overall, at that time 1,100 hectares of land were devoted to waste dumps and waste storage sites, including 800 hectares of mining waste. This includes waste from industry, agriculture, building refuse, and municipal waste.[21] Some 4 to 5 million cubic meters of municipal waste are generated annually, most of which is dumped into legal landfills. But illegal landfills are also common. There is no waste-sorting or treatment facility in the country, and illegal burning of leaves is still common.

A 2008 World Bank study of the country's environmental problems nonetheless concluded:

> The analysis suggests that the key constraints in environmental management in the country are not from the absence of well-defined environmental policies but rather inadequate legislation and bylaws/guidelines to implement specific policies in particular, weaknesses in institutional design, lack of vertical and horizontal coordination, lack of capacity of institutions, and insufficient funding.... The analysis also suggests that policies currently followed do not provide economic incentives for pollution reduction and more efficient use of natural resources.[22]

The problems with the implementation of Tajikistan's environmental legislation are manifold. There are too few inspectors, so it often takes them a year to get back to a business that has been found in violation of an environmental law, reducing any incentive that the entrepreneur involved might have to spend the money to remedy the problem.

Much of the legislation related to environmental protection was poorly drafted, and in some cases it simply restates Soviet-era laws that were designed to respond to very different economic and even environmental conditions. Or, in some cases, the laws provide for long lists of pollutants, such as 197 chemical pollutants for water (including 101 different pesticides) and 123 different pollutants for air quality, but then only develop tests for a handful of them. Other times, the law calls for specific types of hazardous and nonhazardous waste disposal, but factories and businesses are not expected to install monitoring equipment for environmentally polluting emissions, and inspectors are not given such equipment. Consequently, the firm owners and inspectors engage in a bargaining process to ascertain what the discharges may have been, a process made more difficult by the fact that few plants operate at capacity, so inspectors must rely on good-faith estimates of the variation in output over time. In addition, localities fail to create proper waste disposal sites, partly because the revenues they can raise from waste collection are based on rates that are so low (designed to get people to dispose of waste properly) that they are not adequate to equip or maintain waste disposal sites.

Similarly, though the Tajik government has reorganized its various ministries and departments that deal with environmental issues, none of these changes has been anything but cosmetic—shuffling bureaucrats, but failing to address the aspects of the various laws that make them difficult to enforce. One of the major problems that has remained throughout is that very little expertise needs to be demonstrated in order to occupy a post as an environmental expert, even though many jobs (like those with the State Environment Control Service) require special licenses (for example, to manage hazardous wastes, ionized radiation, and pesticides).

Fines have generally been set too low to be effective. Most have been set in multiples of monthly salaries—commonly ten or fifteen times an average salary, which is generally substantially less than the cost of fixing a violation. Fines for the poaching of rare species are the highest of all environmental penalties, going up to roughly $10,000 for killing a wild Bukharan mountain ram, but the government itself is rumored to be the biggest abuser of these rules, by allowing foreign dignitaries to hunt in national preserves.[23] Added to this are very ineffective collection practices on the part of local governments. Then the local governments frequently fail to collect the fines levied, and as these funds are frequently designated to fund environmental agencies or other environmental protection activities, they become increasingly more underfunded. For example, in 2003, just before the World Bank did its study of Tajikistan's environmental problems, Sughd Oblast's local ecology fund had only $2,995 (8,755 somoni).[24]

Environmental agencies can suspend enterprises that are found in violation of the code, and then bring a case to police departments and prosecutors' offices to investigate whether criminal charges should be brought against the owners of the suspended business. According to Tajikistan's Criminal Code, criminal charges can be brought in case of violations of laws concerning environmental safety, poaching, land degradation, pollution, and interference with subsoil resources. But between 1998 and 2008, when the World Bank report was written, only two criminal cases were brought against environmental violators, and they were both dismissed because the enterprises had a bearing on military activities.[25]

As bad as things are, there is a strong likelihood that things will get worse. In Tajikistan, environmental despoliation has increased the effect of natural disasters, whose impact the World Bank also believes is exacerbated by the improper selection of sites for economic activity, which furthers natural disasters by imposing technologies that cause human-made landslides, rock slides, and deep depressions. The World Bank study cites the Shurab coal mine as one such example. It also notes the role played by improperly constructed and exploited irrigation schemes, which in its opinion resulted in landslides in Zakhmatabad (or Ayni, Sughd Province), Kamcha, and Sharora (Rasht Valley in the Region of Republican Subordination)—all of which led to extensive physical damage and numerous deaths. In addition, settlements are routinely built in potentially dangerous landslide areas. Finally, the report notes that the construction of large reservoirs, like Nurek, contributes to local seismic activity and reinforces tectonic movements. This suggests a potential for further damage resulting from the construction of the large reservoir planned for Roghun, which, according to current plans, will be even larger than Nurek. The World Bank study reports 13,306 natural disasters in Tajikistan between 2000 and 2006—with 2,586 deaths, 8,884 injuries, and the destruction of 44,373 houses, 1,339 schools and kindergartens, 357 health centers, 2,356 irrigation canals, 494 bridges, 10,796 kilometers of road, 283 hydropower stations, and 182 kilometers of water supply and sewage systems.[26]

As dismal as this current picture may seem, the future could be much worse, especially if the region's annual temperature continues to rise, causing the country's glaciers, which make up 6 percent of its territory, to melt at an increasingly rapid rate.[27] An estimated 20 percent of these glaciers have retreated, and some have disappeared altogether.[28] Experts predict that at current rates, an additional third of the glaciers' volume may be lost, and some smaller glaciers will disappear in their entirety by 2050. Warming temperatures will also lead to changes in the courses of rivers, through small glaciers drying up and others being formed by mudslides caused by glacial melting.[29] This in turn will put further pressure on the irrigation systems (as evaporation rates increase at the same time that the availability of water is reduced), changing the volume of water available to hydroelectric stations and increasing the tensions between these competing uses of water. It is estimated that 20 percent more water will be needed to produce the same amount of water that was available under 2002 climate conditions, because of increased evaporation of irrigation water due to higher temperatures. The projected changes in global temperatures could substantially reduce agricultural yields in Tajikistan, with cotton yields dropping by 15 percent if 20 to 30 percent less water is available for irrigated agriculture and by 35 percent if the available supply of water for irrigation drops by 50 percent.[30] All this could lead to a substantial amount of population movement both within the country and beyond its borders. In addition, the shrinking of Tajikistan's water supply will also likely increase the incidence of waterborne diseases such as diarrhea and malaria.

Looking at the severity of Tajikistan's environmental problems, the weakness of the regulatory framework it has devised to deal with them, the funding challenges that its government faces in trying to address them, and the general lack of government will and its capacity limitations, it is hard to be optimistic that there will be any meaningful redress of the country's ecological problems. As a result, Tajikistan may well be facing environmental catastrophes in the future.

CAN THERE BE A ROSY FUTURE FOR TAJIKISTAN?

During Emomali Rahmon's first years in office, there was some reason for optimism that Tajikistan would commit to comprehensive economic and political reforms, leading to a privatized economy and a competitive political system. Some of the early signs were quite good; international economic and financial experts were invited in, and given as much access to the countryside as the still-fragile security situation made realistic. Rahmon's willingness to share power with politically independent and opposition groups, even if on an unequal basis, created the preconditions for fostering the development of a democratic society.

Ten years later, by late 2006, the following quotation from the Swiss authors of their country's Cooperation Strategy for Central Asia for 2007–2013 articulated a widely held view among Westerners engaged with Tajikistan:[31]

[At the] end of 2006, Tajikistan's development reached a point where the relative stability, given the consolidated power situation, would theoretically allow the government to speed up reforms of the agriculture and public sectors, to decrease state interference in the economy and to enhance decentralization/power devolution. However, realistically considered, no drastic developments in this direction can be expected and thus, the potential of popular unrest caused by widespread dissatisfaction with poor social services, as well as rampant unemployment may increase during forthcoming years.[32]

By this time, it appears that the Western-dominated international financial institutions basically expected the Tajik authorities to continue to behave in a financially lax, if not corrupt, way, and that this was simply part of the cost of continuing to do business in Tajikistan. And with NATO operating just across the border in Afghanistan, and Western financial institutions deeply entrenched in Afghanistan trying to find a way to rebuild its economy, there was no way that the ADB, the World Bank, the EBRD, the IMF, and Tajikistan's various bilateral donors could withdraw from Tajikistan. To do this would have put their goals in Afghanistan at further risk.

So the strategy for these institutions continued to involve prodding Tajikistan's government and state-owned enterprises to enhance their technical capacity, introduce international financial and statistical standards, and move toward cost recovery models for pricing utilities. Efforts were also made to engage Tajikistan on agricultural reform, but all within procedural and financial constraints.

All the donors working in Tajikistan have had funding constraints, most of which have increased in recent years, given the proliferation of economic crises and humanitarian disasters in other parts of the world. Funding limitations meant that efforts at reform projects focused on pilot projects, which is a preference of international donors that see their role as provoking host governments to take on and expand these projects using their own funds. In Tajikistan, however, such funds are clearly limited. And though donor coordination has increased in recent years, few donors pick up successful pilot projects introduced by other funders (and this is particularly true because many donors use technical experts and program facilitators from their own countries). Thus many of these successful pilot projects are not sustained long enough to build support from local and national political elites. And without that support, there is no hope that these pilot reform programs will receive the necessary Tajik government funding to introduce them at a national level. This problem is further complicated by the cynicism that many Tajik elites have developed about the way international assistance has been disbursed in their country, viewing projects in which a large percentage of the expenses goes to foreign specialists being paid wages that are exponentially higher than what locals earn, and whose travel expenses are also included in financial disbursements that need to eventually be repaid by the Tajik government. The fact that Tajikistan is required to repay all the loans that the international financial institutions offer them also limits the "stick" that these institutions have.

Would Tajikistan have been easier to reform if the international financial institutions and Tajikistan's various promarket and pro–political liberalization bilateral donors committed more funding and followed a more integrated and comprehensive approach to providing technical assistance for economic and political institution building?

For those of us who believe that most people in the world aspire to market-based economies and democratically oriented participatory societies, it is reassuring to imagine that if we do a better job of advocating them through word and deed to governors and the governed alike, more countries would choose to evolve in these ways. And the obverse of this is also reassuring to imagine—that countries that fail to evolve in these ways do so because of the greed and corruption of their rulers and the ignorance of those they ruled who in their poverty or isolation prove vulnerable to extremist ideologies.

There is strong evidence to suggest that President Rahmon has used his time in office to advance his own and his family's economic interests, and it is also clear that the Tajik leader enjoys the trappings of power, seeing his picture on streets and highways and having mini-palaces built for his use in the country's principal regions. But this alone is not a sufficient explanation for the fragile state of Tajikistan's economy and the difficulties that the country has had sustaining political reform.

Tajikistan was something of a perfect storm. The country experienced a debilitating civil war that was not caused by those currently in power. But the current rulers inherited a ruined and fractured economy. Because of this the international nation-building community was welcomed by the ruling elites, who needed to consolidate power and appease or buy off their citizens, whose support they needed to remain in power.

As a result, Tajikistan's government let nongovernmental organizations proliferate and economic planners do their respective things, but the country's leadership had no serious interest in considering the longer-term implications of these reform programs and no real commitment to introducing a genuinely democratic and participatory political system or in supporting the full liberalization or privatization of the economy.

When the Tajik elites—who had no previous exposure to a broader international community and the ideas that dominated in the leading North American, European, and Asian capitals—realized that neither economic nor political reform was in their personal interests or those of their key supporters, this doomed many attempts to reform the country's political institutions, slowed down its economic recovery, and kept its key assets in the hands of the state or nontransparent private groups. In doing this, the ruling elites assumed the continued apathy of the country's citizens, who were either still emotionally exhausted from the war years or so concerned with the challenge of surviving economically that they were disinclined to aggressively seek regime change. At the same time, President Rahmon also sought to reinforce his legitimacy through an appeal to history that he was effectively the founder of a modern Somoni dynasty returning the Tajik people to the glories of an earlier millennium.

For their part, the leading international financial institutions did not do the best job possible selling their vision of economic and political change to the Tajik authorities, even given their own internal constraints. Part of the problem was the basic tension created by the fact that these institutions were pursuing regional goals that had to be sold as consistent with the national strategies of the countries themselves, as advanced by country-based teams of these institutions. But for the Tajiks (and this can also be said of most of the leadership of the other Central Asian states), there is a feeling that those defining the policy priorities for the Western-dominated international financial institutions do not understand or appreciate the worldviews of Central Asians.

In private settings, Central Asian policymakers and their advisers frequently complain that the developmental model being advocated by the Western powers and the international financial institutions that they dominate smacks of the same kind of paternalism imposed by Soviet planners and their Russian successors. The charge is made that these foreign visions of what is best for the Tajiks or the other Central Asian nations is removed from the cultural, social, and economic realities of these countries, and that successfully managing these realities requires different kinds of political solutions—stronger leaders and more predictability—than what is being proposed.

The more distant the advisers are from home, and the more dissimilar the advisers' culture, the less understanding they are likely to have of how their proposed reforms, though aimed at improving medium- and long-term prospects for Tajikistan (or some other Central Asian state), may in fact cause short-term stresses and dislocations, undermining the likelihood that medium- and long-term gains will actually occur.

Admittedly, there is a self-serving quality to some of these remonstrations, as the ruling elites clearly have something to gain from maintaining the status quo or opting for slow-paced change (provided they are not overthrown for their policies). But it is easy to see why some of them feel this way, when confronted with foreigners who come to advise them but who know little of their culture or history and do not speak their languages.

This is not to say that everyone who comes to advise them fits such a profile, but more than a few do; and some in fact display the kind of paternalistic or condescending attitudes toward the Tajiks and other Central Asians of which people in the region accuse them. Sometimes foreigners forget that no one gets to the top echelon of power in Central Asia and retains control without being a wily, skilled political figure with some knowledge of large parts of his own population.

Western advisers like to couch their advice by arguing that it is in the Tajiks' best interests to accept the Bretton Woods developmental model. Tajikistan's leaders are astute enough to recognize that this model's political choices—freedom and democracy—have ideological foundations no less deep than the communist system under which they previously lived, and for many prominent Tajiks, Western ideology may seem no more "universal" than the one they were happy enough to be able to discard.

Similarly, they do not see Western assistance as "altruistic" simply because it is being advanced in the name of global peace and stability. Though Tajik leaders want peace and stability in their region and beyond, they do not want them at the expense of what they consider their own valid national security needs. And they see many of the policies they are being pressed to adopt as serving other countries' agendas at the expense of their own.

For example, the sanctions imposed on Iran by the United States and European Union have not influenced Tajikistan's generally friendly relations with Iran so much as made Iran a less valuable ally than it would otherwise be. Pressure to adopt Western-style laws on religious freedom seem to the Tajiks and other Central Asians as driven by the agendas of Protestant minorities and other Christian Evangelical groups that in their opinion want to deny Hanafi Islam its "proper" role in the region—a role that is more than a thousand years old.

The Tajiks believe that decisions as to whether the World Bank will help fund the construction of the Roghun hydroelectric project is a decision as to which nationality is more valuable to the NATO effort in Afghanistan—the Tajiks or the Uzbeks—and fear that it will be decided in the Uzbeks' favor. Unfortunately, no amount of arguing that the decision will be based on the advice of independent experts will convince them that these experts are more knowledgeable than Tajikistan's own scientists—a position that, of course, the Tajik scientists (rather naively) themselves defend.

Western policies regarding Russia seem even more confusing. The Tajiks are expected to stand firm against Russian pressure when Moscow tries to lobby against overflight rights for NATO forces, but when the United States' relations with Russia are warm, Washington often seems ready to accept Moscow's premise that it is entitled to a "special relationship" with the former Soviet republics in Central Asia. But the reverse is also not true; when the United States and NATO view Russia as a potentially hostile power in the region, they are not willing to offer the Tajiks and their Central Asian neighbors any real security guarantees, providing training and a willingness to sell certain kinds of weapons to them (and the latter is of particular interest to NATO as 2014 approaches, and thousands of tons of weapons and equipment must be shipped westward).

These are some of the reasons why it must often appear easier for Rahmon to deal with Russian, Chinese, Iranian, and Arab interlocutors than with their Western counterparts. The members of the former group offer less advice save in the case of the Russians; provide lands and grants with less conditionality; and are able to argue political and cultural affinities that Western leaders just cannot.

But can any of these interlocutors lead Tajikistan out of its current developmental dilemmas? As this book argues, I believe that many of the Tajik government's policies over the past decade in particular have slowed the pace of the country's economic recovery and possibly even put it permanently out of reach. Similarly, the tightening of political controls is providing a ready-made agenda for political opposition groups, and making them potentially more legitimate even as their exercise of power as political minorities has been made more problematic. One or more of these men, or one of their followers, could emerge as a serious adversary for Rahmon if the security situation in and around Tajikistan deteriorates, or if the next few winters are unusually cold and summers unusually hot.

But this does not mean that better policies from the Rahmon government would have translated into solutions for the problems that he inherited when taking power. Collectively, these problems were effectively unsolvable. Tajikistan's economic problems were created by its unexpected independence, as its economy had been shaped by being a dependent republic that was part of an integrated whole—the USSR. These problems included the collapse of its industries due to the disruption of their production supply chains; the overdependence of agriculture on cotton, combined with the environmental degradation caused by the overproduction of cotton; the deterioration of the irrigation system upon which cotton growing and most other forms of agriculture depended; and the difficulties of bringing goods into and out of Tajikistan, which exacerbated all the usual challenges of creating small businesses in post-Soviet states.

There were also a host of social problems, many of which were the direct consequence of Tajikistan's demographic bulge, created by its population's high birthrates in the 1970s and 1980s, which would have led to a deficit of jobs for the working-age population within the republic even under very good economic conditions. And the Tajik baby boomers are now reproducing, albeit at a slower rate than their parents. They are still having families large enough to put educational and health care systems under considerable additional stress. And this is happening at a time when Tajikistan's social services are seeking to become more compatible with a market economy and simultaneously maintain Soviet-era social welfare guarantees.

The challenges for the education system are particularly acute, for they are juggling the consequences of a brain drain from the country, the difficulty of attracting people to a traditionally low-salary but high-status profession in what is now a capitalist economy, the burden of switching a curriculum from Russian to Tajik, and trying to meet new global technological norms in an environment short of electricity.

Finally, the Tajik political elites are still facing the challenges of learning how to govern and the Tajik population still needs to learn and accept the responsibilities of citizenship and of being governed. And this is all being fashioned by people who once learned their lessons in politics from the Soviet Union, where political rhetoric was a substitute for policy; where the state assumed it had the right to define the population's religious and ideological beliefs, rather than allow religious values and political norms to reflect the public will; and where political patronage, corruption, and criminality were all intermingled.

APPENDIX

GROSS DOMESTIC PRODUCT, 1990–2010

	GDP (Current US$, Million)	GDP GROWTH (Annual %)	GDP PER CAPITA (Current US$)	GDP PER CAPITA GROWTH (Annual %)
1990	2,629	-0.60	495.82	-3.09
1995	1,232	-12.40	213.24	-13.67
2000	861	8.30	139.41	7.10
2001	1,081	10.20	173.41	9.14
2002	1,221	9.10	194.27	8.18
2003	1,554	10.20	245.26	9.31
2004	2,076	10.60	324.85	9.66
2005	2,312	10.49	358.32	9.42
2006	2,830	6.70	433.78	5.53
2007	3,719	7.00	563.18	5.71
2008	5,161	7.80	771.34	6.40
2009	4,978	7.90	733.87	6.44
2010	5,640	3.80	819.95	2.36

Source: World Bank Data, http://data.worldbank.org/country/tajikistan?display=default.

NOMINAL GDP BY SECTOR (%), 1995–2010

	PORTION OF GDP (%)							
	1995	1996	1997	1998	1999	2000	2001	
INDUSTRY	34.1	25.7	22.0	20.1	21.7	33.2	33.5	
AGRICULTURE	36.7	36.0	32.0	25.1	25.4	25.1	23.8	
CONSTRUCTION	3.2	2.6	2.7	3.9	5.4	2.1	2.7	
TRADE	7.6	14.6	20.5	22.1	19.7	10.7	10.5	
TRANSPORT AND COMMUNICATIONS	4.4	4.0	2.9	4.2	7.4	4.8	5.0	
OTHER	0.7	1.6	1.6	1.5	1.1	0.7	0.6	
MARKET AND NON-MARKET SERVICES	8.7	7.9	8.6	15.6	12.0	15.1	15.0	
INDIRECT TAXES	4.6	7.6	9.6	7.6	7.3	8.4	9.0	
TOTAL	100	100	100	100	100	100	100	

Source: Agency on Statistics Under President of the Republic of Tajikistan, "Real'nyy sektor:
Nominal'nyy VVP po otraslyam proiskhozhdeniya, 1995–2010" [Real sector: Nominal GDP
by sector of origin, 1995–2010], http://stat.tj/ru/analytical-tables/real-sector.

NOMINAL GDP BY SECTOR (%), 1995–2010

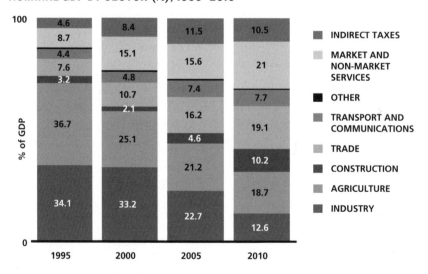

Source: Agency on Statistics Under President of the Republic of Tajikistan, "Real'nyy sektor: Nominal'nyy
VVP po otraslyam proiskhozhdeniya, 1995–2010" [Real sector: Nominal GDP by sector of origin, 1995–
2010], http://stat.tj/ru/analytical-tables/real-sector.

2002	2003	2004	2005	2006	2007	2008	2009	2010
33.1	30.4	23.6	22.7	21.3	18.3	14.2	14.3	12.6
22.2	24.2	19.2	21.2	21.5	19.4	19.9	18.6	18.7
2.0	2.9	7.5	4.6	6.1	8.1	10.3	10.2	10.2
11.4	11.2	16.1	16.2	16.9	16.4	19.4	20.8	19.1
5.5	5.3	6.6	7.4	7.2	9.5	10.1	11.0	7.7
0.7	0.6	0.8	0.7	0.4	0.4	1.0	0.3	0.2
15.1	14.8	15.1	15.6	15.3	15.3	12.5	13.7	21.0
9.9	10.7	11.0	11.5	11.4	12.5	12.6	11.1	10.5
100	100	100	100	100	100	100	100	100

TAJIKISTAN EXCHANGE RATES (Tajik somoni per 1 USD), 2006-2012

2006	2007	2008	2009	2010	2011	2012
31.995	34.265	34.649	34.556	43.714	44.029	47.585

Nominal exchange rates from the first day of the year as reported by the National Bank of Tajikistan.

Source: National Bank of Tajikistan, www.nbt.tj/en/kurs/?c=4&id=28.

AVERAGE ANNUAL NUMBER OF INDIVIDUALS
EMPLOYED BY SECTOR (in thousands)

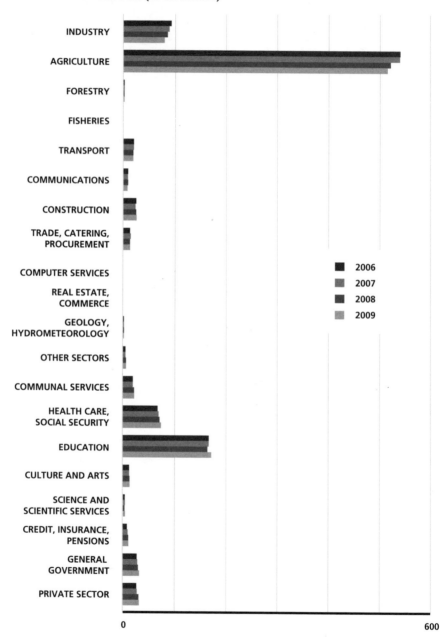

Source: Calculated by author. Data from Agency on Statistics Under President of the Republic of Tajikistan, "Real Sector," http://stat.tj/en/database/real-sector.

AVERAGE ANNUAL INDUSTRY WAGES (in nominal somoni)

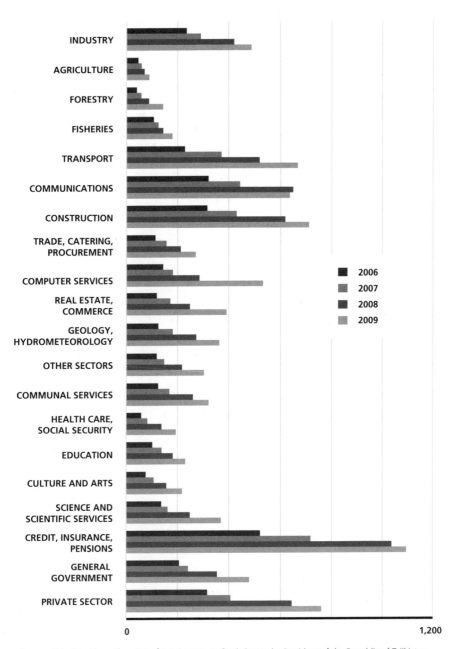

Source: Calculated by author. Data from Agency on Statistics Under President of the Republic of Tajikistan, "Real Sector," http://stat.tj/en/database/real-sector.

POPULATION, LIFE EXPECTANCY, INFANT MORTALITY RATES, 1985–2010

	1985	1990	1995	2000	2001	
POPULATION, TOTAL (THOUSANDS)	4,567	5,303	5,775	6,173	6,233	
POPULATION GROWTH (ANNUAL %)	3.04	2.54	1.46	1.12	0.96	
POPULATION AGES 0–14 (% OF TOTAL)	42.53	43.16	43.65	42.36	41.93	
POPULATION AGES 15–64 (% OF TOTAL)	53.47	53.01	52.51	54.09	54.48	
POPULATION AGES 65 AND ABOVE (% OF TOTAL)	4.01	3.83	3.85	3.55	3.59	
LIFE EXPECTANCY AT BIRTH, TOTAL (YEARS)	63.28	62.86	62.37	63.76	64.10	
LIFE EXPECTANCY AT BIRTH, FEMALE (YEARS)	65.89	66.08	66.30	67.73	68.06	
LIFE EXPECTANCY AT BIRTH, MALE (YEARS)	60.80	59.79	58.64	59.97	60.34	
MORTALITY RATE, UNDER 5 (PER 1,000 LIVE BIRTHS)	121.60	116.40	111.10	93.40	89.70	
MORTALITY RATE, NEONATAL (PER 1,000 LIVE BIRTHS)	—	37.00	36.00	33.00	32.00	

Source: World Bank Data, http://data.worldbank.org/country/tajikistan?display=default.

LITERACY RATES AND SCHOOL ENROLLMENT, 2000–2010

	2000	2001	
LITERACY RATE, YOUTH TOTAL (% OF PEOPLE AGES 15–24)	99.8	—	
LITERACY RATE, ADULT TOTAL (% OF PEOPLE AGES 15 AND ABOVE)	99.5	—	
RATIO OF FEMALE TO MALE PRIMARY ENROLLMENT (%)	93.0	92.8	
RATIO OF FEMALE TO MALE SECONDARY ENROLLMENT (%)	85.9	82.9	
RATIO OF FEMALE TO MALE TERTIARY ENROLLMENT (%)	33.9	31.6	
SCHOOL ENROLLMENT, PRIMARY (% GROSS)*	97.0	96.7	
SCHOOL ENROLLMENT, SECONDARY (% GROSS)*	74.2	76.3	
SCHOOL ENROLLMENT, TERTIARY (% GROSS)*	14.0	13.3	

*Ratio of total enrollment to the population of the age group at the particular level of education.

Source: World Bank Data, http://data.worldbank.org/country/tajikistan?display=default.

2002	2003	2004	2005	2006	2007	2008	2009	2010
6,286	6,337	6,391	6,453	6,525	6,604	6,691	6,783	6,879
0.85	0.81	0.85	0.97	1.10	1.22	1.31	1.37	1.39
41.44	40.92	40.37	39.79	39.21	38.62	38.04	37.50	36.99
54.89	55.32	55.80	56.35	56.96	57.62	58.29	58.94	59.53
3.67	3.76	3.84	3.86	3.83	3.76	3.66	3.56	3.48
64.47	64.85	65.23	65.61	65.97	66.32	66.66	66.97	67.26
68.38	68.69	68.99	69.27	69.54	69.80	70.06	70.32	70.58
60.75	61.19	61.65	62.12	62.58	63.02	63.42	63.78	64.10
86.10	82.90	79.2	76.20	73.20	70.40	67.30	65.30	62.60
31.00	30.00	29	29.00	28.00	27.00	26.00	26.00	25.00

2002	2003	2004	2005	2006	2007	2008	2009	2010
—	—	—	—	—	—	—	99.9	—
—	—	—	—	—	—	—	99.7	—
95.8	95.8	95.7	96.4	95.5	96.2	96.0	96.2	96.4
82.0	82.8	83.7	83.1	83.0	84.0	87.0	88.2	86.6
32.6	33.4	33.1	35.0	36.6	37.7	39.2	40.9	41.1
98.0	100.1	100.0	100.7	100.3	99.9	102.2	101.9	101.9
79.0	81.5	82.4	82.5	83.3	84.8	85.8	86.4	87.2
14.2	15.7	16.9	17.8	18.9	19.9	20.2	19.8	19.7

CELL PHONE, TELEPHONE, AND INTERNET USE, 2000-2010

	2000	2001	2002	2003	
MOBILE CELLULAR SUBSCRIPTIONS	1,160	1,630	13,200	47,617	
PER 100 PEOPLE	0.02	0.03	0.21	0.75	
TELEPHONE LINES	218,516	226,851	237,600	245,192	
PER 100 PEOPLE	3.54	3.64	3.78	3.87	
INTERNET USERS	3,000	3,195	3,486	4,092	
PER 100 PEOPLE	0.05	0.05	0.06	0.06	

Source: World Bank Data, http://data.worldbank.org/country/tajikistan?display=default.

ETHNIC COMPOSITION OF TAJIKISTAN BASED ON CENSUS RESULTS

ETHNICITY	1979	1989	2000
TAJIK	58.8%	62.3%	79.9%
CENTRAL ASIAN TURKS (includes Uzbeks and other groups in 1979 and 1989)	22.9%	23.5%	15.3%
RUSSIAN	10.4%	7.6%	1.1%
KYRGYZ	1.3%	1.3%	1.1%
TURKMEN	0.4%	0.4%	0.3%
TATAR	2.1%	1.6%	0.3%
ARAB	—	0.01%	0.2%
AFGHAN	—	0.04%	0.1%
UIGHUR	—	0.04%	0.1%
UKRAINIAN	0.9%	0.8%	0.1%
KOREAN	0.3%	0.3%	0.03%
GERMAN	1.0%	0.6%	0.02%
KAZAKH	0.3%	0.2%	0.01%
OTHER	1.3%	1.6%	1.4%

Source: Percentages calculated by author. Data from: Mikhail Tul'skiy, "Itogi perepisi naseleniya Tadzhikistana 2000 goda: natsional'noy vozrastnoy, polovoy, semynyy, i obrazovatelynyy sostavy" [Results from the Population Census of Tajikistan in 2000. Composition of national age, gender, family, and education], http://demoscope.ru/weekly/2005/0191/analit05.php.

	2004	2005	2006	2007	2008	2009	2010
	135,000	265,000	2,150,000	2,132,770	3,673,520	4,900,000	5,940,842
	2.11	4.11	32.95	32.29	54.90	72.24	86.36
	273,400	280,200	—	292,730	286,940	347,260	367,693
	4.28	4.34	—	4.43	4.29	5.12	5.35
	4,952	19,275	246,136	475,361	587,506	683,087	794,483
	0.08	0.30	3.77	7.20	8.78	10.07	11.55

MAIN PARTIES INVOLVED IN THE TAJIK CIVIL WAR
in chronological order vertically

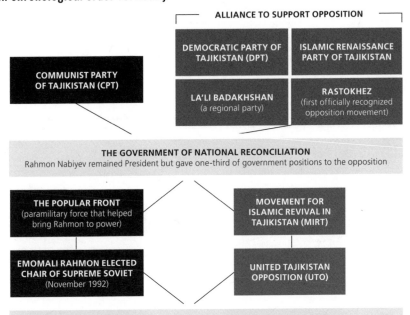

ALLIANCE TO SUPPORT OPPOSITION

DEMOCRATIC PARTY OF TAJIKISTAN (DPT)

ISLAMIC RENAISSANCE PARTY OF TAJIKISTAN

COMMUNIST PARTY OF TAJIKISTAN (CPT)

LA'LI BADAKHSHAN (a regional party)

RASTOKHEZ (first officially recognized opposition movement)

THE GOVERNMENT OF NATIONAL RECONCILIATION
Rahmon Nabiyev remained President but gave one-third of government positions to the opposition

THE POPULAR FRONT (paramilitary force that helped bring Rahmon to power)

MOVEMENT FOR ISLAMIC REVIVAL IN TAJIKISTAN (MIRT)

EMOMALI RAHMON ELECTED CHAIR OF SUPREME SOVIET (November 1992)

UNITED TAJIKISTAN OPPOSITION (UTO)

GENERAL AGREEMENT ON THE ESTABLISHMENT OF PEACE AND NATIONAL ACCORD
Signed in June 1997 by the delegation of the Government of Tajikistan and the UTO

Key: Black: Parties that supported government powers
Dark gray: Parties that supported opposition
Light gray: Peace agreements/reconciliation governments

OFFICIAL DATA ON MIGRATION, 1998–2010

	1998	1999	2000	2001	2002	2003	
ARRIVING							
TOTAL ARRIVING	16,890	14,730	14,482	16,729	17,735	16,923	
GBAO	446	433	334	513	451	308	
SUGHD	5,788	5,459	4,505	5,728	5,423	5,953	
KHATLON	3,317	1,491	1,953	2,282	2,494	2,020	
DUSHANBE	5,248	5,664	5,772	5,486	6,475	5,897	
RRS	2,091	1,683	1,918	2,720	2,892	2,745	
DEPARTING							
TOTAL DEPARTING	32,283	28,823	28,188	29,144	30,219	27,936	
GBAO	830	1,278	964	862	1,212	919	
SUGHD	10,629	10,939	10,481	11,434	10,563	9,995	
KHATLON	8,662	6,899	7,342	7,969	8,364	8,049	
DUSHANBE	7,262	4,715	4,826	4,582	4,750	3,975	
RRS	4,900	4,992	4,575	4,297	5,330	4,998	

Source: Data from Agency on Statistics Under President of the Republic of Tajikistan, "Socio-demographic sector," www.stat.tj/en/database/socio-demographic-sector.

ARRIVING AND DEPARTING MIGRANTS, 1998–2010

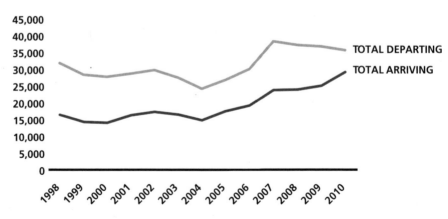

Source: Data from Agency on Statistics Under President of the Republic of Tajikistan, "Socio-demographic sector," www.stat.tj/en/database/socio-demographic-sector.

2004	2005	2006	2007	2008	2009	2010
15,244	17,962	19,646	24,283	24,419	25,563	29,637
193	336	464	427	454	267	531
5,128	5,236	5,772	6,966	7,959	8,767	9,794
2,393	2,714	3,715	4,403	4,883	6,713	6,860
4,869	6,276	5,481	6,475	4,724	3,849	3,396
2,661	3,400	4,214	6,012	6,399	5,967	9,056
24,663	27,311	30,554	38,761	37,651	37,231	36,134
1,205	2,058	1,833	2,518	1,978	1,475	1,751
8,083	8,068	9,648	12,340	13,061	12,459	12,431
8,311	9,217	9,876	11,872	10,789	12,777	11,359
2,974	3,106	3,895	4,129	4,007	3,678	2,925
4,090	4,862	5,302	7,902	7,816	6,842	7,668

MIGRANT REMITTANCE INFLOWS IN MILLIONS US$

2002	2003	2004	2005	2006	2007	2008	2009	2010	2011E
79	146	252	467	1,019	1,691	2,544	1,748	2,254	2,680

Source: World Bank, "Remittance Flows in 2011: An Update," http://web.worldbank.org/WBSITE/
EXTERNAL/TOPICS/0,,contentMDK:21924020~pagePK:5105988~piPK:360975~theSitePK:214971,00.
html#fragment-3.

All numbers are in current (nominal) US$. World Bank staff calculation based on data from IMF Balance of
Payments Statistics Yearbook 2011 and data releases from central banks, national statistical agencies, and
World Bank country desks.

ELECTRICITY OUTPUT AND CONSUMPTION 1980–2010 (in billion kW/h)

	1980	1985	1990	1995	2000	2005	2010
TOTAL OUTPUT	13.6	15.7	18.2	14.8	14.3	17.1	16.4
HYDROPOWER AS SOURCE	12.6	14.4	16.9	14.6	14.1	17	16.4
TOTAL DOMESTIC CONSUMPTION	9.7	15.3	19.4	15.4	15.6	17.3	16.6
INDUSTRY CONSUMPTION	4.6	8.7	11.1	6.6	5.8	7.5	7.3
AGRICULTURE CONSUMPTION	2.7	3.5	4.2	4.6	4.3	3.9	3.6
HOUSEHOLD CONSUMPTION	0.7	1.0	1.3	2.0	2.8	2.7	2.9
LOSSES OF DOMESTIC CONSUMPTION	0.9	1.1	1.6	1.8	2.2	2.7	2.3

Source: Agency on Statistics under President of the Republic of Tajikistan, "Real Sector: Electricity Output, Sale and Consumption, 1980–2010," www.stat.tj/en/analytical-tables/real-sector.

ELECTRICITY GENERATION IN TAJIKISTAN

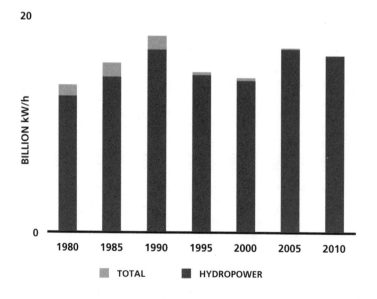

TAJIKISTAN'S INTERNAL ELECTRICITY CONSUMPTION AND TOTAL OUTPUT

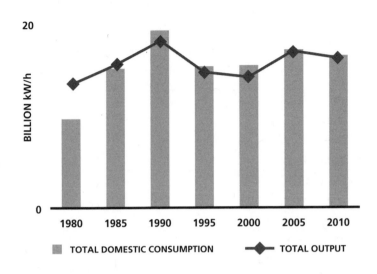

ELECTRICITY CONSUMPTION IN TAJIKISTAN

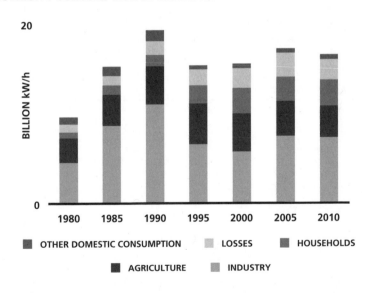

EASE OF DOING BUSINESS IN TAJIKISTAN, 2006–2012, SELECTED TOPICS

TOPIC	TAJIKISTAN	
	2006	**2007**
STARTING A BUSINESS		
PROCEDURES (NUMBER)	14	14
TIME (DAYS)	80	80
COST (% OF INCOME PER CAPITA)	85.1	75.1
DEALING WITH CONSTRUCTION PERMITS		
PROCEDURES (NUMBER)	28	28
TIME (DAYS)	261	261
COST (% OF INCOME PER CAPITA)	3,195.6	2,819.2
REGISTERING PROPERTY		
PROCEDURES (NUMBER)	6	6
TIME (DAYS)	37	37
COST (% OF PROPERTY VALUE)	1.9	1.9
PROTECTING INVESTORS		
STRENGTH OF INVESTOR PROTECTION INDEX (0-10)	1.7	1.7
PAYING TAXES		
PAYMENTS (NUMBER PER YEAR)	69	69
TOTAL TAX RATE (% PROFIT)	79.9	79.9
TRADING ACROSS BORDERS		
DOCUMENTS TO EXPORT (NUMBER)	11	11
DOCUMENTS TO IMPORT (NUMBER)	10	10
ENFORCING CONTRACTS		
TIME (DAYS)	430	430
COST (% OF CLAIM)	25.5	25.5
PROCEDURES (NUMBER)	35	35

*Regional average includes Kazakhstan, Kyrgyz Republic, Russian Federation, Tajikistan, and Uzbekistan.

Source: International Finance Corporation and World Bank, "Historical Data Sets and Trends Data," Doing Business, www.doingbusiness.org/custom-query.

	2008	2009	2010	2011	2012	REGIONAL AVERAGE* 2012
	13	13	12	8	5	5.6
	62	62	38	27	24	19.4
	39.6	27.6	24.3	36.9	33.3	9.2
	28	28	27	26	26	29.2
	261	361	231	228	228	245
	2,315.5	1,614.2	1,165.2	996.1	849.9	271.1
	6	6	6	6	6	6.2
	37	37	37	37	37	40.6
	1.9	1.8	4.6	5.5	5.3	1.7
	1.7	3.3	4.7	5.7	5.7	6.02
	69	69	69	69	69	35.6
	80	83.4	83.8	84	84.5	65.3
	11	11	11	11	11	9.2
	10	10	10	9	9	10.2
	430	430	430	430	430	311.2
	25.5	25.5	25.5	25.5	25.5	22.4
	35	35	35	35	35	37.4

FREEDOM HOUSE RATINGS FOR TAJIKISTAN, 2002–2011

| | FREEDOM IN THE WORLD | | | | FREEDOM OF THE PRESS | |
YEAR	FREEDOM RATING	STATUS	CIVIL LIBERTIES	POLITICAL RIGHTS	PRESS FREEDOM SCORE	PRESS STATUS
2002	6	NOT FREE	6	6	80	NOT FREE
2003	5.5	NOT FREE	5	6	76	NOT FREE
2004	5.5	NOT FREE	5	6	73	NOT FREE
2005	5.5	NOT FREE	5	6	74	NOT FREE
2006	5.5	NOT FREE	5	6	76	NOT FREE
2007	5.5	NOT FREE	5	6	76	NOT FREE
2008	5.5	NOT FREE	5	6	77	NOT FREE
2009	5.5	NOT FREE	5	6	78	NOT FREE
2010	5.5	NOT FREE	5	6	78	NOT FREE
2011	5.5	NOT FREE	5	6	78	NOT FREE

Civil liberties and political rights are ranked from 1 (most free) to 7 (least free). Press freedom is scored between 0 (best) to 100 (worst).

Source: Freedom House, *Freedom in the World and Freedom of the Press*.

ELECTIONS AND REFERENDA

1990 PARLIAMENTARY ELECTION (February 25, 1990)

IN 1990, MEMBERS OF THE COMMUNIST PARTY OF TAJIKISTAN FILLED 96% OF 230 SEATS. NO DETAILED DATA AVAILABLE.

Note: Until 1999, Tajikistan had a unicameral parliament. Both the 1990 and 1995 parliamentary elections were held under a system of absolute majority in single-member constituencies, with possible runoffs between two top-placing candidates.

Source: Dieter Nohlen, Florian Grotz, and Christof Hartmann, *Elections in Asia and the Pacific: A Data Handbook, Volume I* (Oxford University Press, 2002), 462–68.

1991 REFERENDUM (March 17, 1991)

96% VOTED IN FAVOR OF PRESERVING THE SOVIET UNION.

Source: Dieter Nohlen, Florian Grotz, and Christof Hartmann, *Elections in Asia and the Pacific: A Data Handbook, Volume I* (Oxford University Press, 2002), 462–68.

1991 PRESIDENTIAL ELECTION (November 24, 1991)

TURNOUT (%):   84.6

CANDIDATE	PARTY	VOTES	%
RAHMON NABIYEV	COMMUNIST PARTY OF TAJIKISTAN	—	56.9
DAVLATNAZAR KHUDONAZAROV	DEMOCRATIC PARTY OF TAJIKISTAN	—	30.1
DAVLAT USMON*	ISLAMIC RENAISSANCE PARTY OF TAJIKISTAN	—	—
TAKHIR ABDUDZHABBOR*	RASTOKHEZ	—	—
SHODMON YUSUF*	DEMOCRATIC PARTY OF TAJIKISTAN	—	—
AKBAR TURAJONZODE*	INDEPENDENT	—	—

* Won between 0.2% and 5.0% of the vote

Source: Dieter Nohlen, Florian Grotz, and Christof Hartmann, *Elections in Asia and the Pacific: A Data Handbook, Volume I* (Oxford University Press, 2002), 462–68.

1994 PRESIDENTIAL ELECTION (November 6, 1994)

REGISTERED VOTERS: 2,535,777
VOTES CAST: 2,409,330
TURNOUT (%):   95

CANDIDATE	PARTY	VOTES	%
EMOMALI RAHMON	SUPPORTED BY COMMUNIST PARTY OF TAJIKISTAN	1,434,437	59.5
ABDUMALIK ABDULLADZHANOV	—	835,861	34.7
AGAINST ALL CANDIDATES	—	—	—

Source: Dieter Nohlen, Florian Grotz, and Christof Hartmann, *Elections in Asia and the Pacific: A Data Handbook, Volume I* (Oxford University Press, 2002), 462–68.

1994 CONSTITUTIONAL REFERENDUM (November 6, 1994)

90% OF VOTERS APPROVED THE NEW CONSTITUTION. AMONG OTHER MEASURES, THE NEW CONSTITUTION CHANGED THE NUMBER OF SEATS IN PARLIAMENT FROM 230 TO 181.

Source: Dieter Nohlen, Florian Grotz, and Christof Hartmann, *Elections in Asia and the Pacific: A Data Handbook, Volume I* (Oxford University Press, 2002), 462–68.

1995 PARLIAMENTARY ELECTION (February 26 and March 12, 1995)

REGISTERED VOTERS: 2,684,000
VOTES CAST: 2,254,560
TURNOUT (%): 84

PARTY	SEATS
COMMUNIST PARTY OF TAJIKISTAN	60
PEOPLE'S PARTY OF TAJIKISTAN / PEOPLE'S DEMOCRATIC PARTY*	5
PARTY OF POPULAR UNITY AND ACCORD	2
TAJIKISTAN PARTY OF ECONOMIC AND POLITICAL RENEWAL	1
OTHER	113
TOTAL	181

Note: Data on seats won as reported by the Inter-Parliamentary Union. The IPU notes that the figures were not officially confirmed, and no information was available regarding the remaining seats.

* The People's Party of Tajikistan was renamed the People's Democratic Party in 1997 and Emomali Rahmon was elected chairman.

Source: Dieter Nohlen, Florian Grotz, and Christof Hartmann, *Elections in Asia and the Pacific: A Data Handbook, Volume I* (Oxford University Press, 2002), 462–68.

Inter-Parliamentary Union, "Tajikistan Parliamentary Chamber: Shuroi Oly, Elections Held in 1995," www.ipu.org/parline-e/reports/arc/2309_95.htm.

1999 CONSTITUTIONAL REFERENDUM (September 26, 1999)

THE AMENDMENTS, WHICH PASSED WITH 75.3% VOTING IN FAVOR, LEGALIZED RELIGIOUS PARTIES, INTRODUCED A BICAMERAL PARLIAMENT, AND EXTENDED THE PRESIDENTIAL TERM OF OFFICE FROM FIVE TO SEVEN YEARS.

Source: Dieter Nohlen, Florian Grotz, and Christof Hartmann, *Elections in Asia and the Pacific: A Data Handbook, Volume I* (Oxford University Press, 2002), 462–68.

1999 PRESIDENTIAL ELECTION (November 6, 1999)

REGISTERED VOTERS: 2,866,578
VOTES CAST: 2,835,590
INVALID VOTES: 18,774
TURNOUT (%): 98.9

CANDIDATE	PARTY	VOTES	%
EMOMALI RAHMON	PEOPLE'S DEMOCRATIC PARTY OF TAJIKISTAN	2,749,908	97.6
DAVLAT USMON	ISLAMIC RENAISSANCE PARTY OF TAJIKISTAN	59,857	2.1
AGAINST ALL CANDIDATES	—	7,051	0.3

Source: Dieter Nohlen, Florian Grotz, and Christof Hartmann, *Elections in Asia and the Pacific: A Data Handbook, Volume I* (Oxford University Press, 2002), 462–68.

2000 PARLIAMENTARY ELECTION (February 27, 2000)

REGISTERED VOTERS: 2,873,145
VOTES CAST: 2,693,120
TURNOUT (%): 93.7

Note: Figures vary slightly between IPU and Nohlen et al. but both calculate a turnout of between 93 and 94 percent.

PARTY	SEATS
PEOPLE'S DEMOCRATIC PARTY	38
COMMUNIST PARTY OF TAJIKISTAN	12
ISLAMIC RENAISSANCE PARTY	2
INDEPENDENTS	11
TOTAL	63

Note: After a bicameral Parliament was established through the 1999 Referendum, several modifications to the electoral system were adopted in late 1999. The resulting system is still in effect. The Assembly of Representatives (Majlisi Namoyandagon) has 63 deputies, who are directly elected for five-year terms: 22 by proportional representation and 41 in single-member constituencies. The National Assembly (Majlisi Milli) has 33 members, who are either indirectly elected or appointed by the president.

Note: Nohlen et al. give slightly different results: PDP (36), CPT (13), IRP (2), Independents (10), Unfilled seats (2).

Source: Inter-Parliamentary Union, "Tajikistan Parliamentary Chamber: Majlisi Namoyandagon, Elections Held in 2000," www.ipu.org/parline-e/reports/arc/2309_00.htm.

Dieter Nohlen, Florian Grotz, and Christof Hartmann, *Elections in Asia and the Pacific: A Data Handbook, Volume I* (Oxford University Press, 2002), 462–68.

2003 REFERENDUM (June 22, 2003)

SEVERAL CONSTITUTIONAL AMENDMENTS PASSED WITH A 93% YES VOTE, INCLUDING THE REMOVAL OF ARTICLE 65 OF THE CONSTITUTION, WHICH LIMITED THE PRESIDENT TO SERVING ONLY ONE SEVEN-YEAR TERM.

IFES Election Guide, "Overview, Referendum, June 22, 2003," www.electionguide.org/election. php?ID=366.

IRIN, "Tajikistan: Focus on Constitutional Referendum," June 26, 2003, www.irinnews.org/PrintReport. aspx?ReportID=20195.

2005 Parliamentary Election (February 27 and March 13, 2005)

	ROUND 1	ROUND 2
REGISTERED VOTERS:	3,134,666	217,672
VOTES CAST:	2,902,316	194,391
TURNOUT (%):	92.6	89.3

ESTIMATES VARY SLIGHTLY FOR THE FIRST ROUND BUT TURNOUT FOR THE FIRST ROUND IS CONSISTENTLY IN THE RANGE OF 92–94%.

PARTY	ROUND 1		ROUND 2	
	SEATS	%	SEATS	%
PEOPLE'S DEMOCRATIC PARTY	49	64.51	3	74.7
COMMUNIST PARTY OF TAJIKISTAN	4	13.97		
ISLAMIC RENAISSANCE PARTY	2	9.15		
INDEPENDENTS	5			

Source: Inter-Parliamentary Union, "Tajikistan Majlisi Namoyandagon (House of Representatives), Elections in 2005," www.ipu.org/parline-e/reports/arc/2309_05.htm.

2006 PRESIDENTIAL ELECTION (November 6, 2006)

REGISTERED VOTERS: 3,356,221
VOTES CAST: 3,054,573
TURNOUT (%): 91

CANDIDATE	PARTY	VOTES	%
OLIMJON BOBOYEV	PARTY OF ECONOMIC REFORM	190,138	6.23
ABDULHALIM GAFUROV	SOCIALIST PARTY	85,295	2.8
AMIR KARAKULOV	AGRARIAN PARTY	156,991	5.15
EMOMALI RAHMON	PEOPLE'S DEMOCRATIC PARTY OF TAJIKISTAN	2,419,192	79.3
ISMOIL TALBAKOV	COMMUNIST PARTY OF TAJIKISTAN	159,493	5.23

Source: OSCE/ODIHR, "Republic of Tajikistan Presidential Election, 6 November 2006, OSCE/ODIHR Election Observation Mission Report," Warsaw, April 18, 2007, www.osce.org/odihr/elections/tajikistan/24664.

2010 PARLIAMENTARY ELECTION (February 28, 2010)

PARTY	PROPORTIONAL	MAJORITY	TOTAL SEATS
PEOPLE'S DEMOCRATIC PARTY	16	39	55
COMMUNIST PARTY OF TAJIKISTAN	2	0	2
ISLAMIC RENAISSANCE PARTY	2	0	2
AGRARIAN PARTY OF TAJIKISTAN	1	1	2
PARTY OF ECONOMIC REFORMS OF TAJIKISTAN	1	1	2
TOTAL	22	41	63

OSCE REPORTS THE SAME RESULTS, BUT WHEREAS THE OSCE LISTS ONE SEAT FOR INDEPENDENTS, THE IPU LISTS THE SEAT UNDER THE PEOPLE'S DEMOCRATIC PARTY, GIVING THE PDP A TOTAL OF 55 SEATS VERSUS 54 IN THE OSCE REPORT.

Source: Inter-Parliamentary Union, "Tajikistan Majlisi Namoyandagon (House of Representatives), Last Elections," www.ipu.org/parline-e/reports/2309_E.htm.

OSCE/ODIHR, "Republic of Tajikistan Parliamentary Elections, February 28, 2010, OSCE/ODIHR Election Observation Mission Final Report," Warsaw, July 6, 2010, www.osce.org/odihr/elections/69061.

NOTES

CHAPTER I

1   World Bank, "World Development Indicators: Gross National Income Per Capita 2010, Atlas Method and PPP," 2010, http://siteresources.worldbank.org/ DATASTATISTICS/Resources/GNIPC.pdf.

2   This number is from the Tajikistan 2010 Population Census, which put the population of the country at 7,565,000. See Agenstvo po statistike pri prezidente Respubliki Tadzhikistan, "Predvaritel'nye itogi perepisi naseleniya i zhilishchnogo fonda 2010" (Preliminary findings of the population census and housing 2010), Dushanbe, 2011, 3, www.stat.tj/ru/img/689970f6c49dc744ad4bb1001f96a5b0_1306734923.pdf.

3   The U.S. Central Intelligence Agency lists the lengths of Tajikistan's borders as follows: Afghanistan, 1,206 kilometers; China, 414 kilometers; Kyrgyzstan, 870 kilometers; and Uzbekistan, 1,161 kilometers. U.S. Central Intelligence Agency, *World Factbook*, www. cia.gov/library/publications/the-world-factbook/geos/ti.html. Interestingly, Tajikistan's government often cites slightly different lengths for its borders, listing the border with Afghanistan as 1,030 kilometers, with Uzbekistan as 910 kilometers, with Kyrgyzstan as 630 kilometers, and with China as 430 kilometers. See, for instance, RECCA V, "O Tadzhikistane" (On Tajikistan), www.recca2012.tj/ru/news.html.

4   See Appendix.

5   President Rahmon formally changed his name from Rahmonov to Rahmon in 2007, and several other prominent Tajiks have since followed suit. For the sake of consistency, this volume refers to him as "Rahmon" throughout.

6   Economist Intelligence Unit, *Country Profile 2005: Tajikistan* (London: Economist Intelligence Unit, 2005), 5; International Crisis Group, "Executive Summary,"

Tajikistan: An Uncertain Peace, ICG Asia Report 30 (Brussels: International Crisis Group, 2001), www.crisisgroup.org/~/media/Files/asia/central-asia/tajikistan/ Tajikistan%20An%20Uncertain%20Peace.pdf.

7   Of these, 134,046 went to the Russian Federation, 10,000 to Turkmenistan, 8,000 to Uzbekistan, 5,000 to Kyrgyzstan, and 5,000 to Kazakhstan. See United Nations Development Program, *Human Development Report Tajikistan 1995* (Dushanbe: United Nations Development Program, 1995), 51.

8   Ibid.

9   Payam Forough, "Tajikistan," in *Nations in Transit* (New York: Freedom House, 2011), 534, www.freedomhouse.org/sites/default/files/inline_images/NIT-2011-Tajikistan.pdf.

10 John Heathershaw, *Post-Conflict Tajikistan: The Politics of Peacebuilding and the Emergence of Legitimate Order* (New York: Routledge, 2009); Paul Bergne, *The Birth of Tajikistan: National Identity and the Origins of the Republic* (London: I. B. Tauris, 2007); David Lewis, *The Temptations of Tyranny in Central Asia* (London: Hurst, 2008); Kathleen Collins, *Clan Politics and Regime Transition in Central Asia* (New York: Cambridge University Press, 2006); Lena Johnson, *Tajikistan in the New Central Asia: Geopolitics, Great Power Rivalry, and Radical Islam* (London: I. B. Tauris, 2006); Ahmed Rashid, *Descent into Chaos: The United States and the Failure of Nation Building in Pakistan, Afghanistan, and Central Asia* (New York: Penguin, 2008); Ahmed Rashid, *The Resurgence of Central Asia: Islam or Nationalism?* (Oxford: Oxford University Press, 1995); Olivier Roy, *The New Central Asia: The Creation of Nations* (New York: New York University Press, 2000).

11 Regional Bureau for Europe and the Commonwealth of Independent States, United Nations Development Program, "Central Asia Regional Risk Assessment: Responding to Water, Energy, and Food Insecurity," 2009, http://reliefweb.int/ sites/reliefweb.int/files/resources/0D4D43F5273097AC49257583000EC1F4-Full_ Report.pdf.

12 Asian Development Bank, *Asian Development Outlook 2009* (Manila: Asian Development Bank, 2009), http://beta.adb.org/publications/asian-development-outlook-2009.

13 Sangtuda 1 went online in three tranches—in January, July, and November 2008— but the additional electricity produced in January could not fully compensate for the loss of power generating capacity from Nurek hydroelectric station, which was so badly affected by the drought that wintertime generation of electricity had to come to a virtual halt.

14 Regional Bureau for Europe and the Commonwealth of Independent States, United Nations Development Program, "Central Asia Regional Risk Assessment."

15 Financial Tracking Service, "Tajikistan 2008 Total Humanitarian Funding," http://fts. unocha.org/pageloader.aspx?page=emerg-emergencyCountryDetails&cc=tjk&yr=2008.

16 Transparency International, "International Corruption Index 2011," http://cpi. transparency.org/cpi2011/results.

17 In answering the question "And what about the situation of Tajikistan generally: Are you very satisfied, somewhat satisfied, somewhat dissatisfied, or very dissatisfied with the situation in Tajikistan?" 68 percent answered very or somewhat satisfied in 2010, 65 percent provided the same answer in 2004, and only 22 percent gave an analogous answer in 1996. These surveys were done on the eve of parliamentary elections in all three cases, with national samples of 1,500 (1996), 1,404 (2004), and 1,500 (2010). International Foundation for Electoral Systems, *Public Opinion in Tajikistan Survey, 2010* (Washington, D.C.: International Foundation for Electoral Systems, 2010), 6, www.ifes.org/~/media/Files/Publications/Survey/2010/1644/ IFES_TajikistanSurvey_012510.pdf.

18 A total of 83 percent of those surveyed said that they considered Tajikistan a democracy, up from 74 percent in 2004 and 39 percent in 1996; and 63 percent of those surveyed said that a democracy was the preferable form of government, while 25 percent said that "to people like me, it doesn't matter what form of government as long as it provides for its citizens." Ibid., 18.

19 A total of 33 percent said that creating jobs should be the priority, 14 percent said fighting poverty, and 10 percent said improving the economy in general. An additional 10 percent said providing heat and electricity to all citizens, 7 percent said fighting corruption, 5 percent improving the quality of education, 4 percent improving access to health care, 3 percent reinforcing stability and national security, 3 percent protecting the rights of labor migrants abroad, and 2 percent improving the status of women—with an additional 7 percent citing various other things. Ibid., 26.

20 In 2004, 32 percent reported that they had enough money for food and shelter. Overall, respondents seemed better able to meet their basic needs in 2010, because only 4 percent said that they sometimes did not have enough money for three meals a day, versus 25 percent in 2004. Ibid., 9.

CHAPTER 2

1 Swiss Agency for Development and Cooperation, "Cooperation Strategy for the Central Asia Region 2007–2011," 2007, www.deza.admin.ch/ressources/resource_ en_162032.pdf.

2 Constitution of the Republic of Tajikistan, www.legislationline.org/documents/ action/popup/id/6817.

3 Tajikistan has eight registered political parties. (1) The ruling People's Democratic Party of Tajikistan (PDPT), registered in 1994, is led by President Rahmon. (2) The Socialist Party (SPT), which is led by Abdulhalim Gafurov and terms itself a constructive opposition, and (3) the Agrarian Party (APT), founded in 2005, which is led by Amir Karakulov and represents the interests of the agricultural sector, are both generally viewed as propresidential. Traditionally, (4) the Communist Party of Tajikistan (CPT), led by Shodi Shabdolov, has been viewed this way as well, although it does oppose the PDPT on a number of issues. All considered to be opposition parties are (5) the Islamic Renaissance Party of Tajikistan (IRPT), registered in 1991 and reregistered in 1999, and led by Muhiddin Kabiri; (6) the Social Democratic Party (SDPT), founded in 1998, first registered in 1999, and headed by Rahmnatillo Zoiov; and (7) the Democratic Party of Tajikistan (DPT), first founded in 1990 and reregistered in 1999, and led by Masud Sobirov. The DPT, however, has remained divided into factions since the arrest of its former party leader, Mahmadruzi Iskandarov, who was jailed during the 2005 parliamentary campaign. (8) There is also the largely progovernment Party of Economic Reform of Tajikistan (PERT), founded in 2005, which is led by Olimjon Boboev.

4 The observers from the OSCE's Office for Democratic Institutions and Human Rights report cases of spreadsheets reporting vote totals being altered both in favor of Rahmon and in favor of some of his opponents, presumably the latter in order to show that the presidential election was a competitive one. Office for Democratic Institutions and Human Rights, *Republic of Tajikistan: Presidential Election, November 6, 2006—OSCE/ODIHR Election Observation Mission Report* (Warsaw: Organization for Security and Cooperation in Europe, 2007), 20, www.osce.org/odihr/elections/tajikistan/24664.

5 These six nominated candidates were Emomali Rahmon, of the PDPT; Olimjon Boboev, chairman of the Economic Reform Party of Tajikistan; Abdulhalim Gafurov, chairman of the progovernment wing of the Socialist Party of Tajikistan; Amir Karakulov, chairman of the Agrarian Party of Tajikistan; Ismoil Talbakov, a member of the Communist Party of Tajikistan; and Tavarali Ziyoev, a leading member of the progovernment wing of the DPT. Mirhusein Narziyev, of the breakaway wing of the Socialist Party, was denied registration and, after the party split in 2003, the more progovernment branch of the party was registered instead. The SDPT refused to participate in the election because it rejected the 2003 constitutional amendments. The IRPT decided not to nominate a candidate, but agreed to participate in the Presidential Election Commission and the district election commissions. The country's political parties are entitled to representation in the national and district and precinct election commissions. Economist Intelligence Unit, "Country Profile 2008: Tajikistan" (London: Economist Intelligence Unit, 2008), 5–7.

6 Ibid., 9.

7 The blocked websites were www.centrasia.net, www.ferghana.ru, www.tajikistantimes.ru, www.charogiruz.ru, and www.arianstorm.com.

8 "Rajab Mirzo: Authorities Misunderstood Us," NewEurasia.net, November 24, 2006, www.neweurasia.net/politics-and-society/rajab-mirzo-authorities-misunderstood-us.

9 "Like Father, Like Daughter," Radio Free Europe/Radio Liberty, September 3, 2009, www.rferl.org/content/Like_Father_Like_Daughter/1839891.html.

10 Sadulloev is also known as Hasan Azadullozoda, a Tajik translation of his Russian surname.

11 "President's Son Hosts Circumcision Bash," Radio Free Europe/Radio Liberty, March 31, 2011, www.rferl.org/content/chaikhana_blog_on_circumsision/3543047.html.

12 "Tajikistan: A Ruling Family Feud Appears to Turn Bloody," *Eurasia Insight*, May 9, 2008, www.eurasianet.org/departments/insight/articles/eav050908a.shtml.

13 International Crisis Group, *Tajikistan: On the Road to Failure*, ICG Asia Report 162 (Brussels: International Crisis Group, 2009), 8, www.crisisgroup.org/~/media/Files/asia/central-asia/tajikistan/162_tajikistan___on_the_road_to_failure.ashx.

14 International Crisis Group, *Tajikistan: Uncertain Peace*, ICG Asia Report 30 (Brussels: International Crisis Group, 2001), 5, www.crisisgroup.org/~/media/Files/asia/central-asia/tajikistan/Tajikistan%20An%20Uncertain%20Peace.pdf.

15 The law requires that a district election commission be formed by the CCER in each of the 41 single-mandate districts 60 days before the election, to be made up of nine to eleven members proposed by local executive bodies based on recommendations from local political parties.

16 Office for Democratic Institutions and Human Rights, *Republic of Tajikistan: Parliamentary Elections, February 27 and March 23, 2005—OSCE/ODIHR Election Observation Mission Report* (Warsaw: Organization for Security and Cooperation in Europe, 2005), 7, www.osce.org/odihr/elections/tajikistan/15193.

17 Office for Democratic Institutions and Human Rights, *Republic of Tajikistan: Parliamentary Elections, February 28, 2010—Statement of Preliminary Findings and Conclusions—OSCE/ODIHR Election Observation Mission Report* (Warsaw: Organization for Security and Cooperation in Europe, 2010), 3, www.osce.org/odihr/elections/tajikistan/41627.

18 However, when one of the two members stepped down in 2009, the Central Election Commission refused to name a second member from the IRPT, claiming that this was unnecessary because it was the final year of the legislature; this decision was upheld by Tajikistan's Supreme Court, after the IRPT protested it. Office for Democratic Institutions and Human Rights, *Republic of Tajikistan: Parliamentary Elections, February 2010—OSCE/ODIHR Needs Assessment Report, November 9–11, 2009* (Warsaw: Organization for Security and Cooperation in Europe, 2009), 3, www.osce.org/odihr/elections/40739.

19 Office for Democratic Institutions and Human Rights, *Republic of Tajikistan: Parliamentary Elections, February 27 and March 23, 2005*, 5.

20 Ibid., 14–15.

21 Tajik law prohibits individuals who are under investigation or have been convicted of a crime from running for office. The law does not address the severity of the crime committed: "Individuals with minor convictions cannot run as candidates, even if the sentence has been served but not lifted." This eligibility requirement remains despite recommendations by OSCE/ODIHR that it be eliminated. Office for Democratic Institutions and Human Rights, *Republic of Tajikistan: Parliamentary Elections 2010—Final Report* (Warsaw: Organization for Security and Cooperation in Europe, 2010), 12, www.osce.org/ru/odihr/74504.

22 U.S. Mission to the Organization for Security and Cooperation in Europe, *Statement on the Detention of Mahmadruzi Iskandarov in Dushanbe, as Delivered by Ambassador Stephan M. Minikes to the Permanent Council* (Vienna: Organization for Security and Cooperation in Europe, 2005), www.osce.org/pc/15758.

23 Office for Democratic Institutions and Human Rights, *Republic of Tajikistan: Parliamentary Elections, February 27 and March 23, 2005*, 10.

24 Ibid., 14.

25 This allegation was made to the OSCE/ODIHR election monitoring team by representatives of the SDPT and DPT. Ibid., 13.

26 In answer to the question "How fair do you expect the February 2010 election to be?" 26 percent of the 1,500 surveyed said "completely fair," 42 percent said "somewhat fair," 9 percent said "somewhat unfair," 2 percent said "completely unfair," and 20 percent either said "don't know" or gave no response. "Public Opinion Survey in Tajikistan 2010: Findings from an IFES Survey," SHARQ, 22, www.ifes.org/~/media/Files/Publications/Survey/2010/1644/IFES_TajikistanSurvey_012510.pdf.

27 Ibid., 33.

28 Strategic Research Center Under the President of the Republic of Tajikistan, "Report on Corruption in the Republic of Tajikistan (a Public Opinion Survey)," United Nations Development Program in the Republic of Tajikistan, Dushanbe, 2006, www.undp.tj/files/reports/pta_en.pdf.

29 This is at an exchange rate of TJS 4.1437 to $1 in 2010. Agency on Statistics Under the President of the Republic of Tajikistan, "Macroeconomic Indicators," www.stat.tj/ru/macroeconomic-indicators.

30 The OSCE/ODIHR reports that of the 68 nominated candidates who were denied registration in the 2010 election, 50 were rejected because they did not pay the deposit. See Office for Democratic Institutions and Human Rights, *Republic of Tajikistan: Parliamentary Elections 2010—Final Report*, 13.

31 Office for Democratic Institutions and Human Rights, *Republic of Tajikistan: Parliamentary Elections, February 28, 2010—Statement of Preliminary Findings and Conclusions,* 7–8. Each candidate is allowed up to five proxies to represent his or her interests as election observers. Other than these proxies, no domestic observers are permitted.

32 Office for Democratic Institutions and Human Rights, *Republic of Tajikistan: Parliamentary Elections 2010—Final Report,* 15.

33 These include TV Tojikistan, TV Safina, and Jahonnamo TV.

34 The OSCE considers that only *Asia-Plus, Farazh, Narodnaya Gazeta, Millat,* and *Vecherniy Dushanbe* show any interest in these questions, as do Radio Tojikistan, Radio Vatan, and Imruz.

35 Office for Democratic Institutions and Human Rights, *Republic of Tajikistan: Parliamentary Elections, February 28, 2010—Statement of Preliminary Findings and Conclusions,* 8.

36 Ibid., 9.

37 Ibid., 11–12.

38 Republic of Tajikistan, "National Development Strategy of the Republic of Tajikistan for the Period to 2015," draft presented at Regional Conference on MDS based on NDS and PRSP, Dushanbe, March 2007, www.undp.tj/files/reports/nds_eng.pdf.

39 For details see Tomislav Novovic, "Tajikistan: Local Governance and Decentralization: A Project Assessment," United Nations Development Program, 2011, www.undp.org/content/undp/en/home/librarypage/democratic-governance/dgttf/tajikistan_localgovernanceanddecentralisation-aprojectassessment.html, and Ministry of Finance of the Republic of Tajikistan, *The Government Medium-Term Expenditure Framework for 2011–2013.* (Dushanbe: Government of Tajikistan, 2010), www.minfin.tj/downloads/files/MTEFfinalTajikenglish.pdf.

40 Francis Conway et al., "Local Governance and Citizen Participation Program in Tajikistan: Tajikistan—Sub-National Government Assessment, 2009," Urban Institute Center of International Development and Governance, May 2009, 11–16, http://pdf.usaid.gov/pdf_docs/PNADQ959.pdf.

41 Ibid.

42 There were 914 respondents who were aware of upcoming local government elections. In addition to the responses quoted in the text, 39 percent wanted better access to health care, 36 percent sought improved gas supply, 34 percent noted the need for better garbage collection, 17 percent for better fee collection, and 9 percent gave assorted other answers. SHARQ, "Public Opinion Survey in Tajikistan 2010: Findings from an IFES Survey," 25, www.ifes.org/-/media/Files/Publications/Survey/2010/1644/IFES_TajikistanSurvey_012510.pdf.

43 U.S. Embassy in Dushanbe, "USAID Launches Local Governance Project," press release, 2010, http://dushanbe.usembassy.gov/pr_04222010.html.

44 Johannes Linn, "Scaling Up Development Interventions: A Review of UNDP's Country Program in Tajikistan," Brookings Institution, August 24, 2011, 15, as supplied by the paper's author.

45 UNDP Tajikistan, "Tajikistan at a Glance," www.undp.tj/files/Communities%20 Programme%20Information%20Brochure.pdf.

46 Funders for the UNDP's Communities Program include the UK Department for International Development, the government of Germany, the government of Norway, the government of Finland, the Canadian International Development Agency, the Swedish International Development Cooperation Agency, the Swiss Agency for Development and Cooperation, the Czech Trust Fund, the Slovak Trust Fund, the World Bank's International Development Association, the Asian Development Bank, the Global Environment Facility, Technical Assistance for the Commonwealth of Independent States (TACIS), the European Union, the UNDP's Democratic Governance Thematic Trust Fund, the United Nations Development Fund for Women, the United Nations Environment Program, and the International Labor Organization. United Nations Development Program in Tajikistan, "UNDP Communities Program Ongoing Projects in 2012," www.undp.tj/index.php?option= com_content&task=view&id=337&Itemid=125.

47 A total of 33 percent of the 1,500 surveyed said that they had contacted a local *avlod* or *mahalla* official in the last twelve months to address or solve a problem, versus 14 percent who said that they had contacted a public official. SHARQ, "Public Opinion Survey in Tajikistan 2010," 15.

48 Yusuff Yusufbekov, Rustam Babajanov, and Natalya Kuntuvdiy, *Civil Society Development in Tajikistan* (Dushanbe: Aga Khan Development Network, 2007), 18, www.akdn.org/publications/civil_society_tajikistan_development.pdf.

49 This information was provided by Saodat Olimova.

50 International Monetary Fund, *Republic of Tajikistan: Poverty Reduction Strategy Paper, Second Progress Report*, IMF Country Report 06/1 (Washington, D.C.: International Monetary Fund, 2006), 15, www.imf.org/external/pubs/ft/scr/2006/ cr0601.pdf.

51 Bureau of Democracy, Human Rights, and Labor, U.S. Department of State, *2009 Human Rights Report: Tajikistan* (Washington, D.C.: U.S. Government Printing Office, 2010), 3, www.state.gov/j/drl/rls/hrrpt/2009/sca/136094.htm.

52 "Tajik Population Names Anti-Corruption Agency Among the Most Corrupt Bodies," *Asia-Plus*, www.news.tj/en/news/tajik-population-names-anticorruption-agency-among-most-corrupt-bodies; United Nations Development Program and Center for Strategic Studies Under the President of the Republic of Tajikistan, "Corruption in Tajikistan: Public Opinion," 2010, www.undp.tj/files/undpeng.pdf.

53 Bureau of Democracy, Human Rights, and Labor, *2009 Human Rights Report*, 3.

54 Ibid., 2.

55 USAID also funded a project on commercial law reform in Tajikistan as well. USAID, *Program for a Legal Infrastructure for a Market Economy in Kyrgyzstan and Tajikistan (Commercial Law Reform): Final Report* (Washington, D.C.: U.S. Government Printing Office, 2005), http://pdf.usaid.gov/pdf_docs/PDACF844.pdf.

56 USAID reported that 87 percent of the judges and 62 percent of the judicial candidates passed examinations that they helped administer. Ibid., 24.

57 Ibid.

58 Bureau of Democracy, Human Rights, and Labor, *2010 Human Rights Report: Tajikistan* (Washington, D.C.: U.S. Government Printing Office, 2011), 6, www.state.gov/j/drl/rls/hrrpt/2010/sca/154487.htm.

59 Bureau of Democracy, Human Rights, and Labor, *2009 Human Rights Report*, 1.

60 The European Court imposed damages for unlawfully extraditing him. "ECHR Throws Out Appeal by Russian Authorities Over Iskandarov's Case," *Asia-Plus*, April 2011, http://news.tj/en/news/echr-throws-out-appeal-russian-authorities-over-iskandarov-s-case. Bureau of Democracy, Human Rights, and Labor, U.S. Department of State, *2010 Human Rights Report*, 7.

61 Bureau of Democracy, Human Rights, and Labor, *2009 Human Rights Report*, 4.

62 Human Rights Watch, *Tajikistan Country Summary* (New York: Human Rights Watch, 2009), www.hrw.org/en/node/79352.

63 That same year, several Uzbeks were also arrested and convicted on espionage charges. "Tajikistan Sentences Man for Spying for Uzbekistan," Radio Free Europe/Radio Liberty, January 6, 2010, www.rferl.org/content/Tajikistan_Sentences_Man_For_Spying_For_Uzbekistan/1922799.html.

64 "Jurisprudence: CCPR, Rakhmatov, et al. v. Tajikistan," United Nations Human Rights Treaties, www.bayefsky.com/docs.php/area/jurisprudence/node/4/filename/tajikistan_t5_iccpr_1209_1231_2002_1241_2004.

65 Bureau of Democracy, Human Rights, and Labor, *2009 Human Rights Report*, 3.

66 Bruce Pannier, "Tajikistan: Small Jewish Community Fighting to Save Its Synagogue," Radio Free Europe/Radio Liberty, May 27, 2004, www.rferl.org/content/article/1052685.html.

67 Nigina Sharipova, "Tajik Banker Gives Jewish Community Building for Synagogue," Central Asia Online, April 2, 2009, http://centralasiaonline.com/cocoon/caii/xhtml/en_GB/features/caii/features/2009/04/02/feature-04; http://centralasiaonline.com"/cocoon/caii/xhtml/en_GB/features/caii/features/2009/05/11/feature-02.

68 "Dushanbe Synagogue Operating Illegally, Declares Official," Central Asia Newswire, December 29, 2010, http://centralasianewswire.com/Tajikistan/Dushanbe-synagogue-operating-illegally-declares-official/viewstory.aspx?id=2780.

69 Somewhat ironically, Tajikistan was ranked above Kyrgyzstan (125), Kazakhstan (142), Uzbekistan (160), and Turkmenistan (172). Reporters without Borders, "World Press Freedom Index 2009," http://en.rsf.org/IMG/pdf/classement_en.pdf.

70 Bureau of Democracy, Human Rights, and Labor, *2010 Human Rights Report*, 10.

71 Ibid., 6.

72 "Tadzhikskiy oppozitsioner Dododzhon Atovulloyev opasaetsya pohishcheniya" (Tajik opposition member Dododzhon Atovulloyev fears abduction), *Novaya Gazeta*, September 25, 2008, www.novayagazeta.ru/politics/38657.html; "Tajikistan Politics: Media Straining at the Leash," Economist Intelligence Unit, December 16, 2008, www.eiu.com/index.asp?layout=VWPrintVW3&article_id=234321808&printer=printer&rf=0.

73 Konstantin Parshin, "Tajikistan: Journalists Under Pressure as Parliamentary Elections Approach," *Eurasia Insight*, February 5, 2010, http://eurasianet.org/departments/insight/articles/eav020519a..pr.shtml. See also Mavjouda Hasanova, "Issues Related to Legal Protection of Journalists Discussed in Dushanbe," *Asia-Plus*, February 5, 2010, http://old.news.tj/en/news/issues-related-legal-protection-journalists-discussed-dushanbe.

74 This is borne out by results in the IFES 2010 survey, in which 75 percent of those interviewed cited Tajik television as the most frequently used source of information. SHARQ, "Public Opinion Survey in Tajikistan 2010," 44.

75 Bureau of Democracy, Human Rights, and Labor, *2010 Human Rights Report*, 6.

76 Ibid., 6; Bureau of Democracy, Human Rights, and Labor, *2009 Human Rights Report*.

77 This information was provided by Saodat Olimova.

78 Abdullo Rakhnamo, "'Politicheskiy Islam' I Sekulyaristy v Tadzhikistane: Evolyutsiya na Puti k Miru" ("Political Islam" and Secularism in Tajikistan: Evolution on the Path to Peace), Press Klub, http://kemyaesaadat.com/7/index.php?option=com_content&view=article&id=793:l-r-&catid=52:2008-12-09-19-32-22.

79 The Hanafi school of law (*mazhab*) of Sunni Islam is based on the writing of Imam abu Hanaf (699–767). His full name is Nu'mān ibn Thābit ibn Zūtā ibn Marzubān, and he is referred to as Imam Azam, or the great imam in Tajikistan). The Hanafi school, one of four in Sunni Islam, is the dominant one in Central Asia, and it is often viewed as the most tolerant as it has historically been most accepting of the incorporation of pre-Islamic traditions.

80 Salafists, or Salafiya, are Sunni Muslims who reject all four schools of Islamic law and believe that religious interpretations have to be based directly on the Quran and on the Hadiths (the sayings that were directly attributed to the Prophet Muhammad). They are considered to be "fundamentalists" because their intent is to go back to the "fundament" or foundation of the faith, to the faith of their ancestors; hence the term "Salafi."

81 Faragis Najibullah, "Tajikistan Authorities Impose Religious Tests on Imams," Radio Free Europe/Radio Liberty, August 8, 2007, www.refrl.org/featuresarticleprint/2007/08/9a9d6519-fldb-498.

82 Ismaili Muslims are a splinter group of Shi'i Muslims that date from the eighth century, the largest group of which (from the Nizari branch or path) recognizes the Aga Khan as their spiritual leader. It is from this group that Tajikistan's and Afghanistan's Ismailis are drawn.

83 This is as quoted by Felix Corley, "Tajikistan: Restrictive President-Backed Religion Law Reaches Parliament," *Forum 18*, December 17, 2008, www.forum18.org/Archive.php?article_id=1230.

84 For example, *Forum 18* reports that only one Ismaili mosque in Gorno-Badakhshan had been reregistered by October 7, 2009, while six others had not yet received reregistration, and that by December 9, 2009, only 65 or 98 previously registered mosques in the town of Khujand had been granted reregistration. See Mushfig Bayra, "Tajikistan: More Than Half of Religious Communities to Be 'Illegal'?" *Forum 18*, December 10, 2009, www.forum18.org/Archive.php?article_id=1386.

85 "Tajik Children to Take Mandatory Class on Islam," Radio Free Europe/Radio Liberty, August 18, 2009, www.rferl.org/content/Tajik_Children_To_Take_Mandatory_Class_On_Islam/1802115.html.

86 Ibid.

87 Mavjuda Hasanova, "V Tadzhikistane iz shkol'noy programmy ubrali predmet 'Poznaniye islama'" (In Tajikistan the subject "Knowledge of Islam" has been removed from the school curriculum), *Asia-Plus*, February 4, 2011, http://news.tj/ru/news/v-tadzhikistane-iz-shkolnoi-programmy-ubrali-predmet-poznanie-islama.

88 "Imam iz Komsomol'ska-na-amure provel vstrechu s muftiyem Tadzhikistana" (The imam of the Komsomolsk-na-Amur met with the mufti of Tajikistan), *Islam News*, November 30, 2009, www.islamnews.ru/news_21498.html.

89 This information was provided by Saodat Olimova.

90 Said Abdullo Nuri (1947–2006) was a Tajik politician and religious leader of the opposition Islamic Renaissance Party in Tajikistan during the Tajik civil war (1992–1997). Nuri became involved with the IRPT after launching his career as the leader of the illegal Islamic educational organization Nahzat-i Islomi in the 1970s. Following the 1997 peace agreement that put an end to the Tajik civil war, Nuri formed a coalition with President Emomali Rahmon, his former political archenemy, and chaired the Commission on National Reconciliation. He remained head of the IRPT for thirteen years until his death in 2006. See "Said Abdullo Nuri," *Conciliation Resources*, www.c-r.org/our-work/accord/tajikistan/profiles.php.

91 "Imams of Mosques are Certified in Tajikistan," Interfax, December 28, 2011, www.interfax-religion.com/?act=news&div=8952.

92 "Tajikistan: Islamic Party Facing Pressure in Dushanbe," Eurasianet.org, February 3, 2011, www.eurasianet.org/node/62820.

93 "Tajikistan: President's Pocket Pundit Bullies the Opposition," *Central Asia Today*, January 14, 2011, www.eurasianet.org/node/62720.

94 Farangis Najibullah, "Tajik Islamic Party Puts a Face-Lift to the Test," Radio Free Europe/Radio Liberty, February 22, 2010, www.rferl.org/content/Tajik_Islamic_Party_Puts_Face_Lift_To_A_Test/1965070.html.

95 Shonavruz Afzalshoev, "V GBAO vremenno priostanovlena deyatel'nost' 15 mechetey" (In Badakhshan the activities of 15 mosques have been temporarily suspended), *Asia-Plus*, January 25, 2011, http://news.tj/ru/news/v-gbao-vremenno-priostanovlena-deyatelnost-15-mechetei.

96 Mexrangez Tursunzoda, "Nuzhno li regulirovat' temy propovedey v mechetyakh?" (Is it necessary to regulate the themes of sermons in mosques?), *Asia-Plus*, February 1, 2011, http://news.tj/ru/news/nuzhno-li-regulirovat-temy-propovedei-v-mechetyakh.

97 "Tajik Government to Issue List of Approved Sermon Topics," Radio Free Europe / Radio Liberty, January 10, 2011, www.rferl.org/content/tajikistan_government_orders_mosques/2271961.html.

98 Zakon o bor'be s ekstremizmom (Law on Combating Extremism); for its full text, see http://legislationline.org/ru/documents/action/popup/id/14807.

99 Additionally, Presidential Decree 1717 (March 2006) laid out the main goals of Tajikistan's effort to combat terrorism and extremism; for its text, seet www.osce.org/home/71714.

100 "Q&A: Hizb ut-Tahrir," BBC News, August 4, 2007, http://news.bbc.co.uk/2/hi/4127688.stm.

101 "Tajik Hizb ut-Tahrir Leader Sentenced to 18 Years," Radio Free Europe/Radio Liberty, January 22, 2011, www.rferl.org/content/tajikistan_hizuttahrir_members_sentenced/2284242.html.

102 Mavlouda Rafiyeva, "11 Activists of Hizb ut-Tahrir Group Convicted in Sughd," *Asia-Plus*, April 26, 2011, http://news.tj/en/news/11-activists-hizb-ut-tahrir-group-convicted-sughd.

103 "Tablighi Jamaat: An Indirect Line to Terrorism," Stratfor Global Intelligence, January 23, 2008, www.stratfor.com/weekly/tablighi_jamaat_indirect_line_terrorism.

104 Mariya Yanovskaya, "'Tabligi Dzhamaat': Skrytaya ugroza mirnoy propovedi" ("Tablighi Jamaat": The hidden threat of a peaceful preacher), February 11, 2009, www.fergananews.com/article.php?id=6065.

105 "Tablighi Jamaat: An Indirect Line"; Amnesty International, *Tajikistan-Amnesty International Report 2010: Human Rights in the Republic of Tajikistan* (London: Amnesty International, 2010), www.amnesty.org/en/region/tajikistan/report-2010.

106 "Followers of a Sunni Missionary Group Detained in Tajikistan," *Turkish Weekly*, April 17, 2009, www.turkishweekly.net/news/72858/-followers-of-sunni-missionary-group-detained-in-tajikistan.html.

107 Farangis Najibullah, "Tajiks Target Obscure Islamic Group for Persecution," Radio Free Europe/Radio Liberty, May 14, 2009, www.rferl.org/content/Tajiks_Target_Obscure_Islamic_Group_For_Prosecution/1731761.html

108 See http://lenta.ru/news/2010/03/10/jail; and Amnesty International, *Tajikistan–Amnesty International Report 2010*.

109 "V Tadzhikistane osuzhdeny desyatki storonnikov zapreshchennogo dvizheniya" (In Tajikistan dozens of supporters of a banned movement convicted), Lenta.ru, March 10, 2010, http://lenta.ru/news/2010/03/10/jail; Stan Rogers, "Tajik Supreme Court Rejects Appeal by Hizb ut-Tahrir Members," Central Asia Online, August 6, 2010, www.centralasiaonline.com/cocoon/caii/xhtml/en_GB/features/caii/newsbriefs/2010/08/06/newsbrief-10.

110 Farangis Najibullah, "In Central Asia, Unofficial Madrasahs Raise Official Fears," Radio Free Europe/Radio Liberty, January 20, 2010, www.rferl.org/articleprintview/1935068html.

111 Payrab Chorshanbiyev, "Iz Yegipta na rodinu vozvrasheny tadzhikskiye studenty, obuchavshiyesya v religioznyh uchrezhdeniyah ARE" (Tajik students studying in ARE religious institutions returned home from Egypt), *Asia-Plus*, November 10, 2010, http://news.tj/ru/news/iz-egipta-na-rodinu-vozvrashcheny-tadzhikskie-studenty-obuchavshiesya-v-religioznykh-uchrezhden.

112 Edward Lemon, "Tajikistan: Dushanbe Forcing Students to Return Home," Eurasianet.org, November 29, 2010, www.eurasianet.org/node/62460.

113 Mavjuda Hasanova, "Okolo polutora tysyach studentov-nelegalov vozvratilis' na rodinu iz islamskikh stran" (Around a thousand students, illegals return to their homeland from Islamic countries), *Asia-Plus*, January 19, 2011, http://news.tj/ru/ news/okolo-polutora-tysyach-studentov-nelegalov-vozvratilis-na-rodinu-iz-islam-skikh-stran.

114 Lemon, "Tajikistan."

115 Farangis Najibullah, "Tajik Officials Keep a Sharp Eye on Islamic Teaching," Eurasianet.org, August 7, 2010, www.eurasianet.org/node/61682.

116 Bureau of Democracy, Human Rights, and Labor, U.S. Department of State, *Tajikistan: International Religious Freedom Report 2010* (Washington, D.C.: U.S. Government Printing Office, 2010), www.state.gov/j/drl/rls/irf/2010/148805.htm.

117 "V Tadzhikistane shkol'nitsam zapreshchayut prikhodit' na zanyatiya v musul'manskom platke 'rusari'" (In Tajikistan school girls forbidden to attend classes in the Muslim scarf ["rusar"]), Ferghana.ru, September 17, 2009, www.fergananews. com/article.php?id=6303.

118 Bureau of Democracy, Human Rights, and Labor, *2009 Human Rights Report*, 7.

119 "Tajikistan: The Education Ministry Issued Permission to Teachers to Wear Beards and Galoshes," Ferghana.news, September 29, 2009, http://enews.fergananews.com/ news.php?id=1390&print=1.

120 "Tajikistan: From Beards to Mosques, Dushanbe Cracking Down on Suspected Radicals," Eurasianet.org, January 24, 2011, www.eurasianet.org/node/62758.

121 Richard Orange, "Tajik Ban on Children in Mosques Could Be 'Disastrous,'" *Daily Telegraph*, June 23, 2011, www.telegraph.co.uk/news/worldnews/asia/ tajikistan/8594032/Tajik-ban-on-children-in-mosques-could-be-disastrous.html.

122 U.S. Embassy in Dushanbe and U.S. Mission to the OSCE, "Statement at OSCE on Tajikistan's Parental Responsibility Law," June 23, 2011, http://dushanbe. usembassy.gov/sp_07232011.html; Avaz Yuldoshev, "Deputy: Law 'On Parental Responsibility of Children' Needs Mechanism of Implementation," *Asia-Plus*, June 17, 2011, http://news.tj/en/news/deputy-law-parental-responsibility-children-needs-mechanism-implementation.

123 "Tajikistan: Ban on Children in Worship 'Once Ramadan Is Over,'" *Forum 18*, August 16, 2011, www.forum18.org/Archive.php?article_id=1602.

124 Nigina Sharipova, "Regional Head of Criminal Investigations and Insurgent Detention Killed in Tajikistan," Central Asia Online, September 23, 2009, http:// centralasiaonline.com/en_GB/articles/caii/features/2009/09/23/feature-05.

125 "Tajik Islamic Militant Leader Sentenced to Life in Prison," RIA Novosti, October 20, 2009.

126 Farangis Najibullah, "Four Suspected IMU Members Killed in Tajikistan," Radio Free Europe/Radio Liberty, October 20, 2009, www.rferl.org/content/Four_ Suspected_IMU_Members_Killed_In_Tajikistan/1855410.html.

127 "Kyrgyz Border Guards Continue Search for Tajik Insurgents," Radio Free Europe/ Radio Liberty, October 18, 2009, www.rferl.org/content/Kyrgyz_Border_Guards_ Continue_Search_For_Tajik_Insurgents/1854841.html.

128 "Predpolagayemykh chlenov 'Islamskogo dzhikhada' zaderzhali v Tadzhikistane" (Prospective members of the 'Islamic jihad' arrested in Tajikistan), RIA Novosti Ukraina, December 12, 2009, http://ua.rian.ru/CIS_news/20091218/78257554- print.html.

129 "Tajikistan Jails Suspected Al-Qaeda Member," Radio Free Europe/Radio Liberty, February 9, 2010, www.rferl.org/articleprintview/1953111.html.

130 International Crisis Group, *Tajikistan: The Changing Insurgent Threats*, ICG Asia Report 205 (Brussels: International Crisis Group, 2011), 6, www.crisisgroup.org/ ~/media/Files/asia/central-asia/tajikistan/205%20Tajikistan%20-%20The%20 Changing%20Insurgent%20Threats.pdf.

131 Ibid., 2.

132 "Court in Tajikistan Jails 53 for Terrorism," *Moscow Times*, December 28, 2011, www.themoscowtimes.com/news/article/court-in-tajikistan-jails-53-for-terrorism/ 450560.html.

133 International Crisis Group, *Tajikistan: The Changing Insurgent Threats*, 6.

134 Ibid., 7.

CHAPTER 3

1 European Bank for Reconstruction and Development, "Commercial Laws of Tajikistan: An Assessment by the EBRD," July 2008, 3, www.ebrd.com/downloads/ sector/legal/tajik.pdf.

2 In 2010, 49 percent of those surveyed said that corruption was a very serious prob- lem, and 38 percent said that it was a fairly serious problem. This compares with 2004, when 38 percent said it was a very serious problem, and 37 percent said that it was a fairly serious problem. "Public Opinion Survey in Tajikistan 2010: Findings from an IFES Survey," SHARQ, 11, www.ifes.org/~/media/Files/Publications/ Survey/2010/1644/IFES_TajikistanSurvey_012510.pdf.

3   Rahmon does not live in the palace, because it was deemed unsafe, given that its weight is so great that there has been substantial subsidence of the ground on which it was constructed; instead, it is used for ceremonial gatherings.

4   U.S. Embassy, Dushanbe, "Hip Hip Hurrah for President Rahmon," WikiLeaks cable 131447, November 26, 2007, www.cablegatesearch.net/cable.php?id=07DUSHANBE1688&q+rahmon.

5   U. S Embassy in Dushanbe, "A Case-study in Roghun Extortion," WikiLeaks cable 245745, January 27, 2010.

6   Ibid. It describes the pressure exerted on employees of FINCA, the World Bank's small-loan division, which had two branches closed when local employees did not meet their targeted contributions. The FINCA office in the town of Vose was closed by the local authorities when the staff of four could not come up with $5,600, roughly their combined annual salary. It was opened several days later when a "down payment" was received.

7   "Presidential Call to Reflect on Islamic Heritage," Transitions Online, September 24, 2008, www.tol.org/client/article/20014-presidential-call-to-reflect-on-islamic-heritage.html.

8   Swiss Agency for Development and Cooperation, "Cooperation Strategy for the Central Asia Region 2007–2011," 2007, 4, www.deza.admin.ch/ressources/resource_en_162032.pdf.

9   World Bank, "Implementation Completion and Results Report (IDA Grant Nos. H246, H325, H451)," Report ICR00001279, March 23, 2010, www-wds.worldbank.org/external/default/WDSContentServer/WDSP/IB/2010/05/03/000334955_20100503033256/Rendered/INDEX/ICR12790ICR0P01closed0April03002010.txt.

10 World Bank, "Implementation Completion and Results Report (IDA Grant Nos. H246, H325, H451) on Grants in the Amounts of (1) SDR 7.0 Million (US$10.0 Million Equivalent), (2) SDR 6.7 Million (US$10.0 Million Equivalent), (3) SDR 13.3 Million (US$20.0 Million Equivalent) to the Republic of Tajikistan for the Programmatic Development Policy Operations," March 23, 2010, 25, www.wds.worldbank.org/external/default/main?pagePK=64193027&piPK=64187937&theSitePK=523679&menuPK=64187510&searchMenuPK=64187283&siteName=WDS&entityID=000334955_20100503033256.

11 This study, which was based on a survey of Tajikistan's population, was done in consultation with Transparency International, and with colleagues from Kyrgyzstan, Russia, and Bulgaria. It was done under the auspices of the United Nations Development Program, but with the program taking no responsibility for the accuracy of the data.

12 Strategic Research Center Under the President of the Republic of Tajikistan, "Report on Corruption in the Republic of Tajikistan (a Public Opinion Survey)," United Nations Development Program in the Republic of Tajikistan, Dushanbe, 2006, 8, www.undp.tj/files/reports/pta_en.pdf.

13 Ibid.

14 These include the Anti-Corruption Law of the Republic of Tajikistan, December 1991; the Criminal Code of the Republic of Tajikistan from 1998 (the sections "Crimes Against the Interests of Civil Service" and "Crimes in the Sphere of Economic Activity"); and the Decree of the President of the Republic of Tajikistan, "On Additional Measures Aimed at Strengthened Crime Fighting in the Sphere of Economy and Corruption," July 1999. There are also provisions relating to corruption in the following laws: "On the State Service," "On the State Financial Control," "On Auditing," "On the State Support and Development of Entrepreneurship," "On Privatization of the State Property," and the "Tax," "Customs," and "Civil" Codes. Ibid., 12.

15 The report of the Strategic Research Center includes a lengthy examination of how Islamic teachings could be used by the government in an anticorruption campaign, with reference to Quran and Hadith teachings. Ibid., 36–41.

16 Ibid., 8.

17 Ibid., 11.

18 World Bank, "Implementation Completion and Results Report (IDA Grant Nos. H246, H325, H451)."

19 Ibid., 15.

20 Ibid., 17.

21 Ibid., 14

22 Ibid., 13.

23 Ibid., 34.

24 Strategic Research Center Under the President of the Republic of Tajikistan, "Report on Corruption," 45.

25 The entrepreneurs included 145 small business owners (with a turnover of up to 1,500 somoni), 103 medium-sized business owners (with a turnover of up to 15,000 somoni), and 36 larger business owners (with a turnover up to 300,000 somoni).

26 Strategic Research Center Under the President of the Republic of Tajikistan, "Report on Corruption," 20.

27 Ibid., 44.

28 The breakdown of those answering the question on facing corruption in schools and educational institutions was as follows: "Don't face," 43.0 percent; "seldom face," 22.8 percent; "time to time," 16.3 percent; "quite often," 9.7 percent; and "very often," 8.2 percent. Ibid., 55.

29 Strategic Research Center Under the President of the Republic of Tajikistan, "Report on Corruption," 8.

30 Ibid., 62.

31 Christian Aid, "From Local to Global: Stopping Corruption from Stunting Development," December 2008, 15, www.christianaid.org.uk/images/from-local-to-global.pdf.

32 Kambiz Arman, "Tajikistan: IMF Catches Dushanbe in a Creative Accounting Scandal," Eurasianet.org, March 9, 2008, www.eurasianet.org/departments/insight/articles/eav031008.shtml.

33 International Crisis Group, *Tajikistan: On the Road to Failure*, ICG Asia Report 162 (Brussels: International Crisis Group, 2009), 13, www.crisisgroup.org/-/media/Files/asia/central-asia/tajikistan/162_tajikistan___on_the_road_to_failure.ashx.

34 "IMF Resident Representative Answers to Questions from Asia Plus Regarding Misreporting Case of Tajikistan," April 1, 2008, www.imf.org/External/country/TJK/rr/pdf/2008/040108.pdf. This statement also makes reference to the two sets of books kept by the NBT.

35 Ernst & Young Business Advisory Services, *National Bank of Tajikistan: Report on Agreed-Upon Procedures on the Net International Reserves Reported to IMF as of June 30, 2009* (Moscow: Ernst & Young, 2009), 5.

36 Ibid., 4.

37 They discovered that loans were made from NBT branch banks, and that the NBT had also provided guarantees to domestic banks, including Tajprom Bank. Ibid., 7. The report's "Executive Summary" was originally published on the National Bank of Tajikistan's website. However, all references to this audit are no longer available. However, both the full document and the "Executive Summary" can still be accessed through other sites; the full document can be found at www.docstoc.com/docs/51895664/National-Bank-of-Tajikistan-Report-on-Agreed-Upon-Procedures-on-the, and the "Executive Summary" can be found in Russian using a web archive site, http://web.archive.org/web/20101009171648/http://nbt.tj/files/docs/annual_report/rep_rus.pdf.

38 Ibid., 14.

39 Ibid., 8 (paragraph 2.23).

40 Ibid., 18.

41 Ibid., 19.

42 Ibid., 9 (paragraph 2.26).

43 Ibid., 11.

44 Ibid., 16.

45 The cotton factors trading with these two companies were HIMA, Vostochnaya Khlopkovaya Companiya, VEA Somoni, and Olimi Karimzod. Ibid., 13.

46 Ibid., 15.

47 Ibid., 17.

48 Ibid., 23.

49 Ibid., 18.

50 Ibid., 19.

51 National Bank of Tajikistan, "Financial Statements for the Years Ended 30 April 2009 and 2008," www.nbt.tj/files/Fin_State/FinState_en.pdf.

52 European Bank for Reconstruction and Development, *Strategy for Tajikistan*, January 2009, 6, www.ebrd.com/downloads/country/strategy/tajikistan.pdf.

53 The EBRD reference was to the Khujand Packing Project, the first EBRD agribusiness project in Tajikistan, which was also supported by the Central Asian American Enterprise Fund but never managed to secure adequate fruit nectar supplies; from the author's personal archives.

54 U.S. Agency for International Development, "Investigation of International Fraudulent Conspiracy Results in Incarceration for Two Co-Conspirators," November 27, 2002, www.usaid.gov/oig/press/pressrelease_1127_02_132.pdf; Birgit Brauer, "U.S. Missteps Wasted Investments in Central Asian Economies, Critics Say," *New York Times*, September 4, 2009, www.nytimes.com/2001/09/04/world/us-missteps-wasted-investments-in-central-asian-economies-critics-say.html.

55 The author served on the Board of Directors of the Central Asian American Enterprise Fund; some of the worst abuses were in Tajikistan, and a third manager, from Tajikistan, would likely have been charged if he had not been severely disabled from an illness contracted in Tajikistan during the course of the investigations by the U.S. Federal Bureau of Investigation.

56 Strategic Research Center under the President of the Republic of Tajikistan, "Report on Corruption," 25.

57 Ibid., 23–24.

58 Ibid., 51–52.

59 Jafar Olimov, "Informal Economy in Tajikistan," in *National Human Development Report 2007* (Dushanbe: United Nations Development Program and SHARQ, 2007), 38.

60 Ibid., 39.

61   Ibid., 79.

62   "According to statistics from Tajikistan's Drug Control Agency, in the first nine months of 2011, law enforcement agencies seized 3,529 kilograms of narcotics, of which 437 kilograms were heroin, 251 kilograms were opium, and 2,841 kilograms were cannabis. During the same period of 2010, law enforcement agencies seized a total of 2,652 kilograms of narcotics, nominally a 33 percent increase in drug seizures over the past year. However, heroin seizures declined by 32 percent and opium seizures by 58 percent. The decline in opiate seizures was offset by a 103 percent increase in cannabis seizures. During the first nine months of 2011, cannabis accounted for 80 percent of total seizures." Bureau of International Narcotics and Law Enforcement Affairs, U.S. Department of State, *2012 International Narcotics Control Strategy Report: Country Reports–South Africa through Zambia*, March 7, 2012, www.state.gov/j/inl/rls/nrcrpt/2012/vol1/184102.htm#Tajikistan.

63   Letizia Paoli et al., "Tajikistan: The Rise of a Narco-State," *Journal of Drug Issues*, 2007, https://lirias.kuleuven.be/bitstream/123456789/200273/1/Paoli+et+al._Tajikistan_printed+article.pdf.

64   Bruce Pannier, "Tajikistan: Opposition Leader Brought Home to Face Charges, Ex-Interior Minister Imprisoned for 15 Years," Radio Free Europe/Radio Liberty, April 27, 2005, www.rferl.org/content/article/1058667.html.

65   Olga Tutubalina, "Yakub Salimov mezhdu prisyagoy i predatel'stvom" (Yakub Salimov: Between oath and betrayal"), *Asia-Plus*, April 20, 2012, http://news.tj/ru/news/yakub-salimov-mezhdu-prisyagoi-i-predatelstvom.

66   P. Sobirova, "Gaffor Mirzoyev: Srok dlinoyu v zhizn'" (Gaffor Mirzoyev: A lifelong term), CentrAsia.ru, August 6, 2010, www.centrasia.ru/newsA.php?st=1281114120.

67   Paoli et al., "Tajikistan." For more on Mirzoev, see Erica Marat, "Impact of Drug Trade and Organized Crime on State Functioning in Kyrgyzstan and Tajikistan," *China and Eurasia Forum Quarterly* 4, no. 1 (2006): 93–101, www.silkroadstudies.org/new/docs/CEF/Quarterly/February_2006/Erica_Marat.pdf.

68   Filippo De Danieli, "Counter-Narcotics Policies in Tajikistan and Their Impact on State Building," *Central Asian Survey* 30, no. 1 (2011): 129–45, www.tandfonline.com/doi/abs/10.1080/02634937.2011.554067.

69   David Stern, "Young Men Risk Death on Drugs Train to Europe," *Financial Times*, January 9, 2002, http://specials.ft.com/afghanfuture/FT3HWBFK9WC.html (note that Stern misidentifies Sanginov as Saginov); Bruce Pannier, "Tajikistan: Court Sentences Seven for Murder of Minister Sanginov," Radio Free Europe/Radio Liberty, March 28, 2002, www.rferl.org/content/article/1099240.html.

70   Bruce Pannier, "Death of Prominent Tajik Highlights Instability in Central Asia's Southeast," Radio Free Europe/Radio Liberty, July 14, 2009, www.rferl.org/content/Death_Of_Prominent_Tajik_Highlighting_Instability_In_Central_Asias_Southeast/1776540.html.

71 Saodat Mahbatsho, "Tajikistan: Dushanbe Ramps Up Crackdown of Suspected Islamic Radicals," Eurasianet.org, June 15, 2009, www.eurasianet.org/departments/insightb/articles/eav061609a.shtml.

72 Paoli et al., "Tajikistan."

73 There was an agreement reached between Russia and Tajikistan in 2010 to give renewed access to Tajikistan's borders with Afghanistan by providing training, air support, and equipment but not to jointly guard these borders. See U.S. Department of State, *2012 International Narcotics Control Strategy Report: Country Reports–South Africa through Zambia.*

74 U.S. Embassy, Dushanbe, "Tajik President Fires Senior Anti-Narcotics Officer to Protect a Relative From Persecution," WikiLeaks cable 124733, October 4, 2007, www.cablegatesearch.net/cable.php?id=07DUSHANBE1420.

75 "Tadjikistan: Glava UBNON MVD osvobozhden ot zanimayemoy dolzhnosti" (Head of UBNON Interior Ministry dismissed), Fergana.ru, November 21, 2007, www.fergananews.com/news.php?id=7714.

76 Central Asia and the Caucasus Institute, "Tajik Drug Police Burn Half-Ton of Heroin," June 8, 2004, www.cacianalyst.org/newsite/?q=node/2207/print.

77 These data were collected by Alexander Zelichenko with a grant from the Terrorism, Transnational Crime, and Corruption Center. Also see Alisher Latypov, "Drug Dealers, Drug Lords and Drug Warriors-Cum-Traffickers: Drug Crime and the Narcotics Market in Tajikistan," 2011, http://dl.dropbox.com/u/64663568/library/Drug_warriors_in_Takijistan_0.pdf.

78 Ibid., 6.

79 Ibid., 15.

80 Ibid., 12.

81 Max Maksudov, "Drug Trafficking Remains a Serious Problem: Closer Government-Public Co-operation Needed," Central Asia Online, March 14, 2011, http://centralasiaonline.com/en_GB/articles/caii/features/main/2011/03/14/feature-01.

82 United Nations Office on Drugs and Crime, "Summary Report: Second Technical Working Group on the Financial Flows Linked to the Illicit Production and Trafficking of Afghan Opiates," Abu Dhabi, November 2011, 4, www.paris-pact.net/upload/03812ab07336539471ca8e9e99ea7303.pdf.

83 Corruption was cited as the most important problem by 20.6 percent of the population in the Region of Republican Subordination, 17.1 percent in Dushanbe, 8.7 percent in Gorno-Badakhshan, 8.4 percent in Khatlon, and 3.7 percent in Kulyab.

84 Strategic Research Center under the President of the Republic of Tajikistan, "Report on Corruption," 64.

85   Ibid., 78.

86   Bureau of Democracy, Human Rights, and Labor, U.S. Department of State, *2010 Human Rights Report: Tajikistan* (Washington, D.C.: U.S. Government Printing Office, 2011), 10, www.state.gov/j/drl/rls/hrrpt/2010/sca/154487.htm.

CHAPTER 4

1   This figure for GDP per capita is using the Atlas method, and puts Tajikistan in 183 place out of 215 countries; $2,060 in purchasing power parity (PPP) earns Tajikistan a ranking in 173 place. World Bank Indicators Database, "Gross National Income per Capita 2010, Atlas Method and PPP," July 1, 2011, http://siteresources.worldbank.org/DATASTATISTICS/Resources/GNIPC.pdf.

2   Middle East and Central Asia Department, International Monetary Fund, "Caucasus and Central Asia Set for Solid Growth, but Global Risks Loom Large," in *Regional Economic Outlook Update*, April 20, 2012, 4, www.imf.org/external/pubs/ft/reo/2012/mcd/eng/pdf/cca-update0412.pdf.

3   World Bank, *Implementation Completion and Results Report (IDA Grant Nos. H246, H325, H451) on Grants in the Amounts of (1) SDR 7.0 Million (US$10.0 Million Equivalent), (2) SDR 6.7 Million (US$10.0 Million Equivalent), (3) SDR 13.3 Million (US$20.0 Million Equivalent) to the Republic of Tajikistan for the Programmatic Development Policy Operations*, March 23, 2010, 1, www.wds.worldbank.org/external/default/main?pagePK=64193027&piPK=64187937&theSitePK=523679&menuPK=64187510&searchMenuPK=64187283&siteName=WDS&entityID=000334955_20100503033256.

4   European Bank for Reconstruction and Development, *Strategy for Tajikistan*, January 2009, 18, www.ebrd.com/downloads/country/strategy/tajikistan.pdf.

5   This led to decreases of projected imports, and hence less VAT was collected, and it had particularly negative effects on the aluminum industry, which are described at length in the chapter on industry.

6   International Monetary Fund, *Republic of Tajikistan: 2011 Article IV Consultation, Fourth Review Under the Three-Year Arrangement Under the Extended Credit Facility, Request for Waiver of Nonobservance for Performance Criteria and Modification of Performance Criterion—Staff Report; Staff Supplement; and Public Information Notice on the Executive Board Discussion, June 2011*, IMF Country Report 11/130 (Washington, D.C.: International Monetary Fund, 2011), 10, www.imf.org/external/pubs/cat/longres.aspx?sk=24915.0; United Nations Development Program, *National Development Strategy of the Republic of Tajikistan for the Period to 2015* (Dushanbe: United Nations Development Program, 2007), 51, www.undp.tj/files/reports/

nds_eng.pdf; International Monetary Fund, *Republic of Tajikistan: Poverty Reduction Strategy Paper*, IMF Country Report 09/82 (Washington, D.C.: International Monetary Fund, 2009), 41, www.unpei.org/PDF/Tajikistan_PRSP_2009.pdf.

7   This is a year-on-year figure based on the first half reporting in 2010. International Monetary Fund, *Republic of Tajikistan: Third Review Under the Three-Year Arrangement Under the Extended Credit Facility, Request for Waiver of Nonobservance of a Performance Criterion and Request for Modification of a Performance Criterion—Staff Report; Staff Supplements; Press Release on the Executive Board Discussion*, Country Report 10/374 (Washington, D.C.: International Monetary Fund, 2010), www.imf.org/external/pubs/cat/longres.aspx?sk=24522.0.

8   International Monetary Fund, *Republic of Tajikistan: 2011 Article IV Consultation, Fourth Review Under the Three-Year Arrangement Under the Extended Credit Facility, Request for Waiver of Nonobservance for Performance Criteria and Modification of Performance Criterion—Staff Report*, 5.

9   Ibid., 10.

10   Ibid., 4.

11   International Monetary Fund, *Republic of Tajikistan: Fifth Review Under the Three-Year Arrangement Under the Extended Credit Facility, Request for Waiver of Nonobservance of Performance Criteria, and Request for Modification of Performance Criteria—Staff Report; Press Release on the Executive Board Discussion; and Statement by the Executive Director for the Republic of Tajikistan*, Country Report 12/32 (Washington, D.C.: International Monetary Fund, 2012), 13, www.imf.org/external/pubs/cat/longres.aspx?sk=25711.0.

12   Ibid., 5.

13   Ibid., 15.

14   This $372.5 million took the form of loans from the Asian Development Bank, which also had disbursed $33.65 million in technical assistance and $97.27 million in loans.

15   European Bank for Reconstruction and Development, "Strategy for Tajikistan."

16   According to the EBRD's 2009 *Strategy for Tajikistan*, in 2004, Russia and Tajikistan agreed to a debt for equity swap of roughly $207 million, and the same year Pakistan canceled a $13 million debt; in 2006, the IMF offered Tajikistan $99 million of debt relief, Iran postponed debt service of $25 million for two years, and Uzbekistan postponed $8 million of debt service for two years as well.

17   They expect it to fluctuate slightly each year. International Monetary Fund, *Republic of Tajikistan: Fifth Review Under the Three-Year Arrangement Under the Extended Credit Facility, Request for Waiver of Nonobservance of Performance Criteria, and Request for Modification of Performance Criteria—Staff Report*, 18.

18 The SDR is an international reserve asset created by the IMF; its value is calculated as a basket of currencies—the dollar, euro, Japanese yen, and pound sterling. The dollar equivalent is calculated daily.

19 International Monetary Fund, *Republic of Tajikistan: 2011 Article IV Consultation, Fourth Review Under the Three-Year Arrangement Under the Extended Credit Facility, Request for Waiver of Nonobservance for Performance Criteria and Modification of Performance Criterion—Staff Report*, 6.

20 Ibid., 13; also see 16 (box 4).

21 Ibid., 14.

22 International Monetary Fund, *Republic of Tajikistan: Fifth Review Under the Three-Year Arrangement Under the Extended Credit Facility, Request for Waiver of Nonobservance of Performance Criteria, and Request for Modification of Performance Criteria—Staff Report*, 13.

23 Tajikistan received a rating of "moderate" on this indicator. World Bank, *Implementation Completion and Results Report* (IDA Grant Nos. H246, H325, H451), 17.

24 Ibid., 18.

25 Ibid., 23.

26 Ibid., 24.

27 International Finance Corporation, "Business Environment in Tajikistan as Seen by Small and Medium Enterprises," December 2009, 115, www.ifc.org/ifcext/tajikistansme.nsf/Content/Survey.

28 "Statement by Thomas Moser, IMF Executive Director for the Republic of Tajikistan," April 13, 2009. See International Monetary Fund, *Republic of Tajikistan: 2009 Article IV Consultation, Final Review Under the Staff-Monitored Program, and Request for a Three-Year Arrangement Under the Poverty Reduction and Growth Facility—Staff Report; Staff Supplement; Staff Statement; Public Information Notice and Press Release on the Executive Board Discussion; and Statement by the Executive Director for the Republic of Tajikistan*, Country Report 09/147 (Washington, D.C.: International Monetary Fund, 2009), 110–12, www.imf.org/external/pubs/cat/longres.aspx?sk=22995.0.

29 International Monetary Fund, *Republic of Tajikistan: Fifth Review Under the Three-Year Arrangement Under the Extended Credit Facility, Request for Waiver of Nonobservance of Performance Criteria, and Request for Modification of Performance Criteria—Staff Report.*

30 European Bank for Reconstruction and Development, *Strategy for Tajikistan*, 28.

31 International Monetary Fund, *Republic of Tajikistan: 2011 Article IV Consultation, Fourth Review Under the Three-Year Arrangement Under the Extended Credit Facility,*

Request for Waiver of Nonobservance for Performance Criteria and Modification of Performance Criterion—Staff Report, 6.

32 International Monetary Fund, *Republic of Tajikistan: Third Review Under the Three-Year Arrangement Under the Extended Credit Facility, Request for Waiver of Nonobservance of a Performance Criterion and Request for Modification of a Performance Criterion—Staff Report*; International Monetary Fund, *Republic of Tajikistan: 2011 Article IV Consultation, Fourth Review Under the Three-Year Arrangement Under the Extended Credit Facility, Request for Waiver of Nonobservance for Performance Criteria and Modification of Performance Criterion—Staff Report*, 6.

33 International Monetary Fund, *Republic of Tajikistan: Third Review Under the Three-Year Arrangement Under the Extended Credit Facility, Request for Waiver of Nonobservance of a Performance Criterion and Request for Modification of a Performance Criterion—Staff Report*; International Monetary Fund, *Republic of Tajikistan: 2011 Article IV Consultation, Fourth Review Under the Three-Year Arrangement Under the Extended Credit Facility, Request for Waiver of Nonobservance for Performance Criteria and Modification of Performance Criterion—Staff Report*, 7.

34 International Monetary Fund, *Republic of Tajikistan: Third Review Under the Three-Year Arrangement Under the Extended Credit Facility, Request for Waiver of Nonobservance of a Performance Criterion and Request for Modification of a Performance Criterion—Staff Report*, 38.

35 Ibid., 10.

36 Ibid., 9.

37 Ibid., 11.

38 Ibid., 35.

39 Ibid., 36.

40 International Monetary Fund, *Republic of Tajikistan: 2011 Article IV Consultation, Fourth Review Under the Three-Year Arrangement Under the Extended Credit Facility, Request for Waiver of Nonobservance for Performance Criteria and Modification of Performance Criterion—Staff Report*, 9.

41 International Monetary Fund, *Republic of Tajikistan: Fifth Review Under the Three-Year Arrangement Under the Extended Credit Facility, Request for Waiver of Nonobservance of Performance Criteria, and Request for Modification of Performance Criteria—Staff Report*, 13.

42 European Bank for Reconstruction and Development, *Strategy for Tajikistan*, March 13, 2012, 4, www.ebrd.com/downloads/country/strategy/tajikistan.pdf.

43 Ibid., 18.

44 Ibid., 6.

45 Ibid., 3.

46 European Bank for Reconstruction and Development, *Strategy for Tajikistan*, February 13, 2009, 12, www.unece.org/fileadmin/DAM/hlm/prgm/cph/experts/ tajikistan/Documents/EBRD_CountryStrategy_2009.pdf.

47 European Bank for Reconstruction and Development, "Southern Tajikistan Water Rehabilitation Project," Project 37656, April 16, 2012, www.ebrd.com/english/pages/ workingwithus/procurement/notices/project/120416d1.shtml.

48 International Finance Corporation, "Business Environment in Tajikistan," 23. These are the most recent comprehensive data on employment in the private sector, which is generally viewed as accounting for about 50 percent of the employment available in the country.

49 Ibid., 26.

50 These include the avoidance of restrictions on current payments, the avoidance of discriminatory currency practices, the convertibility of foreign-held balances, obligations to collaborate regarding policies on reserve assets, the obligation to furnish information, and the need to engage in consultation between members regarding existing international agreements.

51 International Financial Corporation, *Doing Business 2012: Doing Business in a More Transparent World—Comparative Regulation for Domestic Firms in 183 Countries* (Washington, D.C.: International Financial Corporation, 2011), www.doingbusiness. org/-/media/FPDKM/Doing%20Business/Documents/Annual-Reports/English/ DB12-FullReport.pdf.

52 Ibid., 72.

53 Ibid., 81.

54 Ibid., 10.

55 Ibid., 11.

56 Ibid., 12.

57 European Bank for Reconstruction and Development, *Strategy for Tajikistan*, February 13, 2009, 59.

58 International Financial Corporation, *Doing Business 2012*, 20.

59 European Bank for Reconstruction and Development, *Strategy for Tajikistan*, February 13, 2009, 59.

60 This is based on material obtained from an EBRD survey done in 2005. Ibid., 61.

61 Ibid., 63.

62 European Bank for Reconstruction and Development, *Strategy for Tajikistan*, March 13, 2012, 41.

63 These percentages are the most recent available from the European Bank for Reconstruction and Development. International Finance Corporation, "Business Environment in Tajikistan," 114.

64 Ibid., 24.

65 Ibid., 30.

66 Ibid., 27.

67 Ibid., 11–12.

68 Ibid., 38.

69 Ibid., 45–46, 49, 52; for a list of the licenses in transportation, see 68, and for a more complete list of activities requiring licenses or special licenses, see 81–84.

70 International Finance Corporation, "Business Environment," 86, 88.

71 Ibid., 92–93.

72 Ibid., 95.

73 International Finance Corporation, *Doing Business 2009* (Washington, D.C.: International Financial Corporation, 2008), 138, www.doingbusiness.org/~/media/FPDKM/Doing%20Business/Documents/Annual-Reports/English/DB09-FullReport.pdf; World Bank and International Finance Corporation, "Ease of Doing Business in Tajikistan," 2012, 142, 198, www.doingbusiness.org/data/exploreeconomies/tajikistan.

74 International Finance Corporation, "Business Environment in Tajikistan," 101.

75 World Bank and International Finance Corporation, "Ease of Doing Business in Tajikistan."

76 International Finance Corporation, "Business Environment in Tajikistan," 140–43.

77 Ibid., 114.

78 For example, the NBT reports that the exchange rate in February 2010 was TJS 4.36 = $1, and on May 3, 2012, it was TJS 4.79 = $1. National Bank of Tajikistan, Exchange Rates, www.nbt.tj/en/kurs/?c=4&id=28.

79 International Finance Corporation, "Business Environment in Tajikistan," 133–36.

80   Jafar Olimov, "Informal Economy in Tajikistan," in *National Human Development Report 2007* (Dushanbe: United Nations Development Program and SHARQ, 2007), 8.

81   Ibid., 12.

82   Sergey Medrea, "The Tajik Tax Jungle: Survival of the Fittest," *Central Asia— Caucasus Analyst* 10, no. 13 (June 25, 2008): 14, www.silkroadstudies.org/ docs/080625Analyst.pdf.

83   International Finance Corporation, "Business Environment in Tajikistan," 187; for a comprehensive review of Tajikistan's tax regime, see 213–14. Also see World Bank and International Finance Corporation, "Ease of Doing Business in Tajikistan."

84   International Finance Corporation, "Business Environment in Tajikistan"; World Bank and International Finance Corporation, "Ease of Doing Business in Tajikistan."

85   International Finance Corporation, "Business Environment in Tajikistan," 182.

86   Ibid., 199.

87   Ibid., 205.

88   Medrea, "Tajik Tax Jungle."

89   For the details, see International Finance Corporation, "Business Environment in Tajikistan," 197–202.

90   Olimov, "Informal Economy."

91   Ibid., 46.

92   Ibid., 47.

93   Ibid., 49.

94   Ibid., 51.

95   Ibid., 27.

96   Ibid., 28.

97   Complaints about electricity were greatest in Khatlon Province, where 62.1 percent said that it was a serious problem.

98   Olimov, "Informal Economy," 36–37.

99   Ibid., 75. This included 92.9 percent of those operating transportation services, 81.8 percent of those with communication services, and 70 percent of those in utilities— all areas where operating without permits is very difficult to do. By contrast, only 50 percent of those in health care and social services, 55.7 percent of those in trade and

food catering, and 57.8 percent of those in agriculture said that they had obtained all the necessary permits. And, rather expectedly, the highest incidence of obtaining of permits was in the Region of Republican Subordination (including Tajikistan), where 73.9 percent of the entrepreneurs said that they had received them, and the lowest rate of compliance was in Khatlon, with 44.3 percent, although some of the regional difference is a reflection of the type of enterprises operating in each region.

100 World Bank and International Finance Corporation, "Ease of Doing Business in Tajikistan."

101 Tajikistan's exports have been decreasing as a share of GDP, dropping from 23 percent of GDP in 2006 to 13 percent of GDP in 2009. Imports grew from 58 percent of GDP in 2006 to 72 percent of GDP in 2008, before falling to 56 percent of GDP in 2009. World Bank, "Indicators," http://data.worldbank.org/indicator.

102 World Bank and International Finance Corporation, "Ease of Doing Business in Tajikistan."

103 International Finance Corporation, "Business Environment in Tajikistan," 218.

104 Olimov, "Informal Economy," 42.

105 Ibid., 44.

106 European Bank for Reconstruction and Development, *Strategy for Tajikistan*, March 13, 2012, 20.

107 World Bank, *Migration Remittances and Factbook*, 2nd ed. (Washington, D.C.: World Bank, 2011), http://siteresources.worldbank.org/INTLAC/Resources/Factbook2011-Ebook.pdf.

108 These data were provided by Saodat Olimova.

109 International Monetary Fund, "Regional Economic Outlook, Middle East and Central Asia," *World Economic and Financial Surveys*, October 2009, 32.

110 World Bank, "Tajikistan: Poverty Assessment, December 3, 2009," 42, http://web.worldbank.org/external/default/main?pagePK=51187349&piPK=51189435&theSiteP K=258744&menuPK=64187510&searchMenuPK=287276&theSitePK=258744&enti tyID=000333038_20100118015430&searchMenuPK=287276&theSitePK=258744.

111 International Monetary Fund, *Republic of Tajikistan: Poverty Reduction Strategy Paper*, 25.

112 According to the World Bank's 2009 World Development Indicators, Russia's labor force participation rate is 63 percent, Ukraine's is 58 percent, and Belarus's is 60 percent.

113 This is from research by Jafar Olimov, as provided by Saodat Olimova.

114 World Bank, "Tajikistan: Poverty Assessment, December 3, 2009," 40.

115 In addition, 11.3 percent of the population was self-employed (and including the 17.5 percent who are unpaid family workers, and 0.4 percent were not employed in a classifiable fashion). Ibid., 43.

116 Olimov, "Informal Economy," 56. They also found that 15.2 percent of all households received salaries from state-owned enterprises and organizations.

117 Ibid., 54.

118 Bureau of Democracy, Human Rights, and Labor, U.S. Department of State, *2009 Human Rights Report: Tajikistan* (Washington, D.C.: U.S. Government Printing Office, 2010), 14, www.state.gov/j/drl/rls/hrrpt/2009/sca/136094.htm.

119 European Bank for Reconstruction and Development, *Strategy for Tajikistan*, January 2009, 21.

120 Tajikistan still has two passports—internal and external.

121 United States Department of State, Bureau of Democracy, Human Rights, and Labor, *2009 Human Rights Report: Tajikistan*, March 2010.

122 For demographic changes, see Aaron Erlich, "Tajikistan: From Refugee Sender to Labor Exporter," *Migration Information Source*, July 2006, www.migrationinformation. org/Feature/display.cfm?id=411.

123 A total of 17 percent of those surveyed first went to work abroad in 1998, and 18 percent in 1999, as opposed to 13 percent in 1997 and 9 percent in 2000. Saodat Olimova and Igor Bosc, *Labour Migration from Tajikistan* (Dushanbe: International Organization for Migration, 2003), 21, www.iom.int/jahia/webdav/site/myjahiasite/ shared/shared/mainsite/published_docs/studies_and_reports/Tajik_study_oct_03.pdf.

124 Ibid., 22.

125 Shuttle traders are individuals who make their living traveling to foreign countries to import goods for resale at home. They are not licensed and do not pay taxes or tariffs (unless caught), and they dominated the Tajik wholesale and retail market before the introduction of a functioning customs system at the country's borders.

126 Olimova and Bosc, *Labour Migration*, 27–28.

127 A total of 430,000 "Tajiks" sought refuge in the Russian Federation from 1989 to 1998, but in this case "Tajik" is probably used solely to denote the country of residence rather than the ethnic origin of these people, as the note says that it refers to residence and not to citizenship. Abdul-Ghaffar Mughal, "Migration, Remittances, and Living Standards in Tajikistan," Tajikistan Office, International Organization for Migration, September 2007, 6, www.iom.tj/pubs/Impact%20 of%20remittances%20in%20Khatlon%20by%20Mughal.pdf.

128 International Crisis Group, *Central Asia: Migrants and the Economic Crisis*, Asia Report 183 (Brussels: International Crisis Group, 2010), 1, www.crisisgroup.org/-/media/Files/asia/central-asia/183%20Central%20Asia%20Migrants%20and%20the%20Economic%20Crisis.ashx.

129 International Organization for Migration, *Perspectivy migratsii: Vostochnaya Evropa i Tsentral'naya Aziya—Planirovaniye i upravleniye trudovoy migratsiey* (Perspectives on Migration: Eastern Europe and Central Asia—Planning and managing labor migration) (Vienna: International Organization for Migration, 2006), 110, www.iom.lt/documents/Migr.Perspectives-Russ2006.pdf.

130 The World Bank conclusion presumes that Tajik women who are not employed are either living permanently in Russia or visiting for less than a month, with the latter likely to be pretty exceptional.

131 World Bank, "Tajikistan: Poverty Assessment, December 3, 2009," 52.

132 Ibid., 49.

133 Mughal, "Migration," xviii.

134 *Sbornik normativno-pravovykh dokumentov Respubliki Tadzhikistan v sfere migratsii naseleniya* (Collection of legal documents of the Republic of Tajikistan concerning migration), Dushanbe, 2006, as cited by International Organization for Migration, *Perspectivy migratsii*, 109.

135 The applicable legislation includes the State Migration Policy Concept (1998), the Migration Law of the Republic of Tajikistan (1999), the Statute on the State Migration Service Under the Ministry of Labor and Employment (2000), the External Labor Migration Concept (2001), the Government Decree on the Registration of Labor Migration of Tajik Nationals (2003), and the Government Decree on the Regulation of External Labor Migration (2005).

136 This is in fulfillment of the Government of Tajikistan Resolution 242, "On the Basic Direction of State Policy in the Area of Stimulating Labor Migration," July 9, 2001.

137 I thank Saodat Olimova for this insight.

138 International Organization for Migration, *Perspectivy migratsii*, 111.

139 Other sources show lower total remittances than reported in table 4.4. The authors of "IOM 2005," a study that focused on Khatlon Oblast, reported a total for nationwide remittances for 2004 and 2005, from formal and informal remittances, of $550 million and $735 million, respectively. These numbers were based on National Bank of Tajikistan statistics, which have traditionally included downward adjustments to account for exportables. Mughal, "Migration," xix.

140 This information was provided by Saodat Olimova.

CHAPTER 5

1 Environment Department and Poverty Reduction and Economic Management Unit, Europe and Central Asia, World Bank, *Tajikistan Country Environmental Analysis*, Report 43465-TJ, May 15, 2008, 48, www-wds.worldbank.org/external/default/WDSContentServer/WDSP/IB/2008/06/17/000333038_20080617041000/Rendered/PDF/434650ESW0P1061sclosed0June01302008.pdf.

2 Ibid., 49.

3 Ibid., 52.

4 Ibid., 59.

5 This dollar amount here is based on a 2008 exchange rate of $1 = TJS 3.44.

6 The data I am referencing here deal with employed population, not total population or labor force (labor force = employed + actively seeking employment, but not discouraged workers).

7 This is from the Statistical Agency Under the President of the Republic of Tajikistan.

8 I wish to thank Saodat Olimova for providing this statistic.

9 The European Bank for Reconstruction and Development provides the figure of 900,000 hectares of arable land, but the Food and Agriculture Organization of the United Nations states that there are 960,000 hectares. FAO and Ministry of Agriculture and Nature Protection of the Republic of Tajikistan, *Report of the Tajikistan Emergency Agriculture and Livestock Rapid Assessment (February 8–15, 2008)*, FAO Emergency Agriculture Rapid Assessment Report, Dushanbe, March 6, 2008, http://reliefweb.int/sites/reliefweb.int/files/resources/D718D552F66477364925743C000FD263-Full_Report.pdf.

10 Presidential decrees issued in 1995 and 1997 distributed household plots averaging 0.115 hectares to qualifying rural households to increase food security. All households with holdings less than the national norm of household land were eligible to receive them. See Roy Behnke, *The Socio-Economic Causes and Consequences of Desertification in Central Asia*, NATO Science for Peace and Security Series (Bishkek: NATO, 2006), http://books.google.co.in/books?id=RlnX0JTdg-0C&pg=PA175&lpg=PA175&dq=%22presidential+land%22++tajikistan&source=bl&ots=TPENH_oujG&sig=OEJRadaD1yq2SftsL6pBsaj3yhM&hl=en&sa=X&ei=hqoTT_iuD4LsrAeludieAg&redir_esc=y#v=onepage&q=%22presidential%20land%22%20%20%20tajikistan&f=false, 175; and Obie S. Porteous, "Land Reform in Tajikistan," Emergency Nutrition Network Online, March 2005, http://fex.ennonline.net/24/landreform.aspx.

11   FAO and Ministry of Agriculture and Nature Protection of the Republic of Tajikistan, *Report of the Tajikistan Emergency Agriculture and Livestock Rapid Assessment*, 28.

12   Ibid., 29.

13   The FAO surveyed 276,000 households in thirteen districts, of which 114,300 were judged vulnerable to food insecurity, including 13,000 households headed by women. Ibid., 23–24.

14   Ibid., 27.

15   Ibid., 28.

16   Zvi Lerman and David Sedik, "The Economic Effects of Land Reform in Tajikistan," European Commission under the EC/FAO Food Security Programme—Phase II Food Security Information for Action, October 2008, ftp://ftp.fao.org/docrep/fao/011/aj285e/aj285e00.pdf.

17   U.S. Agency for International Development Tajikistan, *Land Legislation Development Project: Final Report*, December 31, 2005, 12, http://pdf.usaid.gov/pdf_docs/PDACH703.pdf.

18   USAID Tajikistan, "Land Reform and Farm Reorganization in Tajikistan, Policy Issues Paper," (Washington, D.C.: ARD Inc., 2004) http://pdf.usaid.gov/pdf_docs/PNADD469.pdf.

19   Lerman and Sedik, "Economic Effects," 26.

20   Ibid., 28.

21   FAO and Ministry of Agriculture and Nature Protection of the Republic of Tajikistan, *Report of the Tajikistan Emergency Agriculture and Livestock Rapid Assessment*, 8.

22   Personal communications with author.

23   World Bank, "Land Registration and Cadastre System for Sustainable Agriculture Project (LRCSP)," Project P089566, http://web.worldbank.org/external/projects/main?Projectid=P089566&theSitePK=40941&piPK=64302772&pagePK=64330670&menuPK=64282135&Type=Financial.

24   The date of the tax system changes varies among sources; recent Tajik tax documents say that the changes are from 2008; see Tajinvest, "Nalogovyi Kodeks Respubliki Tadzhikistan (s izmeneneiyami, 2008 goda)" (Tax Code of the Republic of Tajikistan with changes from 2008), www.tajinvest.tj/downloads/zakon/014.pdf. The U.S. State Department says that the changes were enacted in December 2009; see U.S. State Department, "2010 Investment Climate Statement—Tajikistan," March 2010, www.state.gov/e/eb/rls/othr/ics/2010/138152.htm.

25 USAID Central Asian Republics, "Land Reform and Market Development Project II: Final Report, Tajikistan, 2008–2009," December 2009, 2, http://pdf.usaid.gov/ pdf_docs/PDACP456.pdf.

26 Parvina Khamidova, "I Did Not Have Financial Interest in Cotton Investment, Says Former Head of NBT," *Asia-Plus*, April 15, 2009. The original interview is no longer available on *Asia-Plus*; however, a BBC Monitoring Report provides a transcript: "(Corrected) Tajik Banker Denies Involvement in Fraud," BBC Monitoring International Reports, April 30, 2009, available at www.accessmylibrary.com/ article-1G1-198839282/corrected-tajik-banker-denies.html.

27 Personal communication with the author.

28 Lerman and Sedik, "Economic Effects," 6.

29 Personal communications with the author.

30 European Bank for Reconstruction and Development, *Strategy for Tajikistan*, January 2009, 28.

31 Lerman and Sedik, "Economic Effects," 18.

32 FARMS Project-Tajikistan, "Dekhan Farms Inside/Out: A Comparative Assessment of Dekhan Farm Growing Models in Sughd Oblast, Tajikistan—Agro Socioeconomic Survey and Baseline Report," Facilitating Agricultural Reform and Marketing in Sughd, Center for International Studies and Cooperation (CECI), November 2006, 21.

33 Personal communications with Saodat Olimova. Her research in Sughd Oblast showed that much of this credit was from private sources, especially from senior military officials.

34 FARMS Project-Tajikistan, "Dekhan Farms Inside/Out," 10.

35 The CECI study found that collective farms had a net profit of 129.3 somoni ($27), individual farms 81.3 somoni ($17), and family farms lost 16.5 somoni ($3.47) in 2004, and all did somewhat better in 2005 because of higher cotton prices, earning 239.0 somoni ($50), 153.0 somoni ($32), and 101.3 somoni ($21.29), respectively, while the profit for wheat in 2005 averaged 175.5 somoni ($36.88); for corn, 667.0 somoni ($140.71); and for onions 1,256.1 somoni ($263.98), FARMS Project-Tajikistan, "Dekhan Farms Inside/Out," 15–16.

36 Personal communications with Saodat Olimova.

37 Lerman and Sedik, "Economic Effects," 54.

38 Ibid., 57.

39 Ibid., 59.

40 FAO and Ministry of Agriculture and Nature Protection of the Republic of Tajikistan, *Report of the Tajikistan Emergency Agriculture and Livestock Rapid Assessment*, 10.

41 World Bank, "Implementation Status and Results Tajikistan Cotton Sector Recovery Project (P098889)," www-wds.worldbank.org/external/default/WDSContentServer/WDSP/ECA/2011/06/25/A885095D5E0D55F3852578BA006B739B/1_0/Rendered/PDF/P0988890ISR0Di025201101309030419393.pdf.

42 FAO and Ministry of Agriculture and Nature Protection of the Republic of Tajikistan, *Report of the Tajikistan Emergency Agriculture and Livestock Rapid Assessment*, 3.

43 Ibid., 9.

44 These numbers can be found using the FAOSTAT database, http://faostat3.fao.org/home/index.html.

45 This has been funded through a USAID program through Michigan State University and the ICARDA project.

46 Personal communications with the author.

47 FAO and Ministry of Agriculture and Nature Protection of the Republic of Tajikistan, *Report of the Tajikistan Emergency Agriculture and Livestock Rapid Assessment*, 15.

48 Ibid., 16.

49 Ibid., 17.

50 Ibid.

51 See USAID, "Productive Agriculture," http://centralasia.usaid.gov/tajikistan/332.

52 Ministry of Agriculture of Republic of Tajikistan, FAO, and World Food Program, *Crop and Food Security Assessment Mission Report Tajikistan 2011* (Dushanbe: FAO and Ministry of Agriculture, 2011), 5, www.fao.org/docrep/015/an110e/an110e00.pdf.

53 The number of hectares here was provided by Saodat Olimova. She estimates that pasturage is five to ten times less productive than previously.

54 FAO and Ministry of Agriculture and Nature Protection of the Republic of Tajikistan, *Report of the Tajikistan Emergency Agriculture and Livestock Rapid Assessment*, 17.

55 GIZ is currently implementing a food security program in Tajikistan. The Swedish International Development Cooperation Agency closed down its operations in Tajikistan in 2009 to focus resources on fewer countries. Helvetas's ongoing Local Market Development Project "aims to develop synergies between public, civil and private actors leading to systemic changes and improvements in selected agricultural sectors, and thus contribute to poverty reduction." See Helvetas, "Local Market Development," www.helvetas.tj/en/project/8.

56   USAID, "AgLinks Final Report: Kyrgyzstan, Kazakhstan, Tajikistan, And
      Turkmenistan," Bishkek, September 2008, 6, http://pdf.usaid.gov/pdf_docs/
      PDACM094.pdf.

57   The three beneficiaries were Tajik Fruit Company, a large-scale fruit producer that
      exports to the United States and Europe, which received funding to improve pruning
      (which virtually doubled their production) and to purchase food processing facilities;
      Askarali Mirzoev Farm Association, for processing grape juice (whose owner decided
      to invest in the project after an AgLinks-sponsored trip to PRODEXPO in Moscow);
      and Umedi Saidburhon Water Users' Association, which began exporting Meyer
      lemons to Afghanistan. USAID, "AgLinks Final Report," 9–11.

58   For details on all these challenges, see the report prepared by the regional office of
      ICARDA in Central Asia in 2009, ICARDA, NARS of Kyrgyzstan, Tajikistan, and
      Iran, and CACSA, "Improving Livelihoods of Small Farmers and Rural Women
      through Value-Added Processing and Export of Cashmere, Wool and Mohair,"
      August–December 2009, www.icarda.org/cac/fiber/files/progress_report_august_
      december_2009_eng.pdf.

59   Katherine M. Kelm and Shuhrat Nurubloev, *Tajikistan: Improving Aid Coordination
      and Portfolio Management (Aid Coordination Component for Farm Debt Resolution
      Strategy)*, Technical Assistance Consultant's Report, Project 38239-02, Asian
      Development Bank, November 2008, 7, www2.adb.org/Documents/Reports/
      Consultant/38239-TAJ/38239-TAJ-TACR.pdf.

CHAPTER 6

1   For complete data on Tajik industrial statistics, see the Statistical Agency Under the
      President of the Republic of Tajikistan, www.stat.tj, the government of Tajikistan's
      statistical service that maintains its databases, with assistance from the United
      Nations Development Program–Tajikistan. Also see International Monetary Fund,
      Republic of Tajikistan: Poverty Reduction Strategy Paper, IMF Country Report 09/82
      (Washington, D.C.: International Monetary Fund, 2009), 35, www.unpei.org/PDF/
      Tajikistan_PRSP_2009.pdf.

2   These statistics come from "Selected Indicators of Industrial Production, 1985–2008,"
      www.stat.tj/english.tables.htm. They were accessed on April 13, 2012, and were the
      most recent data available at that time.

3   International Monetary Fund, *Republic of Tajikistan: Poverty Reduction Strategy
      Paper*, 36.

4   For example, in November 2011 there was an explosion on the Uzbek side of the rail
      link between Uzbekistan and Tajikistan, and the government of Uzbekistan waited

a full two months to begin repairs. See Joshua Kucera, "Railroad Explosion on Uzbekistan-Afghanistan Border 'Terrorist Act,'" Eurasianet.org, November 18, 2011, www.eurasianet.org/node/64544; and "Uzbekistan Begins Repairs at Rail Ridge Blast Site: Tajikistan," *Different Stans*, January 31, 2012, http://3dblogger.typepad.com/different_stans/2012/01/uzbekistan-begins-repairs-at-rail-bridge-blast-site-tajikistan.html.

5   A good source for monitoring Tajikistan's ongoing industrial performance is the blog of the Office of the Senior Economist, http://europeandcis.undp.org/senioreconomist.

6   United Nations Development Program, *National Development Strategy of the Republic of Tajikistan for the Period to 2015* (Dushanbe: United Nations Development Program, 2007), 25, www.undp.tj/files/reports/nds_eng.pdf.

7   International Monetary Fund, *Republic of Tajikistan: Poverty Reduction Strategy Paper*, 37.

8   *Tajik Aluminum Plant* v. *Ermatov et al.* (2005–2008). I wish to thank Paul Hauser of Bryan Cave LLP for sharing the October–November 2008 trial transcripts with me.

9   TALCO (Tajik Aluminum Company), "Osnovnyye tendetsii razvitiya proizvodstvenno-ekonomicheskoy i finansovoy deyatel'nosti GUP 'Tadzhikskaya Alyuminiyevaya Kompaniya' (za 2010 v sravnenii s 2009)" (Main trends of production, economic and financial activities of the SUE "Tajik Aluminum Company" [in 2010 compared to 2009]), January 2011, 12, www.talco.com.tj/index.php?l=2&u=2&mm=2&m2=27.

10   Tajikistan's Embassy in Tokyo reports that aluminum accounted for 53 percent of Tajikistan's exports in 2009. Embassy of the Republic of Tajikistan in Tokyo, "Mineral Resources of the Republic of Tajikistan," January 6, 2009, www.tajikistan.jp/mineral.en.php.

11   TALCO, "Osnovnyye tendetsii," 5.

12   Ibid., 9.

13   RUSAL (an abbreviation for Russian Aluminum) is Russia's largest aluminum company, and with Alcoa and Alcan, one of the three largest aluminum companies in the world, and frequently in first place. It is headed by its founder, Oleg Deripaska. For details on the company and its history, see www.rusal.ru/en/about/history.aspx.

14   Dmitry Ponomarev and Dmitry Glumskov, "Rusal poluchil kontrol' nad TadAZom" (Rusal took control over TadAZ), *Kommersant*, no. 17 (285), January 31, 2004, http://kommersant.ru/doc/445494.

15   "UPDATE 1-Russian Tycoons' Feud Over RUSAL Comes to UK Court," Reuters, April 10, 2012, www.reuters.com/article/2012/04/10/rusal-glencore-idUSL3E8FA2XE20120410.

16 "Professor Nazarov pomirilsya s RusAlom" (Professor Nazarov made peace with RUSAL), Avesta.TJ–Tajik News, May 24, 2007, www.avesta.tj/main/1292-d.html.

17 For basic information about Ashton Commodities, see www.manta.com/ic/mvyld6h/gb/ashton-commodities-ltd. It no longer maintains its earlier website, www.ashtoncommodities.com/about.html, but it can still be located through the Way Back Machine website, http://web.archive.org/web/20080723171222/, www.ashtoncommodities.com/about.html.

18 International Monetary Fund, *Republic of Tajikistan: Selected Issues and Statistical Appendix*, Staff Country Report (Washington, D.C.: International Monetary Fund, 2003), 77.

19 *Tajik Aluminum Plant* v. *Ermatov et al.*, trial transcripts, October 30, 2008, 96.

20 "Hydro Aluminum AS and Tajik Aluminum Plant Settlement Agreement," December 20, 2006, 2, reproduced by John Helmer, "President Rakhmon Forced to End Tajik Aluminum Court Case in London," *Dancing with Bears*, November 27, 2008, http://johnhelmer.net/?p=626.

21 With RUSAL in the picture, the earlier structure became very cumbersome—Ansol and RUSAL supplied alumina to Hamer, which supplied it to TadAZ (RUSAL wanted Ansol dissolved, but they had too well defined a supplier and client base. See *Tajik Aluminum Plant* v. *Ermatov et al.*, 2005, EWHC 2241 (Ch), HC05C01237, 98, www.bailii.org/cgi-bin/markup.cgi?doc=ew/cases/EWHC/Ch/2005/2241.html&query=TAJIK%20ALUMINIUM%20PLANT). RUSAL also wanted Hydro to agree to off-take the aluminum in return for Hydro providing TadAZ with the necessary financial guarantees. The 2003 barter agreement basically gives RUSAL a tripartite guarantee, replacing the 2000 agreement with TadAZ-Hamer-Hydro. It consisted of several parts—an aluminum agreement between Hydro and Ansol from September 25, 2003, whereby Ansol agreed to sell aluminum to Hydro in exchange for Hydro providing financial backing to Ansol to enable it to finance the supply of raw materials and services to TadAZ; an agreement between TadAZ and Hamer from April 15, 2003, whereby Hamer supplied raw materials to TadAZ and made payments for TadAZ in exchange for aluminum; and an agreement between Ansol and Hamer, whereby Hamer supplied Ansol with aluminum delivered by TadAZ to Hamer.

22 *Tajik Aluminum Plant* v. *Ermatov et al.*, 2006, EWHC 2374 (Comm), 2006 folio 271 QB, 41, www.bailii.org/ew/cases/EWHC/Comm/2006/2374.html.

23 Ibid., 43. Ansol is also rumored to have received $70 million for this.

24 *Tajik Aluminum Plant* v. *Ermatov et al.*, 2006, EWHC 2374 (Comm), 2006 folio 271 QB, 49.

25 *Tajik Aluminum Plant* v. *Ermatov et al.*, 2005, EWHC 2241 (Ch), HC05C01237, 114.

26   Ibid., 155.

27   *Tajik Aluminum Plant* v. *Ermatov et al.*, 2006, EWHC 2374 (Comm), 2006 folio 271 QB, 55.

28   *Tajik Aluminum Plant* v. *Ermatov et al.*, trial transcripts, November 6, 2008, 81.

29   *Tajik Aluminum Plant* v. *Ermatov et al.*, 2006, EWHC 2374 (Comm), 2006 folio 271 QB, 57–58.

30   *Tajik Aluminum Plant* v. *Ermatov et al.*, 2005, EWHC 2241 (Ch), HC05C01237, 180.

31   *Tajik Aluminum Plant* v. *Ermatov et al.*, trial transcripts, October 31, 2008, 122.

32   Ibid., 106–108.

33   Hydro Aluminum AS and Tajik Aluminum Plant Settlement Agreement.

34   *Tajik Aluminum Plant* v. *Hydro Aluminum AS*, 2006, EWHC 1135 (Comm) QB.

35   Ibid., 31.

36   John Helmer, "EBRD Wraps Secrecy Around Aluminum Dealing," *Dancing with Bears*, July 11, 2006, http://johnhelmer.net/?p=3587.

37   *Tajik Aluminum Plant* v. *Ermatov et al.*, trial transcripts, November 3, 2008, 26.

38   At the time of the agreement, 43.8 percent of the shares of Hydro, which trades on the New York Stock Exchange, were held by the Norwegian government, with several U.S. banks either directly or as nominees controlling approximately 12 percent of Hydro shares. John Helmer, "Global Tizz Over Tajik Aluminum Deal," *Asia Times*, November 27, 2007, www.atimes.com/atimes/Central_Asia/IK21Ag01.html.

39   John Helmer, "Tajik Mine Resource Promotion Mystification," *Dancing with Bears*, November 28, 2007, http://johnhelmer.net/?p=301.

40   *Tajik Aluminum Plant* v. *Ermatov et al.*, trial transcripts, November 3, 2008, 37–40.

41   John Helmer, "A Missing Aluminum Trick Worth Half a Billion Dollars Goes to High Court," *Dancing with Bears*, January 11, 2008, http://johnhelmer.net/?p=315.

42   *Tajik Aluminum Plant* v. *Ermatov et al.*, trial transcripts, November 3, 2008, 44.

43   Ibid., 30.

44   Ibid., 35.

45   "Hydro Aluminum AS and Tajik Aluminum Plant Settlement Agreement":

5.4 Hydro irrevocably and absolutely undertakes, covenants and agrees that it shall not, without the prior written consent of TadAZ sue on or otherwise bring or threaten any Claims of *whatever* nature against any or all of CDH, Hamer, the RUSAL Group and/or Ansol (save in the case of Ansol, in relation to the Aluminium Agreement dated 25 September 2003 (as amended) or its predecessor agreement) provided that TadAZ is not in breach of its obligations under the Agreement and that TadAZ has not remedied such breach within 30 days of receipt of a notice from Hydro requiring it to do so. In the event of any breach by Hydro of this provision Hydro agrees to indemnify TadAZ against any losses suffered by TadAZ as a consequence (whether direct or indirect and including any claims for contribution) of Hydro's actions.

6.1 Hydro acknowledges the possibility that Hamer may, following the date of this Agreement, contend that TadAZ is liable to it in respect of a particular shipment or shipments of alumina or aluminum in respect of which TadAZa has determined to be liable to Hydro pursuant to the Arbitration Award (the Hamer Claims). In the event that a Hamer Claim is threatened or brought by Hamer, Hydro agrees that it shall so far as reasonably possible co-operate with and assist TadAZ in resisting the Hamer Claim, such cooperation and assistance to include:

6.1.1 confirming in writing to TadAZ and/or Hamer in a form previously approved by TadAZ (acting reasonably) the grounds upon which Hydro does not consider that Hamer has any valid claim against TadAZ in respect of the shipments of alumina or aluminum to which the Arbitration Award relates:

8 Co-operation Against the Fraud Action Defendants, the RUSAL, The RUSAL Group and/or Hamer

8.1 Hydro shall as far as reasonably possible co-operate with and assist TadAZ in:

8.1.1 pursuing the Fraud Action to recover damages: and

8.1.2 pursuing companies with the RUSAL Group and Hamer to recover damages; and

8.1.3 pursuing any further actions against Ansol and/or the other defendants to the Fraud Action to recover damages (the "Additional Ansol Claims")

8.2 The cooperation and assistance to be provided by Hydro pursuant to Clause 8.1 above shall include...

8.2.2 permitting TadAZ or its representatives to interview employees or (if they agree) other representatives, consultants or agents of Hydro or the Norsk Hydro Group (in the presence of Hydro's legal representatives if Hydro sees fit) in relation to any issues raised in the Fraud Action, in prospective or actual claims by TadAZ against companies in the RUSAL Group and/or Hamer, or in the Additional Ansol Claims (whether such claims are prospective or actual);

8.2.3 making available employees or (if they agree) other representatives, consultants or agents of Hydro or the Norsk Hydro Group to give evidence for TadAZ in the Fraud Action in or any proceedings brought by TadAZ against companies in the RUSAL Group and/or Hamer, or in connection with the Additional Ansol Claims, provided that Hydro's legal advisers are given permission to attend any hearings in such proceedings which are in any way relevant to the evidence of such individuals. TadAZ shall give reasonable notice to Hydro of such hearings. From Hydro's part, it is important to note that they have left options for refusing assistance to TadAZ as well, particularly through

8.2.1 promptly disclosing to TadAZ any further non-privileged requests by TadAZ (such documents or classes of documents to be identified with reasonable specificity) save where Hydro considers acting reasonably and in good faith that disclosing such documents would not be practicable and/or would involve a disproportionate effort on Hydro's part and/or would materially prejudice Hydro's interests (in which event Hydro shall promptly inform TadAZ of the reasons for its refusal to provide the relevant documents).

46 Hydro, "The Hydro Integrity Program Handbook on Corruption and Human Rights," 13, www.hydro.com/upload/7233/Integrity_handbook_2010_EN.pdf.

47 "RUSAL Agrees to Settlement to End TadAZ Dispute," *Metal Bulletin*, May 3, 2007, www.metalbulletin.com/Article/1528776/Rusal-agrees-settlement-to-end-TadAZ-dispute.html.

48 "Tajik Aluminum Plant vs. Rusal," Worldal.com, July 7, 2007, www.worldal.com/news/russia/2007-07-07/126398484217494.shtml.

49 "RUSAL Sued by TALCO on BVI," *Kommersant*, July 19, 2007, www.kommersant.com/p783705/r_500/industrial_corruption.

50 "RUSAL Files Lawsuits Claiming $312 Mln from TALCO, Related Cos.," *Highbeam Business*, July 2, 2007, http://business.highbeam.com/407705/article-1G1-165945579/rusal-files-lawsuits-claiming-312-mln-talco-related.

51 Ansol was then ordered on July 2006 to neither destroy nor tamper with these documents. *Tajik Aluminum Plant* v. *Ermatov et al.*, 2005, EWHC 2241 (Ch), HC05C01237.

52 Ibid., 163.

53 Ibid., 177.

54 Ibid., 179.

55 Ibid., 180.

56 Ibid., 182.

57 *Tajik Aluminum Plant* v. *Ermatov et al.*, trial transcripts, October 30, 2008, 22.

58 Ermatov was said to own three apartments in Moscow purchased for $1.1 million, and a Mayfair apartment in London worth $10 million. Ibid., October 27, 2008, 5.

59 Ibid., October 30, 2008, 113.

60 Ibid., 114.

61 Ibid., October 29, 2008, 127.

62 Ibid., 120.

63 Schedule 3 was not published.

64 Amended Revised Defense of Defendants 2, 3, 4, 5, 6, 8, and 9 (the Ansol/Ashton Defendants) in *Tajik Aluminum Plant* v. *Ermatov et al.*, 2006, EWHC 2374 (Comm), 2006 FOLIO 271 QB.

65 *Tajik Aluminum Plant* v. *Ermatov et al.*, trial transcripts, October 30, 2008, 115.

66 Ibid., 110–11.

67 Ibid., 111–12.

68 *Tajik Aluminum Plant* v. *Ermatov et al.*, 2005, EWHC 2241 (Ch), HC05C01237, 63.

69 *Tajik Aluminum Plant* v. *Ermatov et al.*, trial transcripts, October 29, 2008, 113.

70 John Helmer, "Tajik Aluminum Court Case Ends in London Defeat for President Rahmon," *Dancing with Bears*, November 27, 2008, http://johnhelmer.net/?p=632.

71 U.S. Geological Survey, *2007 Minerals Yearbook: Tajikistan*, 42.3, http://minerals. usgs.gov/minerals/pubs/country/2007/myb3-2007-ti.pdf.

72 "Tadzhikistan sokratil proizvodstvo i eksport alyuminiya" (Tajikistan reduced production and export of aluminum), *All About Aluminum*, October 30, 2009, www.aluminiumleader.com/serious/news/2009/10/30/talco301009.

73 TALCO, "Osnovnyye tendetsii," 13.

74 Ibid., 4.

75 Ibid., 13.

76 TALCO (Tajik Aluminum Company), "Tajik Aluminum Company Received the 'Best Enterprises in Europe' Award," February 28, 2009, www.talco.com.tj/index. php?l=4&action=newslist&id=115&page=2.

77 See the Europe Business Assembly website, www.ebaoxford.co.uk.

78 TALCO (Tajik Aluminum Company), "Board of Directors of Tajik Aluminum Company Conducted First Meeting in Dushanbe," May 6, 2008, http://talco.com.tj/ index.php?l=4&action=newslist&id=14&page=6.

79 Operations Policy and Services Unit, Europe and Central Asia Region, World Bank, *Tajikistan Country Financial Accountability Assessment*, Report 29693-TJ, June 22, 2004, 27, www-wds.worldbank.org/servlet/WDSContentServer/WDSP/IB/2004/08/ 13/000090341_20040813112914/Rendered/PDF/296930TJ.pdf.

80 These are profits/losses before taxation. After taxation, there was a total loss of $11,669 in 2007, as opposed to $7,456 profit in 2006. Tajik Aluminum Company (formerly Tajik Aluminum Plant), "Abbreviated Financial Statements for the Year Ended December 31, 2007," July 31, 2010, 6, www.talco.com.tj/UserFiles/FS%20 audit%202007%20Eng.pdf.

81 Ibid., 7.

82 Ibid., 24.

83 TALCO, "Osnovnyye tendetsii," 10.

84 "TALCO Management Secures Promising Al Premiums for H2," *Metal Bulletin*, August 14, 2009, www.metalbulletin.com/Article/2274002/Talco-Management-secures-promising-Al-premiums-for-H2.html.

85 For more information, see www.thisisnoble.com.

86 Alaska Metals AG, "About Us: The Business," www.alaskametals.com/about.php.

87 Rustam Makhmudov, "Alyuminiyevyye ogurtsy na uzbekskikh gryadkakh" (Aluminum cucumbers in Uzbek vegetable gardens), *Tsentr Asia*, April 4, 2011, www.centrasia.ru/newsA.php?st=1302863880.

88 Arkady Dybnov, "Prosecutor General of Tajikistan Blames Russian Company Ansol for Involvement in Organization of the Turnover," Fergana.ru, April 12, 2005, http://enews.fergananews.com/article.php?id=908.

89 In a WikiLeaked U.S. State Department cable, Ambassador Jon Purnell makes reference to Salim as a mafia figure; see "Mafia Boss Fixes GOU Tenders and Jobs, U.S. Embassy Tashkent Cable 06TASHKENT902," May 5, 2006, http://wikileaks.org/cable/2006/05/06TASHKENT902.html.

90 Michael Chernoy was active in the Russian metals industry at the time of the collapse of the USSR, has reputed ties to the Russian mafia, and is embroiled in legal proceedings with Oleg Deripaska in London. Donald Macintyre, "Clash of the Oligarchs," *Independent*, July 20, 2009, www.independent.co.uk/news/uk/home-news/clash-of-the-oligarchs-1753022.html?action=Popup. Also see "Salim-bai: Chempion po druzhbe" (Salimboi: A friendship champion), *Tsentr Asia*, September 28, 2004, www.centrasia.ru/newsA.php?st=1096382220.

91 "Roghun & TadAZ, Chast' 7: Gubitel'naya poezdka v Tashkent" (Roghun & TadAZ, Part 7: Disastrous trip to Tashkent), *Avesta.TJ–Tajik News*, September 13, 2008, www.avesta.tj/main/1454-d.html.

92 Anna Lander, "Ekologicheski chistaya vstrecha" (Ecologically clean meeting), *Vremya Novostei*, May 12, 2005, www.vremya.ru/2005/226/8/140574.html.

93 Rukhshona Ibragimova and Shakar Saadi, "Uzbekistan and Tajikistan Argue Over TALCO Emissions," Central Asia Online, April 19, 2010, http://centralasiaonline.com/en_GB/articles/caii/features/politics/2010/04/19/feature-01.

94 "India, Tajikistan Discuss Cooperation in Mineral Sector," *Highbeam Research*, August 3, 2006, www.highbeam.com/doc/1P3-1088518671.html.

95 Debarati Roy, "Nalco Seeks to Buy Tajik Aluminum to Double Capacity (Update 1)," Bloomberg, July 3, 2008, www.bloomberg.com/apps/news?pid=newsarchive&sid=aA4wd2bML.Ac&refer=india.

96 Alexander Sodiqov, "India's Relations with Tajikistan: Beyond the Airbase," *Eurasia Daily Monitor* 8, issue 36 (February 22, 2011), www.jamestown.org/single/?no_cache=1&tx_ttnews%5Btt_news%5D=37545&tx_ttnews%5BbackPid%5D=512.

97 "China, Tajikistan Agree to Build New Bauxite-Producing Plants," Interfax China, May 22, 2008, www.interfax.cn/news/2619; "TALCO Started the Project on Change to Local Raw Materials," Interfax China, May 1, 2008.

98 Tianchen Engineering Corporation first showed strong interest in the project in 2008. "Chairman Wang Zhi Yuan Visits Republic of Tajikistan," China Tianchen Engineering Corporation, September 25, 2009, www.china-tcc.com/en/news/en/e_news_detail.asp?id=633.

99 The plant is to become the property of TALCO after eight years of operation. TALCO (Tajik Aluminum Company), "Press-Reliz po itogam deyatel'nosti Gosudarstvennogo Unitarnogo Predpriyatiya Tadzhikskaya alyuminiyevaya kompaniya v 2010 godu" (Press release on the results of 2010 activities of the Tajik Aluminum Company State Unitary Enterprise), February 2, 2011, http://talco.com.tj/index.php?l=2&action=newslist&id=161&page=1&act_back=press.

100 TALCO (Tajik Aluminum Company), "O khode realizatsii program GUP 'TALCO' po ispol'zovaniyu proizvodstvennykh moschnostey Tadzhikistana i perekhodu na mestnoye syr'ye" (On the process of realizing SUE 'TALCO's' program of utilization of Tajikistan's manufacturing resources and shift to local natural resources: Addendum No. 1 to the press release of February 4, 2011), February 4, 2011, 1, http://talco.com.tj/UserFiles/prilojeny1_ru.doc.

101 Nargis Khamraabyeva, "V Tadzhikistane poyavyatsya zavody po proizvodstvu ftoristogo alyuminiya i kriolita, Pekin obeshchal" (Aluminum fluoride and cryolite production facilities will be built in Tajikistan, Beijing has promised), *Tsentr Asia*, May 21, 2008, www.centrasia.ru/newsA.php?st=1211338860.

102 Alexandr Shustov, "Rossiya i Kitay v Tsentral'noi Azii: Konkurentsiya ili sotrudnichestvo?" (Russia and China in Central Asia: Competition or collaboration?), *Fond strategicheskoi kul'tury*, May 28, 2008, www.fondsk.ru/article.php?id=1410.

103 U.S. Geological Survey, "Bauxite Reserves in China Are Estimated to Be 830,000 Tons," Mineral Commodity Summaries, Bauxite and Alumina, January 2012, http://minerals.usgs.gov/minerals/pubs/commodity/bauxite/mcs-2012-bauxi.pdf; "Chinese Bauxite Export Market Continues to Tighten," *Metal Bulletin*, March 11, 2011, www.metalbulletin.com/Article/2785582/Chinese-bauxite-export-market-continues-to-tighten.html.

104 Nuclear Threat Initiative, "Country Profiles: Tajikistan," www.nti.org/country-profiles/tajikistan.

105 Alexander Sodiqov, "India's Intensified Interest in Tajikistan Driven by Pursuit of Airbase and Uranium," *Central Asia-Caucasus Institute Analyst*, September 16, 2009, www.cacianalyst.org/?q=node/5182.

106 "Uranovyy poryv s pritselom na perspektivy" (Uranium aspirations focused on future prospects), *Echo Planety*, June 22, 2010, www.ekhoplanet.ru/world_500_6943.

107 "Tajikistan Renews Uranium Processing," Country.TJ: News portal of the Republic of Tajikistan, http://country.tj/engnews.php?id=4.

108 Cassady B. Craft, Suzette R. Grillot, and Liam Anderson, "The Dangerous Ground: Nonproliferation Export-Control Development in the Southern Tier of the Former Soviet Union," *Problems of Post-Communism* 47, no. 6 (November–December 2000): 39–51.

109 Ramakrishna Upadhya, "India to Explore Uranium in Tajikistan," *Deccan Herald*, September 10, 2009, www.deccanherald.com/content/24350/india-explore-uranium-tajikistan.html.

110 "Rosatom Ready to Cooperate with Tajikistan in Developing Uranium Deposits," iStockAnalyst, November 13, 2009, www.istockanalyst.com/article/viewiStockNews/articleid/3636345.

111 *Interfax Daily Business Report* 9, issue 136 (2309), July 21, 2000; in "Chinese Corporation Eyes Tajik Uranium complex," FBIS document CEP20000720000242.

112 "China Company Eyes Uranium Deposits in Tajikistan," *New Europe*, July 21, 2008, www.neurope.eu/articles/89015.php.

113 Operations Policy and Services Unit, Europe and Central Asia Region, World Bank, "Tajikistan Country Financial Accountability Assessment," 27.

114 "Tadzhikistan: za shpionazh v pol'zu Uzbekistana zaderzhan direktor GUP 'Vostokredmet' (Tajikistan: SUE "Vostokredmet's" director detained on charges of spying for Uzbekistan), Fergana,ru, July 23, 2009, www.fergananews.com/news.php?id=12503.

115 "Tajikistan: Zhitely Chkalovska prosyat amnistirovat' osuzhdennykh rukovoditeley 'Vostokredmeta'" (Tajikistan: Chkalovsk residents petition for amnesty for convicted managers of "Vostokredmet"), Fergana.ru, October 3, 2009, www.fergananews.com/news.php?id=13351.

116 Payrav Chorshanbiyev, "Comsup Commodities Inc. to Build Metallurgical Enterprise in Tajikistan," *Asia-Plus*, May 19, 2011, http://news.tj/en/news/comsup-commodities-inc-build-metallurgical-enterprise-tajikistan.

117 John Helmer, "Antimony Has Billion-Dollar Potential in Tajikistan," *Dancing with Bears*, October 22, 2007, http://johnhelmer.net/?p=281.

118 Bruce Pannier, "Beijing Flexes Economic Muscle Across Central Asia," Radio Free Europe/Radio Liberty, May 29, 2008, www.rferl.org/content/article/1347810.html.

119 "Zijin Mining Could Invest $100 Mln in Tajik Gold JV," *Highbeam Business*, July 10, 2007, http://business.highbeam.com/407705/article-1G1-166243361/ zijin-mining-could-invest-100-mln-tajik-gold-jv.

120 Chris Oliver, "China's Zijin Mining Buys Tajikistan Gold Rights," *Market Watch*, June 29, 2007, http://articles.marketwatch.com/2007-06-29/news/30681860_1_ tajikistan-gold-mining-and-exploration-rights.

121 "Tajikistan Discovers Two Large Gold Deposits," Agence France-Presse, January 13, 2011, *China and Eurasia Forum Quarterly: News Digest*, www.chinaeurasia.org/news-digest/722-tajikistan-discovers-two-large-gold-deposits.html.

122 U.S. Geological Survey, *2007 Minerals Yearbook: Tajikistan*, 42.2.

CHAPTER 7

1 The EBRD has labeled Armenia, Azerbaijan, Belarus, Georgia, the Kyrgyz Republic, Moldova, Mongolia, Tajikistan, Turkmenistan, and Uzbekistan as "early transition countries," because more than 50 percent of the people in these countries live below the national poverty line and each country faces significant economic and political reform challenges in their transition from its Communist past. See European Bank for Reconstruction and Development, "Early Transition Countries Initiative," December 1, 2011, www.ebrd.com/pages/about/where/etc.shtml.

2 Pamir Electric customers have also benefited from subsidies from the World Bank's concessional facility, the International Development Association.

3 See Pradeep Mitra, Marcelo Selowsky, and Juan Zalduendo, *Turmoil at Twenty: Recession, Recovery, and Reform in Central and Eastern Europe and the Former Soviet Union* (Washington, D.C.: World Bank, 2010), 225. Additionally, the World Bank reports that losses have dropped to 13.7 percent of electricity generated and 14.6 percent of gas generated by 2009 from higher figures of 18.7 and 21.9 percent, respectively, in 2004. See World Bank, *Implementation Completion and Results Report (IDA Grant Nos. H246, H325, H451) on Grants in the Amounts of (1) SDR 7.0 Million (US$10.0 Million Equivalent), (2) SDR 6.7 Million (US$10.0 Million Equivalent), (3) SDR 13.3 Million (US$20.0 Million Equivalent) to the Republic of Tajikistan for the Programmatic Development Policy Operations*, March 23, 2010, 15, http://documents. worldbank.org/curated/en/2010/03/12179652/tajikistan-first-second-third-program-matic-development-policy-grant-operation-project.

4 For a succinct discussion of the Soviet-era water management practices and modifying them to regional and national control regimes, see Stephen Hodgson, "Strategic Water Resources in Central Asia: In Search of a New International Legal Order," *EU Central Asia Monitoring*, no. 14, May 2010, www.eucentralasia.eu/fileadmin/ user_upload/PDF/Policy_Briefs/PB14.pdf.

5   These include the February 18, 1992, agreement between the five newly independent states, "On Cooperation in the Field of Joint Water Resources Management and Conservation of Interstate Sources." World Bank, "Water Energy Nexus in Central Asia: Improving Regional Cooperation in the Syr Darya Basin," January 2004, http://siteresources.worldbank.org/INTUZBEKISTAN/Resources/Water_Energy_Nexus_final.pdf.

6   In the Soviet Union, both water and electricity were effectively provided free of charge to the republics, and supervision for both sectors was the responsibility of all-union ministries working in Moscow.

7   Regional Bureau for Europe and the Commonwealth of Independent States, United Nations Development Program, "Central Asia Regional Risk Assessment: Responding to Water, Energy, and Food Insecurity," January 2009, 31, http://reliefweb.int/sites/reliefweb.int/files/resources/0D4D43F5273097AC49257583000E C1F4-Full_Report.pdf.

8   UNICEF, "Tajikistan: Living Standards Measurement Survey 2007—Indicators at a Glance," Dushanbe, 2009, www.google.com/url?sa=t&rct=j&q=&esrc=s&source=we b&cd=1&ved=0CE8QFjAA&url=http%3A%2F%2Fwww.tojikinfo.tj%2Fen%2Fdo wnload%2Ffiles%2FUNICEF%2520TLSS%2520Report%2520Eng.pdf&ei=wAy0T 7GTMcnB6AGb3IHcDw&usg=AFQjCNG2VbfrrRHjMFoaMtrCVyvMI3F3JA.

9   This was calculated by the author based on December 30, 2007, exchange rates, where $1 = TJS 3.4649, as found at the National Bank of Tajikistan's website, www.nbt.tj/en/kurs/?c=4&id=28.

10 Oxfam, "Water Management in Tajikistan," Dushanbe, December 2007, 8, http://tajwss.tj/site/images/reports/Water-Management-in-Tajikistan-eng.pdf.

11 "Multiple Indicator Cluster Survey (MICS 2005)," Tajikistan, 2005, www.childinfo.org/files/MICS3_Tajikistan_FinalReport_2005_Eng.pdf.

12 Environment Department and Poverty Reduction and Economic Management Unit, Europe and Central Asia, World Bank, *Tajikistan Country Environmental Analysis*, Report 43465-TJ, May 15, 2008, 36, www.google.com/url?sa=t&rct=j&q=&esrc=s&frm=1&source=web&cd=1&ved=0CCMQFjAA&url=http%3A%2F%2Fwww-wds.worldbank.org%2Fexternal%2Fdefault%2FWDSContentServer%2FWDSP%2 FIB%2F2008%2F06%2F17%2F000333038_20080617041000%2FRendered%2FP DF%2F434650ESW0P1061sclosed0June01302008.pdf&ei=P5O5TvvBNOaw2QXt 5fzbBw&usg=AFQjCNFuFkVNCMWXlpWJzDPCOWtkcr29Yw.

13 World Bank, "Dushanbe Water Supply Project," World Bank Project P057883, www.worldbank.org/projects/P057883/dushanbe-water-supply-project?lang=en.

14 Ibid.

15 European Bank for Reconstruction and Development, *Strategy for Tajikistan*, January 26, 2009, 14, www.ebrd.com/downloads/country/strategy/tajikistan.pdf.

16   Swiss Agency for Development and Cooperation, "Khujand Water Supply Project,"
      November 11, 2009, www.swiss-cooperation.admin.ch/centralasia/en/Home/
      Activities_in_Tajikistan/BASIC_INFRASTRUCTURE/Khujand_Water_Supply;
      EBRD, "Tapping Tajikistan's Water Resources," June 1, 2011, www.ebrd.com/pages/
      project/case/asia/tajikistan_khujand.shtml.

17   EBRD, *Strategy for Tajikistan*, 16.

18   I thank Saodat Olimova for this information.

19   These statistics vary depending upon the definition of "reasonable hygiene facilities,"
      which varies from source to source. World Bank data show almost no difference
      between the urban and rural in availability of hygiene facilities.

20   The *dachas* of the upper middle class are being built with indoor plumbing, almost
      regardless of location, but outside toilets are the norm in rural Tajikistan, although
      many households do not maintain proper septic fields. World Bank, "Tajikistan:
      Poverty Assessment, December 3, 2009," 95–96, http://web.worldbank.org/external/
      default/main?pagePK=51187349&piPK=51189435&theSitePK=258744&menuPK=6
      4187510&searchMenuPK=287276&theSitePK=258744&entityID=000333038_201
      00118015430&searchMenuPK=287276&theSitePK=258744.

21   The same survey found that 74 percent of the schools and 68 percent of the health
      care facilities also lacked heat in winter. Regional Bureau for Europe and the
      Commonwealth of Independent States, United Nations Development Program,
      Central Asia Regional Risk Assessment.

22   Saodat Olimova reports that Soviet-era data concluded that the Soviet Republic of
      Tajikistan had 113 million tons of oil and 863 billion cubic meters of gas.

23   U.S. Geological Survey, "Tajikistan," *2007 Minerals Yearbook*, 42.4, http://minerals.
      usgs.gov/minerals/pubs/country/2007/myb3-2007-ti.pdf.

24   "Tajikistan Overview," INOGATE, www.google.com/url?sa=t&rct=j&q=&esrc=s&
      source=web&cd=1&ved=0CDcQFjAA&url=http%3A%2F%2Fwww1.inogate.org%
      2Fenergy_themes%2Ftadjikistan%2Fcountry-overview%2FTAJIKISTAN_
      OVERVIEW.doc%2Fdownload&ei=HLizT-LHMcnB6AHorIngBg&usg=
      AFQjCNExk_B3ZzTUlK80hN7eYWXvnmq2sw&sig2=AnU
      bHl_JPk3V8G8QriY3Ow.

25   The largest of these is the Sarikamysh field. "Major Natural Gas Find in Tajikistan
      Set to Change Regional Dynamic," Oilprice.com, December 22, 2010, http://
      oilprice.com/Energy/Natural-Gas/Major-Natural-Gas-Find-in-Tajikistan-Set-to-
      Change-Regional-Dynamic.html.

26   Gazprom, "Cooperation with Tajikistan," www.gazprom.com/about/production/
      central-asia.

27   "Uzbekistan Increases Price of Gas to Tajikistan," Central Asia Newswire, August 2,
      2011, www.universalnewswires.com/centralasia/viewstory.aspx?id=4559.

28 Roman Kozhevnikov, "Uzbekistan Resumes Gas Prices to Tajikistan," Reuters Africa, April 16, 2011, http://af.reuters.com/article/energyOilNews/idAFL6E8FG3YL20120416.

29 Khosiyat Komilova, "Podacha gaza vozobnovlena" (Gas service reestablished), Stan TV, *Informatsionnyivideoportal*, December 24, 2009, www.stan.tv/news/13909.

30 Much of this work is supported by the World Bank Energy Reduction Program (PO89244), which had disbursed $10.91 million of an allocated $15.47 million. The program runs from June 30, 2005, until June 30, 2012.

31 World Bank, *Implementation Completion and Results Report (IDA Grant Nos. H246, H325, H451)*, 15.

32 "Tajikistan: Early Blackouts Generate Electricity Anxiety," Eurasianet, October 18, 2011, www.eurasianet.org/print/64322; Avaz Yuldoshev, "Tajikistan to Celebrate Navrouz Under Conditions of Shortage of Electricity," *Asia-Plus*, March 20, 2012, http://news.tj/en/print/118604.

33 World Bank, "Central Asia Regional Electricity Export Potential Study," December 2004, www.adb.org/Documents/Reports/CAREC/Energy/CA-REEPS.pdf, 8.

34 United Nations Development Program, *National Development Strategy of the Republic of Tajikistan for the Period to 2015* (Dushanbe: United Nations Development Program, 2007), 33, www.undp.tj/files/reports/nds_eng.pdf.

35 "President Rahmon Inaugurates South–North Power Grid," *Times of Central Asia*, November 30, 2009.

36 EBRD, *Strategy for Tajikistan*, 24.

37 Ben Slay, "Are Kyrgyzstan and Tajikistan Ready for Winter?" *Development and Transition*, December 2010, www.developmentandtransition.net/Gotovy-li-Kyrgyzstan-i-Tadzhikistan-k-zime.53+M51b2f57df99.0.html.

38 "Emomali Receives Malaysian and Czech Ambassadors," *Khovar*, April 21, 2011, http://khovar.tj/eng/archive/158-emomali-rahmon-receives-malaysian-and-czech-ambassadors.html; "Czech Firm to Finance Sarband Hydropower Plant in Tajikistan," *Hydroworld*, January 24, 2011, www.hydroworld.com/index/display/article-display/4073927931/articles/hrhrw/hydroindustrynews/rehabilitationandrepair/2011/01/czech-firm_to_finance.html.

39 "Earn Power Station with Food Waste in Tajikistan," *Khovar*, August 24, 2011, http://khovar.tj/eng/energetics/2071-earn-power-station-with-food-waste-in-tajikistan.html.

40 "Iran Will Build a Hydel Power Plant in Tajikistan," *Construction Update*, 2011, www.constructionupdate.com/Default.aspx?Tags=vOvzvWubU2hHmcwdkr/MPlsjgsBlOn5TfCK9uyOn0Iym/O508qBRbUjIjV52OSjr&NewsType=Ayni-hydroelectric-power-station-India-Sector.

41 In 2003, average price for electricity in Tajikistan was 0.5 cents, with a cost recovery at the retail level of 2.1 cents; this compares with 1.4 cents and 2.3 in Kyrgyzstan, 2.6 cents and 2.8 cents in Kazakhstan, and 2.2 cents and 3.5 cents in Uzbekistan. Poverty Reduction and Economic Management Unit Europe and Central Asia Region, World Bank, "Tajikistan Trade Diagnostic Study," December 3, 2005, http://siteresources.worldbank.org/INTRANETTRADE/Resources/Pubs/ TajikTradeStudy.pdf.

42 Rukhshona Ibragimova, "Tajikistan Raises Electrical Rates," Central Asia Online, January 30, 2010, http://centralasiaonline.com/en_GB/articles/caii/features/ main/2010/01/30/feature-02.

43 This was calculated by the author based on average December 2009, 2010, and April 2012 exchange rates, where $1 equals approximately TJS 4.4, TJS 4.4, and TJS 4.8, respectively, as found at the National Bank of Tajikistan's website, www.nbt. tj/en/kurs/?c=4&id=28. "Since April 1, Tajik Population to Pay by New Tariffs of Electricity," Avesta.tj, March 7, 2012, www.avesta.tj/eng/goverment/1857-since-april-1-tajik-population-to-pay-by-new-tariffs-of-electricity.html.

44 Ibragimova, "Tajikistan Raises Electricity Rates."

45 Ibid. Also see Office of the Senior Economist, United Nations Development Program, "Household Energy Access and Affordability in Kyrgyzstan and Tajikistan," http://europeandcis.undp.org/senioreconomist/show/2801DF39-F203-1EE9-BC73C347BB247275.

46 Michael J. G. Cain, "Tajikistan's Energy Woes: Resource Barriers in Fragile States," *Washington Review of Turkish and Eurasian Affairs*, January 2011, www. thewashingtonreview.org/articles/tajikistans-energy-woes-resource-barriers-in-fragile-states.html.

47 World Bank, *Lights Out? The Outlook for Energy in Eastern Europe and the Former Soviet Union* (Washington, D.C.: World Bank, 2010), http://siteresources.worldbank. org/ECAEXT/Resources/258598-1268240913359/Full_report.pdf.

48 Asian Development Bank, *Republic of Tajikistan: Strengthening Corporate Management of Barki Tojik*, Technical Assistance Consultant's Report (Manila: Asian Development Bank, 2009), www.adb.org/Documents/Reports/Consultant/40623-TAJ/40623-TAJ-TACR.pdf.

49 Ibid.

50 Ibid., 2–3, 12.

51 Barki Tojik, "Audit of OSHC 'Barki Tojik' Consolidated Financial Statement," January 25, 2008, www.barkitojik.tj/rus; www.barkitojik.tj/eng.

52 Ibid.

53 These include the modernization of TES-1, the HPS-2 Cascade Varzob HPS, the modernization of the Kayrakkum HPS and the Perepadnaya HPS, and some sixteen other projects that were featured at the Power 2010 international exhibition held in Dushanbe in October 2010. For the details, see GIMA, "Power Tajikistan 2010," Dushanbe, 2010, www.gima.de/en/Events.html.

54 "CASA-1000 Feasibility Study Update, Interim Report Presentation," September 25, 2010, SNC-Lavalin.

55 "Afghan–Tajik Electricity Transmission Line in Operation," Universal Newswire, October 27, 2011, www.universalnewswires.com/centralasia/international/viewstory. aspx?id=10540.

56 World Bank, "Tajikistan: Trade Diagnostic Study, December 3, 2005," 47, www. google.com/url?sa=t&rct=j&q=&esrc=s&frm=1&source=web&cd=1&ved=0CCQQF jAA&url=http%3A%2F%2Fsiteresources.worldbank.org%2FINTRANETTRADE %2FResources%2FPubs%2FTajikTradeStudy.pdf&ei=sPayTuDQB8jY0QHFi6mZB A&usg=AFQjCNEd-91ODWcS3_zDfoMusgIYQtQybQ.

57 The Central Asia–South Asia Regional Electricity Market framework is an initiative launched by the ADB, the EBRD, the International Financial Corporation (IFC), the Islamic Development Bank (IsDB), and the World Bank, Kyrgyzstan, Tajikistan, Afghanistan, and Pakistan to produce an electricity market in which Kyrgyzstan and Tajikistan serve as exporters of electricity and Pakistan and Afghanistan become importers. A memorandum was signed in 2007 between the countries involved and several technical meetings have been held thereafter.

58 Baipaza (generating 600 MW), Golovnaya (240 MW), Perepadnaya (30 MW), and Tsentral'naya 15 MW) were all built and continue to function.

59 World Bank, *Tajikistan: Trade Diagnostic Study*, 42.

60 Kai Wegerich, Oliver Olsson, and Jochen Froebrich, "Reliving the Past in a Changed Environment: Hydropower Ambitions, Opportunities and Constraints in Tajikistan," *Energy Policy* 35 (2007): 3817.

61 Ibid., 3819.

62 World Bank, "Tajikistan: Trade Diagnostic Study, December 3, 2005," 43.

63 Ibid.

64 Anna Nikolaeva and Aleksei Nikolskiy, "Rossiya poluchit bazy v Tadzhikistane" (Russia to get military bases in Tajikistan), *Vedomosti*, June 7, 2004.

65 World Bank, "Central Asia Regional Electricity Export Potential Study," December 2004, 57, www.adb.org/Documents/Reports/CAREC/Energy/CA-REEPS.pdf.

66. "Rossiya grozitsya ostanovit' Sangtudinskuyu GES v Tadzhikistane iz-za dolgov" (Russia threatening to shut down Tajikistan's Sangtuda hydropower plant because of debts), Fergana.news, November 13, 2009, www.fergananews.com/news.php?id=13432.

67. "Sangtuda-2 Began to Generate Electricity," Avesta.tj, January 1, 2012, www.avesta.tj/eng/business/1453-sangtuda-2-began-to-generate-electricity.html.

68. Embassy of Tajikistan to Austria, "The Rogunskaya Hydropower Station: Performance Characteristics," www.tajikembassy.org/images/roghun.pdf.

69. R. Schmidt, S. Zambaga-Schulz, and M. Seibitz, "Bankable Feasibility Study for Roghun HEP Stage 1 Construction Completion in Tajikistan," in *Dams and Reservoirs, Societies and Environment in the 21st Century* (London: Taylor & Francis, 2006), 408.

70. Ibid.

71. "Onwards and Upwards," *Water Power Magazine*, June 4, 2008, 4, www.waterpowermagazine.com/story.asp?storyCode=2049809. There are four kinds of dams: rock-fill embankment dams, concrete-faced rock-fill dams, arch gravity, and concrete arch dams.

72. Ibid., 7.

73. Wegerich, Olsson, and Froebrich, "Reliving the Past," 3823.

74. "Onwards and Upwards," 8.

75. The 335-meter project would produce a total of 3,600 MW of electricity annually, 1,200 MW more than the Roghun version of the project. Farangis Najibullah, "Energy Dreams Drive Tajikistan to Desperate Measures," Radio Free Europe/Radio Liberty, November 24, 2009, www.rferl.org/content/Energy_Dreams_Drive_Tajikistan_To_Desperate_Measures/1886750.html.

76. World Bank, "Management Response to Request for Inspection Panel Review of the Tajikistan Energy Loss Reduction Project, IDA Credits 40930-TJ and HI7S0-TJ," http://siteresources.worldbank.org/ECAEXT/Resources/258598-1297718522264/UZ_Management_Response_Full.pdf.

77. The terms of reference demonstrate Uzbek concerns for complete seismological information and a detailed study of possible variations in the water reserves reflecting different climate change scenarios. World Bank, "Management Response to Request for Inspection Panel Review of the Tajikistan Energy Loss Reduction Project, IDA Credits 40930-TJ and HI7S0-TJ. Annex 2," 9 and 65, http://siteresources.worldbank.org/ECAEXT/Resources/258598-1297718522264/UZ_Management_Response_Full.pdf.

78. World Bank, "Tajikistan," www.worldbank.org/tj.

79   International Monetary Fund, *Tajikistan, IMF Country Report 10/203* (Washington, D.C.: International Monetary Fund, 2010), www.imf.org/external/pubs/ft/scr/2010/cr10203.pdf.

80   Bureau of Democracy, Human Rights, and Labor, U.S. Department of State, *2009 Human Rights Report: Tajikistan* (Washington, D.C.: U.S. Government Printing Office, 2010), www.state.gov/j/drl/rls/hrrpt/2009/sca/136094.htm.

81   International Monetary Fund, "Statement at the Conclusion of an IMF Staff Mission to the Republic of Tajikistan," Press Release 10/37, February 12, 2010, www.imf.org/external/np/sec/pr/2010/pr1037.htm.

82   International Monetary Fund, *Republic of Tajikistan: First and Second Review Under the Three-Year Arrangement Under the Extended Credit Facility, Request for Waiver of Performance Criteria, and Request for Augmentation of the Arrangement*, IMF Country Report 10/203 (Washington, D.C.: International Monetary Fund, 2010), 13, www.imf.org/external/pubs/ft/scr/2010/cr10203.pdf.

83   Ibid., 8.

84   Ibid.

85   Ministry of Finance of the Republic of Tajikistan, "Operatsii OAO 'Rogunskaya GES' za pervoye polugodiye 2010g" (Operations of Rogun Hydro Power Plant for the first half of 2010), http://minfin.tj/downloads/files/operacii_2010.pdf.

86   World Bank, "Tajikistan: Trade Diagnostic Study," Report 32603-TJ, December 3, 2005, 46, www.google.com/url?sa=t&rct=j&q=&esrc=s&frm=1&source=web&cd=1&ved=0CCQQFjAA&url=http%3A%2F%2Fsiteresources.worldbank.org%2FINTRANETTRADE%2FResources%2FPubs%2FTajikTradeStudy.pdf&ei=sPayTuDQB8jY0QHFi6mZBA&usg=AFQjCNEd-91ODWcS3_zDfoMusgIYQtQybQ.

87   "Obshchaya summa aktsiy Rogunskoy GES v Tadzhikistane sostavila okolo $1,37 mlrd" (Roghun HPP shares totaled $1.37 billion), CA-News.org, www.ca-news.org/news/285401.

88   World Bank, "Roghun Hydropower Project Techno-Economic Assessment," May 15, 2011, 13, http://siteresources.worldbank.org/ECAEXT/Resources/258598-1304704143712/3_TEAS_POE_Eng.ppt.

89   Suhrob Majidov, "World Bank Advises Tajikistan to Halt Construction of Hydropower Station," *CACI Analyst*, August 31, 2011, www.cacianalyst.org/?q=node/5624.

90   World Bank, "World Bank and Independent Panels of Experts Visited Tajikistan to Review Progress of Roghun Assessment Studies," August 15, 2011, http://web.worldbank.org/WBSITE/EXTERNAL/COUNTRIES/ECAEXT/TAJIKISTANEXTN/0,,contentMDK:22982591~menuPK:258749~pagePK:2865066~piPK:2865079~theSitePK:258744,00.html.

91 "Rakhmon Discussed with a Representative of the World Bank Project Roghun," Avesta.tj, August 28, 2011, www.avesta.tj/eng/rogun/386-rakhmon-discussed-with-a-representative-of-the-world-bank-project-rogun.html.

92 World Bank, "World Bank Update on the Status of the Roghun Assessment Studies," December 15, 2011, http://web.worldbank.org/WBSITE/EXTERNAL/ COUNTRIES/ECAEXT/0,,contentMDK:23071412~menuPK:2246556~pagePK:28 65106~piPK:2865128~theSitePK:258599,00.html.

93 Timur Rahmatullin, "Rogunskaya GES o bor'be politicheskoy boli s tekhnicheskoy logikoy" (Roghun against political pain with technical logic), *Nezavisimyy obozrevatel' stran Sodruzhestva*, no. 2, 2007.

94 Several independent experts have written that the potential loss of irrigated agriculture could cost Uzbekistan roughly 2.2 percent of its gross domestic product per year if the Tajik version of the Roghun project is developed. Shokhrukh-Mirzo Jalilov, Thomas M. DeSutter, and Jay A. Leitch, "Impact of Roghun Dam on Downstream Uzbekistan Agriculture," *International Journal of Water Resources and Environmental Engineering* 3, no. 8 (September 2011): 164–65.

95 The EBRD reports a fixed teledensity figure of five percent, which is much lower than the proportion served by mobile connections. EBRD, *Strategy for Tajikistan*, 32.

96 Ibid.

97 Christina Lin, "PLA on Board an Orient Express," Asia Times Online, March 29, 2011, www.atimes.com/atimes/China/MC29Ad03.html.

98 *CAREC* Federation of Carrier and Forwarder Associations, "Corridor 1: Map," http://cfcfa.net/carec-transport-corridors.

99 EBRD, *Strategy for Tajikistan*, 39.

100 Joshua Kucera, "Did Uzbekistan Bomb Its Own Railway?" Eurasia.net, December 1, 2011, www.eurasianet.org/node/64617.

101 International Monetary Fund, *Republic of Tajikistan: Poverty Reduction Strategy Paper, IMF Country Report 09/82* (Washington, D.C.: International Monetary Fund, 2009), 33, www.unpei.org/PDF/Tajikistan_PRSP_2009.pdf.

102 Ibid., 37.

103 World Bank, "Implementation Completion and Results Report (IDA Grant Nos. H246, H325, H451)," 18.

104 Ibid.

105 Ibid.

CHAPTER 8

1   International Monetary Fund, *Republic of Tajikistan: Staff Report for the 2011 Article IV Consultation, Fourth Review Under the Three-Year Arrangement Under the Extended Credit Facility, Request for Waiver of Nonobservance for Performance Criteria and Modification of Performance Criterion, IMF Country Report 11/130* (Washington, D.C.: International Monetary Fund, 2011), 12, www.imf.org/external/pubs/ft/scr/2011/cr11130.pdf.

2   Pradeep Mitra, Marcelo Selowsky, and Juan Zalduendo, *Turmoil at Twenty: Recession, Recovery, and Reform in Central and Eastern Europe and the Former Soviet Union* (Washington, D.C.: World Bank, 2010), 92–93.

3   The Human Development Index is calculated from a life expectancy index, an education index (including adult literacy), and a GDP index (GDP per capita at purchasing power parity, private consumption, government spending, investment, and net exports).

4   World Bank, "Tajikistan: Poverty Assessment," Report 51341-TJ, December 3, 2009, 14, http://web.worldbank.org/external/default/main?pagePK=51187349&piPK=51189 435&theSitePK=258744&menuPK=64187510&searchMenuPK=287276&theSitePK =258744&entityID=000333038_20100118015430&searchMenuPK=287276&theSit ePK=258744.

5   Ibid., 17.

6   Ibid., 16.

7   By contrast, if income-based rather than consumption-based poverty measures are used, then Khatlon is poorer than Sughd, with 72 percent of the population ranked as poor and 43 percent extremely poor. World Bank, "Tajikistan: Poverty Assessment," 32.

8   The Region of Republican Significance had 20.2 percent of the poor population and 22.1 percent of the total national population; Dushanbe, 7.6 percent of the poor and 9.4 percent of the national population; and the Gorno-Badakhshan Autonomous Oblast, 2.5 percent of the poor and 3.1 percent of the national population. Sughd also had a poverty headcount rate of 68.8 percent, in contrast to 47.3 percent in Khatlon, 48.8 percent in the Region of Republican Significance, 43.4 percent in Gorno-Badakhshan, and 43.3 percent in Dushanbe. World Bank, "Tajikistan: Poverty Assessment," 26.

9   World Bank, "Tajikistan: Poverty Assessment," 27.

10   A total of 65.5 percent of poor people and 47 percent of non-poor people reported themselves as not satisfied with their financial situation. World Bank, "Tajikistan: Poverty Assessment," 32.

11 This was very close to the national average of 135 somoni ($28) per month, which was reported in the national survey as the minimum necessary to satisfy basic food and non-food needs. By contrast, the average answer of those considered to be consumption poor was that 123 somoni ($26) was needed. World Bank, "Tajikistan: Poverty Assessment," 32.

12 At TJS 3 = $1, in 2007. World Bank, "Health Indicators," http://data.worldbank.org/indicator.

13 Agriculture also included forestry and fishing. World Bank, "Tajikistan: Poverty Assessment," 44.

14 Ibid., 45.

15 Given the importance of home production in contributing to household income, the World Bank believes that consumption indexes of poverty are more effective indicators than income-based indicators. World Bank, "Tajikistan: Poverty Assessment," 31.

16 Ibid., 21.

17 Ibid., 28.

18 Poverty headcounts for poverty and extreme poverty then drop to 42.6 and 13 percent, respectively, as opposed to 54.4 and 17.4 percent, with the latter being virtually identical to the general population, with 53.5 and 17.1 percent, respectively. World Bank, "Tajikistan: Poverty Assessment," 28.

19 EBRD, *Strategy for Tajikistan*, February 13, 2009, 23.

20 World Bank, "Tajikistan: Poverty Assessment," 3.

21 Mitra et al., *Turmoil at Twenty*, 165.

22 International Monetary Fund, *Republic of Tajikistan: Poverty Reduction Strategy Paper, IMF Country Report 09/82* (Washington, D.C.: International Monetary Fund, 2009), 68, www.unpei.org/PDF/Tajikistan_PRSP_2009.pdf.

23 This benefit, for which 25 million somoni ($5,250,000) is paid out yearly, goes directly to the national gas and electricity companies, and most people do not know that their income qualifies them for it; moreover, many of those who qualify on the basis of income lack connections to either the electricity or the gas network. World Bank, "Tajikistan: Poverty Assessment," 60.

24 Ibid., 59.

25 Ibid., 64.

26 The text of the law can be found at Zakon Respubliki Tadzhikistan o prozhitochnom minimume (Republic of Tajikistan, law regarding a living wage), Akhbori Madzhlisi Oli of the Republic of Tajikistan, 2009, no. 5, article 328, Dushanbe, May 19, 2009, www.mmk.tj/ru/legislation/legislation-base/2009.

27 "Tajik Parliament Adopts Subsistence Level Law," Central Asia Online, April 28, 2009, http://centralasiaonline.com/en_GB/articles/caii/features/2009/04/28/feature-08.

28 World Bank, "Tajikistan: Poverty Assessment," 62–64.

29 Ibid., 65.

30 By contrast, the Russian Federation spent 8 percent, Kazakhstan spent 11 percent, the Kyrgyz Republic spent 11 percent, Uzbekistan spent 9 percent, and Turkmenistan spent 10 percent. World Health Organization, Global Health Expenditure Database, http://apps.who.int/nha/database/DataExplorerRegime.aspx.

31 The Tajik figure of $49 for 2010 compares with $82 in Uzbekistan, $53 in the Kyrgyz Republic, $106 in Turkmenistan, $393 in Kazakhstan, and $525 in the Russian Federation. The Turkmen and Kazakh figures reflect the cost of opening and maintaining a few state-of-the-art medical facilities in selected specialties in the nations' capitals. "Total health expenditure is the sum of public and private health expenditures as a ratio of total population. It covers the provision of health services (preventive and curative), family planning activities, nutrition activities, and emergency aid designated for health but does not include provision of water and sanitation. Data are in current U.S. dollars." World Bank, "Health Indicators."

32 Ibid.

33 Ibid.

34 Those from the poorest quintile make just under 0.8 outpatient visits per year, whereas those in the richest quintile make approximately 1.3 visits. World Bank, "Tajikistan: Poverty Assessment," 90.

35 World Bank, "Health Indicators."

36 World Bank, "Tajikistan: Poverty Assessment," 90.

37 Also, a lack of finances was cited in 50 percent of the cases of people refusing to get medical care when referred for treatment in hospitals. World Bank, "Tajikistan: Poverty Assessment," 90.

38 Ibid., 95.

39 Ibid., 85.

40 Tajikistan has 6.1 hospital beds per 1,000 people, compared with 4.3 in Turkmenistan, 5.2 in Uzbekistan, 5.1 in Kyrgyzstan, 7.8 in Kazakhstan, and 9.7 in the Russian Federation (2005–2006 data). Tajikistan has 2.0 physicians per 1,000 people, compared with 2.4 in Kyrgyzstan, 2.5 in Turkmenistan, 2.7 in Uzbekistan, 3.9 in Kazakhstan, and 4.3 in the Russian Federation (2005–2006 data). Tajikistan is second only to Turkmenistan in how few nurse midwives it has—5.0 per 1,000, as compared with 4.7 in Turkmenistan, 5.8 in the Kyrgyz Republic, 7.6 in Kazakhstan, 8.5 in the Russian Federation, and 10.9 in Uzbekistan (2005–2006 data). World Health Organization, "Core Health Indicators," http://apps.who.int/whosis/database/core/core_select.cfm.

41 World Bank, "Tajikistan: Poverty Assessment," 94.

42 Ibid., 86.

43 Andrew Dabalen and Waly Wane, *Informal Payments and Moonlighting in Tajikistan's Health Sector*, Policy Research Working Paper 4555 (Washington, D.C.: World Bank, 2008), 13, www-wds.worldbank.org/servlet/WDSContentServer/WDSP/IB/2008/03/12/000158349_20080312150046/Rendered/PDF/wps4555.pdf.

44 World Bank, "Tajikistan: Poverty Assessment," 86.

45 In Sughd, the Region of Republican Subordination, and Gorno-Badakhshan, 38 percent were stunted. World Bank, "Tajikistan: Poverty Assessment," 90.

46 Ibid., 89.

47 These data were provided by Saodat Olimova.

48 These 2009 data were provided by Saodat Olimova.

49 United Nations Office on Drugs and Crime, *World Drug Report 2009* (Vienna: United Nations Office on Drugs and Crime, 2009), 53, www.unodc.org/documents/wdr/WDR_2009/WDR2009_eng_web.pdf.

50 OSCE, "International Election Observation Mission, Republic of Tajikistan, Parliamentary Elections, 28 February 2010: Statement of Preliminary Findings and Conclusions," Dushanbe, March 1, 2010, 10, www.osce.org/odihr/elections/tajikistan/41627.

51 These compare to approximately 39.6 percent under 19 in Uzbekistan, 40.3 percent in Turkmenistan, 40.5 percent in Kyrgyzstan, and 31.2 percent in Kazakhstan (all data from 2009). U.S. Census Bureau, International Database, www.census.gov/population/international/data/idb/informationGateway.php.

52 World Bank, "Tajikistan: Poverty Assessment," 87.

53 Ibid., 75.

54 Ibid., 29–30.

55 Environment Department and Poverty Reduction and Economic Management Unit, Europe and Central Asia, World Bank, *Tajikistan Country Environmental Analysis*, Report 43465-TJ, May 15, 2008, 36, www-wds.worldbank.org/external/default/WDSContentServer/WDSP/IB/2008/06/17/000333038_20080617041000/Rendered/PDF/434650ESW0P1061sclosed0June01302008.pdf.

56 Angela Baschieri and Jane Falkingham, *Child Poverty in Tajikistan* (Dushanbe: UNICEF Country Office, 2007), 34, www.unicef.org/tajikistan/Child_Poverty.pdf.

57 World Bank, *Tajik Child Health: All Hands on Deck*, Europe and Central Asia Knowledge Brief (Washington, D.C.: World Bank, 2009), 2, www-wds.worldbank. org/external/default/WDSContentServer/WDSP/IB/2010/01/21/000334955_20100 121032053/Rendered/PDF/527970BRI0TJ0E10Box345583B01PUBLIC1.pdf.

58 Maternal mortality was 86 per 100,000 live births, versus 81 in the Kyrgyz Republic, 45 in Kazakhstan, 77 in Turkmenistan, 39 in the Russian Federation, and 30 in Uzbekistan, according to 2008 figures from UNICEF, adjusted "to account for the well-documented problems of underreporting and misclassification of maternal deaths." UNICEF, "Country Data," www.unicef.org/statistics/index_countrystats.html.

59 The Tajik figure of 10 percent low birth weight compares with 6 percent in Russia, 6 percent in Kazakhstan, 5 percent in the Kyrgyz Republic, 5 percent in Uzbekistan, and 4 percent in Turkmenistan (2006–2010 data). Ibid.

60 The World Bank puts prenatal care for Tajik women at 80 percent for 2006, versus the 88 percent figure provided by the 2007 TLSS. This compares unfavorably with the other four Central Asian countries: 100 percent for Kazakhstan, 97 percent for Kyrgyzstan, and 99 percent for Turkmenistan and Uzbekistan (Tajikistan data for 2008, all other countries from 2006). World Bank, "Health Indicators."

61 The official Tajik government figure for maternal mortality was 97 per 100,000 in 2005. The Poverty Reduction Strategy set the goal of cutting this figure to 70 per 100,000 by 2009. International Monetary Fund, *Republic of Tajikistan: Poverty Reduction Strategy Paper*, 17.

62 The Tajik figure of 93 percent for diphtheria immunization compares with 95 percent in the Kyrgyz Republic, 98 percent in Uzbekistan, 96 percent in Turkmenistan, and 98 percent in Kazakhstan and in Russia (2009 data). World Bank, "Health Indicators."

63 The figure of 85 percent of Tajik children inoculated for measles compares with 99 percent for all the Central Asian countries, except Uzbekistan, where it is 95 percent (2009 data). Ibid.

64 United Nations Development Program, *National Development Strategy of the Republic of Tajikistan for the Period to 2015* (Dushanbe: United Nations Development Program, 2007), 51, www.undp.tj/files/reports/nds_eng.pdf.

65 Baschieri and Falkingham, *Child Poverty in Tajikistan*, 5.

66 Ibid., 46.

67 These data are from the 2003 TLSS, as cited by Baschieri and Falkingham, *Child Poverty in Tajikistan*, 41.

68 A total of 15 percent of boys under three and 14 percent of all girls under three had been treated for diarrhea in the four-week period before the 2003 survey, as opposed to 63 percent of the boys and 54 percent of the girls being treated for a common cold. Baschieri and Falkingham, *Child Poverty in Tajikistan*, 47.

69   The 2003 TLSS reported that only 23 percent of Tajik mothers breastfed exclusively, although only 5 percent of Tajik infants were completely weaned, with the remainder combining breast feeding with various combinations of food, milk, and water. Baschieri and Falkingham, *Child Poverty in Tajikistan*, 45.

70   World Bank, "Tajikistan: Poverty Assessment," 97.

71   UNICEF, "Progress Donor Report: Iodine Deficiency Disorders Elimination in Tajikistan," January 2006, http://pdf.usaid.gov/pdf_docs/PDACH771.pdf.

72   Baschieri and Falkingham, *Child Poverty in Tajikistan*, 3, 26.

73   Firuz Saidov, *Children's Voices: A Qualitative Study of Poverty in Tajikistan* (Dushanbe: UNICEF Country Office, 2007), 6, www.unicef.org/tajikistan/Childrens_Voices.pdf.

74   Ibid., 7.

75   Ibid., 11–12, 47.

76   According to UNICEF's 2005 Multiple Indicator Cluster Survey, only 5 percent of these children work 28 hours or more per week on these chores, with the majority working under 4 hours per day. Baschieri and Falkingham, *Child Poverty in Tajikistan*, 58.

77   This is roughly 3.6 percent of their age cohort. Ibid., 8.

78   Ibid., 59.

79   Ibid.

80   School of Oriental and African Studies, University of London, *What Has Changed? Progress in Eliminating the Use of Forced Child Labour in the Cotton Harvests of Uzbekistan and Tajikistan* (London: University of London, 2010).

81   As quoted in Baschieri and Falkingham, *Child Poverty in Tajikistan*, 58.

82   Bureau of Democracy, Human Rights, and Labor, U.S. Department of State, *2009 Human Rights Report: Tajikistan* (Washington, D.C.: U.S. Government Printing Office, 2010), www.state.gov/j/drl/rls/hrrpt/2009/sca/136094.htm.

83   Baschieri and Falkingham, *Child Poverty in Tajikistan*, 63.

84   International Monetary Fund, *Republic of Tajikistan: Poverty Reduction Strategy Paper—Second Progress Report*, IMF Country Report 06/1 (Washington, D.C.: International Monetary Fund, 2006), 18, www.imf.org/external/pubs/ft/scr/2006/cr0601.pdf.

85   Saidov, *Children's Voices*, 8.

86 Amnesty International, *Tajikistan: Amnesty International Report 2010—Human Rights in Republic of Tajikistan* (London: Amnesty International, 2010), www.amnesty.org/en/region/tajikistan/report-2010.

87 Human Rights Watch, "World Report 2012: Tajikistan," in *2009 Country Reports on Human Rights Practices: Tajikistan,* edited by the U.S. Department of State, www.hrw.org/world-report-2012/world-report-2012-tajikistan.

88 Amnesty International, *Violence Is Not Just a Family Affair: Women Face Abuse in Tajikistan* (London: Amnesty International, 2009), 23, www.amnesty.org/en/library/asset/EUR60/001/2009/en/59bb6e9b-727d-496b-b88d-1245a750d504/eur600012009en.pdf.

89 Baschieri and Falkingham, *Child Poverty in Tajikistan,* 8.

90 Ibid., 8.

91 "Tsena potrebitel'skoy korziny" (Cost of Consumer Basket), *Stan,* December 23, 2009, www.stan.tv/news/13898.

92 In 2001, 88 percent of the Tajiks surveyed in a national nutrition survey reported eating three meals a day, but by 2003, 58 percent reported eating only two meals a day, and in the 2003 TLSS, 85 percent said that they ate one to two meals per day. Baschieri and Falkingham, *Child Poverty in Tajikistan,* 37.

93 All data are for 2005–2007, except for Kazakhstan data, which are for 2002–2007. Food and Agriculture Organization of the United Nations, "Food Security Statistics," www.fao.org/economic/ess/ess-fs/en.

94 The data for Tajikistan are from 2005, and for the other countries for 2006. World Bank, "Health Indicators."

95 World Bank, "Tajikistan: Poverty Assessment," 33.

96 Ibid., 34.

97 Food and Agriculture Organization of the United Nations, "Number of Undernourished Persons," *Food Security Data and Definitions,* October 31, 2011, www.fao.org/economic/ess/ess-fs/fs-data/ess-fadata/en.

98 UN Representative in Tajikistan, *Social and Economic Survey of Zerafshan Valley, Republic of Tajikistan: Report on Survey Results* (Dushanbe: United Nations, 2007), 24, www.undp.tj/files/Socio-economic%20survey%20in%20Zerafshan%20eng.pdf.

99 Regional Bureau for Europe and the Commonwealth of Independent States, United Nations Development Program, "Central Asia Regional Risk Assessment: Responding to Water, Energy, and Food Insecurity," January 2009, 25, http://reliefweb.int/sites/reliefweb.int/files/resources/0D4D43F5273097AC49257583000EC1F4-Full_Report.pdf.

100 Of those who said that they could read and write only with difficulty, 28.3 percent said that they had no education, 32.7 percent said that they had primary education (grades 1–4), and 17.5 percent said that they had basic education (grades 1–8 or 1–9).

101 In a survey of approximately 2,500 people, 8.7 percent of the housewives and unemployed; 7.1 percent of the farmers, 2.7 percent of seasonal employees, and 2.4 percent of those who were employed full time. UN Representative in Tajikistan, *Social and Economic Survey of Zerafshan Valley*, 11.

102 Ministry of Education of the Republic of Tajikistan, "National Strategy for Education Development of the Republic of Tajikistan (2006–2015)," Dushanbe, August 2005, http://planipolis.iiep.unesco.org/upload/Tajikistan/Tajikistan%20Education%20 Plan%202006-2015.pdf.

103 "Natsional'naya programma Ministerstva Obrazovaniya Respubliki Tadzhikistan" (National Program of the Ministry of Education of the Republic of Tajikistan), 2009, 30, as provided by Saodat Olimova.

104 There is some discrepancy over the actual percentage of GDP spent by the Republic of Tajikistan on education, with Goskomstat reporting in 2009 that the Tajik government spent 2.7 percent of GDP on education in 2004, 3.4 percent in 2005, 3.4 percent in 2006, 3.4 percent in 2007, and 4.1 percent in 2008. Data provided by Saodat Olimova.

105 Strategic Research Center Under the President of the Republic of Tajikistan, "Report on Corruption in the Republic of Tajikistan (a Public Opinion Survey)," United Nations Development Program in the Republic of Tajikistan, Dushanbe, 2006, 56, www.undp.tj/files/reports/pta_en.pdf.

106 International Monetary Fund, *Republic of Tajikistan: Poverty Reduction Strategy Paper*, 41.

107 Ibid., 35.

108 United Nations Development Program, *National Development Strategy*, 35.

109 These data were provided by Saodat Olimova from TLSS 2007.

110 U.S. Department of State, *2009 Country Reports on Human Rights Practices: Tajikistan*.

111 This information was provided by Saodat Olimova.

112 Ibid. Olimova reports that this reflected effectively no growth from 2003 to 2004, when there were 53 private schools, in which 14,126 students were studied.

113 World Bank, "Tajikistan: Poverty Assessment," 73–74.

114 Among the poorest quintile of students, 9 percent were reported to have paid for specialized secondary education and 39 percent for higher education, versus 38 and

52 percent, respectively, in the highest quintile. World Bank, "Tajikistan: Poverty Assessment," 74.

115 Ibid., 72.

116 Ibid., 70–71.

117 Information provided by Saodat Olimova from "Ob utverzhedenii pravil normativnogo podushevogo finansirovaniya obsheobrazovatel'nyh uchrezhdeniy" (Regarding the Approval of Regulations for Normative Per Capita Financing of Educational Institutions), Resolution RT, no. 505, October 3, 2007.

118 United Nations Development Program, *National Development Strategy*, 46.

119 There were 34,000 students enrolled in PTUs (vocational technical schools) in Tajikistan in 2009, as compared with 40,700 students in 1992. Goskomstat Respubliki Tadzhikistan, "Obrazovaniye v Respublike Tadzhikistan," 2009, 49, as provided by Saodat Olimova.

120 World Bank, "Tajikistan: Poverty Assessment," 76.

121 Ibid., 126.

122 International Monetary Fund, *Republic of Tajikistan: Poverty Reduction Strategy Paper*, 41.

123 Christopher M. Whitsel, "Counting the Costs: Informal Costs and Corruption Expenses of Education in Post-Soviet Tajikistan," *Problems of Post-Communism*, May–June 2011, 28–38.

124 World Bank, "Tajikistan: Poverty Assessment," 79.

125 Ibid., 78.

126 UN Representative in Tajikistan, *Social and Economic Survey of Zerafshan Valley*, 34.

127 Ministry of Education of the Republic of Tajikistan, "Pravitel'stvo Respubliki Tadzhikistan: Postanovleniye ot 27 avgusta 2008 goda, no. 436, g. Dushanbe," *Gosudarstvennaya programma stroitel'stva, remonta i rekonstruktsii shkol na 2000–2015 gody* (Government of the Republic of Tajikistan: Resolution of August 27, 2008, no. 436, Dushanbe, 2000–2015, Government program on school construction, repair, and reconstruction, Dushanbe, 2009), http://maorif.tj/barnomai_sokhtmon_russ.pdf.

128 World Bank, "Education Modernization Project, Project ID P069055," http://web.worldbank.org/external/projects/main?pagePK=64283627&piPK=73230&theSitePK=40941&menuPK=228424&Projectid=P069055.

129 This observation, which is my own, was triggered by a conversation with Saodat Olimova.

130 International Monetary Fund, *Republic of Tajikistan: Poverty Reduction Strategy Paper—Second Progress Report*, 18.

131 World Bank, "Tajikistan: Poverty Assessment," 81.

132 In Khatlon, 18 percent of the schools reported such closure, as did 10 percent in the Region of Republican Subordination. World Bank, "Tajikistan: Poverty Assessment," 81–82.

133 Ibid., 82.

134 Baschieri and Falkingham, *Child Poverty in Tajikistan*, 58.

135 According to UNICEF's 2005 Multiple Indicator Cluster Survey, only 5 percent of these children work 28 hours or more per week on these chores, with the majority working under 4 hours per day. Ibid., 58.

136 Ibid., 7–8.

137 Ibid., 63.

138 Statistics provided by Saodat Olimova from Gosstatagentstvo Respubliki Tadzhikistan, *Obrazovaniye v Tadzhikistane* (State Agency on Statistics of the Republic of Tajikistan, Education in Tajikistan), 2009.

139 World Bank, "Tajikistan: Poverty Assessment," 82.

140 United Nations Development Program, *National Development Strategy*, 37.

141 "Kak vernut' domoy obrazovannuyu molodezh?" (How to bring well-educated youth back home), *Stan*, December 25, 2009, http://stan.tv/news/13953?REID=g4ik7n7hh kimv0en4nb2rovp76.

142 Baschieri and Falkingham, *Child Poverty in Tajikistan*, 63.

143 "Tajik Adolescents Prey to Human Traffickers," IWPR, January 17, 2011, http://iwpr. net/report-news/tajik-adolescents-prey-human-traffickers.

144 OSCE, "High-Level Dialogue on Human Trafficking in Tajikistan Focuses on Partnership and Participation," November 10, 2010, www.osce.org/tajikistan/74125.

145 "Human Trafficking Plagues Tajikistan," Central Asia Online, May 26, 2010, http://centralasiaonline.com/cocoon/caii/xhtml/en_GB/features/caii/features/ main/2010/05/26/feature-01.

146 U.S. Department of State, *2009 Country Reports on Human Rights Practices: Tajikistan*.

147 International Organization for Migration, *Perspectivy migratsii: Vostochnaya Evropa i Tsentral'naya Aziya—Planirovaniye i upravleniye trudovoy migratsiey* (Perspectives on Migration: Eastern Europe and Central Asia—Planning and managing labor migration) (Vienna: International Organization for Migration, 2006), 110, www.iom.lt/ documents/Migr.Perspectives-Russ2006.pdf.

148 Saodat Olimova and Igor Bosc, *Labour Migration from Tajikistan* (Dushanbe: International Organization for Migration, 2003), 65, www.iom.int/jahia/webdav/ site/myjahiasite/shared/shared/mainsite/published_docs/studies_and_reports/Tajik_ study_oct_03.pdf.

149 Embassy of the Republic of Tajikistan in the Russian Federation, "Pamyatka grazh-daninu Tadzhikistana, pribyvshemu v Rossiyskuyu Federatsiyu: Migratsionnyy uchet grazhdan Respubliki Tadzhikistan v Rossiyskoy Federatsii" (Information for Tajik nationals arriving in the Russian Federation: Migration Registration for Citizens of Tajikistan in the Russian Federation), www.tajembassy.ru/pamyatka-grazhdaninu-tadzhikistana-pribivshemu-v-rossiyskuiu-federatsiiu/stranitsa-2.html.

150 "Nuzhny li Rossii deti migrantov?" (Does Russia Need the Children of Migrants?) Fergana News, April 5, 2012, www.fergananews.com/article.php?id=7330.

151 "Russia Deports 300 Tajik Workers after Pilot Incarceration," RIA Novosti, November 15, 2011, http://en.rian.ru/russia/20111115/168716845.html.

152 "Tajikistan Releases Russian and Estonian Pilots," BBC, November 22, 2011, www. bbc.co.uk/news/world-europe-15835483.

153 International Crisis Group, *Central Asia: Migrants and the Economic Crisis,* Asia Report 183 (Brussels: International Crisis Group, 2010), 13, www.crisisgroup.org/~/ media/Files/asia/central-asia/183%20Central%20Asia%20Migrants%20and%20 the%20Economic%20Crisis.ashx.

154 Olimova and Bosc, *Labour Migration*, 95.

155 International Crisis Group, *Central Asia*, 15. In early December 2010, Moscow mayor Sergei Sobyanin placed the new quota for migrant workers in the city at 200,000 in 2011, down nearly 50 percent from 2010. Countrywide, Russia's work permit quota for labor migrants in 2011 was 1.6 million, down from around 6 mil-lion in 2007. "Central Asian Labor Migrants Facing Uncertain Year," Transitions Online, January 11, 2011, www.tol.org/client/article/22077-central-asian-labor-migrants-facing-uncertain-year.html?utm_source=TOL+mailing+list&utm_ campaign=a5d96803b5-TOL_newsletter1_13_2011&utm_medium=email.

156 Abdul-Ghaffar Mughal, "Migration, Remittances, and Living Standards in Tajikistan," Tajikistan Office, International Organization for Migration, September 2007, 84, www.iom.tj/pubs/Impact%20of%20remittances%20in%20Khatlon%20 by%20Mughal.pdf.

157 International Crisis Group, *Central Asia*, 15.

158 If all categories were added up, the total was actually 1,215,091.5 people. Mughal, *Migration*, 85.

159 Olimova and Bosc, *Labour Migration*, 105.

160 International Organization for Migration, *Perspectivy migratsii*, 112.

161 Institute for War and Peace Reporting, "Nezavidnoye polozheniye 'pokinutykh zhen v Tadzhikistane" (The difficult situation of Tajikistan's "abandoned wives"), December 16, 2010.

162 "Tajik Fatwa Bans SMS Divorce," Radio Free Europe/Radio Liberty, April 11, 2011, www.rferl.org/content/tajik_fatwa_bans_sms_divorces/3553754.html.

163 Olimova and Bosc, *Labour Migration*, 108.

164 International Organization for Migration, *Perspectivy migratsii*, 112.

165 International Crisis Group, *Central Asia*; S. Olimova and M. Olimov, *Vozdeystviye global'nogo krizisa na trudovuyu migratsiyu iz Tadzhikistana* (The Impact of the Global Crisis on Labor Migration from Tajikistan). (Dushanbe: Research Center Sharq, 2009).

166 International Crisis Group, *Central Asia*, 3.

167 Ibid., 5.

CHAPTER 9

1 Tajik citizens were the first citizens of a country belonging to the Commonwealth of Inpendent States (CIS) to be required to get visas to visit Uzbekistan; then Uzbekistan reciprocated when the Turkmen introduced a visa regime for all CIS citizens, adding Turkmen to the list of those requiring visas for entry in Uzbekistan. There has also been a visa regime for residents of Kyrgyzstan, but that was eliminated.

2 The TIR system is an international customs transit system for goods carried by road, adopted under the auspices of the United Nations Economic Commission for Europe. ("TIR" is the abbreviation for "Transports Internationaux Routiers," French for "International Road Transports.") The system guarantees that goods are carried in secure containers, irregular duties and taxes are secured by an international guarantee chain, goods are accompanied by harmonized control document, control measures taken in the country of departure are accepted by countries of transit and destination, the system is controlled by competent authorities, and goods are traceable (via an electronic risk management system).

3 The Eurasian Economic Community, or EurAsEC, was founded by the presidents of Belarus, Kazakhstan, Kyrgyzstan, the Russian Federation, and Tajikistan in Astana on October 10, 2000. In January 2006, Uzbekistan also joined the community, later withdrawing 2008. In May 2002, Moldova and Ukraine were granted observer status; and in April 2003, Armenia was also granted this status.

4   Sergei Lavrov, "Russia Wants 'Post-Soviet Tajikistan Integration,'" RIA Novosti. April 24, 2012, http://en.rian.ru/world/20120424/173012162.html; "Tajikistan May Join Customs Union Only After Kyrgyzstan, Says Russian PM," *Asia-Plus*, October 20, 2011, http://news.tj/en/news/tajikistan-may-join-customs-union-only-after-kyrgyzstan-says-russian-pm; "Regional Leaders Meet in Moscow for Eurasian Union Summit," Central Asia Newswire, March 19, 2012, www.universalnewswires.com/centralasia/viewstory.aspx?id=11617.

5   The monetary amounts in this sentence are based on the 2008 exchange rate, at $1 = TJS 3.44.

6   Indoor air pollution is largely the result of the use of solid fuels (such as dung) to heat buildings.

7   Environment Department and Poverty Reduction and Economic Management Unit, Europe and Central Asia, World Bank, *Tajikistan Country Environmental Analysis*, Report 43465-TJ, May 15, 2008, 23, www-wds.worldbank.org/external/default/WDSContentServer/WDSP/IB/2008/06/17/000333038_20080617041000/Rendered/PDF/434650ESW0P1061sclosed0June01302008.pdf.

8   Ibid., 26.

9   Constitution of the Republic of Tajikistan, Chapter 1, Article 13: "The earth, its resources, water, the atmosphere, flora, fauna, and other natural resources are the exclusive property of the state, and the government guarantees their effective utilization in the interests of the people." Chapter 2, Article 38: "Each person has the right to health care. This right is ensured through free medical assistance in governmental health care institutions, measures to improve the condition of the environment, formation and development of mass athletics, physical fitness, and other sports. Other forms of medical assistance to be provided are determined by law." See Constitution of the Republic of Tajikistan, http://unpan1.un.org/intradoc/groups/public/documents/untc/unpan003670.htm.

10   Environment Department and Poverty Reduction and Economic Management Unit, Europe and Central Asia, World Bank, "Tajikistan Country Environmental Analysis," 73.

11   Some of these have been reorganized over time, such as the Ministry of Agriculture and Nature Protection (which was previously the Ministry of Nature Protection and the State Committee for Environmental Protection and Forestry).

12   This material was provided by Saodat Olimova.

13   Environment Department and Poverty Reduction and Economic Management Unit, Europe and Central Asia, World Bank, "Tajikistan Country Environmental Analysis," 70.

14   Ibid., 71.

15 International Finance Corporation and World Bank, "2009 Enterprise Survey: Running a Business in Tajikistan," Country Note 4, Enterprise Surveys Country Note Series, 2009, 71–72, www.enterprisesurveys.org/Reports.

16 International Monetary Fund, *Republic of Tajikistan: Poverty Reduction Strategy Paper, IMF Country Report 09/82* (Washington, D.C.: International Monetary Fund, 2009), 57, www.unpei.org/PDF/Tajikistan_PRSP_2009.pdf. As of this writing, this was the most recent strategy available.

17 Environment Department and Poverty Reduction and Economic Management Unit, Europe and Central Asia, World Bank, "Tajikistan Country Environmental Analysis," 44.

18 Constitution of the Republic of Tajikistan.

19 This is in Khujand, Chkalovsk, and Taboshar; all three sites are at a high risk of causing environmental pollution. United Nations, "Uranium Tailings in Central Asia: Extended Summary," 2009, www.un.org.kg/index2.php?option=com_resource&task=show_file&id=7609.

20 Environment Department and Poverty Reduction and Economic Management Unit, Europe and Central Asia, World Bank, "Tajikistan Country Environmental Analysis," 46.

21 Ibid., 45.

22 Regional Bureau for Europe and the Commonwealth of Independent States, United Nations Development Program, "Central Asia Regional Risk Assessment: Responding to Water, Energy, and Food Insecurity," January 2009, 69, http://reliefweb.int/sites/reliefweb.int/files/resources/0D4D43F5273097AC49257583000EC1F4-Full_Report.pdf.

23 The author watched a large group of dignitaries from the Arabian Peninsula leave on such a hunt in 2009.

24 Environment Department and Poverty Reduction and Economic Management Unit, Europe and Central Asia, World Bank, "Tajikistan Country Environmental Analysis," 81.

25 Ibid., 77.

26 Ibid., 60–62.

27 From 1957 to 1980, Soviet scientists reported that the Pamir-Alay mountain ranges—of which Tajikistan forms an important part—lost 1114.9 square kilometers of glaciers, or 11.7 percent of their ice capacity. Ibid., 64.

28 Oxfam, "Reaching Tipping Point? Climate Change and Poverty in Tajikistan," February 17, 2010, 7, www.oxfam.org/en/policy/climate-poverty-tajikistan.

29 Tajikistan has nineteen dams that help create nine large reservoirs with a capacity of more than 500 million cubic meters each. The largest reservoirs are Nurek on the Vakhsh River, Kayrakkum on the Syr Darya River, and the Lower Kafirnigan reservoir on the Kafirnigan River.

30 Environment Department and Poverty Reduction and Economic Management Unit, Europe and Central Asia, World Bank, "Tajikistan Country Environmental Analysis," 65.

31 Switzerland heads the Bretton Woods consultative group for Tajikistan.

32 Swiss Agency for Development and Cooperation, "Cooperation Strategy for the Central Asia Region 2007–2011," 2007, 6, www.deza.admin.ch/ressources/resource_en_162032.pdf.

BIBLIOGRAPHY

Amnesty International. *Women and Girls in Tajikistan: Facing Violence, Discrimination, and Poverty.* Dushanbe: Amnesty International, 2009.

Andrienko, Iorii. "Analiz migratsii v Rossii" [Analysis of migration in Russia]. Tsentr ekonomicheskikh i finansovykh issledovaniy i razrabotok v Rossiyskoy ekonomicheskoy shkole, no. 23, Aprel' 2006. Series: "Analiticheskiye razrabotki i otchety."

Asian Development Bank. *Country Operations Business Plan: Tajikistan 2008–2010.* Washington, D.C.: ADB, 2007.

———. *Kyrgyz Republic and Republic of Tajikistan: Regional Customs Modernization and Infrastructure Development Project.* Washington, D.C.: Asian Development Bank, 2009.

———. *Republic of Tajikistan: Cotton Processing and Market Development Project.* Washington, D.C.: Asian Development Bank, 2009.

———. *Tajikistan: Improving Aid Coordination and Portfolio Management: Aid Coordination for Farm Debt Resolution Strategy. Technical Assistance Report.* Dushanbe: Asian Development Bank, 2008.

Baschieri, Angela, and Jane Falkingham. *Child Poverty in Tajikistan.* January 2007. Dushanbe: UNICEF, 2007.

Berdikeeva, Saltanat. "Organized Crime in Central Asia: A Threat Assessment." *China and Eurasia Forum Quarterly*, vol. 7, no. 2 (2009): 75–100. Washington, D.C.: CACI, 2009.

Bergne, Paul. *The Birth of Tajikistan: National Identity and the Origins of the Republic.* London,: I.B. Taurus & Co. Ltd., 2007.

Bleuer, Christian. "Instability in Tajikistan? The Islamic Movement of Uzbekistan and the Afghanistan Factor." Central Asia Security Policy Brief 7. Geneva: Geneva Center for Security Policy and OSCE Academy, 2012. http://osce-academy.net/uploads/docs/bleuer_policy_brief7.pdf.

Briller, Vladimir. *Tajikistan Country Case Study*. Paris: UNESCO, 2008.

Brownbridge, Martin, and Sudharshan Canagarajab. "How Should Fiscal Policy Respond to the Economic Crisis in the Low Income Commonwealth of Independent States? Some Pointers from Tajikistan." Policy Research Working Paper. Washington, D.C.: World Bank, 2009.

Bureau of Democracy, Human Rights, and Labor. *Tajikistan: International Religious Freedom Report 2010*, November 17, 2010. Dushanbe: Bureau of Democracy, Human Rights and Labor, 2010.

Bureau on Human Rights and Rule of Law. *Overview of the Human Rights Situation in Tajikistan* (1–31 March, 2009). Dushanbe: Bureau on Human Rights and Rule of Law, 2009.

Collins, Kathleen. "Clans, Pacts, and Politics in Central Asia." *Journal of Democracy*, vol. 13, no. 3, July 2002.

———. *Clan Politics and Regime Transition in Central Asia*. Cambridge: Cambridge University Press, 2006.

———. *Tajikistan: Bad Peace Agreements and Prolonged Civil Conflict*. Cambridge: Cambridge University Press, 2006.

Cummings, Sally N., ed., *Oil, Transition and Security in Central Asia*. London: RoutlegeCurzon, 2003.

Dukovny, Victor. *Interstate Commission for Water Coordination of Central Asia: Achievements and Challenges of the Future: Water Cooperation on the Way to Sustainable Development*. Tashkent: Interstate Commission for Water Coordination of Central Asia, 2007.

Dukovny, Victor, Nazir Mirzaev, and Vadim Sokolov. "IWRM Implementation: Experiences with Water Sector Reforms in Central Asia." In *Central Asian Waters*, edited by Muhammad Rahaman and Olli Varis. Tashkent: Water & Development Publications 2008. 19–31.

Dukovny, Victor, and A. G. Sorokin. "Otsenka vliyaniya Rogunskogo vodokhranilishcha na vodnyy rezhim Amudar'i" [An evaluation of the impact of the Rogun reservoir on the Amudarya River]. Prepared for the Scientific Informational Center of the Interstate Commission for Water Coordination of Central Asia. Tashkent: CICW, 2007.

Djalili, Mohammad-Reza, Frederic Grare, and Shirin Akiner. *Tajikistan: The Trials of Independence*. New York: St. Martin's Press, 1997.

Dorofeev, Vladislav, and Tatiana Kostileva. *Printsip Deripaski* [Deripaska's Principle]. Moscow: Biblioteka Kommersant, 2010.

Economist Intelligence Unit. *Tajikistan: Country Profile 2005*. London: Economist Intelligence Unit, 2005.

Embassy of Japan in Kazakhstan. "Sustainable Use of Natural Resources of Central Asia, Environmental Problems of the Aral Sea and Surrounding Areas." Proceedings of the International Scientific Conference, September 9–11, 1997, Almaty, Kazakhstan. Almaty: Tethys, 1998.

Emerson, Michael, and Evgeny Vinokurov. "Optimisation of Central Asian and Eurasian Trans-Continental Land Transport Corridors." Working Paper 2007. Brussels: EUCAM, 2009.

European Bank for Reconstruction and Development. *Strategy for Tajikistan*, November 2005. London: EBRD, 2005.

———. *Strategy for Tajikistan*, 2009. London: EBRD, 2009.

———. *Transition Report 2009: Tajikistan*. London: EBRD, 2009.

———. *Transition Report 2006: Tajikistan*. London: EBRD, 2006.

European Training Foundation. *Country Report: Overview of the Relationship between Human Capital Development and Equity in Tajikistan*. Dushanbe: European Training Foundation, 2010.

European Union. *Joint Progress Report by the Council and the European Commission to the European Council on the Implementation of the EU Central Asia Strategy*. Brussels: European Union, 2010.

Food and Agriculture Organization. *Report of the Tajikistan Emergency Agriculture and Livestock Assessment* (8–15 February 2008). Dushanbe: Food and Agriculture Organization, 2008.

Fumagalli, Matteo. "Framing Ethnic Minority Mobilization in *Central Asia: The Cases of the Uzbeks in Kyrgyzstan and Tajikistan*." Europe Asia Studies, vol. 59, no. 4 (June 2007): 567–90.

Gavrilis, George. *The Dynamics of Interstate Boundaries*. Cambridge: Cambridge University Press, 2008.

Goodhand, Jonathan. "Bandits, Borderlands, and Opium Wars: Afghan State-Building Viewed from the Margins." DIIS Working Paper 2009. Copenhagen: DIIS, 2009.

Gleason, Gregory. "The Struggle for Control over Water in Central Asia: Republican Sovereignty and Collective Action." Radio Free Europe/Radio Liberty Research Institute, June 21, 1991.

Granit, Jakob, Anders Jagerskog, Rebecca Lofgren, and Andy Bullock. *Regional Water Intelligence Report Central Asia: Baseline Report.* Paper 15. Stockholm: UNDP, 2010.

Gray, Cheryl, Joel Hellman, and Randi Ryterman. "Anticorruption in Transition 2: Corruption in Enterprise-State Interactions in Europe and Central Asia 1999–2002." Washington, D.C.: World Bank, 2004.

Gupta, Raj, Kirsten Kienzler, Christopher Martius, Alisher Mirzabaev, and Theib Oweis. "Research Prospectus: A Vision for Sustainable Land Management Research in Central Asia." ICARDA CAC Program. Tashkent: ICARDA, 2009.

Harris, Collette. *Control and Subversion: Gender Relations in Tajikistan.* London: Pluto Press, 2004.

———. *Muslim Youth: Tensions and Transitions in Tajikistan.* Oxford: Westford Press, 2006.

Hartog, Merijn, ed. *Security Sector Reform in Central Asia: Exploring Needs and Possibilities.* (Greenwood Paper 25). Groningen, Netherlands: Center for European Security Studies, 2010.

Hodgson, Stephen. "Land and Water—The Rights Interface." Working Paper. Washington, D.C.: Food and Agriculture Organization of the United Nations, 2004.

International Crisis Group. *Central Asia: Border Disputes and Conflict Potential.* Asia Report no. 33, April 4, 2002. Brussels: International Crisis Group, 2002.

———. *Central Asia: Crisis Conditions in Three States.* Asia Report no. 7, August 7, 2000. Brussels: International Crisis Group, 2000.

———. *Central Asia: Drugs and Conflict.* Asia Report no. 25, November 26, 2001. Brussels: International Crisis Group, 2001.

———. *Central Asia's Energy Risks.* Asia Report no. 133, May 24, 2007. Brussels: International Crisis Group, 2007.

———. "Central Asia: Islamists in Prison." Asia Briefing no. 97, December 15, 1997. Brussels: International Crisis Group, 1997.

———. *Central Asia: Water and Conflict.* Asia Report no. 34, May 30, 2002. Brussels: International Crisis Group, 2002.

———. *Central Asia: Decay and Decline.* Asia Report no. 21, February 3, 2011. Brussels: International Crisis Group, 2011.

———. *The Curse of Cotton: Central Asia's Destructive Monoculture.* Asia Report no. 93, February 28, 2005. Brussels: International Crisis Group, 2005.

———. *Tajikistan: An Uncertain Peace.* Asia Report no. 30, December 24, 2001. Brussels: International Crisis Group, 2001.

———. *Tajikistan: A Roadmap for Development*. Asia Report no. 51, April 24, 2003. Brussels: International Crisis Group, 2003.

———. *Tajikistan: On the Road to Failure*. Asia Report no. 162, February 12, 2009. Brussels: International Crisis Group, 2009.

International Finance Cooperation. *Business Environment in Tajikistan as Seen by Small and Medium Enterprises*. December 2009. Dushanbe: International Finance Cooperation, 2009.

International Monetary Fund. *Tajikistan: Letter of Intent, Memorandum of Economic and Financial Policies, and Technical Memorandum of Understanding*. April 19, 2011. Washington, D.C.: International Monetary Fund, 2011.

———. *Tajikistan: First and Second Review Under the Three-Year Arrangement Under the Extended Credit Facility, Request for Waiver of Performance Criteria, and Request for Augmentation of the Arrangement—Staff Report: Staff Statement: Press Release on the Executive Board Discussion; and Statement by the Executive Director for Tajikistan*. Country Report No. 10/201, July 2010. Washington, D.C.: International Monetary Fund, 2010.

———. *Regional Economic Outlook May 2010: The Caucasus and Central Asia: Incipient Recovery*. Washington, D.C.: International Monetary Fund, 2010.

———. *Republic of Tajikistan, IMF Country Report No. 08/197, June 2008*. Washington, D.C.: International Monetary Fund, 2008.

———. *Republic of Tajikistan—2009 Article IV Consultation, Final Review Under the Staff-Monitored Program, and Request for a Three-Year Arrangement Under the Poverty Reduction and Growth Facility—Staff Report; Staff Supplement; Staff Statement; Public Information Notice and Press Release on the Executive Board Discussion; and Statement by the Executive Director for the Republic of Tajikistan. June 2009*. IMF Country Report no. 09/174. Washington, D.C.: International Monetary Fund, 2009.

International Organization for Migration. "Baseline Research on Smuggling of Migrants in, from, and through Central Asia." Vienna: International Organization for Migration, 2006.

Jawad, Nassim, and Shahrbanou Tadjbakhsh. *Tajikistan: A Forgotten Civil War*. Manchester: Minority Free Press, 1995.

Jonson, Lena. *Tajikistan in the New Central Asia*. New York: I.B. Tauris & Co. Ltd., 2006.

KasWag AgriConsulting Worldwide. *Desk Study: Rural Sector Reform and Legal Aid in Tajikistan, June 2008*. Basilea, Australia: KasWag, 2008.

Khublaryan, Martin G., ed. *Water Resources*, vol. 26, no. 1, January-February 1999.

Khudonazarov, Daviat. "The Conflict in Tajikistan: Questions of Regionalism." Washington, D.C.: Eisenhower Institute, 2002.

Kobori, Iwao, and Michael H. Glantz, ed. *Central Eurasian Water Crisis: Caspian, Aral, and Dead Seas.* New York: United Nations University Press, 1998.

Laruelle, Marlene. "Central Asian Labor Migrants in Russia: The "Diasporization of the Central Asian States?" *China and Eurasia Forum Quarterly*, vol. 5, no. 3 (2007): 101–19.

Lerman, Zvi, and David Sedik. "Agricultural Development and Household Incomes in Central Asia: A Survey of Tajikistan, 2003–2008." *Eurasian Geography and Economics* 50, no. 3, (2009): 301–26.

Lewis, David. *The Temptations of Tyranny in Central Asia.* New York: Columbia University Press, 2008.

Luong, Pauline Jones. "Political Obstacles to Economic Reform in Uzbekistan, Kyrgyzstan, and Tajikistan: Strategies to Move Ahead." Paper presented at the Lucerne meeting of the CIS-7 Initiative, January 20–22, 2003.

Majidov, Suhrob. "Audit Leads to Scandal for Tajik National Bank." Central Asia-Caucasus Institute Analyst. May 6, 2009. www.cacianalyst.org/?q=node/5103.

Maredia, Karim M., and Dieudonne Baributsa. "Ecologically-Based Participatory and Collaborative Research and Capacity Building in Integrated Pest Management Program in the Central Asia Region." Regional Collaborative IPM Program, Michigan State University. East Lansing, Michigan: Michigan State University, 2009.

Maredia, Karim M., and Dieudonne Baributsa, ed. "Integrated Pest Management in Central Asia: Proceedings of the Central Asia Region Integrated Pest Management Stakeholders Forum, May 27–29, 2007," held in Dushanbe, Tajikistan. Dushanbe: USAID, 2007.

Michalopoulos, Constantine. "The Integration of Low-Income CIS Members in the World Trading System." Paper presented at the CIS-7 Conference, January 2003. CIS: 2003.

Micklin, Phillip. *Managing Water in Central Asia.* London: Royal Institute of International Affairs. 2000.

Ministry of Agriculture of the Republic of Tajikistan. *Cotton Sector Project Restructuring, Environmental Management Framework.* Dushanbe: Ministry of Agriculture, 2009.

Ministry of Education of the Republic of Tajikistan. *National Strategy for Education Development for the Republic of Tajikistan, 2006–2015*, August, 2005. Dushanbe: Ministry of Education of Tajikistan, 2005.

Mitra, Pradeep. *Innovation, Inclusion, and Integration: From Transition to Convergence in Eastern Europe and the Former Soviet Union*. Washington, D.C.: World Bank, 2008.

Mitra, Pradeep, Alexander Muravyev, and Mark Schaffer. "Convergence in Institutions and Market Outcomes: Cross-Country and Time-Series Evidence from the Business Environment and Enterprise Performance Surveys in Transition Economies." Policy Research Working Paper 4819. Washington, D.C.: World Bank, 2009.

Mitra, Pradeep, Marcelo Selowsky, and Juan Zalduendo. *Turmoil at 20: Recession, Recovery, and Reform in Central and Eastern Europe and the Former Soviet Union*. Washington, D.C.: World Bank, 2010.

Najibullah, Farangis. "Tajik Audit Reveals Huge National Bank Shortfalls." Radio Free Europe/Radio Liberty. April 15, 2009. www.rferl.org/articleprintview/1609233.html.

Nakaya, Sumie. "Aid and Transition from a War Economy to an Oligarchy in Post-War Tajikistan." *Central Asian Survey*, vol. 28, no. 3 (September 2009): 259–73.

National Democratic Institute. "Strengthening Political Parties in Tajikistan: USAID Cooperative Agreement No. 119-A-00-05-00023-00(05153) Final Report." Washington, D.C.: NDI/USAID, 2009.

Nellis, John, and Ira Lieberman. 2009. "Privatization in Transition States: Lessons for Latecomers." Background Paper. Washington, D.C.: World Bank, 2009.

Nichol, Jim. "Tajikistan: Recent Developments and U.S. Interests." CRS Report for Congress, February 10, 2011. Washington, D.C.: Congressional Research Service, 2011.

Novovic, Tomislav. "Tajikistan: Local Governance and Decentralization: A Project Assessment." Dushanbe: United States Development Program, 2009.

Office for Democratic Institutions and Human Rights. *Republic of Tajikistan: Parliamentary Elections February 28, 2010: Election Observation Mission Final Report*. Warsaw: OSCE, 2010.

O'Hara, Sarah L., and Tim Hannan. "Irrigation and Water Management in Turkmenistan: Past Systems, Present Problems, and Future Scenarios." *Europe-Asia Studies*, vol. 51, no. 1, 1999. 21–41.

Olcott, Martha Brill. "NATO and Security in Central Asia." *Security Sector Reform in Central Asia* (2010): 63–72. www.isn.ethz.ch/isn/DigitalLibrary/Publications/Detail/?ots591=0c54e3b3-1e9c-be1e2c24-a6a8c7060233&lng=en&id=119154.

Olimov, Jafar. *Informal Economy in Tajikistan*. Dushanbe: UNDP, 2007.

Olimova, Saodat. "Paper 3: Impact of External Migration on Development of Mountainous Regions: Tajikistan, Kyrgyzstan, Afghanistan, and Pakistan." International Workshop, Dushanbe, Tajikistan, June 6–10, 2005.

Open Society Institute. *Tajikistan: Refugee Reintegration and Conflict Prevention.* Washington, D.C.: Open Society Institute, 1998.

OSCE. "Common Framework for Addressing Water Issues in Central Asia: Towards a Shared Vision & Joint Approach among Water Sector Partners." December 2008. Vienna: OSCE, 2008.

Osmonaliev, Kairat. "Developing Counter-Narcotics Policy in Central Asia: Legal and Political Dimensions." Silk Road Paper, January 2005. Washington, D.C.: CACI, 2005.

Peyrouse, Sebastian. "The Hydroelectric Sector in Central Asia and the Growing Role of China." *China and Eurasia Forum Quarterly,* vol. 5, no. 2, 2007.

Power Tajikistan 2010. "The 4th International Exhibition in Tajikistan Power and Lighting." Dushanbe: Power Tajikistan, 2010.

Rahaman, Muhammad Mizuar, and Olli Varis, ed. *Central Asian Waters: Social, Economic, Environmental and Governance Puzzle.* Helsinki: Water and Development Publications, 2008.

Republic of Tajikistan. *Poverty Reduction Strategy of the Republic of Tajikistan for 2000–2012.* Dushanbe: 2010.

Rowe, William Campbell. "'Kitchen Gardens' in Tajikistan: The Economic and Cultural Importance of Small-Scale Private Property in a Post-Soviet Society," *Human Ecology,* vol. 37, no. 6 (2009): 691–703.

Sanderson, Thomas M., Daniel Kimmage, and David A. Gordon. *From the Ferghana Valley to South Waziristan: The Evolving Threat of Central Asian Jihadists. A Report of the CSIS Transnational Threats Project.* March 2010. Washington, D.C.: CSIS, 2010.

Schmidt, Roland. "Onwards and Upwards." *International Water Power and Dam Construction Magazine.* May 2008.

Sewall, Bella Katy. "Transboundary Water Management in Central Asia: Have Donors Made a Difference?" Academic Thesis. Harvard University, March 1998. Cambridge, Mass.: Harvard University, 1998.

Sharma, Raghuveer. "Tajik Energy Utilities Reform Review." Washington, D.C.: World Bank, 2005.

SHARQ Research Center. Musul'manskiye lidery: sotsial'naya rol' i avtoritet. Materialy kruglogo stola [Muslim leaders: social roles and authority. Roundtable materials]. Dushanbe: SHARQ/Friedrich Ebert Foundation, 2003.

Sievers, Eric W. *The Post-Soviet Decline of Central Asia.* London: RoutledgeCurzon, 2003.

Slater, Dan. "Can Leviathan be Democratic? Competitive Elections, Robust Mass Politics, and State Infrastructural Power." *Studies in Comparative International Development*. no. 43 (August, 2, 2008): 252–72.

Smith, R. Grant. "Russia to Invest in Tajikistan." *Central Asia-Caucasus Institute Analyst*. December 15, 2004. www.cacianalyst.org/view_article.php?article=2908.

State Statistical Committee of the Republic of Tajikistan. Natsional'nyy sostav naseleniya Respubliki Tadzhikistan po dannym Vseobshchey perepisi naseleniya 2000 goda [National composition of the population of the Republic of Tajikistan based on data from the 2000 Population Census]. Dushanbe: 2000.

"Strategies for Development and Food Security in Mountainous Areas of Central Asia." International Workshop. Dushanbe: Aga Khan Foundation 2005.

Swiss Agency for Development. *Cooperation Strategy for the Central Asia Region 2007–2011*. Berne: SDC/SECO, 2007.

Tan, Vivian. "Tajik Returnees." *UNHCR Refugees* no. 143, issue 2, 2006, 12–13, www.unhcr.org/44b64fac2.pdf.

Turajonzoda, Qadi Akbar. *Religion: The Pillar of Society*. Washington, D.C.: Eisenhower Institute, 2002.

United Nations. "Development Assistance Framework for Tajikistan, 2010–2015." New York: United Nations, 2009.

United Nations Children's Fund. (UNICEF). *Child Poverty in Tajikistan*. January 2007. Dushanbe: UNICEF, 2007.

———. *Children's Voices: A Qualitative Study of Poverty in Tajikistan*. Dushanbe: UNICEF, 2003.

———. *Tajikistan Country Profile: Education in Tajikistan*. Washington, D.C.: UNICEF, 2008.

———. *Tajikistan: Living Standards Measurement Survey 2007*. Dushanbe: UNICEF, 2007.

———. *The State of Women and Children in Tajikistan*. Comparative Analysis of MICS 2000 and MICS 2005 Results. June 2008. Dushanbe: UNICEF, 2008.

United Nations Office on Drugs and Crime. *Afghanistan: Opium Survey 2004*. Vienna: UNODC, 2004.

———. "Caspian Sea and Turkmen Border Initiatives, November 2008." Working paper. (Washington, D.C.: UNODC, 2008).

"Central Asia Intelligence-Sharing Centre Inaugurated in Kazakhstan." UNODC, December 9, 2009. Vienna: UNODC, 2009.

————. "Securing Central Asia's Borders with Afghanistan." November 2008. New York: UNODC, 2008.

————. "Targeting Precursors used in Heroin Manufacture." November 2008. New York: UNODC, 2008.

————. *World Drug Report 2009.* New York: United Nations, 2009.

UNDP. *Central Asia Human Development Report: Bringing Down Barriers: Regional Cooperation for Human Development and Human Security.* Bratislava, Slovakia: UNDP, 2005.

————. *Central Asia Human Development Report: Bringing Down Barriers: Regional Cooperation for Human Development and Human Security.* Dushanbe: UNDP, 2005.

————. *Challenges and Recommendations at the Inter-Ministry Level of the Republic of Tajikistan in Rural Drinking Water Supply. Report June 2009.* Dushanbe: UNDP, 2009.

————. *Communication Strategy for Agricultural Reforms Intended to the Independent Commission.* Dushanbe: UNDP, 2007.

————. *Country Programme Action Plan between the Government of Tajikistan and the United Nations Development Programme, 2010–2015.* Dushanbe: UNDP, 2010.

————. *Country Programme Action Plan between the Government of Tajikistan and the United Nations Development Program, 2010–2015.* New York: UNDP, 2010.

————. *Human Development Report 2007: Informal Economy in Tajikistan.* Dushanbe: UNDP, 2007.

————. *Issues and Recommendations for Community Level Rural Water Supply in Tajikistan Report, February 2009.* Dushanbe: UNDP, 2009.

————. *Public Opinion Survey: Report on Corruption in the Republic of Tajikistan, Dushanbe 2006.* Dushanbe: UNDP, 2006.

————. "Recent Trends in Socio-Economic and Water/Energy Vulnerability in Central Asia." December 3, 2009. New York: UNDP, 2009.

————. "Risk Monitoring and Warning Report Tajikistan: July 2009." UNDP, 2009.

————. "Strategy and Project Activities to Support Improved Regional Water Management in Central Asia. July 2004." New York: UNDP, 2004.

UNEP. *Environment and Security in the Amu Darya Basin.* Nairobi: UNEP, 2011.

USAID. "Collaborative Research Support Program for Integrated Pest Management in Central Asia." IPM-CRSP. Washington, D.C.: USAID, 2009.

———. "Land Reform and Market Development Project 11 Final Report–Tajikistan–2008–2009." Washington, D.C.: USAID, 2009.

———. "Local Governance and Citizen Participatory Program in Tajikistan: Sub-National Government Assessment—2009." Washington, D.C.: USAID, 2009.

———. "Program for a Legal Infrastructure for a Market Economy in Kyrgyzstan and Tajikistan (Commercial Law Reform) Final Report, September 2005." Washington, D.C.: USAID, 2005.

———. Tajikistan: *Country Health Statistical Report, May 2009.* Washington, D.C.: USAID, 2009.

U.S. Department of State. *Human Rights Report 2009, Tajikistan.* Washington, D.C.: U.S. Department of State, 2009.

———. *Human Rights Report 2010, Tajikistan.* Washington, D.C.: U.S. Department of State, 2010.

U.S. Government. "2009 Report to Congress of the U.S.-China Economic and Security Review Commission. One Hundred Eleventh Congress, First Session, November 2009." Washington, D.C.: U.S. Government Printing Office, 2009.

Van Atta, Don. "King Cotton Freezes Tajikistan." *Central Asia-Caucasus Analyst Institute.* March 19, 2008. www.cacianalyst.org/?q=node4819.

———. "'White Gold' or Fool's Gold? The Political Economy of Cotton in Tajikistan." *Problems of Post-Communism,* vol. 56, no. 2. (March/April 2009): 17–35.

Wegerich, Kai. "Hydro-hegemony in the Amu Darya Basin." Netherlands: Wageningen University, 2007.

———. "Water and Conflict in Central Asia" Netherlands: Wageningen University, 2007.

———. "Passing Over the Conflict: The Chu Talas Basin Agreement as a Model for Central Asia?" In *Central Asian Waters.* Helsinki: Water and Development Publications, 2008. 117–31.

Wegerich, Kai, Oliver Olsson, and Jochen Froebrich. "Reliving the Past in a Changed Environment: Hydropower Ambitions, Opportunities and Constraints in Tajikistan." Energy Policy, vol. 35, 2007.

Weigand, Christine, and Margaret Grosh. "Levels and Patterns of Safety Net Spending in Developing and Transition Countries." World Bank, SP Discussion Paper no. 0817, June 2008. Washington, D.C.: World Bank, 2008.

Weinthal, Erika. "Water Conflict and Cooperation in Central Asia." UNDP Human Development Report Office Occasional Paper. New York: UNDP, 2006.

Wiegmann, Gunda. "Socio-Political Change in Tajikistan: The Development Process, Its Challenges Since the Civil War and the Silence Before the New Storm?" Ph.D. Thesis. University of Hamburg, Institute for Political Science. Hamburg, Germany: University of Hamburg, 2009.

World Bank. "Agricultural Activities, Water, and Gender in Tajikistan's Rural Sector: A Social Assessment of Konibodom, Bobojon Ghafurov, Yovon." World Bank Water Resource Management Project. Washington, D.C: World Bank, 2009.

———. Concessional Finance & Global Partnerships. *Tajikistan Country Report*, FY09-FY11, Q1, IBRD/IDA Trust Funds. Washington, D.C.: World Bank, 2011.

———. *Doing Business in Tajikistan, 2010 Data*. Washington, D.C.: World Bank Group, 2010.

———. "Implementation Status & Results: Tajikistan: Ferghana Valley Water Resource Management Project." Washington, D.C.: World Bank, 2011.

———. "Implementation Status & Results: Tajikistan: Community Agriculture & Watershed Management Project." Washington, D.C.: World Bank, 2011.

———. *Integrating Environment in Key Economic Sectors in Europe and Central Asia*, Washington, D.C.: World Bank, 2011.

———. "International Development Association Program Document for a Proposed Grant in the Amount of SDR 7 Million (US$10 Million Equivalent) to the Republic of Tajikistan for a Programmatic Development Grant, May 9, 2006." Washington, D.C.: World Bank, 2006.

———. *Infrastructure in Europe and Central Asia Region*. Washington, D.C.: World Bank, 2006.

———. "Levels and Patterns of Safety Net Spending in Developing and Transition Countries." Safety Nets Primer Series, no. 30. January 2009. Washington, D.C.: World Bank, 2009.

———. "Republic of Tajikistan: Country Financial Accountability Assessment, June 22, 2004." Operations Policy & Services Unit, Europe and Central Asia. Washington, D.C.: World Bank, 2006.

———. "Republic of Tajikistan: Poverty Assessment." Washington, D.C.: World Bank, 2009.

———. "Republic of Tajikistan. Key Priorities for Climate Change Adaptation." Policy Research Working Paper. World Bank, 2010. Washington, D.C.: World Bank, 2010.

———. "Republic of Tajikistan. Country Partnership Strategy Progress Report 2007." Washington, D.C.: World Bank, 2006.

————. "Republic of Tajikistan: Poverty Assessment." Washington, D.C.: World Bank, 2010.

————. "Restructuring Paper on a Proposed Project Restructuring of the Community Agriculture & Watershed Management Project to the Republic of Tajikistan. April 27, 2011." Washington, D.C.: World Bank, 2011.

————. "Restructuring Paper on a Proposed Project Restructuring of Community & Basic Health Project Grant to the Republic of Tajikistan, December 12, 2005." Washington, D.C.: World Bank, 2011.

———. "Restructuring Paper on a Proposed Project Restructuring of Fast Track Initiative Catalytic Fund Grant-3 Project Grant to the Republic of Tajikistan, March 8, 2011." Washington, D.C.: World Bank, 2011.

————. "Restructuring Paper on a Proposed Project Restructuring of the Emergency Food Security and Seed Imports Project, Republic of Tajikistan." Washington, D.C.: World Bank, 2011.

————. *Tajikistan, Review of the Air Transport Sector in Tajikistan, A Policy Note.* Washington, D.C.: World Bank, 2011.

————. *Tajikistan Trade Diagnostic Study.* Washington, D.C.: World Bank, 2005.

————. "Water Energy Nexus in Central Asia: Improving Regional Cooperation in the Syr Darya Basin." January 2004. Washington, D.C.: World Bank, 2011.

Zurcher, Christoph. "Analysis of Peace and Conflict Potential in Rasht Valley, Shurabad District and GBAO, Tajikistan." Academic Report. Deutsche Gesellschaft für Technische Zusammenarbeit (GTZ). Berlin: Deutsche Gesellschaft fur Technische Zusammenarbeit, 2008.

INDEX

ABOUT THE AUTHOR

Martha Brill Olcott is a senior associate with the Russia and Eurasia Program at the Carnegie Endowment in Washington, D.C., and co-director of the al-Farabi Carnegie Program on Central Asia in Almaty, Kazakhstan.

Olcott specializes in the problems of transitions in Central Asia and the Caucasus as well as the security challenges in the Caspian region more generally. She has followed interethnic relations in Russia and the states of the former Soviet Union for more than twenty-five years and has traveled extensively in these countries and in South Asia. She is the author of *Central Asia's Second Chance, Kazakhstan: Unfulfilled Promise?*, and *In the Whirlwind of Jihad*.

CARNEGIE ENDOWMENT FOR INTERNATIONAL PEACE

The Carnegie Endowment for International Peace is a private, non-profit organization dedicated to advancing cooperation between nations and promoting active international engagement by the United States. Founded in 1910, its work is nonpartisan and dedicated to achieving practical results.

Carnegie is pioneering the first global think tank, with flourishing offices now in Washington, Moscow, Beijing, Beirut, and Brussels. These five locations include the centers of world governance and the places whose political evolution and international policies will most determine the near-term possibilities for international peace and economic advance.

In 2011 the Carnegie Endowment for International Peace and al-Farabi National University established the al-Farabi Carnegie Program on Central Asia, which aims to generate a deeper dialogue between policy institutes, business leaders, and governments in Kazakhstan and the Central Asia region, and to engage international audiences on a wide range of issues.